CHRIST AND CUL

Challenges in Contemporary Theology

Series Editors: Gareth Jones and Lewis Ayres
Canterbury Christ Church University College, UK and Emory University, US

Challenges in Contemporary Theology is a series aimed at producing clear orientations in, and research on, areas of 'challenge' in contemporary theology. These carefully co-ordinated books engage traditional theological concerns with mainstreams in modern thought and culture that challenge those concerns. The 'challenges' implied are to be understood in two senses: those presented by society to contemporary theology, and those posed by theology to society.

These Three are One: The Practice of Trinitarian Theology   David S. Cunningham

After Writing: On the Liturgical Consummation of Philosophy   Catherine Pickstock

Mystical Theology: The Integrity of Spirituality and Theology   Mark A. McIntosh

Engaging Scripture: Theology, Politics, and the Body of Christ   Stephen E. Fowl

Torture and Eucharist: A Model for Theological Interpretation   William T. Cavanaugh

Sexuality and the Christian Body: Their Way into the Triune God   Eugene F. Rogers, Jr.

On Christian Theology   Rowan Williams

The Promised End: Eschatology in Theology and Literature   Paul S. Fiddes

Powers and Submissions: Spirituality, Philosophy, and Gender   Sarah Coakley

A Theology of Engagement   Ian S. Markham

Alien Sex: The Body and Desire in Cinema and Theology   Gerard Loughlin

Scripture and Metaphysics: Aquinas and the Renewal of Trinitarian Theology
Matthew Levering

Faith and Freedom: An Interfaith Perspective   David Burrell

Keeping God's Silence   Rachel Muers

Christ and Culture   Graham Ward

Theology in the Public Square: Church, Academy, and Nation   Gavin D'Costa

Rewritten Theology: Aquinas After His Readers   Mark D. Jordan

CHRIST AND CULTURE

Graham Ward

Blackwell
Publishing

BLACKWELL PUBLISHING
350 Main Street, Malden, MA 02148-5020, USA
9600 Garsington Road, Oxford OX4 2DQ, UK
550 Swanston Street, Carlton, Victoria 3053, Australia

First published 2005 by Blackwell Publishing Ltd

1 2005

Library of Congress Cataloging-in-Publication Data

Ward, Graham, 1955–
    Christ and culture / Graham Ward
        p. cm.—(Challenges in contemporary theology)
    Includes bibliographical references and index.
    ISBN-13: 978-1-4051-2140-8 (hardback : alk. paper)
    ISBN-10: 1-4051-2140-8 (hardback : alk. paper)
    ISBN-13: 978-1-4051-2141-5 (pbk. : alk. paper)
    ISBN-10: 1-4051-2141-6 (pbk. : alk. paper)
    1. Jesus Christ—Person and offices. 2. Christianity and culture.
    3. Incarnation. I. Title. II. Series.
    BT203 W37 2005
    232—dc22   2005005884

A catalogue record for this title is available from the British Library.

Set in 10.5 pt Bembo
by The Running Head Limited, Cambridge
Printed and bound in India
by Replika Press Pvt Ltd., Kundli

The publisher's policy is to use permanent paper from mills that operate a sustainable forestry policy, and which has been manufactured from pulp processed using acid-free and elementary chlorine-free practices. Furthermore, the publisher ensures that the text paper and cover board used have met acceptable environmental accreditation standards.

For further information on
Blackwell Publishing, visit our website:
www.blackwellpublishing.com

to Rowan

CONTENTS

ACKNOWLEDGEMENTS

These essays represent ten years of reflection upon the work of Christ and the operation of redemption. They also represent ten years of ongoing conversation with friends, students, colleagues and opponents. Drafts of some of them appeared in journals (particularly *Literature and Theology* and *Modern Theology*) or edited collections, such as Paul Heelas, *Religion, Modernity and Postmodernity* (Oxford: Blackwell, 1998) and Robert Gibbs and Elliot Wolfson, *Suffering Religion* (London: Routledge, 2002); the others were given as papers at conferences or colloquiums and have remained unpublished. Many people have been involved in commenting upon them, referring me to material I did not know, and pointing out inadequacies. I owe a debt of gratitude to all of these people, and I have learnt so much from others. I particularly wish to thank Marcella Althaus-Reid, Page du Bois, Michael Hoelzl, David Jasper, Todd Klutz, Gerard Loughlin, Walter Lowe, John Milbank, Dale Martin, Stephen Moore, Peter Oakes, Catherine Pickstock, and all those who belong to the Thursday night Krobar group, without whom life would be a lot less fun and intellectually challenging. Mention must also be made of my copy-editor, David Williams, at The Running Head, who saved me a great deal of embarrassment in his meticulous handling of the final draft. I dedicate this book to Rowan Williams, whose trust I have valued.

INTRODUCTION

God is not known to us in His nature, but is made known to us from His operations. (*Summa Theologiae*, I.Q13.8)

Taking our cue from this statement by Aquinas, the Christological question begins not with *who* is the Christ or *what* is the Christ; it begins with *where* is the Christ. The Christological enquiry therefore does not begin with the identity of the Christ, what in dogmatics is the nature as distinct from the work of Christ; it begins with an analysis of the operations whereby Christ is made known to us. And in being made known we participate in him. The Christological work then in these essays is orientated towards questions concerning soteriology, rather than personhood – and as such they are trying to correct a tendency in Christological thinking since at least Schleiermacher. Christ, as second person of the Trinity, is the archetype of all relation. All relations, that is, participate in and aspire to their perfection in the Christological relation. Not only in him is all relation perfected, but the work and economy he is implicated in is relation: that is, the reconciliation of the world to God, summed up in the consummation of the covenant. Christology is concerned, then, with solidarity, mutuality and reciprocity; aspects of relationality. Several corollaries follow from this.

First, Christological enquiry is a profoundly hermeneutical one – no appeal can be made to immediate knowledge of God. This means, *pace* Barth, Christ cannot be an 'epistemological principle [*Erkenntnisprinzip*]'[1] for we have no access to how Christ views and knows things. We only have access to interpretations of the way Christ views and knows things; interpretations which may participate in God's grace, but which we cannot claim to be so inspired without scandal (*skandolon*). Secondly, the focus of this hermeneutical enquiry is the nexus of relations in which the historical, social and cultural engage with the divine. Every statement about Christ

---

[1] *Die Kirkliche Dogmatik*, IV.1 (Zürich/Zollikon: Evangelischer Verlag, 1953), p. 21; *Church Dogmatics*, IV.1, tr. G. W. Bromiley (Edinburgh: T. & T. Clark, 1956), p. 21.

cannot be reduced to, but is, nevertheless, a statement about ourselves and the times and cultures we inhabit. Thirdly, the enquiry itself is governed by the time and circumstances within which it takes place. For to speak of operations is to speak of what has been observed in the past but always in the present. Operations are conducted grammatically in present continuous action. Hence we arrive at the principle of the studies presented here: that the engagement of Christ with culture and the enquiry into that engagement are inseparable. To do Christology is to engage in a Christological operation; to enquire is to engender Christ; to enter the engagement is to foster the economy whereby God is made known to us. To do Christology is to inscribe Christ into the times and cultures we inhabit. It is therefore an operation of redemption undertaken in obedience to witness by faith, in grace. But, in the wake of corollaries 1–3, what is needed is a methodology that can facilitate the examination of the relations and operations that constitute this matrix – and this is where these essays situate themselves.

To some extent the nature of Christological enquiry as I have set it out has been recognised by other theologians. We can take two examples two hundred years apart. The first is from Lessing's famous essay 'On the Proof of the Spirit and of Power'. Lessing, writing of the time of Origen, observes:

> Origen was quite right in saying that in this proof of spirit and of power the Christian religion was able to provide a proof of its own more divine than all Greek dialectic. For in his time there was still 'the power to do miraculous things still continued' among those who lived after Christ's precept … But I am no longer in Origen's position. I live in the eighteenth century in which miracles no longer happen. If I even now hesitate to believe anything on the proof of the spirit and of power, which I can believe on other arguments more appropriately to my age.[2]

The second is from Wolfhart Pannenberg's study *Jesus – God and Man* and forms part of his analysis of modern Christologies that emphasise 'Revelational Presence':

> That the entire problem of the concept of revelation and especially of the connection between Revealer and what is revealed in God's self-revelation has been thought through only in more modern theology – indeed, fully only in the present – is probably connected with the fact that the existence of God in general was self-evident in earlier periods and appeared to be secured by the philosophical proofs for God. One began with such a given concept of God and simply asked how this God could have come into the flesh. Thereby

---

[2]   Henry Chadwick tr., *Lessing's Theological Writing* (Stanford University Press, 1972), p. 52.

one was already stuck in the middle of insoluble difficulties. Since the destruction of the old theistic picture of the world by the Enlightenment and by Kant, such a procedure is no longer possible … For this reason, the problem of revelation has become the fundamental question in modern theology, that is, the only possible basis for speaking about God himself.[3]

Allow me to make three observations, pertinent to this study, with respect to these two statements.

First, in talking about Christ and culture we are concerned with *discourses* on Jesus Christ; representations that are reflective of because embedded within, and also productive of, specific sets of cultural values and assumptions. Dogmatically, we are working on doctrines that constitute Christology – incarnation, atonement, sin, sanctification, the new community – as the Church has formulated them through its historically situated meditations upon Scripture, the proclamations of the Ecumenical Councils and its liturgical practices. Lessing examines Origen's understanding of Christ and recognises Origen's beliefs are no longer believable. He prepares the stage for a presentation of his own Enlightenment Christology. Pannenberg views Barth's understanding of Christ, assessing it in terms of a credible response to the rejected rational Christology of Kant (and by extension Lessing) and 'the contemporary intellectual situation'.[4]

It follows from this, secondly, that the problem which gives rise to reassessments of Jesus Christ, for both Lessing and Pannenberg, is time: time past (the Christ event) and time present ('my age'), and the relationship between the two. With Lessing there is something of a nostalgia for a time that is lost; his sentiments express the long sigh of the labourer who sees the extent of the reconstructive work that lies ahead. If he opens the ugly ditch between the Jesus of history and the Christ of faith, both Pannenberg and Barth are, in their different ways, working to close it. Nevertheless, each of these theologians is embroiled with a problematic about time that is being interpreted according to agendas set by history as a human science. And though Schweitzer, while praising the achievements of historiography in the service of dogma, pointed to the enormous limitations of tracking down the historical Jesus, the tracking continues.[5] The historical Jesus has dominated Christology because of the way systematic theologians have relied upon historico-critical investigations into the Gospels in order to

---

[3] *Jesus – God and Man*, tr. Lewis L. Wilkins and Duane A. Priebe (London: SCM, 1968), p. 131.

[4] Ibid., p. 132.

[5] Norman Perrin's work is usually associated with the 'second' quest for the historical Jesus in the 1960s, and E.P. Sanders, John P. Meier and N.T. Wright with the third and still ongoing quest.

establish the identity of Jesus of Nazareth and the faith of the first Christian Churches. We can see this even with the Roman Catholic theologian, Walter Kasper, who rightly sets about answering the question, 'Where and how do we meet Jesus Christ today?'[6] Kasper, nevertheless, spends most of his book going through accounts of 'The Earthly Jesus' and his resurrection. Of course, no Christology can avoid what the Scriptures say about Christ, but the historico-critical tools used hermeneutically are not without presuppositions. They are secular tools that *prima facie* offer a veneer of scientific realism. In wielding them a sense arises that somehow we have access to empirical truths (and that these kinds of truths are the very mark of truth itself). What starts to be forgotten is that acts of interpretation are taking place, and, as we have learnt from Gadamer, these acts of interpretation are governed as much by our own cultural standpoint (and its predispositions) as any past being investigated.[7]

The predispositions and assumptions that situate either historian or theologian become evident, thirdly, in the way the Christological investigation in the wake of the Enlightenment develops categories that reflect the turn to the human subject that grounded Enlightenment thinking. Christ becomes a figure to be treated in terms of personhood, modern views of what constitute human nature, and notions of identity. Theologians may no longer set themselves up as amateur psychoanalysts – as some nineteenth-century writers of kenotic Christologies did – but, nevertheless, Christology in this cultural climate, whether expounded by Lessing, Pannenberg or even Barth,[8] focuses on defining 'who is this Jesus, called the Christ?' From this the dogmatic enquiry proceeds then to ask about the work done as the

---

[6] *Jesus the Christ*, tr. V. Green (London: Burns & Oates, 1976), p. 24.

[7] Barth is aware of the limitation of verification through historicism (*Die Kirkliche Dogmatik*, IV.1, pp. 316–23; *Church Dogmatics*, IV.1, pp. 335–41). Nevertheless, he uses the positivist findings of historical criticism if not to prove his thesis then certainly to lend his exegesis professional credibility (possibly having learnt the need to do this following the debates among New Testament scholars over the two editions of *Der Römerbrief*). It is this desire to make a reading 'creditable' by borrowing the symbolic capital from the results of form, redaction and source criticism that I am referring to – using this material as if it was beyond interpretation and dealt only with facts.

[8] I say 'even Barth' because Barth was consciously challenging traditional dogmatic enquiry (*Die Kirkliche Dogmatik*, IV.1, pp. 135–40; *Church Dogmatics*, IV.1, pp. 123–8). In particular, he questions having Christology as a section that is entirely distinct from 'what we have to say concerning man and the Church' (p. 135/124). He also questions the distinction between the person and work of Jesus Christ (p. 139/127). Nevertheless, he opens his Christology with an investigation into the divine nature, although the identity of the Christ lies for him in a praxis (obedience, servitude) rather than a certain kind of subjectivity. As I will detail below, his dialectical method militates against examining this praxis in terms of what it produces and for whom. The dialectical method forces Barth into treating Christ as either an absolute subject (considered in himself) or object (considered with respect to either God as Father or the Christian community).

Christ and then the consequences of that work for humanity. The founding dogmatic question concerns the nature of identity. What follows, as Barth recognised, is that Christological examinations 'concerning Him always move in either the one direction or the other, from above downwards or from below upwards'[9] – in Rahner's terms, Christology from below or Christology from above. Of course, it could be argued that the identity question is an old question, already hotly debated in the Council of Chalcedon, and answered in the formulation *vere homo, vere Deus*. But I would contend that Chalcedon was following through the double knowledge of Christ found in the Gospel letters: to know Jesus Christ 'according to the flesh' and 'according to the spirit' (see Rom. 1.3; I Tim. 3.16; I Pet. 3.18). This double mode of knowing is developed into the two natures that are the objects of such knowing. Not that these modes of knowing and these natures are dualistically distinct from one another. While they cannot be conflated with one another, an analogical relation binds them in the same way as, from Origen onward, there is a spiritual sensing that is analogically related to a carnal sensing. The relation makes possible a double operation recorded in the work of other pre-Chalcedonian Fathers like Tertullian and Clement of Alexandria: 'God lived with men as man that man might be taught to live the divine life: God lived on man's level that man might be able to live on God's level';[10] 'I say, of God, who became man that you may learn from a man how it may be that man should become God.'[11] What Chalcedon discusses and formulates, then, is *phusis* or *substantia* itself in Jesus Christ, and by extension all creation conceived and known *en Christo*. This is quite different from the identity concerns constituting the parameters of the Christological discussions in the eighteenth and nineteenth centuries that still hold sway over modern Christian dogmatics.

From these three observations concerning Christology's association with discourse, time and history, and the cultural specificity of certain concepts for and methods of investigation, we can concur with Walter Kasper: 'in Christology we are ultimately concerned with the Christian understanding of reality in the broadest sense of the word. Christology has to do at least in rudimentary terms with the relation between Christianity and culture, politics and so forth.'[12] This being the case, the Christological task is always to ask two questions: not only 'What sense do we make of the Christ event today?' but also 'How are we making that sense for today and what does that

---

9   Ibid., p. 149/136.
10   Tertullian, *Adversus Marcionem,* ii.27.
11   Clement of Alexandria, *Protrepicus,* 1.8, 4.
12   *Jesus the Christ,* p. 20.

making itself point to?' Not that the past is irrelevant, for the horizons of today's questions are always configured by what has been handed down to us – including the historical Jesus himself recorded in the Scriptures. But because Jesus Christ is a confession of faith, and faith is a present operation with respect to salvation, then God is made known by us today in ways that differ from the time of Lessing, or Pannenberg, or Barth. We are no longer bound by Enlightenment rationalism, nineteenth- and twentieth-century preoccupations with subjectivism, psychologism, historical positivism, humanism, ameliorism, liberalism and the pursuit of freedom. We are no longer bound by the way such a culture conceives Christology anthropolog-ically, employing pseudo-scientific tools to achieve the 'effects' of a rational demonstration. Not only is God made known by us differently, God is made known to us in new ways – for the effects of the operations of God are today's effects, not last century's.[13] It is because, then, the Christ-event is always culturally inflected that our two questions arise and determine inves-tigations into what sense this event makes in our own times, with our own ideologies and cultural agendas and what relationship holds between the sense we 'make' today of that event and the senses of that event that were 'made' in the past.[14]

Beyond Dogmatic Enquiry

If what I am setting out is a different agenda for Christology today, these essays are only exercises that go towards fulfilling such an agenda. Nothing here is systematic, but the essays written here over the last ten years are trying to clear a space in which a more systematic work can appear. Never-theless, it would be worthwhile indicating as clearly as possible how, specifically, does the approach to Christology in these essays differ from (and supplement) the approach found in more traditional dogmatics. I will do

---

[13] The distinction between being made known by us (*a nobis*) and to us (*nobis*), I take from 1a12 of Aquinas's *Summa Theologiae* where he moves between both terms.

[14] In a fascinating study on 'The Face and Physique of the Historical Jesus', the New Testament scholar Stephen D. Moore, in his book *God's Beauty Parlor: And Other Queer Spaces in and around the Bible* (Stanford University Press, 2001), examines the presentations of Jesus Christ from Warner Sallman's *Head of Christ* (1940), *The Lord Is My Shepherd* (1943), *Christ Our Pilot* (1950) and *Portrait of Jesus* (1966) to Willem Dafoe's performance of 'Jesus as a Zen hippie' (p. 125) in Martin Scorsese's *Last Temptation of Christ* (1988) and the jacket illustrations of John P. Meiers, *A Marginal Jew: Rethinking the Historical Jesus*, vols. 1 (1991) and 2 (1994) and E.P. Sanders's *The Historical Figure of Jesus* (1995). Moore points to the idealised figures of male virtue and beauty, to the implicitly gay iconography of 'the radiantly handsome hero' (p. 129). What his essay illustrates is the ongoing pro-duction of Christology, a production inseparable from wider cultural concerns, values and agendas.

this through briefly examining the construction of Christology by Karl Barth, for Barth too was responding to the historicist method of treating Christology evident in his own teacher Wilhelm Hermann, and wished to emphasise revelation as an ongoing event or action. But by proceeding this way I can point up how my own approach differs, and why, and with what results. In what follows I am not then invalidating dogmatic enquiry but showing how it requires supplementation. For Barth, this supplementation will entail challenging the heart of his dialectical method.

Karl Barth's most detailed examination of Jesus Christ is located in *Church Dogmatics* I.2, IV.1 and IV.2 – that is, with his expositions of the doctrine of the Word of God and his elaboration of the doctrine of reconciliation (*Versöhnung* – atonement). In particular, I will treat volumes I.2 and IV.1, although Barth would be the first to remind us that since all our knowledge of God issues in and through the revelation of God in Jesus Christ, his Christology actually knits together (and makes possible) the whole of the *Church Dogmatics*. In what follows, the doctrine of Jesus Christ that Barth offers is not my foremost concern. I will not be arguing, then, with whether this doctrine is Alexandrian, Antiochene, Nestorian or just downright incoherent (as some critics have argued).[15] Nor am I concerned with whether the resulting dogmatics is Christocentric or Christomonistic (as other critics have argued).[16] My concern is to give an account of the ways by which his doctrine of Christ emerges, the implicit philosophical assumptions or values implicit in his approach, and the limitations that accrue from it.

We can begin with a telling exegetical remark concerning John 3.16 – 'God so loved the world that He sent his only begotten Son, that whosoever believeth in Him shall not perish, but have everlasting life.' Barth observes: '[T]he divine loving in the form of the sending of the Son is the confirmation of the will of God not to acquiesce in this [*nicht bewenden zu lassen*] ['this' = the lostness of human beings] but to cause [*haben zu lassen*] man to

---

[15]   Given the centrality of Christology to Barth's dogmatics, the critical literature on his Christology is legion. See John Thompson, *Christ in Perspective: Christological Perspectives in the Theology of Karl Barth* (Edinburgh: St Andrew's Press, 1978); Charles T. Waldrop, *Karl Barth's Christology: Its Basic Alexandrian Character* (New York: Mouton Publishers, 1984); Bruce Marshall, *Christology in Conflict: The Identity of a Saviour in Rahner and Barth* (Oxford: Blackwell, 1987); Jeffery C. Pugh, *The Anselmic Shift: Christology and Method in Karl Barth's Theology* (New York: Peter Lang, 1990); Bruce McCormack, *Karl Barth's Critically Realistic Dialectical Theology: Its Genesis and Development* (Oxford University Press, 1995), pp. 327–463; George Hunsinger, 'Karl Barth's Christology: Its Basic Chalcedonian Character' in John Webster ed., *The Cambridge Companion to Karl Barth* (Cambridge University Press, 2000), pp. 127–42.

[16]   See George Hunsinger, *How to Read Karl Barth* (Oxford University Press, 1991), especially his conclusion on Christ as the centre, pp. 225–33.

have the eternal life which he has forfeited.'[17] The revealing clause is 'to cause man to have eternal life'. It is revealing because it states the purpose of God's act – a purpose that because of the sovereignty of God's will will necessarily come about – but it tells us nothing about the process of that act, namely, how God causes human beings to participate in him and have eternal life. Barth insists that there is a participation,[18] but the effect of not giving an account of the process, or economy, of redemption is that relations between God and human beings appear autocratic. The qualification that human beings respond 'by faith' in this act of divine sovereignty is only a partial answer, especially when that faith paradoxically 'even in its emptiness and passivity … has [*trägt*] this character of supreme fullness and activity'.[19] For faith is itself an operation; it is a relational process whereby something comes to pass. Faith is time-bound. Furthermore, it is an engagement that can take many different forms, not just passive obedience. What is missing from Barth's account of faith is the experience and practices in which faith becomes operable and evident: the formation of the one who is being faithful. What is missing is a sociology and a phenomenology of believing. On its own, 'by faith' is simply a theological abstraction. Faith is a response to that which constitutes a relation with; response and engagement enable participation in an economy that is shared. We can agree with Barth that God is the initiator of this redemption, and we do not wish either to deny the ontological difference between creator and creation or to fall into some Pelagian heresy. But faith, I would argue, is an operation in response to a recognition of love, and what is missing in Barth's account is the process whereby love is received and responded to. We might put this in another way (a way that finds repeated expression in the essays that follow): there is in Barth no account of the economy of desire and the productions of faith, discipleship, and personal formation.

There is a second consequence of this failure to account for how redemption is brought about. That is, for all Barth's emphasis on covenant, 'God for us' and his 'being present and active in the world in Christ',[20] he constitutes God as an alienated acting subject, even when it is God incarnate. The heart of the matter here concerns the human nature of Jesus Christ. For while we can admit that all our conceptions of what it is to be human (and in *Church Dogmatics* III Barth labours the point that to be human is not to be a solitary individual but to be in relation) find their perfect expression in Christ,

---

[17]   *Die Kirkliche Dogmatik*, IV.1, p. 77; *Church Dogmatics*, IV.1, p. 72.
[18]   Ibid., pp. 79–80/74–5.
[19]   Ibid., p. 711/636.
[20]   Ibid., p. 80/75.

nevertheless equivocity cannot dictate two uses of the term human: a use for Christ and a use for other human beings. We may, in the manner of Aquinas, have to admit our ignorance of what it means to be human if Christ is the perfection of that humanity, but without an analogical relation between these two uses of 'human' how does the operation of redemption take place? How would human beings ever know it had taken place?[21] The problem here concerns what Hegel would call 'recognition' – to recognise demands an exchange in which one *is* recognised. One can observe in descriptions by Barth of the 'yawning abyss [*ein weit aufgerissener Abgrund*]'[22] between God and creation a tendency towards equivocity:

> Those who believe in Jesus Christ will never forget for a single moment that the true and actual being of reconciled man [*Menschen*] has its place in that Other who is strange, and different from them, and that that is why they can participate in it [the reconciliation between human beings and God] with a fullness and clarity the knowledge of which would be broken if they were to look aside to any other place.[23]

There is a double-bind here in which Christians are caught. It has two characteristics. First, radical difference *enables* participation. Second, the logic of that enablement is neither *prima facie* nor open to human investigation. Even putting aside this double-bind, Barth's language itself distinguishes between being human and being other, strange and different. In other words, the uniqueness of Jesus Christ always separates him from the world he entered into which was his own (John 1.11).

It is at this point that we have to turn to *Church Dogmatics* I.2, for Barth would justify the theo-logic of this double-bind on the basis of a unique Christological formula – *anhypostasis–enhypostasis*.[24] Following Bruce Mc-Cormack's narrative of the *anhypostasis–enhypostasis* as the turning point in

---

[21] On the difficulties of Barth's notion of 'analogy' see Hans Urs von Balthasar, *Karl Barth: Darstellung und Deutung: Seiner Theologie* (Cologne: Verlag Jakob Hegner, 1951), pp. 93–181; Horst Georg Poehlmann, *Analogia Entis oder Analogia Fidei? Die Frage der Analogie bei Karl Barth* (Göttingen: Vanderhoeck & Ruprecht, 1965); Henri Chavannes, *L'analogie entre Dieu et le monde selon saint Thomas d'Aquin et selon Karl Barth* (Paris: Saint-Paul, 1969); and my *Barth, Derrida and the Language of Theology* (Cambridge University Press, 1995).

[22] *Die Kirkliche Dogmatik*, IV.1, p. 87; *Church Dogmatics*, IV.1, p. 82.

[23] Ibid., p. 98/92.

[24] Barth himself does not view his formulation as innovative, but see U.M. Lang, 'Anhypostatos–Enhypostatos: Church Fathers, Protestant Orthodoxy and Karl Barth', *Journal of Theological Studies* 49 NS, pt. 2, October (1998), pp. 630–57: 'If there is indeed anything like a "dual formula" *anhypostasis–enhypostasis*, it is Barth's own innovation rather than that of Protestant orthodoxy', p. 632.

Barth's theology,[25] a debate ensued concerning the coherence of Barth's Christology with regard to Christ as both *anhypostasis* and *enhypostasis*. The debate opened with F. LeRon Shults's essay, 'A Dubious Christological Formula: From Leontius of Byzantium to Karl Barth',[26] the main thrust of which claimed that Barth had received this doctrine through Heinrich Heppe's and Heinrich Schmidt's summaries of Protestant Scholasticism. For Shults, Barth's account is incoherent and badly misinterprets the Patristic thinking on this doctrine. Subsequently, two detailed articles appeared: the first by U.M. Lang[27] and the second by Matthias Gockel.[28] The argument of these essays – which involved extensive exegetical treatment of the doctrine by the Church Fathers – is that the Protestant Scholasticism that Barth worked through to formulate his Christological position was very much in line with the more traditional readings of this teaching. In fact, Gockel even compares the Christologies of Aquinas and Barth that rehearse the *anhypostasis–enhypostasis* formula and declares they are entirely congruent. Significantly, neither Lang nor Gockel return to Barth's text in *Church Dogmatics* I.2 to examine Barth's examination of the teaching. Furthermore, neither Lang nor Gockel explain how, given practically identical Christologies between John Damascene, Aquinas and Barth, both Damascene and Aquinas develop highly participatory accounts of the relationship between the Creator and Creation such that they articulate a *sacramentum mundi*.

In returning to Barth, we have to recognise that his adoption of the 'dual formula' (that he alone is the innovator of[29]) was determined by its dialectical character. Having set out, in #15 of I.2, that the theological necessity for revelation of God lay in God becoming fully human ('His complete solidarity with us'[30]), Barth then strikes the dialectical chord: 'In becoming the same as we are, the Son of God is the same in quite a different [*ganz anders*] way from us.'[31] It is from this point in his argument that he outlines how the Word 'assumes' true human existence (to which the commission of sin is not attributable[32]). What he will finally outline as *enhypostasis* is this 'assump-

---

[25] *Karl Barth's Critically Realistic Dialectical Theology*, pp. 327–463. This essay has been developed in F. LeRon Shults, *Reforming Theological Anthropology: After the Philosophical Turn to Relationality* (Grand Rapids, Mich.: Eerdmans, 2003), pp. 147–50.

[26] *Theological Studies* 57 (1996), pp. 431–46.

[27] 'Anhypostatos–Enhypostatos', pp. 630–57.

[28] 'A Dubious Christological Formula? Leontius of Byzantium and the *Anhypostasis–Enhypostasis* Theory', *Journal of Theological Studies* NS, 51 pt. 2, October (2000), pp. 515–32.

[29] Lang, 'Anhypostatos–Enhypostatos', p. 632.

[30] *Die Kirkliche Dogmatik*, I.2, p. 167; *Church Dogmatics*, I.2, p. 153.

[31] Ibid., p. 170/155.

[32] Ibid., p. 170/156.

tion': 'the Word of God becomes flesh, assumes [*Annahme*] or adopts [*Aufnahme*] or incorporates [*Hineinnahme*] human being into unity with His divine being'.[33] Putting to one side the range of Christological positions opened by those three different prefixes 'an-', 'auf-', and 'hinein-', to the German verb *nehmen* (translated as assumes, adopts, incorporates), *enhypostasis* defines this *unio personalis* – according to the Protestant Scholastics Quenstedt and Hollaz. And, if the arguments of Lang and Gockel are correct, then this understanding of *enhypostasis* is in accord with Patristic (and Aquinas's) teaching. But Barth goes further – and this going further results in the innovation of the 'dual formula'. He writes, with important theological consequences: 'Jesus Christ is described primarily as an *unio personalis sive hypostica* and only secondarily as an *unio naturarum*.'[34] This hierarchy of descriptions – primary and secondary – then allows not only for the positive teaching of the *enhypostasis* but also for the negative teaching of the *anhypostasis*: 'Apart from the divine mode of being whose existence it [Christ's human nature] acquires it has none of its own; i.e., apart from its concrete existence in God in the event of the *unio*, it has no existence of its own, it is *anhypostasis*.' *Anhypostasis* safeguards two theological axioms for Barth: first, the utter uniqueness of this unity and, second, the lack of a point of contact between God and human beings in creation. *Anhypostasis* accords emphasis to a *unio personalis sive hypostica* rather than a *unio naturarum*. *Anhypostasis* withdraws the Godhead deep into its own mystery; *enhypostasis* speaks of an indwelling human being in Christ – just as all things exist in and through Christ. The reason why this dual formula and distinction between primary and secondary description is important for Barth is that *enhypostasis* can then not suggest a *communis participatio* – which he views as the Lutheran error in Christology. For such *enhypostatic* unity, 'does not this give us a kind of reciprocal relation between Creator and creature?'[35] In fact, there is a wide range of distinctions to be made between 'reciprocity' and 'relation'. There can be a relation between Creator and creatures without that being reciprocal (understood as symmetrical). There can be an asymmetrical relation in which creation is sustained in its utter gratuity from God while nevertheless responding eucharistically to such grace. This is a *communio* rather than a *communis participatio*; theologically it makes possible a sacramental and participatory understanding of the relationship between Creator and creation. But Barth's inability to think through an asymmetrical relation that would bind more closely a *unio personalis sive hypostica* with a *unio naturarum* –

---

[33]   Ibid., p. 175/160.
[34]   Ibid., p. 176/161.
[35]   Ibid., p. 179/164.

Barth's modern and uncritical construal of 'nature' – forestalls such an exploration.

As such the work of Christ cannot be characterised in terms of the ordinary human operations of that world – its politics, economics, social and cultural milieu, his friends, his family, his enemies, his admirers. Christ becomes the perfect expression of Cartesian subjectivity: autonomous, self-determining, self-defining, the atomised subject of a number of distinct properties or predicates;[36] as Barth himself puts it, the 'epistemological principle'.[37] Christ becomes either the absolute subject or the absolute object: he 'who is the subject and object of the basic act of God, the subject and object of the consummating act of God that reveals that basis'.[38] The self-authenticating nature of Christ is reflected in the self-referential nature of the dogmatic enquiry. For Barth can only characterise the work of this Jesus Christ in terms of a number of theologumena, namely, intra-ecclesial abstractions such as grace, covenant, atonement, sin and revelation. And so, despite the matrix of relations in which the New Testament situates Jesus Christ, Barth's Jesus Christ is not a social animal; he is an other, an alien, a 'pure act[s] of [the] divine grace'[39] of God.[40]

The question raised here is where is this figure of Christ as the 'epistemological principle' and the 'pure act' to be found? How do we have access to the principle or the pure act so that we recognise them to be such? In these terms are we not dealing with logical inferences, speculative inferences, that Barth himself has made on the basis of his exegeses of the Scriptures? Are we not dealing with a construction, a portrayal of Christ that is Barth's own? For Barth is clear, we have no immediate access to Jesus Christ. All we know

[36] See Bruce Marshall, *Christology in Conflict*, for an examination and analysis of Barth's Christology in terms of a particularised subject of certain unique predicates, the first and most fundamental of which is 'incarnation'. *Enhypostasis*, as George Florovsky observes, does not occur by itself. It therefore cannot be conceived in Cartesian terms. It is constituted by an interaction of natures, so that our being in Christ is *enhypostasis*. See *The Byzantine Fathers of the 6th to 8th Centuries*, tr. Raymond Miller et al. (Vaduz: Büchervertriebsanstalt, 1987) especially chapter four (pp. 191–203) on Leontius of Byzantium, who defined *en-* and *an-hypostasis*. *Enhypostasis* (which determines incarnation from the human perspective by defining a theological anthropology) is a condition of being in relation. We might then understand the incarnation of God in Jesus Christ as the bringing into being of a new relation. Relations, as these essays demonstrate, are not static states but continual operations.

[37] *Die Kirkliche Dogmatik*, IV.1, p. 21; *Church Dogmatics*, IV.1, p. 21.

[38] Ibid., p. 361/327. See also footnote 7.

[39] Ibid., p. 53/50.

[40] In terms of the Chalcedonian Creed, it is difficult to avoid concluding that Barth's theological position approximates to that of Eutyches, who refused to accept that Christ is *homoousios* with us in all things 'sin only accepted'. See R.U. Seller's classic study *The Council of Chalcedon: A Historical and Doctrinal Survey* (London: SPCK, 1953), p. 212.

we know as mediated. Charges of revelatory positivism cannot be levied against Barth at this point in his theological thinking. But here, with his construal of mediation, we reach the heart of the matter.

It is interesting, and significant, that in Barth's wish to argue for a description of Christ's atonement in terms of the judge judged in our place – as distinct from a priestly, sacrificial understanding of atonement that is important to Roman Catholic theologies of divine reconciliation – he writes of the need for 'a salutary reminder that in dogmatics we cannot speak down from heaven in the language of God [*Sprache Gottes*], but only on earth as strictly and exactly as we can in human language [*Menschensprache*]'.[41] The old priestly and cultic metaphors in the New Testament present 'a form which is now rather remote from us'.[42] Here are signs that Barth is conscious of the mediation of both the New Testament material and contemporary dogmatics. But his investigations into this mediation are limited. In fact, there is a sense in which mediation itself is fallenness for Barth; something we must get beyond. That there is a place where interpretation stops finds two particular locations in Barth. Not in order of importance, the first concerns those places in the Scriptures (like the resurrection narratives) where we no longer are dealing with a time, materiality and human perception as we know it. Here we are advised to 'stick to that which is told us, not trying to replace it by something that is not told us on the pretext that it needs interpreting'.[43] The second location is in the final *parousia* itself when the living presence of Jesus Christ is directly encountered. As such, to look towards the *eschaton* is to live 'with a burning longing [*brennenden Sehnsucht*] for the sight denied them in this time, for the liberation and redemption which are still to come, for an immediacy of contact [*Unmittelbarkeit ihrer Beziehung*] with the Lord without the help or the distraction of mediation [*Mittelbarkeit*]'.[44] Mediation, then, like the world, is something to be overcome.

The root of this response to mediation (which is so unlike Augustine, Aquinas, or any Christian theologian with a developed sense of the *sacramentum mundi*) lies in the way Barth focuses any theological attention to mediation on Jesus Christ himself – Jesus Christ as the mediator of God to humanity and humanity to God. Two consequences follow from this, both of which are further outworkings of his theological method. First, the processes of mediation are never materially delineated – they are only theologically delineated in terms of Barth's pneumatology: the Spirit's noetic

---

[41] *Die Kirkliche Dogmatik/Church Dogmatics*, IV.1, p. 301/274.

[42] Ibid., p. 302/275.

[43] Ibid., p. 377/342.

[44] Ibid., p. 360/326.

working out of a new ontology wrought by Christ. Secondly, the fallenness of humankind is such that Jesus Christ can only mediate himself to himself: all human perception and modes of thinking are inadequate. The depth of the alienation of the world from Christ renders mediation impossible unless Christ himself does it (what Barth terms God's 'self-attestation') – and even then there is a question of how we would ever recognise or understand such mediation. Of course, Barth is not oblivious to this question. In fact, as so often in his work, he anticipates it:

> The kernel of the question is simply the incompatibility of the existence of Jesus Christ with us and us with Him, the impossibility of the co-existence of His divine–human actuality and action and our sinfully human being and activity, the direct collision between supreme order and supreme disorder.[45]

But to raise the question does not necessarily mean that it is answered decisively. And it cannot be answered decisively because any answer is pre-determined by the dialectical method that divides the subject from its opposite, and seals not only the truth of Christ within the self-attestation of Christ himself but also dogmatic thinking within the endless hermeneutical spiralling between Christ and his Church. The hermeneutical spiralling may not, as Barth claims, constitute a vicious circle, but I suggest it limits theological reflection somewhat. Most particularly, it limits operations. Because there is inadequate enquiry given to the mediation itself, there is no space open for evaluating the extent to which one's figuring of Christ is itself profoundly imbued with the values, assumptions (or the reactions to those values and assumptions) of the culture in which it was conceived.

To sum up, then, Barth's dogmatic approach to Christology (a) all too thinly defines the economies of salvation in which the gracious love of Christ finds a responding desire; (b) this finds expression in the thinness of his account of mediations (c) such that his mediating Christology remains tied to specific cultural assumptions about the subject and nature; (d) this binds Christology to the logic of dualism, itself a product of a certain cultural heritage in modernity;[46] (e) this logic and these assumptions, on the basis of which he develops his dialectical method, render him unable to reflect upon his own cultural production of Christology. The world is so lost, so secularised, so ignorant of God that both Christ and subsequently a theology of Christ operate above and beyond such a world, in contradistinction

---

[45] Ibid., p. 385/348.

[46] For the relationship between Barth's theological thinking and modernity see my 'Barth, Modernity and Postmodernity' in John Webster ed., *The Cambridge Companion to Karl Barth* (Cambridge University Press, 2002), pp. 274–95.

to it. Dogmatics is fundamentally a countercultural activity. Hence, for him, Christian apologetics is an anathema.[47]

To some extent, the problem here lies with the nature of modern dogmatics itself and the professionalisation of systematic theology such that every theologian worth his or her salt must attempt at least a three-volume enterprise. For modern dogmatics has an inherent tendency to pursue the normative, to essentialise, to seek to present a theology and therefore a religion such as Christianity as a self-contained doctrinal system. This tendency emerges from – to go back no further – Protestant Scholasticism and, later, Enlightenment rationalism. Evident in Kant's *Religion within the Limits of Reason Alone*, it is summed up in a distinction used by Tocqueville in *Democracy in America* between 'dogma itself, which is the substance of religion' and 'worship [which] is only the form'.[48] This idealist tendency, fostered by Enlightenment rationalism that separates doctrine as substance from praxis as form, is amplified when theology appeals only to its own theological resources in order to define itself (as in Barth). The Patristic scholar Richard Hanson makes a valid point when he observes with respect to second- and third-century Christian theologians: 'it is impossible to interpret the Bible in the vocabulary of the Bible'.[49] If Christianity is to offer a different approach – an approach that can nevertheless acknowledge imaginative inflections and alternative possibilities while still speaking in accordance with a grammar of the faith – it has to move beyond modern dogmatics.

Christology and Apologetics

It is important for the essays in this collection that Christological discourse arose not in dogmatics but apologetics.[50] I am not wishing to state either

---

[47] For an examination of both his attack on apologetics and yet also the way his own theological thinking cannot seal itself off from the influences and significances of other discourses, see my *Cultural Transformation and Religious Practice* (Cambridge University Press, 2004), pp. 15–57.

[48] *Democracy in America*, tr. Harvey C. Mansfield and Delba Winthrop (University of Chicago Press, 2000), p. 422.

[49] 'The Achievement of Orthodoxy in the Fourth Century AD' in Rowan Williams ed., *The Making of Orthodoxy: Essays in Honour of Henry Chadwick* (Cambridge University Press, 1989), p. 148.

[50] Apologetics were not simply something undertaken by Christians; there are a variety of apologetic forms so there were a variety of apologetic perspectives. See Mark Edwards, Martin Goodman and Simon Price eds., *Apologetics in the Roman Empire: Pagans, Jews, and Christians* (Oxford University Press, 1999) for a collection of critical essays demonstrating the variety of apologetic viewpoints and styles. The collection serves to remind us that apologetics was not simply a matter of missionising but also the integration of identities that cultural heterogeneity and mobility across wide geographical spaces fragmented and rendered complex.

that the second-century Apologists developed Christologies free from doctrinal errors[51] or that we should return to their concerns with Middle-Platonism. The point I wish to make is that Christological reflection was not simply an intra-ecclesial discourse concerned with articulating the logic of the faith with respect to New Testament titles like the Christ, the Son of God, the Word, the Son of Man and their association with Jesus of Nazareth.[52] It was that as well, as the commentary work of Origen makes clear, and the later work of the Councils of Nicaea and Chalcedon are examples of the working of this intra-ecclesial purpose. Though, even here, it has to be recognised that anyone wishing to understand the forging of orthodoxy in the fourth century 'must perforce plunge into a jungle of Greek philosophical terms ... Very often the debate seems to be remote from the vocabulary and the thought of the New Testament.'[53] But early Christological thinking, following that composed by the authors of the New Testament, developed extra-ecclesially and with conscious reference to the cultural situation in which and to which it spoke. This thinking drew on the Scriptures but also 'on the commonplaces of Hellenistic rhetoric and on the language of Middle-Platonist (and Stoic) religious cosmology and theology ... [In order to] present their faith in a way that might make it appear comprehensible and tolerable, if not attractive, to hostile readers.'[54] Justin Martyr read Jesus in the light of Socrates and Hermes, and draws explicitly on Plato's *Timaeus*; Theophilus employed terms attributed to the Stoics; Irenaeus borrowed technical terms from Greek rhetoric; Clement describes Christ as a new Orpheus and was not adverse to using material from either the Gnostics or Merkabah mysticism; and the feisty Tertullian insisted on the need to use secular culture for furthering the gospel.[55] Evidently, it is in this second kind of Christological discourse that Christ and culture are most explicitly associated. Origen, for example, draws upon his knowledge of the

---

[51]   See Jean Daniélou, *A History of Early Christian Doctrine: Volume Two, Gospel Message and Hellenistic Culture*, tr. John Austin Baker (London: Darton, Longman & Todd, 1973), pp. 157–94 and 354–86 for a sharp discussion of some of the difficulties the Christological debates from Justin to Origen engendered.

[52]   On the whole, this is the approach in James D.G. Dunn, *Christology in the Making: An Inquiry into the Origin of the Doctrine of the Incarnation* (London: SCM, 1980).

[53]   Hanson, 'The Achievement of Orthodoxy in the Fourth Century AD', p. 148.

[54]   Richard A. Norris Jr., 'The Apologists', in Frances Young, Lewis Ayres and Andrew Louth eds., *The Cambridge History of Early Christian Literature* (Cambridge University Press, 2004), pp. 36–7. For a more detailed account of the social, philosophical and religious context being addressed by the Apologists see Eric Osborn, *The Emergence of Christian Theology* (Cambridge University Press, 1993), pp. 1–38.

[55]   See J.C. Fredouille, *Tertullien, et la conversion de la culture antique* (Paris: Études Augustiennes, 1972), p. 357.

philosophical schools of the day, current modes of argument and rhetoric, literature from the classical traditions and late antiquity, and discussions with contemporary rabbis. Furthermore, Origen works on the basis of cultural assumptions shared by himself and other non-Christian readers like Celsus in order to point out to them the various errors and absences in their arguments and present them with an alternative interpretation of Jesus Christ and the teaching of the Church that he inaugurated.[56] He refers to common beliefs about dreams and demons, and medical lore, for example. Christological discourse was born not simply for catechesis but for mission. This is fundamental for the work involved in the essays that follow, for apologetic borrowing is not a simple matter of assimilation. While the early Church Apologists sought to persuade, they also sought to critique and to justify – to tell the story of what is in a better, more coherent, way. In particular, their critique concerned idolatry.[57] Apologetics, then, is implicated in what I call a cultural politics. Its engagement with its cultural contexts offers a *Kulturkritik*.[58]

The basis for this engagement between Christ and culture is significant, in the light of Barth's dialectical method, and the resulting Christology is significant also (even if later developments in Trinitarian theology helped to formulate more adequately a non-subordinatist doctrine of Christ).[59] The theological basis lies in a certain analogy that pertains between the uncreated God and creation, Christ and human beings. It is an analogy that can pertain because we are made in the image of God and therefore, as Jean-Louis Chrétien understands, '[i]t is the transcendence in us that knows the transcendent'.[60] Irenaeus, with his teaching on the first and second Adam and Christ as the recapitulation of all righteous human beings and prophets, states the case briefly:

> [I]f the first Adam was indeed taken from the earth, and moulded by the Word of God, then it was necessary that that same Word, when he made recapitulation of Adam in himself, should have a likeness of the same manner of

---

[56]   See Henry Chadwick's magisterial edition and translation of *Contra Celsum* (Cambridge University Press, 1953).

[57]   See Karen Jo Torjesen, 'Social and Historical Setting: Christianity as Cultural Critique' in *The Cambridge History of Early Christian Literature*, pp. 181–99.

[58]   In my *Cultural Transformation and Religious Practice* (Cambridge University Press, 2004), I present a detailed account of Christian *Kulturkritik* that examines its similarities to and differences from that social critique developed by the Frankfurt School. I will not cover the same ground in this volume.

[59]   See here Hanson, 'The Achievement of Orthodoxy in the Fourth Century AD' and Osborn, *The Emergence of Christian Theology*, pp. 142–96.

[60]   *The Ark of Speech*, tr. Andrew Brown (New York: Routledge, 2004), p. 66.

birth. Why then did not God again take clay, but instead caused the moulding to be done through Mary? In order that that which was formed should not be different, nor that which was saved, but that first man should be recapitulated, the likeness being preserved.[61]

The resulting Christologies from this engagement between Christ and culture, on the basis of this (still yet to be determined) analogy, were cosmological, metaphysical and orientated to soteriology. In fact, the language of *oikonomia*, *dunamis* and *energeia* dominated Christological thinking of this period, giving rise to what one recent scholar has termed a 'power theology'.[62] In a small but incisive article on Christology in Gregory of Nyssa, Brian E. Daly concludes that Nyssa's main interest

> is *not* to identify precisely what is one and what is manifold in Christ, but to explore the conditions of possibility for our sharing in his triumph over death and human corruption … [H]is real interest is in our salvation: in what happens in human *nature* – to *to anthropion*, the common reality all of us concretely share – when it is brought into contact with *to theion*, the transcendent reality of God.[63]

This aptly describes my own Christological preoccuptations and why the questions I am asking concern the operations of God as a cultural and hermeneutical activity.

The Cultural Approach to Christology

I would like to think that the essays collected here share something of the imaginative energies that characterised those early Christian apologetics. Like them, I seek to define a Christology through a defence of the Christian faith. That defence necessarily means an engagement that is at times polemical, for it is always concerned with responding to conditions that pertain to

---

[61] *Adversus Haereses*, 3.21, 10.

[62] Michel Barnes, *Dunamis in Gregory of Nyssa's Trinitarian Theology* (Washington, D.C.: Catholic University of America Press, 2001), pp. 94–172, gives a detailed account of the language of power as it arose from expositions of Wisdom literature and Scriptural texts such as 1 Cor. 1.24 and Luke 1.35 in early Christian thinkers up to Gregory of Nyssa. 'Power theology' was concerned with the generation of the Son in Trinitarian theology; I am extending 'power theology' in terms of soteriology.

[63] 'Divine Transcendence and Human Transformation: Gregory of Nyssa's Antiappollinarian Christology' in *Modern Theology* 18 (4), October (2002), pp. 497–506, p. 502.

our contemporary culture. Like them I seek not just an engagement with but also a transformation of culture. Like them I take the specific Christian resources of the Scriptures but employ the tools of other discourses to interpret them – seeking to understand doctrine not in terms of some sealed-off Christian discourse (like the post-liberals and the neo-Barthians) but in terms of negotiating an understanding of the Christian faith in the world in which we live. That runs risks, but theological thinking must always run risks for two reasons. First, it must run risks because it has no proper discourse of its own, as Aquinas knew.[64] Secondly, it must run risks because understandings and receptions of the Word frequently atrophy; they cease to surprise and they cease to scandalise. The Word then must be made strange again.[65] For we have no simple or single access to either the historical and acculturated figure of Jesus Christ or to the mystery of Trinitarian relations. There is no simple access because on all the levels we have we must treat questions of interpretation, methods of interpretation, mediated revelation and speculation. There is no single access because the body of Jesus is no longer available and so we handle figurations of that body: the Gospels, reflections upon that body beginning with Paul, the Church, and the liturgy of the mass. And even here what we handle are various traditions in which this historical and acculturated body is figured; figured in ways that cannot but disseminate that body through other times, places and cultural habitudes. The Jesus we encounter, as Christian theologians, is always the Jesus of faith – the Jesus made available to us through the practices of faith by others; the Jesus who is the product of faith who we relate to ourselves only through a similar faith. That does not deny what the Council of Trent came to call the 'real presence' of Jesus Christ; participation is a participation in the real Jesus Christ, embodiment in the operations of his body. But all our thinking and figuring is post-Easter, and so to make a distinction between Jesus of Nazareth and the Son of God is to set up a pseudo-problem and pursue an intellectual will-o'-the-wisp. Even though we might develop the tradition of a proto-Gospel (Q) or even a collection of Jesus-sayings, we are enmeshed in interpretation, methods of interpretation, revelation and speculation; we are caught up in the reflections of myriad communities of faith who have delivered us to the place from which such a distinction is made. We cannot winnow the historical from the theological, in the belief that the

---

[64] *Summa Theologiae*, 1a1.5.

[65] There is an allusion here to John Milbank's very fine collection of essays, *The Word Made Strange* (Oxford: Blackwell, 1998), but Barth too opines: 'we must try to find some way of making the accustomed unaccustomed again, the well-known unknown and the old new' (*Kirkliche Dogmatik*, IV.1, p. 246; *Church Dogmatics*, IV.1, p. 224).

historical is 'nearer the truth'.[66] We move always within the circle of faith
and the economy of redemptive response; within a hermeneutical activity
that I wish to call 'discernment' to distinguish it from the philosophical goal
of interpretation, 'understanding'.

As such the Jesus we enquire into is always the Jesus who makes himself
known to us today. The Jesus we figure forth and discern is always a contemporary Jesus. The 'history of traditions' school of investigation uncovers
for us a Jesus coloured by apocalypticism, rabbinic teachings and Hellenism,
but even these 'traditions' are fashioned according to our contemporary
values and predilections.[67] Since, then, all our figuring issues from within
the matrices of our own cultural embeddedness, Christology is always a cultural undertaking.

But that does not mean it is *only* a cultural undertaking, for two reasons.
First, it must always return to a past it cannot recover and which nevertheless remains fundamental: today's negotiations with Jesus as Christ stand in
the line of two millennia of such negotiations with that historical embodied
exousia that proclaimed he was the revelation of God. We may not have
simple access to that past, but the sheer brute contingency of Jesus's existence, and the Scriptural witness to it, legitimates and governs all our
subsequent reflections. Secondly, and concomitantly, that which relates the
past event of Jesus to the *kerygma* and traditions of the Church, and the
present-day negotiations, is the truth of that *exousia* itself: the divine power
and authority of Jesus as Christ who is both Alpha and Omega – the potentate of time. The significance of Jesus for us now – the reason why we
continue to negotiate and encounter this man as God – is inseparable from
the original apocalyptic trajectories within which he is situated (by the
writers of the Gospels) and may indeed have situated himself. If today is not
some further realisation of the incarnation of God in Jesus Christ and an
intimation of a consummating fulfilment at the end of time, then all our figurations are no more than consolations for a body that is lost.[68] Our enquiry

---

[66] See Wolfhart Pannenberg, *Jesus – God and Man*. He assumes throughout that Q is an authentic
collection of the sayings of Jesus and that this can be appealed to as some kernel of the historical.
The assumptions here are twofold: that 'history' is a record of the past's empirical facts and that these
facts constitute the truth of the matter. Both of these assumptions are historiographically and philosophically questionable.

[67] We can appreciate something of 'fashion' and 'trend' in the attention paid by Biblical scholars to
the historical and cultural background of Scriptural texts when we recognise today a move away
from categories such as 'Gnosticism' and the new interest in the ancient practices of medicine and
magic.

[68] See Michel de Certeau's Lacanian reading of the lost body of Christ in 'How Is Christianity
Thinkable Today?' in Graham Ward ed., *The Postmodern God* (Oxford: Blackwell, 1997), pp. 142–55.

then, while being culturally circumscribed and infused, does not simply take place on a plane of historical immanence.

As such the enquiry into the relationship between Christ and culture is not an indifferent one. That is, it is not an enquiry that places the object of its enquiry at a cool and rationalised distance. Because it is an enquiry in, through and concerned with faith it receives its own legitimation only insofar as it is conducted within those apocalyptic trajectories and with respect to the *exousia* that marks Jesus as the Christ. On the other hand, the means whereby the enquiry can take place at all are culturally given. As H. Richard Niebuhr correctly diagnosed over fifty years ago,

> for Christianity, whether defined as church, creed, ethics, or movement of thought, moves between the two poles of Christ and culture. The relations of these two authorities constitute its problem. When Christianity deals with the question of reason and revelation, what is ultimately in question is the relation of the revelation in Christ to the reason which prevails in culture.[69]

What then is the relationship between Christ and culture? Niebuhr famously proposed a number of models for that relationship: Christ and culture can been seen as antithetical (Christ against culture), correlational (the Christ of culture), hierarchical (Christ above culture), paradoxical (Christ and culture) or transformative (Christ the transformer of culture). The models are not discrete, as he himself is aware, but they tend to operate on a governing binary: there is Christ and there is culture, and how the two relate.[70] The difficulty here is that Christ is already a cultural event. We have no access to a Christ who has not already been encultured. So what if we take another approach to this question, and instead of providing a typology of the various theological answers to a binary problematic, actually begin a theological enquiry; begin, that is, to think through the grammar of Christian believing on the basis that there can be no distillation of Christ from culture. What if we pursue a certain theo-logic announced in the final lines of Niebuhr's

---

[69] *Christ and Culture* (New York: Harper & Row, 1951), p. 11.

[70] It is almost a logistical problem. Two positions are sketched, A and B, and then the question raised as to the various relations between them: A ~ B are incommensurate; A = B; A / B; A and B are in dialectic tension; A + B = C (transformation). Niebuhr's own 'concluding unscientific post-script' advocates none of the models he proposes and finds insights in all of them – though he warms particularly to the A + B = C paradigm. '[T]he problem of Christ and culture can and must come to an end only in the realm beyond all study in the free decisions of individual believers and responsible communities', he writes (p. 233). And the rest of that final chapter defends this position, drawing an important – but in this context theologically weak – distinction between positions being 'relative to' each other rather than 'relativistic'.

book: 'the world of culture – man's achievement – exists within the world of grace – God's kingdom'?[71]

If all things exist in Christ, then the cultural is not something entirely separate from him; the cultural is that through which God's redemptive grace operates. Christ, we could say, is the origin and consummation of culture, in the same way as he is both the prototype and the fulfilment of all that is properly human. Where can we begin to contemplate the mystery of this relationship? Athanasius, in *Contra Arianos*, writes: 'We are called "the image and the glory of God" not on our own account; it is on account of the image and true glory of God that dwells in us, namely his Word who later became flesh for us, that we have the grace of this designation.'[72] All the essays in this collection reflect this concern with being 'made in the image of'; if we make enquiry into what a culture is we find that it is a system of symbols and practices involving symbols, a constellation of interrelated meanings that can only be meaningful – and be communicated and taught as meaningful – because they have material form. The character of the form is manifold: a gesture, an event, a word, a sign. But there can only be culture where there is figuring. It is, then, because as human beings we are image makers that we fashion as expressions of ourselves the cultures we inhabit.

Succinctly, how does this differ from Barth's approach? Barth, as I have read him, falls victim to his own dialectical method that tends to hypostasise two distinct positions. In a suggestive little essay written jointly by Jean-Luc Nancy and Philippe Lacoue-Labarthe, reference is made to Adorno's construal of negative dialectic: 'The dialectic is a rigorous consciousness of non-identity', they quote.[73] Barth's construal of dialectic similarly works towards a certain non-identity (of both Christ and ourselves). He too, like Adorno, 'attempts … not to *maintain* the contradiction but to bear its rupture'.[74] In other words Barth's Christology is a negotiation of what Gillian Rose called 'the broken middle'[75] in terms of a unique person (Jesus Christ). What I am attempting in these essays is to see how in and across this broken middle there is constructed a set of relations, a divine and dynamic operation that constitutes an embodiment (the body of Christ, the body of the Church, the sacramental body, the social body and the physical bodies of each of us). It is a glorious embodiment, which like the body of Christ in the garden

[71] Ibid., p. 256.
[72] *Contra Arianos*, iii.10.
[73] 'Noli Me Frangere' in *The Birth to Presence*, tr. Brian Holmes (Stanford University Press, 1993), p. 271.
[74] Ibid., p. 272.
[75] *The Broken Middle* (Oxford: Blackwell, 1992).

encountered by Mary Magdalene can both be there and not there. In Nancy and Lacoue-Labarthe's words (they treat the same Scriptural passage): 'the glorious body ... offers nothing to know or touch. It's there, and it slips away.'[76] Where these essays run against Nancy and Lacoue-Labarthe's claim is in trying to wrestle with what it is that can be known ... before this body slips way. They view incarnation not as a fundamental identifying predicate of this unique subject (Jesus Christ) but as a Trinitarian operation with respect to the world.

Conclusion

Let me conclude by repeating that these essays do not present a Christology in a systematic manner. Rather, they bring together a series of investigations that bear upon the doctrine of Christ. Had I been able I would have included two further investigations. The first, 'The Displaced Body of Jesus Christ' formed part of a chapter in my volume *Cities of God*[77] and would have been an extension to part two, 'Engendering Christ'. The second, 'Beauty and the Son of God', appeared in a collection alongside essays by John Milbank and Edith Wyschogrod[78] and would have provided an extension into aesthetics in part three, 'The Living Christ'. The essays collected here, along with these other pieces, tackle the major issues that constitute Christology – incarnation, atonement, the economics of the Trinity, what it is to be human, the Church – with a particular emphasis upon embodiment, the operation of desire, mediation and interpretation. The investigations testify to the fundamental role Christ plays within my theological thinking, and how that understanding of Christ can never be separated from closely examining what the Scriptures yield to us of the historical Jesus. It is Jesus of Nazareth who is the Christ. Albert Schweitzer, in his critiques of both Wrede's and Bultmann's historical exegeses, points to what is incontrovertible: all four Gospels concur that above the cross Jesus's sentence of death was inscribed 'Jesus of Nazareth, the King of the Jews'.[79] The death of Jesus makes no sense outside of his historical claim to be the Christ; a claim that the Church accepts as foundational in the manner Peter accepted it at Caesarea Philippi (Mark 9.27–33).

I am more than aware of the limitations of the investigations collected

---

[76] '*Noli Me Frangere*', p. 275. For my own account of this Scriptural passage see chapter four, pp. 120–6.

[77] London: Routledge, 2001, pp. 97–116.

[78] *Theological Perspectives on God and Beauty* (Harrisburg, Pa.: Trinity Press International, 2003).

[79] *The Quest for the Historical Jesus* (London: SCM, 2000), p. 71, n. 8.

here. There are three in particular. First, I am not trained in New Testament scholarship and I do not try to situate the texts either in terms of the cultures they arose in or the communities that gave them expression and shape. Partly (as I suggested earlier in this Introduction) this is a reaction against the way certain historicist tools have bound modern Christological thinking. There have been times when, to deepen my own Scriptural exegesis, I have foraged among the detailed commentary work undertaken, and in certain cases I have drawn upon the expertise of colleagues working in the area of New Testament studies in the Department of Religions and Theology at my own university. But I am aware that many of my readings of Scripture might appear idiosyncratic and debatable. My earlier training was in philology and literary criticism that, in the Cambridge English Faculty, centred upon close readings of texts in the original languages. I have followed the dictates of this training: my interpretations are close readings of the Scriptural texts – but I am more than aware of my philological limitations with Greek and my historical limitations concerning the cultural conditions in which these texts were brought to birth and transmitted. Secondly, more might have been made of the difference between my approach to Christology and that of other theologians working in dogmatics. Following in the wake of investigations into the historical Jesus, studies of Christ by dogmatic theologians abound. I am most aware of the presentations of Christ by Balthasar, Rahner, Kasper (from the Catholic perspective) and Barth, Pannenberg and Moltmann (from the Protestant perspective). But in these essays I have only engaged with these theologies tangentially. I sense now the lack, for example, of a detailed interchange with Moltmann's early work, *Theology of Hope* and *The Crucified God*, because, like the Hegel he champions, Moltmann is more Trinitarian and, in some ways, has a more Eastern Orthodox approach to God as *dunamis*. But what I have attempted in these essays is not to facilitate a discussion with dogmatic theologians so much as a discussion with contemporary philosophy and social/cultural theory. For that discussion I simply want to generate new ways of looking, new categories of thinking, new possibilities of conceiving the event of Christ. And certainly, the results shall be wrong, or challengeable, or in need of correction, further work, whatever. That is not the point. The point is to think Christ now. For that is where Christ is. In wishing to develop my own perspective I have drawn upon these systematic theologies (perhaps more from the Catholic than the Protestant tradition). But I have not taken the further critical step of contrasting my position with theirs in advocating my own position. There may well be a time when that is possible. Thirdly, I have not engaged in the question of Christ with respect to our multi-faith culture. In a book concerned with Christ and culture that is a major consideration. But I am quite simply not sure how to do this. I would welcome the necessary engagement with those who are able to enter such a discussion from their own faith position. But I cannot presume to speak for them or about their traditions. I offer these reflections as a way of clarifying my own position the better for such an engagement. As I said, the engagement is absolutely necessary and is already continuing. It may be there are other Christian theologians better placed for such engagements, and that my task is only to provide reflections that may assist them. But if I were to decide to treat the doctrine of Christ more systematically it would be necessary to rectify these three shortcomings. As it is I have simply attempted to sketch ways of thinking about Christ today; to think as suggestively and imaginatively as possible that others might engage with this figure whose life, death, work and claims have coloured every aspect of western culture.[80]

At the crux of the Christological reflections offered lies an account of desire and mimesis. Reflections on desire and mimesis run through each of these essays, being conjugated in different ways. I view both categories, and reflections upon them, as fundamental to understanding God as love and to developing a theological anthropology that issues from that understanding of God when we are conceived as created 'in the image of'. We desire because we are desired, infinitely desired. We create because we are creatures caught up in a creation suspended in the creativity of the Godhead. There is a long tradition of theological meditation upon desire and mimesis in Origen and Gregory of Nyssa, in Augustine and Aquinas, and more recently in de Lubac and de Certeau. It has not been a Protestant tradition. I situate my own thinking within this Catholic tradition, a tradition now informed by a number of poststructural and phenomenological philosophies of desire – from Irigaray and Kristeva, from Lacan and Deleuze, from Lévinas and Foucault, among others. These provide the cultural context in which Christ is refigured. Hence I open my Christological reflections with a group of essays outlining what I call the economy of response. This is fundamental for the way I approach the doctrine of Christ. The second group of essays develops the notions of desire and mimesis with respect to embodiment and sexuality in order to ground materially the examination of the operations of God and the economics of desiring. The final group of essays is essentially ecclesiological – the examination of the body of the historical Christ gives way to an examination of the continuing life of that body in and as the Church. In this third group sensuous Christian living, incarnational living, is explored through a series of essays concerned with the ethics, aesthetics and

---

[80] See Jaroslav Pelikan, *Jesus through the Centuries: His Place in the History of Culture* (New Haven, Conn.: Yale University Press, 1985).

politics of discipleship. These essays take the effects of the Christic operation in the life of the Church into an engagement with the life of the world.

The theological method throughout is both hermeneutical and phenomenological; for ultimately, the reductions performed by phenomenology have to be *read* theologically, they do not render visible the theological as such. Nevertheless, in the Preface to the *Phenomenology of Perception*, Merleau-Ponty concludes that the task of phenomenology is 'to reveal the mystery of the world and of reason'.[81] The statement might have come from the writings of his contemporary, the Catholic theologian, Henri de Lubac. But de Lubac's approach to the same 'mystery of the world and of reason' was through excavating and examining the Biblical exegeses of the Greek and Latin Fathers. While appreciating the concerns in phenomenology for exploring the complexity of our relationship to the world, I have wished to read this complexity through the lenses of Scriptural exegesis. Of course, this hermeneutical practice is circular: my mode of exegesis is also governed by the reflections of the philosophers of desire I am drawn to. But this circularity is not vicious, I believe, because it is itself a theological engagement in the life of the world: it is a theological practice vis-à-vis a specific cultural context. If the life and thinking of any Christian is a communication of their theology with respect to the social conditions in which they have been placed, then what I am doing here is no more (and no less) than doing theology in the intellectual situation in which I am placed. And, in this sense, Christ is engaged in the contemporary cultural milieu; a milieu that (as several essays demonstrate) is often engaging in Christian themes and symbolics. And so the pursuit of truth continues – creatively, polemically, politically, and apologetically.

---

[81] *Phenomenology of Perception*, tr. Colin Smith (London: Routledge & Kegan Paul, 1962), p. xxiv.

Part One

THE ECONOMY OF RESPONSE

Chapter One

CHRISTOLOGY AND MIMESIS

En ho metro metreite metrethesetai umin kai prostethesetai umin. (Mark 4.24)

The Economy of Response

No commentator has adequately been able to 'explain' it. 'The difficulty about 4.24 still remains; [Mark] must have brought it in, though it is hardly relevant, because he wished to use the latter saying [v.25]'.[1] Most commentators look outside the text to an alleged source in the scattered sayings of Q in order to expand upon their difficulty in commentating upon it and their difficulty in understanding it within its context.[2] A number of commentators have drawn attention to its obscurity.[3] Several have assumed that its rewrite in Matthew 7.2 and Luke 6.38, where it is understood as a proverb about judgement, is the closest we get to understanding Mark's original intention.[4] So that, overall, this verse could be said to sum up Mark's clumsiness as an editor.[5]

What I wish to draw attention to are three ambiguities in this verse and how the writer relates (and represses) them through his style. For the verse has a distinct rhythm that arises from the writer's use of assonance, alliteration and balanced clausing.

First, there is the problem of understanding the character of the *en*, which is often interpreted as an instrumental dative. But I would suggest that the *en* bears something of a locative connotation also – that the measure (or the

---

[1]   E. Best, *Mark: The Gospel as Story* (Edinburgh: T. &. T. Clark, 1983), p. 126.

[2]   See Hugh Anderson, *The Gospel of Mark* (Grand Rapids, Mich.: Eerdmans, 1981); Rudolf Pesch, *Das Markusevangelium*, Teil 1 (Freidburg: Herder, 1976).

[3]   D.E. Nineham, *The Gospel of Mark* (London: A. & C. Black, 1963); Eduard Schweitzer, *The Good News According to Mark*, tr. Donald H. Maduig (London: SPCK, 1971).

[4]   C.E.B. Cranfield, *The Gospel According to St Mark*, rev. edn (Cambridge University Press, 1972); Morna D. Hooker, *The Gospel According to St Mark* (London: A. & C. Black, 1991).

[5]   'Mark is not sufficiently master of his material to be able to venture on a systematic construction himself'; R. Bultmann, *The History of the Synoptic Tradition*, tr. John Marsh (Oxford: Blackwell, 1963), p. 350. This is partly true, but for reasons other than Bultmann considers, as we shall see.

measuring) is understood both instrumentally and as a state or condition
that can be inhabited.[6] The measure is not simply an object to be applied (in
order to facilitate judgement), it is a state within which we are already
located. It is an active state which, should we continue to participate in it,
will affect where and who we will be.

Secondly, there is the difficulty of identifying the *umin*, the you that is the
subject of the sentence. The *umin* is always already within the process of a
measuring that is locating and identifying it. Who are the *umin*? Jesus, who
is set apart (*kata monas*), is speaking in the midst of his twelve appointed
ones, but at the request of 'those around him with [*sun*] the twelve' (4.10).
Umin could then refer to several communities of listeners, including the
congregation of the church listening to the reading of the gospel. The
Markan text is scattered throughout with what might be called suspended
pronouns, pronouns referring to subjects that are not stably identified (see
1.45, 2.15 and 3.2 for others). This *umin* reaches out concentrically, passing
through and beyond several referents. It is always being added to (and
prostethesetai carries with it the sense of 'to continue to do something').

Thirdly, there is the question of the verb 'to measure'. What is the act of
measuring within the context of understanding parables; within the context
also of listening as an act of obedience (*akouete*)? Listening for what, to what?
We hear not a proposition but a carefully orchestrated set of phonemes. The
verse performs far more than it states. What we obey is the call to perform
(by listening) the rhythm of the sentence. What we obey is the call to participate in, by responding to, a poetic economy, a metre. *Metron* can, of course
mean 'metre' – metre in the context of *melos* (tune) and *rhythmos* (time) in
classical poetics. And the sentence has a distinctive anapaestic rhythm.

The effect of these three ambiguities is to render prepositional logic sub-
servient to (because subverted by) rhetoric.[7] Of course the sentence refers to

---

[6]   In *The Greek of the Gospel of Mark* (Philadelphia, Penn.: Scholar Press, 1961), John Charles
Doudna draws attention to Mark's 'extensive use of the local sense' (p. 25) of *en* and the dative. In
1.23 and 5.2 it is used with the sense of 'in the power of …' or 'in the possession of …'. Though he
does not include 4.24 (which he classifies as an instrumental dative), within the context of the
Gospel, where there is a correspondence between the Spirit that drives forward and the pace of the
narrative, perhaps we can see in 4.24 that the involvement with 'measuring' and its promotion is
driven by a power (an important Markan word) both beyond and within the 'measuring' itself.
[7]   The first commentary in English, as far as I am aware, that analysed Mark's gospel in terms of its
'rhythm' was Austen Farrer's *A Study in Mark* (London: Dacre Press, 1951). It is a complex study of
cycles, patterns and numbers, which sometimes makes highly tenuous connections, but nevertheless
it remains important and insightful. It anticipates by almost thirty years Jean-François Lyotard's
observation in *The Postmodern Condition* (Manchester University Press, 1986), that 'Narrative form
follows a rhythm; it is the synthesis of a metre beating time in regular periods and of accent modify-
ing the length and amplitude of certain of those periods' (p. 21).

an intelligible object and process; it is not nonsense. But its reference is neither simple nor single and, in the absence of a determinative context, its semantic openness promotes a crisis of representation. For its meaning cannot be decoded; we understand nothing specific beyond the fact that it seems to describe an apodictic law (moral? spiritual? existential?) of response, of responding. It points to, without elaborating, an economy of response. It presents and performs the experience of circling back upon oneself, of being caught up with a repetition of what one is already familiar with. We are already 'measuring', we have already measured, as we participate in the ongoing process of Mark's narrative that bears us towards some promised eschatological judgement – that future, final and absolute measurement.

What we have in this little phrase, I suggest, is a parable of the readers of/listeners to the Gospel, who correspond to the ones who sat and listened to Jesus himself. It is, in cameo, the mimetic process whereby the hermeneut, the one engaged in hearing and re-creating the story, moves out towards that which has already been given and will now be reappropriated anew. The 'measuring' is the act of engagement in an economy of response. The 'measure' is the rhythm of the mimetic process (linked to metre) that enables one to judge and to understand, but not as one who is outside; only as one who is inside, who, by participating, moves towards that which will be given to him or her. Mimesis is the measure. Jesus *kata monas* does not simply speak but generates the call to be involved, to interpret, interpret from within the process. The call is therefore an empowering – of the twelve, those vaguely suggested ones who are with the twelve, the writer himself, Mark's own listeners (the Christian Church in its local particularity and its universal extension). We are all caught up in the representational process, within a mimetic schema that calls forth and calls for interpretation and reinterpretation. Mimesis, I suggest, is the nature of revelation itself (a revelation inseparable from its mediation).

What follows in this chapter is an argument for the rootedness of both the character of Mark's Christ (who has been sent as God's representative) and the character of Mark's Gospel in a theology of mimesis and *poiesis*.[8]

---

[8] Past readers have identified some correlation between Christology and narration. R.H. Lightfoot, in his suggestive *The Gospel Message of St Mark* (Oxford University Press, 1950), repeats a phrase used in connection both with Christ and with the Gospel. For, while acknowledging that 'the Person [of Jesus Christ] and the portrait [is] deeply human it is true, but also profoundly mysterious and baffling' (p. 3), he also recognises that 'the book ends as it began, with extreme abruptness; and indeed from first to last it is mysterious and baffling' (p. 14). Nevertheless, Lightfoot, like many others, failed to follow through and delineate this correlation. The Gospel itself identifies the correlation far more explicitly in 8.35 (*emou kai tou euangeliou*) and 8.38 (*me kai tous emous logous*).

Mimesis and Narrative

The approach being adopted needs some clarification, at this point. Mimesis has the body of an eel and a literary/reader–response analysis of the Gospel is far from original.[9]

Mimesis concerns the character of representation. That character can be understood in three inseparable ways: the kind of world presented in the narrative; the way that world is portrayed and communicated to the readers/listeners; and the way that kind of world and its portrayal is reconstituted and reportrayed in the minds and imaginations of those who read/listen.[10] Mimesis is, then, both a literary and a social praxis. Aristotle already saw this: 'imitation' was both what the text did vis-à-vis the world 'out there' (*Poetics* 1448a) and an anthropological *a priori* whereby human beings were educated and socialised (*Poetics* 1448b5). It is the nature of the correspondence between aesthetic/rhetorical activity and social activity that has provoked so much debate over the centuries since Aristotle. The work today of René Girard, Paul Ricœur, Jean-François Lyotard and Philippe Lacoue-Labarthe indicates that mimesis remains at the forefront of contemporary debates on representation or the symbolic process. For Aristotle, there was an analogical relationship whereby words referred to a world distinct from them and so – 'art ... imitates the works of nature' (*Physics* II) – it represents them. But Aristotle also saw that 'art ... completes that which nature is unable to bring to completion' (ibid.). Art, therefore, idealises and, in this sense, does not strictly mirror what is but imitates what should be or will be. Art here presents rather than represents, for it moves beyond what it repre-

---

[9]   Literary approaches to Mark's Gospel began to proliferate from the early 1970s, in the wake of and partly as a reaction to redaction criticism. At the same time, historico-critical scholars revisiting the historical Jesus question began to examine closely the community in which and for whom the Gospels were being written (see H.C. Kee's attempt to reconstruct Mark's community in *Community of the New Age*, London: SCM, 1977). The extent of how established and interrelated these approaches now are can be seen from studies of Mark executed in the late 1980s. Mary Ann Beavis's *Mark's Audience* (Sheffield Academic Press, 1989) employs reader–response criticism to identify the kind of audience Mark is writing for. Christopher D. Marshall's *Faith as a Theme in Mark's Narrative* (Cambridge University Press, 1989) uses literary analysis to show how the text's representation of the disciples speaks also for and to all subsequent followers of Christ. Morna Hooker's commentary on Mark (which appeared in 1991) repeatedly draws attention to literary aspects of the text and its effect upon readers/listeners, although in 1950 R.H. Lightfoot was already calling for an appreciation of the Gospel's literary language, ordering of the *pericopae* and use of rhythm. In 1951, as we have already noted, Austin Farrer published *his* literary appreciation of Mark (building, in part, on the earlier work of Lightfoot).

[10]   These three aspects correspond, to some extent, to Ricœur's anaysis of what he terms mimesis 1, mimesis 2 and mimesis 3. See *Time and Narrative* vol. I, tr. Kathleen Blamey (University of Chicago Press, 1984), pp. 52–8. The extent of that correspondence can be judged by referring to footnote 42.

sents to the presentation of an ideal form that is otherwise unavailable. The complex character of mimesis begins here – for the aesthetic/rhetorical activity mediates between presentation, representation and absence. Language (or whatever the artistic medium) mediates the natural, the ideal and the unnameable. It mediates several orders of the real.

Mimesis, the character of this mediation, is, then, associated with knowledge and the process whereby we come to know (Aristotle's imitation). It is also associated with form, for all representation (or presentation) is the representation *of something*. The form represents an object, but an object caught between the way it acts upon (the one who represents it) and the way it is acted upon (by the one who represents it). The object is always and only imitated through the twin activities of reception and projection – that is, within the economy of response. The form is always of an action, and is, therefore, an element in a narrative. Hence in *Poetics* all the roads of representation lead into a discussion about drama. Mimesis is inseparable from *muthos* and *poiesis* (the process whereby language bodies forth its representation). Some philosophers would take this further and claim narrative as a fundamental category for epistemology – that there is no knowledge that is not mediated and part of 'the way we tell the story' of what we know. As John Milbank put it towards the end of his *magnum opus*: 'narrative is simply the mode in which the entirety of reality presents itself to us: without the story of the tree, there is no distinguishable, abiding tree'.[11] This is a shift in part away from Aristotle who, at one level, maintained that language *referred* to nature, it did not invent it.[12] But it is also a development of Aristotle's notion that art presents what is otherwise unavailable to us (the idealised reality). It presents by performing, and the negotiation between performance and reception facilitates a discovery, a disclosure of what is otherwise absent.

Mimesis is, therefore, a slippery term, but by foregrounding the mimetic operation in Mark's Gospel I wish to show how the narrative as a whole not only imitates the character and teaching of the Christ within it, but through the economy of response it provokes and engages *our* imitation of that character and teaching of Christ (our discipleship). Furthermore, I wish to show how this 'imitation' is one of the most comprehensive understandings of the Gospel. For it relates Jesus's role (and subsequently our role) as the representative and presentation of the Gospel, to the Gospel as a representation and presentation of Jesus and the process of following him.

This is not, therefore, simply another reader–response analysis of Mark's

---

[11] *Theology and Social Theory* (Oxford: Blackwell, 1991), p. 358.
[12] Though it has to be emphasised here that John Milbank is no linguistic idealist, as he himself makes plain in the introduction to his book.

Gospel. It is not primarily concerned with Christology as a story or narrative theology. Others have already done that and I enter into their labours.[13]
I wish to build upon the awareness that narrative theology provides for us;
that parables and stories always generate a surplus of meaning and that any
final grasp of Mark's Christology is always beyond us because of that. I wish
to engage theologically with the way the narrative has conscious designs
upon its readers/listeners, calling them to participate in its telling, and how
Mark's awareness of this informs his Christology, informs his understanding
and presentation of the economies of response, discipleship and salvation.
Robert Scharlemann has distinguished between theoretical, practical aesthetic and acoluthetic forms of reason. He equates acoluthetic reason with
Christological reason. 'Christological reason is ... that form of reason in
which the inward I is related to the existential I through the authority
[exousia] that enables the following.'[14] My argument is that there is a relationship between this acoluthetic reason and Mark's narrative. Scharlemann
defines aesthetic reason as similar to acoluthetic reason in that both perform
relations within an exstantial I, but aesthetic reason identifies so completely
with this exstantial I that it forgets itself. Acoluthetic reason maintains this
tension between the inward I and the exstantial I. I would argue that in
Mark's Gospel there is a continual movement between Scharlemann's acoluthetic and aesthetic reason, Christological reason and mimesis; that it
becomes impossible to separate the two. The nature of narrative and mimesis,
I wish to argue, is being read by Mark Christologically. The sending, the

---

[13]   Several of the literary analyses of the text have pointed to the mimetic character of the narrative.
The acuity of the perception and yet the limits of its detailed examination are evident in David
Rhoads's and Donald Michie's pioneering *Mark as Story* (Philadephia, Penn.: Fortress Press, 1982).
Here the recognition that 'the writer has told the story in such a way as to have certain effects upon
the reader. The reader experiences much of the same bafflement and reversals as do the characters'
(p. 1) is analysed in terms of the poetics of narrative, the rhetorical techniques employed by the
author. The reader's experience is again foregrounded in the Conclusion, which expands the observation that 'The reader experiences a story-world in which God's ways are hidden' (p. 137) and 'the
narrative leads the reader to be a faithful follower of Jesus' (p. 139). But these observations are not
examined theologically in relation to the Christology that is the main focus of the Gospel and what
Morna Hooker describes as 'Mark's story [a]s a story about the meaning of discipleship' (*The Gospel
According to St Mark*, 1991, p. 21). The same can be said of observations such as Christopher D. Marshall's: 'By the use of irony, paradox, chiasmus and intercalation, framing verses and duplication,
suspense, shock, surprise, riddles, rhetorical questions, ambiguity and double meaning, foreshadowing and allusion, the narrator is able to tell his stories in a way that communicates both the rational
content of faith and the experienced feel of such a disposition' (pp. 132–3). Mimesis, in both these
analyses, is an end in itself. What I wish to ask in this essay is why mimesis is so important to the
writer of Mark's Gospel – what theological end does it serve?

[14]   *The Reason of Following: Christology and the Ecstatic I* (University of Chicago Press, 1991), p. 124.
'Acoluthetic' comes from the Greek verb 'to follow'. The 'I' who is summoned by the command 'to
follow' lives byond itself. It is in this sense that Scharlemann speaks of the 'exstantial I'.

mediation of Jesus Christ, provides grounds for the very possibility of the Church. What I arguing for is not a narrative theology but a theology of narrative (which is also a theology of reading and interpreting).

We now need to examine how mimesis is the measure of Mark.

Mediation and the Kingdom of the In-between

The opening of Mark's Gospel draws attention to the fact that it is no beginning at all. The first word, *Arche*, is anarthrous, and the noun (or its verbal form) recurs throughout the narrative (31 times in Mark compared to 17 in the much longer Gospel of Matthew). One could either say the narrative is always trying to define a beginning (and cannot), or that all beginnings are pragmatic for Mark (i.e. there is no true beginning at all). In the opening 14 verses of the Gospel there are no fewer than five beginnings. First there are the opening words about 'beginning', and then there is an opening pre-text (Isaiah's prophecy) that frames our understanding of what is to follow. There is to be a path (*odos* – also 'journey', 'way') prepared, upon which Christ will tread and along which he will subsequently walk. In the beginning, then, there is the narrative and the narrative records a past speaking proleptically about the present. The past is re-presented. The opening words of Mark's Gospel are outside time, their perspective is omniscient and so able to relate pasts to presents, types to their final fulfilment. Hence there is no main verb in that opening sentence – as the RSV translation makes plain. In the beginning there is representation and without representation nothing can be said to have begun. The 'beginning' appeals to all that has come before it, which it re-presents as it also moves forward with the temporal flow of continuation.

We begin Mark's Gospel, then, *in medias res*; it is this mimesis that constitutes the realm of the in-between, which (as will become evident) governs the thematic and geographical structure of the gospel/Gospel.[15] Thus there

---

[15] There is a difference between gospel as 'the good news' and Gospel as a technical term for the verbal transmission of that 'good news'. Morna Hooker dismisses the notion that Mark's use of *evangelion* is purposefully ambivalent (see p. 35 of her commentary) and then draws attention to its use as a technical word (p. 243). E. Best is, I believe, much closer to the truth when he distinguishes between the gospel of Jesus Christ (subjective genitive) – that is, the good news proclaimed by Jesus – and the gospel of Jesus Christ (objective genitive) – that is, the good news about Jesus. Furthermore, Best hints at, but does not develop in his book, an association between this subjective and objective genitive: 'the risen Jesus may be said to speak in the Gospel; through his words and actions as reported in the Gospel Jesus lives again and speaks to and acts among men' (*Mark: The Gospel as Story*, p. 39). This association between the subjective and the objective genitive in 'the Gospel of Jesus Christ' is central to my thesis that there is a correlation between the mimetic-representation and the Christology in Mark.

are no origins for this Christ, no birth narratives and no genealogies, but instead the abrupt appearance of a voice from the past (the voice of one who sends, the voice of God speaking through the flesh of human words and his representative, Isaiah), followed by the equally abrupt appearance of a figure on an empty stage. The story now begins for the third time: '*egeneto Johannes ho baptizon en te eremo*' (1.4). The River Jordan is a place of liminality, between the wilderness and the Promised Land, and baptism is a rite of passage through the zone of that liminality. John's name means 'gift'. Before the beginning God gives and in the beginning we represent. John too represents, and not just God's word to his representative Isaiah. He is an echo of other ancient prophets – Elijah, for example. In the same way Jesus is an echo of Joshua (and Elijah). He is caught, and so are we as readers/listeners, within the mirroring folds of time and representation. John stalks through the no-man's-land of the desert and commandeers the geographical in-between. It is an in-between where the brute contingencies of the historical moment cross the transcendent significance of typology.

John acts out the gift he represents in the gift of baptism, and in doing so performs the rite of a prologue, an initiation. In the beginning, then, there is a narrative and the narrative is a liturgy. 'Prepare ye' (*etoimasate*) stands at the portal of the good news which is the message of Jesus Christ presented as the story of Jesus Christ. The ritual of baptism (the prefigurement of the sacrament of baptism, itself a prefigurement of the eschatological redemption) brings us to a fourth beginning of the Gospel, when Jesus enters. It prepares 'the way of the Lord' (a double genitive, meaning both the Lord's way and the way about the Lord, or the narrative).[16] It prepares the way by announcing repentance (*metanoia*) that leads into (*eis*) the state of being forgiven, a new beginning. This involves two processes: the confession of sins, which is the retelling of one's life story, the representation of one's past; and the famous 'change of mind'. The way is prepared and paved by people laying down their lives as they later lay down their clothes (11.8). *Metanoia* is not simply a moral category but an epistemological one. It is a compound of *noeo*, like *eunoeo* ('to be well-disposed towards'), *katanoeo* ('to observe attentively'), *pronoeo* ('to foresee') and *uponoeo* ('to surmise'). What John's liturgy calls for, and what the reader's/listener's engagement with the narrative provides, is an epistemological transformation. From seeing the world in one way (which is often the literal, material way) one will begin to see the world in an entirely new way (which is often the symbolic and transfigured way). This is what John's baptism introduces, this is what Jesus's ministry teaches,

---

[16] Though the way is to be made straight, the only straight way in the Gospel is the narrative movement itself. Jesus's way criss-crosses through Galilee and only becomes straight when the direction is uniform and purposed (on the way to the cross).

this is what the reader's/listener's involvement in the story-world promotes. The measure of one's engagement with the mimetic operations of the Gospel is the economy of salvation itself. There is a close association, I would argue, between one's capacity for *metanoia* and one's capacity to engage imaginatively, entering the economy of response; just as, in the Gospel, there is a close association between teaching, exorcism, healing and redemption.

'*Erchetai … Kai egeneto … elthen Jesous*' (1.7–9). A third person now enters, a person who has stepped into the in-between and the place of transitions *apo Nazareth tes Galilaias*, and who will carry the narrative out of the in-between, back into the geographically and historically specific. Jesus here is Joshua entering the Promised Land. The narrative will not enter the realm of specifics, nor will the gospel be proclaimed, until Jesus has had his experience of the nature of the in-between deepened. The Spirit, that divine propelling and compelling agency whose presence the narrative traces through time and history, drives him into the wilderness, and he will emerge into his ministry from the wilderness as John did before him. The wilderness is the experience of living with ambivalence, of battling with cosmological divisions and uncertainties. Caught between the demonic and the angelic, between chaos and order, there is no resolution or final victory in Mark's temptation scene. Jesus will continue to experience the wilderness and the battle throughout the text, with the spiritual and institutional conflicts he will encounter. There are other in-between places (what Michel Foucault would call 'heterotopias') throughout the narrative – the sea, the mountain tops and being 'on the way'; the *eremon topon* will reappear in 1.35, on the mountain of 6.46 and in the isolation of Gethsemane. The realm of the in-between is the realm where prayer and spiritual discipline and illumination are brought to birth. The specific teaching to the disciples will take place 'on the way', between Caesarea Philippi and Jerusalem (8.27–10.52). In terms of narrative time and plot correlation, Jesus will not be allowed to emerge from that wilderness and into ministry until John is incarcerated. When he emerges in verse 14 we have our fifth beginning to the story; already there is a foreshadowing of the end. For John's betrayal (*paradothenai*) is a prophecy of Jesus's own destiny.

In the beginning, therefore, there is repetition, mirroring and typology.[17]

---

[17] The observation substantiates (it does not depend upon) Philippe Lacoue-Labarthe's conclusion that 'Everything "begins" *also* by representation, and religion, in one way or another, cannot be done with it'; *Typography: Mimesis, Philosophy, Politics* (Cambridge, Mass.: Harvard University Press, 1989), p. 117. Theology must confront, and in Mark's Gospel does confront, its own rhetorical strategies. See David Jasper's "Wherever I said Aristotle I meant St. Paul" in Martin Warner ed., *The Bible as Rhetoric* (London: Routledge, 1990), for an examination of the community constituted by and entextualised in Mark's rhetoric. Jasper makes the profound theological observation, central to this reading of Mark's Gospel, that 'The Church is continually stirred into radical reflection by that which, standing outside, necessitates and engenders its rhetoric, its entextualising' (p. 149).

There is a complex inter-association of memory, event and prediction. 1.14 is the fifth attempt to begin the story, the fifth echo of a sending out, a representation that is part of an evolving clarification or fulfilment. It is a representation and fulfilment not simply of the opening prophecy, but more particularly of the original sender of 'salvation' (*apostello ton angelon*) – which is the Hebrew meaning of the name 'Isaiah'. It is a representation of the one who is the origin of the 'gift' – which is the Hebrew meaning of the name 'John': the voice of God who instituted the unlocatable *arche*.

As we have all come to see, in the end there is no ending. The dead do not die, the tomb gapes into an ominous but silent future and the narrative focus returns us to Galilee. An apocalyptic urgency directs us towards a final manifestation that is not represented, whose representation is deferred, suspended. The resurrection can have its prefigurements, but its fulfilment is as unrepresentable as the Hebrew God. The second coming is postponed yet imminent – for Galilee is only a few days' journey away. Our reading passes into an ambiguous silence in which there is a reversal of expectation: not the joy and release of finally understanding, nor the recognition of the fulfilment that promotes obedience and crystallises faith. The silence is both the women's dumbstruck fear and their refusal to pass on the message. The silence is also the reader's response to that concentrated perplexity that concludes the narrative with the broken and elliptical *ephebounto gar*. These silences are taut with paradox – for the Gospel of Mark has been written and what we have read cannot logically exist if the women had remained silent. Unless, that is, the narrator is God himself and the narrative a product of his omniscience.

At the 'end' as in the 'beginning' there is a question about origins and authorship. And the final 'ending' is deferred and doubled.[18] Narrative, which is always governed by a teleology, is cheated of its apocalyptic telos, and so is the reading experience. In the end there is a crisis (a prefigurement of the final crisis which has already been prefigured in chapter 13) from which faith must emerge. It is the crisis of interpretation and response – for how was the gospel proclaimed, has the Christ risen, have the signs been read properly, has the lesson of the fig tree been learnt? It is a crisis of representation – and paradox, like irony, is the condensing of such a crisis – in two senses: first, because there is no representation of the risenness, the completion of the narrative process; secondly, because the meaning of what

---

[18] Parallels between chapter 13 and the Passion narrative were identified by Lightfoot, but with Norman Perrin's observation that Mark's Gospel closes with a 'twin climax' – the apocalptyic discourse and the Passion narrative – we appreciate Mark's spliced 'ending' (*The New Testament: An Introduction*, New York: Harcourt Brace Jovanovich, 1974, p. 159).

has been represented throughout (that this carpenter from Nazareth is the Christ), without the final revelation, is put in doubt. It is the crisis of representation, in its two senses, that perpetuates the need for continually reinterpreting, continually rereading the text, the representation of Jesus as the Christ. It is this crisis of representation that is the focus of the Gospel (as both literary form and *kerygma*) and the very character of the reading experience created by the Gospel. Confronting the crisis of representation is, as we shall see, the very character of Mark's mimesis.

At the 'end' the narrative folds back upon its mirroring depths. There is no end-stopping corpse nor any end-stopping apotheosis. Rather, there is a young man (*neaniskos*), dressed in white and sitting at the right side of the tomb. We are returned to the transfiguration with the white robe and the three witnesses (women this time). We are returned also to the night of the arrest and two prophecies. For the words the young man utters are a repetition of Jesus's words to the disciples after the Last Supper (14.28). And it was Jesus (or was it the Psalmist and Jesus was quoting, and so Mark quotes Jesus quoting what God had spoken to the Psalmist? a familiar pattern in the narrative as we have seen) who said: 'you will see the Son of Man seated at the right hand of power' (14.62). And these words follow the arrest in the Garden of Gethsemane which ends with the flight, and the first appearance of a young man. There, in a scene echoing Joseph's flight from Potiphar's wife, the young man prefigures the risen Christ.[19] For he leaves behind a linen sheet (*sindon*) – the same word used to describe Jesus's grave-clothes in 15.46 – and evades (*ephugen*) the religious authorities. Here, clothed like the new man – *nean-iskos* – in the community of the baptised, he sits enthroned in glory. Is this a fulfilment of Jesus's prophecy? Do we read this representation aright? Do the women? We are left, in the end, to rethink the whole narrative again. For what cannot be represented is prefigured and this prefigurement of the resurrection stands at the end of a series of such prefigurements – Jairus's daughter, the repetition of the very word *egeiro*, each healing and exorcism narrated. We close the story with another substitution for the true event, with a representation of the unrepresentable. We end in a complex but highly suggestive weave of questions that riddle the Gospel and generate hermeneutic enigmas.

The enigma of the final scene only parallels enigmas throughout the text – the enigma of the young man in the garden, the enigma of the parable

---

[19] The specific reference to Christ's resurrection here can be seen more clearly when 14.52 is compared with the Septuagint account of Joseph and Potiphar's wife in Genesis 39.12. There we have '*katalipon ta himatia autou ... ephugen*' and in Mark '*katalipon ten sindona ... ephugen*'. Thus Mark deliberately wishes to use *sindon* prefiguratively rather than as an allusion back to *himatia*.

of the fig tree and the parables more generally (prototypically 4.24), the
enigma of Jesus walking upon the water and meaning to pass them by (6.48)
when the disciples faced a head wind, and the enigma of the Messianic
secret.[20]

It is the crisis of representation that constitutes such enigmas. Morna
Hooker's commentary often describes the hermeneutical somersaulting as
one encounters such an enigma and, without pressing further, at one point
observes the very source of the crisis. On 14.51–2 about the young man
who flees from the garden, she writes: 'Mark gives no hint as to the identity
of the young man – or if he does, we do not recognise it.'[21] The crisis of representation issues from what we have already observed about Mark's way of
telling the story: his frequent refusal to identify, his refusal to link a sign with
a single signified. We see this with his use of suspended pronouns, we will
see this again with the parables. By not framing the reference (for example,
to the young man) with a context whereby the appearance of the young
man becomes comprehensible, we can read about the incident and we can
understand the incident *qua* description, but we cannot interpret what we
have understood. We then experience (and fulfil) Jesus's words in 4.12 –
seeing but not perceiving, hearing but not understanding. The meaning of
the incident is suspended. It is not given a conclusiveness, a fixed point of
reference. By doing this Mark frequently creates the effect known as semiosis – where an object, incident or statement is imbued with the possibility
of many meanings or none at all; no single possibility remains definitive.
Semiosis is the crisis of representation – for it suggests that the representation
is meaningful while simultaneously refusing to define its meaning. We have
to create the meaning and when we are left to do that there is always the
possibility of eisegesis (rather than exegesis) and paranoia. The representation is both meaningful and meaningless. What the crisis of representation
does is to generate the need and the desire to interpret, to engage with the
text, to participate in its telling – as the flowering of commentaries and the
spawning of interpretative methods for resolving these enigmas in Mark's
Gospel are ample witness. The shortcut here is to say that this is an example
of Mark the clumsy editor or Mark the preserver of traditions. But it is the
highly sophisticated way in which these incidents (such as the appearance of
the young man) are woven into the language of the text, the verbal echoes
and rhythms which riddle the text, that continually suggest the possibility of

---

[20] See in this context John Drury's fine display of interpretative acumen when trying to resolve the
riddle of the bread in 8.14–21: 'Mark' in Robert Alter and Frank Kermode eds., *The Literary Guide
to the Bible* (London: Collins, 1987), pp. 414–16.
[21] *The Gospel According to St Mark*, p. 352.

meaningfulness, of these events being symbolic. The crisis of representation, the mimetic crux (and cross) of the narrative, calls in Mark's Gospel for a response of faith and therefore discipleship. It could otherwise generate a sense of paranoia.[22]

There is in the 'end' no final release from the rhythm of the narrative. The book cannot be closed and put away as if the telling of the tale has finished. We, like the disciples and contemporary representations of discipleship, return to Galilee to learn again, to reinterpret. We, like the disciples, remain caught within the nets of the Christian story (and its telling and re-telling). And in doing so we continue the story, rewrite it anew in our own lives and so generate further acts of signification. Like the three women, we take flight from the sheer intractability of comprehending that there is no end, no finality, there is only and ever perdurance and continuation. We too cannot stare for too long into the dark hole of the eternal. But we have to take note that without either an identifiable beginning or a resolved ending, there are only the ambiguities and ephemeralities of the in-between. The Gospel of Mark concentrates upon, is a theology of, the in-between – of mediation (understood as Christology) and representation (understood as rhetoric). The Gospel's other themes – faith, discipleship, the polarisation governing institutional and cosmological conflicts – are tangents of this circle of Christology and mimesis, as we are beginning to see.

The In-between and the Economy of Faith

The realm of the in-between concentrates its narrative attention upon what is done rather than on the space itself. In-between is a process before being

---

[22] We arrive here at the portals of Kafka's castle and the auction-room in Thomas Pynchon's *The Crying of Lot 49*. Mimesis is established with the crisis of representation, where Jesus's question to the disciples 'Do you still not understand?' (8.12) echoes endlessly, and endlessly cannot be answered. When is something understood? When do we know we have now understood? The crisis of representation (a crisis which representation is always in, for representation is forever seeking for the ground, the *arche*, the origin that would allow it to understand itself and to be legitimate) leads either to faith or madness. Again, the other side of mimesis provoking faith is the provocation of paranoia. Postmodern thinkers like Philippe Lacoue-Labarthe wish to stress *this* side of mimetic activity: 'madness is a matter of mimesis' (*Typography*, p. 138). He points out that 'Possession … is the monstrous, dangerous form of a *passive mimesis*, uncontrolled and unmanageable' (p. 264). The two sides of the crisis of representation are evident in Mark's Gospel in the polarisation between the Kingdom of God and the chaotic madness of the demonic realm. The victims of possession and the unpredictable storms are portrayals of the instability of meaning that mimesis as representation in crisis provokes. The religious and political institutions in the narrative offer a pragmatic but arbitrary order which the presence of Jesus renders illegitimate. In the crisis of representation only faith in God as the *arche* and origin will suffice.

a place. That process is the process of representation. Discipleship could be
described as learning (that is being subject to, disciplined by participation in
what is being mediated) how to represent aright. The recognition of one's
own participation is also the recognition of being inscribed within what is
being mediated of the Father through the Son, Jesus Christ. We are written
into a story, a metanarrative. Our recognition is that we are always only
in-between. Similarly, one reads of Andrew and Simon entering into a discipleship, but a discipleship that is a continuation of what they have been
doing formerly. The verbs of 1.16–18 – *paragon, amphiballontas, poieso umas
genesthai* and *aphentes* – are all verbs emphasising transition and movement.
Fishers they were and fishers they will remain, for it is while they engage in
the narrative of their occupation that they issue into the narrative of Jesus
Christ.[23] It is not that narrative meets metanarrative, but that narrative is
always complicit with metanarrative – and it is that complicity that Jesus
calls his disciples to understand. To become fishers of human souls is to
enter the narrative of their occupation from another perspective. It is to be
taught the metaphorical association between two forms of activity; to enter
into the crisis of representation that the metaphorical always engenders. But
within that crisis there is also the entrance, through the parabolic and
figural, into new articulations of identities and the configuration of the
world. And so they must recognise that, in being part of this new narrative,
they are not just fishers (those in control, those mastering their own economic destinies), they are fish (servants) caught by Christ in the nets of a
narrative within which he too has been and is being and will be caught, by
God the Father, the unrepresentable origin of the *arche*, the Sender, the
Giver.[24] The disciples, while plying their trade, are informed of the fact that
they are woven into God's meta-text, a story of Trinitarian inscription

---

[23] See Robert Scharlemann, *The Reason of Following*, particularly chapter 6, 'Explication of Acoluthetic Reason', in which he outlines the phenomenological relation between the first-order self and
the second-order self as they adhere to the process of following.

[24] In the section of the Gospel which treats discipleship (8.27–10.52) there is a story of the man of
great wealth who addresses Jesus as 'Good'. Jesus's reply, 'No one is good except God alone' (10.18),
indicates, as Morna Hooker observes, that 'Jesus makes no claims to independent authorship,' as
God's representative he 'point[s] away from himself to the character and demands of God' (*The
Gospel According to St Mark*, p. 241). His being a representative is part of his nature as a son. James
Dunn, in the second edition of his book *Christology in the Making* (London: SCM, 1989), points out
the relation between this representative sonship and the sonship of those who follow him. '[T]here
is sufficiently good testimony that Jesus taught his disciples to regard themselves as God's sons in the
same intimate way, but also that he regarded their sonship as somehow *dependent* upon his own, that
he thought of their sonship as somehow "derivative" of his' (p. 32). The relationship between
Christology and mimesis that I am attempting to uncover here provides a better description of the
nature of that 'somehow' in Dunn.

where God is author, Christ is performer and the Holy Spirit is the performance.[25] We, as readers/listeners, are not external and excluded. For our act of reading 'concretises' another performance.[26] We too are caught by the power of the story-telling. Being held by the story is analogous to being part of the liturgy. Our participation is then a liturgical praxis of sacramental and soteriological significance.

Christology: The Performer and the Performance

Framing the calling of the first four disciples (1.16–20) are accounts of the cosmological importance of Jesus's work – the unresolved conflict with Satan in the wilderness and the casting out of the unclean spirit from the man in the synagogue at Capernaum. Framing the ordaining (*epoiesen*) of the Twelve (3.13–19) are accounts again of the cosmological importance of Jesus's work – the unclean spirits reveal that he is the Son of God and the accusation by the Jerusalem scribes that he is the agent of Beelzebub (which issues into the parable of binding the strong man). Personal histories are

---

[25] Austin Farrer has observed that 'the control of the Spirit is visible and evident; it issues in precisely that shaping and patterning, that unfolding of symbol and doctrine, which the Gospel exhibits' (*A Study in Mark*, p. 9). My thesis would agree with this – what I am suggesting, and requiring, is an appreciation of the operation of the Trinity in Mark's Gospel. Not that there is an explicit doctrine of the Trinity in the Gospel, but there needs to be some awareness of the inter-relationship between Father, Son and Holy Spirit for the association between Christology and mimesis to be coherent. Certainly Mark insists upon the singleness of God (10.18; 12.29, 32), Jesus as God's representative (and therefore dependent on the Father) and the Holy Spirit as mediating the power by which Jesus's representativeness can be substantiated. The baptism scene, as Walter Kasper observes, 'has a clear Trinitarian structure' (*The God of Jesus Christ*, London: SCM, 1984, p. 245). There is no analysis of the Trinity in Mark's Gospel because no analysis is possible. The key relationship in such an analysis is the relationship between Jesus of Nazareth, Jesus the Christ and the Godhead. That is, the Christological relationship. And it is the impossibility of completely understanding that relationship which is the burden of Mark's Gospel.

[26] See Wolfgang Iser's influential concluding chapter – 'The Reading Process: A Phenomenological Approach' – in his book *The Implied Reader* (Baltimore, Md.: Johns Hopkins University Press, 1974). He takes up the concept of 'concretising' from the work of Roman Ingarden. Ricœur, in volume I of *Time and Narrative*, relates this reader–response approach to the Aristotelian categories of mimesis and *muthos*. 'Mimesis … as an activity, the mimetic activity, does not reach its intended term through the dynamism of the poetic text alone' (p. 46). In 'concretising' the textual performance, then, the reader completes the mimetic operation within the text. The narrative's mimetic activity is a net within which the reader is caught. See Terence R. Wright's 'Margaret Atwood and St Mark: The Shape of the Gaps' in Robert Detweiler and William G. Doty eds., *The Daemonic Imagination: Biblical Text and Sacred Story* (Atlanta, Ga.: Scholar's Press, 1990) for an analysis of what the implied reader in Mark's Gospel is expected to supply in the account of the healing of the demoniac.

translated into a cosmological story being worked out in the kingdom of the in-between: the in-between the polarity of good and evil, God and Satan, order and chaos, being inside and being outside. It is this process of translation which is important; this process of transfiguration which is related to the initial call for *metanoia* – the movement into an alternative epistemology. It is a translation associated with imitating the teacher, the performer.

The disciples' commission is the extension of Jesus's own mission: they too are given authority 'to cast out demons'. And *ekballein* echoes throughout the latter part of chapter 3, as it does throughout the latter part of chapter 1 and in chapter 9 – two other chapters important for the calling and commissioning of the disciples. But Jesus Christ is not just the teacher/ performer, in commissioning others he is also the author (*poieo*)[27] of a continuing performance. He both acts and directs the action; he is both a representative (as the Father's agent, as God's performer) and author of the representational. There is created, then, in this story, through this story, a chain of substitutions – from the Father to the Son, from the Son to the Twelve, from the Twelve to the Church. Christ comes to initiate this chain and, as Philippe Lacoue-Labarthe has observed, 'the "essence" of mimesis [is] precisely about vicariousness, carried to the limit … endless and groundless – something like an infinity of substitution and *circulation* …: the very lapse "itself" of essence'.[28] Without any beginning and without any end, there is only substitution, there is only the chain of representation. This chain *is* the mimesis and the *poiesis*; this chain *is* the nature of narrative; this chain, in Mark's narrative, *is* Christological.

For Christology, like narration and mimesis, concerns representation in two interrelated forms. First, it is about constitutional representation – the standing-in of an official substitute for the actual presence of another. In this case, Jesus enacts a double constitutional role, the first properly ascribed to God the Father by the Jewish authorities and the unclean spirits. Jesus acts not in his own name, but in the name of God. In this connection see 1.24 and the double genitive of the title Holy (Person) of God; and 2.7 where God is the sole forgiver of sins. Jesus, in this sense, is the outward and mediating sign of a God and an author who cannot be represented; just as the Gospel (as text) is the mediating and substituting chain of signifiers for the absent Jesus Christ – the one who is ascended. But he also represents us – humankind – before the Father. If the first constitutional act is the basis for

---

[27]   The Word in this Gospel bears something of the power and creativity of the classical notion of *poiesis*, which Aristotle associates directly with mimesis in *Poetics*. For an examination of this association see Ricœur, *Time and Narrative*, vol. I, pp. 45–51.

[28]   *Typography*, p. 116.

our understanding of the incarnation, the second constitutional act is the basis for our understanding of atonement. Secondly, Christology is about literary representation – the employment of language to represent the nature of that constitutional representation, to enquire into its character. Jesus's life is the performance within which the salvation promised by God is made effective for all; just as the narration of Jesus's life, work and teaching is the performance (re-enacted by each reader/listener) by which the salvation effected by God in Christ is made available to all. Both these forms of representation are associated through the doctrine of incarnation. Each is the Word made flesh, though the discursive representational activity only receives its power and creative authority on the basis of the prior incarnation of God. There is an analogical relation between these two forms of representation.

Characters are transformed in the text (just as readers/listeners are by the text) through assuming their new identity as representatives, as paradigms. Simon becomes Peter, James and John become Boanerges, and the restitution of sight to a blind Jew on the road to Jerusalem becomes parabolic of epistemological change. The same occurs within the language performing the representation. Words are transfigured and given new, more ambivalent meanings. The encounter with the scribes from Jerusalem and the subsequent clarification of Jesus's mission to bind Satan, concludes with Jesus's natural family 'standing outside' (with the added irony of them sending [*aposteilan*] for him). But Jesus turns to those he had appointed 'that he might send them out' (3.14) and informs them that *they* are his mother and brothers. 'Whoever does [*poiese*] the will of God is my brother, and sister, and mother' (3.35). Words become dislodged from their conventional settings – and we are now at the crux of Mark's Christology: Jesus the teacher, Jesus the performer, Jesus the teller of parables and a parable himself.

When signifiers become detached from, and assume more importance than, identifiable signifieds, or when signifiers hang only loosely related to a signified, only two responses are possible. One is to have faith which believes the two are related in some hidden way; a faith which participates in the crisis of meaning that Jesus Christ has come to heal. (We see this in the way the Syro-Phoenician woman enters into the kind of discourse Jesus is employing. She does not seek to understand the new symbolic relations being drawn between 'children', 'bread', 'dogs' and their conventional meanings. She does not attempt to interpret or resolve the enigma at all. She takes up the mode of thinking and speaking (and perceiving the world) that Jesus performs.) The other possible response is to dismiss the detaching that is being done, the *poiesis*, as madness. (We see this in attempts to claim Jesus is possessed and the observation by his friends (the irony!) that 'he is beside himself' (3.21).) The parabolic teaching (*haggadah*) stands directly opposed to the Pharisiac literalism (of what Lacan would call 'the discourse of knowledge') of their *halacha*. Items and actions and roles commonly understood by a community – lamps and wine-skins, seed and grapes, crop growing and vineyard management, physicans and bridegrooms – become dislodged from conventional contexts, their meaning set afloat on the tides of storytelling. They become part of a performance that draws disciples and readers into their suggestive depths. It is not so much a way of life that Jesus is teaching – we cannot reduce the parables to a simply ethical or *halachic* content. Jesus teaches a way of thinking and perceiving, a *meta-noia*, a way of reading and understanding (or living without possession of total understanding). The parables follow and foster conflict.

The parables are forms of testing, or temptation, that draw the reader/listener away from the towns and cities of familiarity and into the wilderness, the storms at sea, the place in-between and under-defined. The question that surfaces – for us as readers, for Mark who sews his traditions together, for those disciples listening to the teacher – Jesus perceives in his spirit and pronounces (while refraining from answering): 'How are you going to understand all the parables?' (4.13). For in a world of floating signifiers, where meaning is only potential and where the lesson of the fig tree must be learnt in order to be saved, a hermeneutic must be found to stabilise the vertigo of semiosis. Jesus as historical person destabilises, deconstitutes the familiar world – this is the character and effect of his performance. As the Christ, the performer, he will bring salvation from this effect. It is his authority as the Son of God that controls the raging storms, the dark thrashing of the sea of chaos which the parables issue into (4.36–41). Christ sent from God as God's representation, rescues readers from the turmoil of endless interpretation. He is salvation because he is the hermeneutic. He performs, for us who participate in the jostling crowds and the fevers of possible meaning, an act of healing which is an act of judgement.[29] Reading/listening/interpreting becomes a form of ongoing exorcism; it performs an increasingly realised, but never finalised, eschatology. The one who reads is being and will be saved.

The performer is inseparable from the performance, the person from the

---

[29] For Karl Barth, Jesus Christ is 'the judge judged in our place', but he recognises also that this judgement is not simply negative: to make a judgement is to bring order and understanding. For Barth the essence of the sin for which Christ came to atone is the human belief in the freedom of judgement – that unaided by the grace of God, we can read aright and understand the situations that confront us truly. See *Die Kirkliche Dogmatik*, IV.1 (Zürich/Zollikon: Evangelischer Verlag, 1953), pp. 231–311; *Church Dogmatics*, IV.1, tr. G.W. Bromiley (Edinburgh: T. & T. Clark, 1956), pp. 211–83.

work done. The telling of the parable is inseparable from the telling of that telling. And Jesus Christ as the representation of God is inseparable from the narrative's representation that makes that representation possible. The power of the parabolic cannot be contained, it overflows the teaching of Jesus and informs the whole of the Gospel of Mark. For the power of the parabolic is the drive towards death and resurrection – the death and the resurrection of one's understanding, one's understanding of oneself and the events of the world. And so the storm at the end of chapter 4 is not only a prefiguration of Christ's entrance into death and exit into the post-apocalyptic calm. It is a prefiguration also of baptism – our entrance into death and exit into the parabolic realm, the realm of the liminal, where *noeo* is transformed (*meta*) into *metanoia*. Serious readers must take up the cross that operates within the mimesis.[30]

It is a cross that operates within the Christology also – and not simply in terms of the historical crucifixion of Christ. The historical is always emblematic in a world where the parabolic is the order of the true. The question emerges "Who then is this …?' (4.41) – *outos* being yet another indefinite demonstrative pronoun. The question is a response by both the disciples and the readers/listeners to the parables and to an engagement in the performance of Christ as the ruler of creation. The question articulates the crisis at the heart of Christology in Mark: who is this man, this Christ? This is a crisis without textual resolution. The nature of Christ receives no unambivalent definition. Any Christology issues only in and through the economy of response, with representation providing the basis for engagement. The crisis is promoted by two means: first, the Christological titles; secondly, Mark's 'scandalous' presentation of Jesus. Again, what is foregrounded in both means is Christology as an enigma to be drawn into, worked at, but never mastered.

The titles and allusions to identity are always ambivalent. Hence there are papers and books on the meaning of the 'Son of Man' and whether Jesus did or did not intend to allude to himself as the I AM in 6.50, 13.6 and 14.62. There are shifting Christological perspectives throughout the narrative – Jesus the Son of Man, the Son of God, the *theios aner*, the Son of David, the king, the apocalyptic teacher and the Messiah. There is no single overarching focus for these perspectives. There is no single unambivalent presentation of Jesus Christ. Ambivalence is essentially what Mark is aiming

---

[30] This is a theme that could well relate to the historical *Sitz im Leben* proposed by Martin Hengel in his *Studies in the Gospel of Mark* (London: SCM, 1985). The Gospel 'was written in a time of severe affliction in Rome after the persecution of Nero and before the destruction of Jerusalem, probably during AD 69' (p. 30).

for, because it fosters the crisis of representation which the coming of Christ, God's representation, engenders. The mystery of Christ's nature cannot ever be resolved and so theological investigations into this nature (beyond the bare markers set out in the Nicean and Chalcedonian creeds) are exercises in speculation, in imagination. One Christological model is qualified by another, as T.J. Weeden's thesis – that Hellenistic Christology is at odds with 'Mark's own suffering Christology presented in his *theologia crucis*'[31] – demonstrates. One Christological model is contextualised, modified, even ironised by another: see the way the suffering Son of Man is played out in parallel with the clearer presentation of the Son of God in the Passion narrative, and the way the Messianic and Royal Christologies are both foregrounded and undermined in the closing chapters.[32] But each model, crystallising in a title, stands. Jesus Christ is the focus for them all. He promoted them and the narrative now keeps them in play. The Christology is not explained nor defined, and, in this sense, Mark's narrator shows that he is not the master of his material; that there is no human position possible whereby one could understand, explain and define the representative nature of Jesus Christ.

In the same way, Mark's representation of Jesus Christ is graphic and sharp-edged, but often puzzling because it disrupts and scandalises our expectations. Jesus is passionately and emotionally human – feeling anger and hunger and grief. Yet he is also in possession of prophetic insight and supernatural abilities. Mark continually surprises us by the actions and reactions of this character. Jesus is never the man we expect. His behaviour is not predictable. We are not given a character the logic of whose motivation and reasoning is made evident. There is no stated reason (although commentators are forever trying to supply one) why Jesus tells one man to say nothing about his healing (1.44) and another to go and proclaim it (5.19). There is no stated reason why Jesus asked the blind man, 'Can you see anything?' (8.23), as if he doubted his own ability to heal. There is no evident explanation why

---

[31] 'The Heresy that Necessitated Mark's Gospel' in W. Telford ed., *The Interpretation of Mark's Gospel* (London: SPCK, 1985).

[32] My argument here challenges that of Jack Dean Kingsbury in his book *The Christology of Mark* (Philadelphia, Penn.: Fortress Press, 1983). He defined two main Christological lines in Mark: the first is a confessional and secret identity (encompassing the titles of Davidic Kingship, the Messiah and the Son of God); the second is a public identity (encompassing the title of Son of Man). These two Christologies 'do not infringe upon, or undermine' each other (p. 175), they are complimentary. The reading I am proposing suggests there is more irony, tension and ambivalence in the use and treatment of these titles. Nevertheless Kingsbury recognises the concern in Mark to engage the reader/auditor and the relationship of that concern to Christology: 'hearing aright the gospel-story of the divinely wrought destiny of Jesus … is indispensable for understanding aright his identity' (p. 174). Unfortunately he does not pursue this in any depth.

Jesus should be so abrupt and rude to the Syro-Phoenician woman; or why he should turn so viciously on what is at worst a naïve remark by Peter (8.33); or why he should be so tolerant to someone driving out demons in his name when he is not a follower (9.39). There is no evident explanation why Jesus should curse the fig tree for something it was unable to do. Again, commentators are not slow at putting forward an explanation for all these irregularities, but that is the point – the irregularities foster and encourage comment, engagement in an economy of response. They make the character of Jesus hard to grasp because his actions and reactions do not adapt easily to our conventions (and the conventional readings and portraits we have created of him). Just when we think we are getting somewhere, understanding the identity of this Christ, we are continually confronted with an enigma, narrative aporia and seeming inconsistency.[33]

Christology, which is attempting to fathom the nature and work of Christ as the representation of God, is and remains a riddle in Mark. It is a riddle that is part of and encourages the crisis of representation, the character of mimesis, evident throughout the Gospel and pre-eminent in the parables. The power of the parabolic, that gave authority to the teaching of Christ, continually spills over into the Gospel as a whole and the parable of Jesus Christ that Mark is narrating. So the parables and the narrative events have a curious way of impacting upon each other – the man among the Gadarene swine is prefigured in Jesus's parable of the strong man who needs to be bound. Parable-telling and the chronicling of events are both forms of story-telling and representation. The stories told and enacted, like Christ the performer and the work of Christ as the performance, cannot be made distinct. Each echoes the other. In such a mirroring maze of imitation, it is the intimate relationship between the way *of* Jesus Christ and the way *of* Mark's Gospel and the way in which the readers/listeners/followers must listen and to which they must conform (or be conformed) that legitimises the authorship and canonises the text. The genitives are always double-sided.

Eschatology and the Economy of Desire

Mimesis (like allegory and irony) always functions through mirroring – repetition that creates significances and, by associating one object or event

---

[33] This is a good place to introduce a book whose presence has been, for the most part, subliminal throughout this study: Frank Kermode's *The Genesis of Secrecy* (Cambridge, Mass.: Harvard University Press, 1979). Kermode's fundamental observation about Mark's Gospel – 'a good deal of the story seems concerned with failure to understand the story' (p. 69) – is axiomatic for this theological analysis.

with another, opens up alternative readings. Repetition displaces chrono-
logical time. What has been called the 'rhetoric of temporality'[34] disturbs
temporality, driving it into semiosis. *Chronos* (twice mentioned in Mark) is
transfigured by *kairos* (mentioned five times in Mark), just as Jesus of
Nazareth, the carpenter (or his son?) is transfigured by his Messiahship. A
theology of history invests the geographical and historical contingency with
transcendental significance. Thus, as one commentator has put it, 'the plot
as a whole is eschatological time'.[35] The 'sea' is not just a stretch of water,
eating 'bread' is not just the satisfaction of a physical appetite, and being
'healed' is not just the restoration to biological health. Critical time (*kairos*)
is narrative time (which is mimetic time) – and it always poses both an
eschatological fulfilment and an eschatology question. There is an eschatological fulfilment because critical time says 'now' is significant. Jesus begins
his preaching with, 'The time [*kairos*] is fulfilled [*peplerotai*]' (1.15). But
this 'fulfilled' is an ambivalent Greek perfect – it has already been fulfilled in
an unpresented past with present implications. When, then, was it fulfilled?
The realised eschatology of the *kairos* is past and unpresentable in the
same way as the future *eschaton* is unpresentable. There is a post-fulfilment
announcement here just as there is a pre-fulfilment announcement in
chapter 13; but it is a representation that mediates and substitutes for what
cannot be presented. Representation is haunted by intimations of the apocalyptic that act as a consciousness of its own limitations and imminent crisis.
Chapter 13 is a proleptic representation of the final crisis, the ruin of all that
has been the vehicle for the narrative's symbolism. There we have the break-
down of the family and the Temple, the collapse of the universal and created
order, the destruction of the house, the abandonment of clothes and
children and the proliferation of signs and wonders which are false and mis-
leading. The movement is towards dissolution, the dissolution of meaning.
It is a dissolution the reverberations of which reach back into the present
writing and the narrative's semiosis.

Kairos appears again, significantly, at the end of the eschatological discourse and in the negative: 'You do not know when the time is.' Again,
when one cannot tell the time, the beginning and endings become arbitrary.
The eschatological paradox is the paradox of representation itself – always

---

[34] Paul de Man, 'The Rhetoric of Temporality' in *Blindness and Insight* (London: Methuen, 1983),
pp. 187–228.

[35] Dan O. Via Jr. in *The Ethics of Mark's Gospel – in the Middle of Time* (Philadelphia, Penn.: Fortress
Press, 1985), p. 32. Through his analysis of the apocalyptic in Mark, Via emphasises Mark's commitment to the processes of history, the 'temporality of eschatology' (p. 63). For Via too this means that
'revelation is both given and withheld' (p. 57).

offering as present what is only a memory, and always promising a future it cannot possibly deliver. '[L]'apocalypse johannique, n'est-ce pas aussi celle de toute scène d'écriture en général? ... l'apocalyptique, ne serait-il pas une condition transcendentale de tout discours, de toute expérience même, de toute marque ou de toute trace?' Derrida asks.[36] The question here in Mark's Gospel receives an affirmative answer. The apocalyptic in Mark (in Jesus's ministry) is part of a general theology of representation. The Christian Gospel presents a theology of narrative.

As I said, within this eschatological paradox of representation there is repetition, folding and doubling. Time folds, rumpling the surface of the text until it seems we walk on water. There are rewinds (Herod's flashback to the execution of John is triggered by a conviction that Jesus is John *redivivus*), replays (the conversation at Herod's court on who Jesus is foreshadows Jesus's conversation with his disciples on the way to Caesarea Philippi) and fast-forwards (chapter 13). What is is a reflection of what was and what will be; and what is is a reflection itself of what occurred as Jesus lived. We are caught as readers/listeners in the mirroring of time and representation, in a land between, in a process that is always 'on the way'.[37]

It is the theme of journeying that relates these references to critical time. It is Jesus Christ's journeying which begins with the prophetic *odos* (1.2). And the word gathers a density of pedagogical, ethical, geographical and eschatological reference as the narrative proceeds. There is an imbrication of three distinct 'ways': the 'way' of Jesus teacher, the *methodos*; the 'way of God' (the *Derek* of God's righteousness); and the 'way' of the narrative which traces the geographical path and the response of the world (corporeal and incorporeal) to the other two 'ways'. The overlapping of these three ways participates in a larger, destined movement towards climax and crisis: the journey towards Jerusalem and death. The dynamic of the movement is governed by an eschatological promise that keeps us continually expecting a revelation and resolution that can never be presented. Its very absence is the precondition for representation – representation that is forever mourning the loss in that absence and desiring its recovery. The eschatological promise of chapter 13, prefigured in each miracle and 'raising', is the theological figuring of the indwelling desire that accompanies all writing and reading. The

---

[36] *D'un ton apocalyptique adopté naguère en philosophie* (Paris: Galilée, 1983), pp. 77–8.

[37] See here Elizabeth Struthers Malbon's book *Narrative Space and the Mythic Meaning in Mark* (Sheffield Academic Press, 1991), in which, having examined three forms of space within the narrative (geopolitical, topological and architectural), she concludes: '"on the way" ... is, finally, the key mediator of the various Markean manifestations of the fundamental opposition ORDER and CHAOS ... [the] conflict between the chaos and the order of life is overcome not in arriving, but being on the way' (pp. 166–8).

desire keeps us alert to the need to read the signs; throughout Mark's representation of apocalyptic dissolution we are commanded to watch, to be awake and to distinguish what are true signs from what are false.[38] The economy of the representation (the movement of the narrative and the Christology) is always also a theology of representation that moves towards and generates an economy of faith. From a discipleship perspective history, Christology and imitation are interwoven through the economy of faith that works within them, interprets them for itself and makes them part of its own Christian praxis. Theologically, history, Christology, imitation and the economy of faith are inter-associated (intertextualised) through the operation of the Spirit.

Christology, Mimesis and the Economy of the Spirit

It is in Mark's Passion narrative that the complex inter-association of Christology, story-telling, discipleship and a theology of history (realised through the working of the Holy Spirit) achieves its most profound expression. The movement of the Spirit through historical contingencies, that has governed the sending and now the handing-over of the Christ, is paralleled by the operation of faith (in the disciples and in the readers of/listeners to the narrative). Both movements or economies participate in and foster the continuation of the economy of mimetic desire. The economy of mimetic desire is the power (*dunamis*) of the story-telling to elicit response (faith) and the power of the representation to promise, partially present and continually forestall the anticipated conclusion,[39] the final resolution and demystification.

There are two related and focusing nodes of mystification. One is theological: who is this Jesus of Nazareth, how does he relate to the Christ, and what legitimises or authorises that relationship? The other one is literary:

---

[38]   As Malbon points out, "'Watch" (*gregoreite*, from *gregoreo*) and "risen" (*egerthe*, from *egeiro*) have a linguistic root in common and thus, perhaps, have some elements of meaning in common. *Gregoreo* was a new formation in Hellenistic Greek from *egregoria*, the perfect of *egeiro*, their shared significance is "to be awake"' (*Narrative Space*, p. 152). Watching, the action characteristic of discipleship, is then a participation in an eschatological unfolding – both a prefigurement of one's own resurrection and an imitation of Jesus's.

[39]   The forestalling is continuous, for from the beginning when the fulfilment is proclaimed, through each miracle performed, through to the transfiguration, Jesus's entry in Jerusalem, his purging of the Temple, his arrest, his trial, his provocation on the cross and early on the first morning of that new week, a resolution, a final revelation and vindication of Jesus's Messiahship is expected, longed-for, and yet deferred.

what relationship does this representation of the life and work of Jesus Christ bear to the generating events themselves, and what legitimises or authorises that relationship? The structure of the theological and literary problems is the same. In fact, they cannot be separated – for they are two forms of expressing the operation of the narrative, the economy of mimetic desire. For both, the nature of the problem is the nature of the problem for all representations, whether political – Jesus as the constitutional representative of God – or aesthetic – Mark's representation of Jesus Christ. The problematic is this: who or what legitimises or authorises that representative status?[40] What I am suggesting throughout this essay is that one legitimises and authorises the other. Just as God legitimises Jesus's representational function (at his baptism and at his transfiguration), so Jesus legitimises the Gospel's representational function ('for my sake and the gospel's'). And legitimation for both Jesus and the Gospel takes the same form, the origin of the one in the other, the extension of one into the other – God in Christ and Christ in the Gospel. The nature of Jesus Christ as representative authorises, through the Spirit, further forms of representational engagement with the gospel – in terms of the narrative of the Christ event, witnessing to that original event, and the disciples as representatives and disseminators of the truth of the gospel. The representative nature of the Gospel is both testimony to the meaningfulness of the Christ event and a vindication of the true identity of Jesus of Nazareth. Therefore one authorises (in a strong sense of that term) the truth of the other. And both forms of representation are caught up in the economics of the Trinity.

The economy of mimetic desire in Mark's Gospel traces the work of the spiritual powers in the cosmos – the Holy Spirit, the spirit of Jesus and the unclean spirits. The narrative begins when the Spirit descends (in prophecy to Isaiah first and then as a material object, the dove); once it has descended it immediately 'drives' and initiates the gospel story, the sending of the Christ. The success of the driving forward is countered by conflicts with religious officials and disciples (who at no point are said to have spirits of their own, to possess an independent spirituality), and the unclean spirits. The conflicts are overcome or transcended by the Spirit operating in and through Jesus – the divine *dunamis*, the Holy Spirit. The unclean, the unbelieving open to believing, the deprived who desire and know their need for salvation, are all either overcome or transfigured by Jesus. That is, until the Passion narrative – until the move into the crisis of death (the death of the will challenged and overcome is prior to any physical or spiritual death

---

[40] See Jean-François Lyotard, *The Postmodern Condition*, for a discussion of the relationship between legitimation and narrative.

on the cross). The spiritual generates events, provides scenes for action. The material (and literal) provide a constative body which the spiritual inhabits and is potentially disruptive of. In and of itself the corporeal is static – the scene for sleep, paralysis, literalism and non-commitment (unbelief).

In the Passion narrative Jesus gives up his flesh to be sacrificed and bequeaths his spirit, the Holy Spirit, to those who, like David in 12.36 or those in chapter 13, will testify and speak not of themselves (13.11). It is the Holy Spirit then who promotes the telling and the retelling of the Christ-event, who promotes the prophecies and testimonies to the coming and coming again of Christ. The economy of response is governed by the operations of God as Spirit. The mimetic experience, informed and legitimated by the Spirit, is always an anticipation of a revealed Christ.

Though the performer retreats in the Passion narrative, the performance continues (under someone else's initiative – the chief priest's and the Romans'). Jesus's injunctions to the disciples to preach repentance and follow are supplanted by the injunctions to beware and to watch. A new economy of responding and a new type of narrative are emerging from the old. A new set of protagonists propels the plot from the opening verses of chapter 14: they usurp the narrative and dictate the terms of its action. A violence both to the narrative and within the narrative is being perpetrated: the violence is evident in the increasingly ironic portrayal of Jesus that is foregrounded. It is almost as if someone else were narrating,[41] or another spirit were speaking within the narrator, a spirit darker and more uncertain than the spirit that fired within the narrative when Jesus's action governed it. The darkness deepens, likewise the uncertainty and ambivalence. Though briefly, when Jesus appears before Pilate, there is daylight, the Last Supper, the agony in the garden, the arrest, the Jewish trial and the crucifixion all develop a theme of deepening night that breaks in the resurrection dawn. Then the light will draw attention to itself through self-conscious circumlocution: 'very early on the first day … when the sun had risen'.

Along with the darkness, the change in protagonists and the new passivity of Christ, there is a widening of narratorial perspective. An omniscient

---

[41] Martin Kahler's idea in 1892, that Mark as an editor wrote an extended introduction to a Passion narrative, is a testimony to the dramatic change in narrative key in chapter 14. In *The Rhetoric of Irony* (University of Chicago Press, 1974) Wayne Booth recognises the complexity of narratorial position as the portayal of Jesus becomes ironic. A double irony is involved as Mark reports the sardonic remarks about Christ as King ironically. Booth makes the important observation that Mark's intention is 'to build, through ironic pathos, a sense of brotherly cohesion' (p. 28). For irony is elitist, only 'insiders' can recognise it. The crisis of representation, then, promoted through the ironic discourse at this point, fosters discipleship and exercises those who, by faith, are on the inside.

narrator (who has appeared at other moments in the text) becomes dominant as the drama widens in its religious and political complexity. A universal perspective is assumed in which Jesus is seen as only one among several major figures. The modification and expansion of narratorial perspective corresponds to the more detailed presentation of Jesus's own omniscience (which again has been evident before). Jesus predicts the future fame of the woman who anoints him, he predicts the future outcome for the disciples who will go to the city and encounter a man carrying a water jar, and he predicts the disciples' flight and Peter's denial – as well as his own impending death. At his Jewish trial he will predict his own glorification; finally, a *neaniskos* informs us that he will go before the disciples to Galilee. The one who predicts or prophesies is always the one who goes before, who is ahead, who is at the head of those who follow after. And the one who is at the head controls all that comes after. Jesus is the potentate of time.

Furthermore, in these closing chapters Jesus also demonstrates (again) his ability to read the hearts and minds of those around him – he knows what Judas has done and the logic of events that will now occur: 'the hour has come ... See, my betrayer ... And immediately Judas came.' Jesus, the potentate of time, also then speaks words that create and represent[42] events prior to their occurrence. His position as the one beyond time and the one whose words engender, parallels the position of the narrator, the work of the narrator, and the experience of that narration as it is re-created and represented in the event of reading/listening. But the inseparability of Christology and mimesis now enters the crisis of ironic and sometimes sardonic representation. (Irony can be understood as mimesis aware of its own paradoxical

---

[42] Jesus's words as both creating and representing events that have not yet but will now occur, portray, *in nuce*, the paradox of mimesis. The words are reported – that is, they are in the past and represented to us by the narrator. But the promise these words contain, what they suggest, is Jesus Christ, the Word of God, is the locus for what Ricœur terms the paradigmatic (mimesis 1) and the syntagmatic (mimesis 2) axes of mimesis (*Time and Narrative*, vol. I, p. 66). That is, Jesus Christ as author or creator both presents and re-presents, and incarnates the condition whereby one can move from presentation to representation. He portrays the 'two sides of poetic configuration' (ibid., p. 45). Ricœur wishes to relate these two sides through the act of reading that constitutes a third level of representation (mimesis 3). This act of reading 'completes the work' (ibid., p. 77) and the 'narrative has its full meaning when it is restored to the time of action and the times of suffering in mimesis 3' (ibid., p. 70). Lacoue-Labarthe, on the other hand, wishes to see no completion or fulfilment as possible: 'the logic of the paradox ... is nothing other than the very logic of mimesis ... the logical matrix of paradox is the very structure of mimesis ... Hence the disquiet to which mimesis gives rise' (*Typography*, p. 260). In terms of Mark's Gospel, I would argue that Lacoue-Labarthe's disquieting mimesis has the upper hand. The paradox of representation remains, the questions remain and the reading does not resolve them. The narrative's meaning is forever withheld, although the narrative encourages a faith that participates in and looks forward to a Ricœurean restoration. The paradox of mimesis is then the paradox of the Word of God.

nature and unnerved by it.[43]) There is a crisis of meaning. Jesus the miracle worker, the *theios aner*, has disappeared. Jesus the Son of David, the Davidic king, the Messiah, is portrayed in terms of contradiction and parody. Jesus the Son of God only reappears on the lips of a man with no past association, in terms of Mark's text, with the disciples; a man, therefore, who (as others in the Gospel) speaks something he does not fully understand (as 10.38) or a man who has received a revelation. And if this is a revelation it is far from being unambiguous – not simply because Romans were familiar with 'sons of God' terminology, nor simply because the 'son' is anarthrous and could be translated 'a son' or just 'son'. But it is ambiguous because it is quite emphatically in the past tense. If this man *was* the Christ, the Son of God, then he is that no longer. There is certainly no suggestion of either victory or a return; no sense the presence of this son of God will continue in some way. There is, in fact, with this anagnorisis, a sudden plunge of the narrative towards tragedy. As for Jesus the Son of Man, *that* title holds the field, but as an epitaph over the suffering and thoroughly human character of Jesus. Pilate's *ecce homo* reverberates throughout. As Morna Hooker observes, 'Mark ... does not treat it [the title] as a christological title comparable to "Christ" or "Son of God".'[44] It describes more the role he is playing as a symbol of

---

[43]   See Paul de Man ('The Rhetoric of Temporality'): 'Allegory and irony are ... linked in their common demystification of an organic world postulated in a symbolic mode of analogical correspondences or in a mimetic mode of representation in which fiction and reality could coincide. It is especially against the latter mystification that irony is directed' (p. 222). In other words, irony destabilises what we consider true representations of our world, representations that can be understood literally. The possibility of irony is the possibility that the literalism is only an interpretation, not a correspondence with facts 'out there'. Irony is, then, representation's reflection upon its own constitutive crisis – that it cannot present that which would legitimate its action. I would agree, then, with Stanley Fish's criticism of Wayne Booth's attempt to stabilise irony. In his essay, 'Short People Got No Reason to Live: Reading Irony' in *Doing What Comes Naturally* (Oxford University Press, 1989), he argues that irony too is an interpretation. But its possibility draws attention to a need always for interpretation – and that precipitates the crisis of representation. This possibility challenges Rorty's strict dichotomy between ironists and metaphysicians in *Contingency, Irony and Solidarity* (Cambridge University Press, 1989). There Rorty separates ironists who hold to the contingency of language from the metaphysicians who believe in the possibility of achieving closer and more accurate representations of what is (see pp. 76–7). My own view, and Fish's, suggest that no such separation can be made – the metaphysical perspective and the ironic perspective are two moments that constitute the nature and crisis of representation. But Rorty's construal of ironism is wide and frequently synonymous with perspectivism – in which case, the ironist's position can embrace the metaphysician's rather than merely counter it. If that is so, then Rorty too accepts a similar view of irony to that I am suggesting here. Markan irony releases the forces of the need for endless interpretation and redescription – forces only held in check by Jesus Christ and guided by faith and the Holy Spirit. Without these theological cornerstones, there is only pragmatic meaning in the face of an infinite regress of unstable interpretation. Upon these theological cornerstones a realism is made possible – but it is a theological, not a philosophical realism.

[44]   *The Gospel According to St Mark*, p. 89.

the suffering community of Israel than the Messianic victor. Christology loses its way in these last chapters, while simultaneously being given more attention.[45]

In our reading, we re-enact this crisis in Christology, the crisis of identity. We are caught up in the crisis of faith among the disciples, those who follow. For 'follow me' is a demand made by both Christ and the narrator of the Gospel. Following is the action of reading and participating in the event of reading (and forever rereading) the narrative of Jesus Christ.[46] Christ's identity, the disciples' identities, the readers'/listeners' identities, are all caught up in and kept in play by the process of representation. One cannot be abstracted or divorced from the other. All the forms of representation are searching for a legitimating fatherhood or origin. The crises of faith and Christology are co-extensive at this point with a bewildering semiosis that infects the narrative. *Logos* as both Christ and the gospel[47] appears to collapse towards *legion* (both demonic host and a Roman army). For there is a surfeit of potential, but no explicit meaning. The representation generates only the effects of meaning – not its understanding. The narrative moves between faith (which embraces and employs an analogical imagination) and paranoia. For no event or character stands alone or means merely what is written.

In the final chapters the refraction and ricochet of possible meaning revolve not just around duplication (there are two trials, two beatings, two betrayals, two cock-crows and the garden of Gethsemane is an ironic inversion of the scene of the transfiguration), but they revolve around triplication. Three times Jesus comes to the disciples (three of them) in the garden. Three times Peter denies him. At the first trial three questions are put to Jesus by the High Priest. At the second trial Pilate too asks three questions. In threes the hours of the crucifixion pass (15.25, 33, 34). The three guilty male protagonists (Judas, Peter and Barabbas – a name parodying 'Son of the Father') stand juxtaposed to three righteous male

---

[45] Morna Hooker: 'the true identity of Jesus becomes clearer the closer we move to the Cross' (ibid., p. 252).

[46] This is Scharlemann's acoluthetic reason, his Christological reason as it adheres to aesthetic reason.

[47] The word *logos* appears 23 times in the Gospel with a variety of different nuances. In the first reference – 1.45 – it appears to be a synonym for Jesus's preaching (*kerussein*). In 5.36 it appears to mean words spoken by one person (here the servant of the synagogue chief) to another. In 7.13 it is the Word of God as the Law. In 7.29 it signifies the manner of the Syro-Phoenician woman's reply. In 9.10 it refers to the content of the transfiguration. In 11.29 Jesus's word is associated with calling into question. In 13.31 it is synonymous with prophecy. One could suggest, therefore, that Mark's Gospel is part of a logocentric vision that perceives analogies between Jesus Christ as God's Word sent into the world and the true meaning of events and human discourse.

protagonists (Simon of Cyrene, the centurion and Joseph of Arimathea) and the three women who come to the tomb. One event may redeem another, one event may reinforce another or deepen the significance of the other, one event may be parallel and contradict another (the woman's anointing is followed by Judas's betrayal, both of which prepare for Jesus's death). What I wish to argue, though, is that there is a descent, in the closing chapters, towards a madness born of imitation, of duplication, or representation, of semiosis, irony and parody – a madness, that is, or a divine logic radically at odds with our own and our representation's. It is within this divine madness, counterpart to the final eschatological crisis of chapter 13, that a faith is born which clutches at significance without fully understanding what it is significant of. And the narrative itself is the first sign that that significance believed in *is* significant of something. For the centurion's cry is ambivalent and the women run away and say nothing, but the narrative speaks and vindicates the significance of what has transpired; that *something* has, in fact, transpired. The narrative is the first indication that a salvation has been wrought. In fact, it makes (*poiesis*) that salvation available. The salvation, the saving event, is again unpresentable. The representation substitutes for what has already taken place – without the representation there would be no salvation. The representation is, then, the search for, the witness to, and the producer of the process of salvation. There is, then, no need for a resurrection, for the narrative itself is the enactment (or is it the re-enactment?) of Christ's resurrection life. The narrative has become Christological, the means of grace.

Conclusion

Christology is and remains a riddle in Mark's Gospel, just as the parables are and remain a riddle, and the Gospel *tout court* is and remains a riddle. The riddles play with and emerge from the crisis of representation. The narrative performs the riddle of Christology and representation that involves the reader/listener, that forces the reader/listener to be alert and watchful. It is a watchfulness and alertness that has to move towards the edge of madness and paranoia, crisis, the cross and death in order that faith may arise. But the effect upon the reader/listener who participates in the riddling, in the economy of the mystery and a response to it, is the operation of a divine soteriology as it moves towards the final eschatological moment when the reader/listener who is now 'on the way' and following, meets up with the one who is returning to encounter her. Soteriology is inseparable from Christology, narratology (one's own narrative as a rereading of Jesus's narrative) and the 'rhetoric of temporality'. Mimesis is therefore the measure of our understanding of the Christ.

The effectiveness of Christ (his *Heilbedeutsamkeit*, which is a central concern of Christology) can only *de jure*, not *de facto*, be distinguished from the effectiveness of the narrative of Christ. Jesus Christ and the Gospel (they are both the Word) participate in a divine creativity, in a Holy Spirit who 'drives'. But the original and generative act lies concealed and unrepresentable. In the beginning, as we saw, there is no beginning, there is only representation; and that representation expresses the eschatological and narrative desire to reveal the author who gave rise to it. Representation is promoted and produced by the absent and unrepresentable. History (of Jesus) and narrative (of Jesus) are inseparable. Their inseparability promotes discipleship, promotes training and being disciplined in the continuing representation of that which is unrepresentable. All discipleship is readership – the participation in the reading and rereading of this one man's representative life and work and teaching as it is narrated. All serious reading engages in an economy of response, and as such it is a liturgy, a prayer, sacramental.

Chapter Two

THE SCHIZOID CHRIST

The term 'Godhead' is significant of operation, and not of nature. (Gregory of Nyssa)[1]

Despite the allusion to a certain psychopathology – schizophrenia – this is not an essay attempting to psychoanalyse Jesus of Nazareth. In fact, nothing could be further from the intention of this essay than an investigation into the historical Jesus and what consciousness he may or may not have had of being the Christ. Such investigations assume the autonomy of the liberal individual, that consciousness is a unified field, and that this individual, in possession of this consciousness, forms a specific sense of self: an identity. This is the subject-in-control; the subject of liberal understandings of freedom who is in subjection to no one. The focus of this essay is working against these assumptions, for the essay is concerned with sketching certain operations in which Jesus is the Christ. 'Operations' is the key term here and is employed synonymously with the word 'economy'. To rehearse Christology in terms of operations and economies raises all sorts of questions and dogmatic enquiries about the nature of the God-Man or the nature of the bodies of Christ (the historical and distinctively gendered Jew, Jesus of Nazareth and the body of the incarnate God) and their co-inherence. These questions and enquiries have courted the opprobrium of 'heresy' in the past. Since the turn to the subject and the cult of the human that emerged as a dominant cultural theme from the seventeenth century onwards, Christology has been treated in terms of defining the subjective personhood of Christ – his consciousness, his autonomy, his history, his mission, his embodiment of the Godhead. But I wish to step out of that way of understanding and examining the incarnate God and think Christology from another direction; to step outside of the turn to the subject and the cult of

---

[1] 'On "Not Three Gods"' in *Select Writings and Letters of Gregory, Bishop of Nyssa*, trs. William Moore and Henry Wilson (Oxford: Parker and Company, 1893), p. 333.

the human. I wish to avoid reducing 'Jesus', 'Christ' or 'body' to identifiable and locatable entities, and to examine this profound theological nexus as a mobile site for the production of desire and belief, love and hope. For Deleuze and Guattari, the schizo is a desiring-machine: 'continually wandering about, migrating here, there, and everywhere as best he can, he plunges further into the realm of deterritorialisation, reaching the furthest limits of the decomposition of the socius on the surface of his own body without organs'.[2] This essay is an attempt to view Christology in terms of the operations of the schizo, whose desire is liquid and viscous, passing through 'relationships of intensities' in a way that demands the surrender of the ego, of the subject-in-control.[3] It takes up Deleuze and Guattari's challenge that 'schizophrenisation' is therapeutic; and examines the operations of Jesus the Christ as performing such a form of healing.

There are points where Deleuze's thinking about space and flows touches upon Scriptural reasoning and narrative, enabling us to reconnect the ministry to the person and view Christology as a relational praxis. In other words, our thinking-through of central concepts in a doctrine of Christ – incarnation, atonement and community – emerges from a participation in which we are responding to representations of this figure. This participation and responding I will call the Christic operation. And that is where I wish to begin, developing three characteristics of this Christic operation – touch, flows and relations – on the basis of Scriptural exegesis. Let us take the

[2]   *Anti-Oedipus: Capitalism and Schizophrenia*, tr. Robert Hurley et al. (London: Athlone Press, 1984), p. 35. See Philip Goodchild, *Gilles Deleuze and the Question of Philosophy* (London: Associated University Presses, 1996), pp. 59–65 and his *Deleuze and Guattari: An Introduction to the Politics of Desire* (London: Sage Publications, 1996) pp. 73–105, 165–9 for commentary upon this notion of the schizo as developed by Deleuze and Guattari. In English 'schizo' may have derogatory connotations. I am certainly not wishing to use it in that way. I use the word here and throughout only because it is their word and the same word is employed in all secondary discussion.

[3]   I need to add here that unlike Deleuze and Guattari I am not suggesting the dissolution of the subject. I wish to retain notions of self, subject, personhood and identity. But I wish to make these notions radically relational – both in their nature and in the way in which we come to understand them. The surrender of the ego is not its disappearance, but it does mean that all our understandings of what that ego is are mediated, are interpretations that are mobile insofar as they arise from being continually contextualised and recontextualised. It is not then that Christ does not have a divine nature, but we can only gain understanding of that nature (and our own) through observing and participating in interpretations of his operations. To a certain extent this accords with the first part of Karl Barth's Christology in which Christ's divinity lies in his radical subjection to the Father. Revisiting Christology in terms of kenosis, Barth views Christ's humanity in terms of the surrender of his will to be in control. '[W]e must determine to seek and find the key to the whole difficult and heavily freighted concept of the "divine nature" at the point where it appears to be quite impossible … – the fact that Jesus Christ was obedient unto death' (*Die Kirkliche Dogmatik*, IV.1, p. 218; *Church Dogmatics*, IV.1, p. 199). In terms of a more traditional dogmatic division, we only come to understand the nature and work of Christ through an economy of response.

account in Mark (5.24–34) of the woman with the unstoppable flow of blood:

> … a great crowd pressed upon [Jesus]. Among them was a woman who had suffered from haemorrhages [*en rusei aimatos*] for twelve years; and in spite of long treatment by many doctors, on which she had spent [*dapanesasa*] all she had, there had been no improvement. On the contrary, she had grown worse. She had heard what people were saying about Jesus, so she came up from behind and touched him; for she said to herself 'If I touch even his clothes, I shall be cured.' And there and then the source [*pege*] of her haemorrhages dried up [*exeranthe*] and she knew in herself [*egno en somati*] that she was cured of her trouble. At the same time [*euthus*] Jesus, aware [*epignous en eauto*] that power [*dunamin*] had gone out of him [*exelthousan*], turned round and asked, 'Who touched my clothes?' His disciples said to him, 'You see the crowd pressing upon you and yet you ask, "Who touched me?"' Meanwhile he was looking round to see who had done it. And the woman, trembling with fear when she grasped what had happened to her [*eiduia o gegonen aute*], came and fell at his feet and told him the whole truth [*pasan ten aletheian*]. He said to her, 'My daughter [*thugater*], your faith [*he pistis sou*] has cured you [*sesooken se*]. Go in peace, free for ever from this trouble.'

Matthew (9.20–2) reduces this complex and detailed scene to three verses and completely erases the extended use of the metaphor of the flowing spring that proceeds from the woman and is met by a force proceeding from Jesus which dries it up.[4] Luke (8.43–8) reduces it to five verses but maintains the metaphor (*en rusei … he rusis*) which in fact is a citation from the Septuagint of Leviticus 12.7 concerning the purity laws. Luke also turns into a highly reflective form of direct speech what had been only a description in Mark: 'Jesus said, "Someone did touch me, for I felt that power had gone out of me [*ego gar egnon dunamin exeleluthuian*)"'.[5] The comparative reflexivity of Luke's over Mark's Greek draws attention to the action and

---

[4]   Matthew nevertheless does observe the relation between touch and the distribution and reception of divine power: 'They besought [Jesus] that they might only touch the hem of his garment: and as many as touched were made perfectly whole' (14.36).

[5]   Nevertheless, it is Luke who records unambiguously what is central to my interpretation of this passage in Mark: 'And the crowd sought to touch him [Jesus], for power came forth from him and healed them all' (6.19). In both 6.19 and 8.46 Luke uses different prepositions to describe the passage of the power – *para* (with the genitive) in 6.19 and *apo* (with the genitive) in 8.46, where Mark uses *ex* (with the genitive). Each can mean 'from' but, as Morna Hooker observes with respect to the Markan account, *ex autou* is difficult to render into English because 'the phrase "out of him" belongs to power and not to the verb: Jesus is the source of the power and does not simply act like the conductor of an electric current' (*The Gospel According to St Mark*, London: A. & C. Black, 1991, p. 149).

the subject with respect to it: the strong presence of the 'I' with respect to a passive verb and a dynamic object (power). By its self-consciousness, it constitutes a highly significant insight not only into Jesus as a person but also into the operations in which he is situated, operations that pass through him. Luke recognises that, telescoping the encounter with the woman with the haemorrhages into that one observation. But it is Mark's account that remains more subtle. For Mark maintains a balance of relations between the woman and Jesus. Being ritually unclean means social as well as religious ostracisation – which is why both Augustine and Ambrose saw in this woman a figure for the Gentile Church.[6] The woman is alienated, but Mark's attention to both persons in this exchange culminates in the relational term 'daughter'. The 'cure' effected, the 'peace' found, the 'trouble' resolved – the whole economy of the woman's salvation [sesooken] – is captured, even produced, in the intimacy of his words to her and the new relationship that is established between them. The redemption lies in the translation from alienation and anonymity ('You see the crowd pressing upon you and yet you ask, "Who touched me?"') to kinship. And it is with this translation, I suggest, that we can come to understand the Christological operation; the divine as it works in, through, with and as the body of this Jewish man who is the Christ. For, after all, the Messiah in Jewish and then Christian thinking is not just a person but an eschatological operation. The person is identified only in the mission. But more of this later. For the moment, I wish to make a number of observations about the flows of blood and power, and their different economies, as this passage suggests them to us.

First, there is a relation between the flow of blood and the spending of money. Both operations, the biological and the economic, represent the woman's life and livelihood. She is being drained or undergoing a kenosis, an emptying out. This is something that is happening to her. Her body is situated in these two consumptions. Nevertheless, she responds to what she hears about Jesus and actively places herself within another operation – the movement of the entourage around Jesus as he walks from the shores of the Sea of Galilee to the house of Jairus, one of the rulers of the synagogue. The whole event takes place in transit between two points. What links the two points, passing through the woman herself, is water, touch (for Jairus wishes Jesus to lays hands on his daughter) and the kinship of father and daughter. For Jesus was 'nigh unto the sea' (5.21) and the water motif is picked up by

---

[6] For an account of the early Church's exegesis of this passage, see what is the most detailed study of it: Marla J. Selvidge, *Woman, Cult and Miracle Recital: A Redactional Critical Investigation on Mark 5.24–34* (Lewisburg, Pa.: Bucknell University Press, 1990).

the metaphors of the spring and the stream of blood (*rusis* – flow, stream; *pege* – running water, spring), and he is on his way to heal Jairus's daughter. The encounter occurs, then, at an intersection of several movements; movements within which the woman is caught. The salvation of the body takes place *en passant*. The body is never stationary. It is never there as such. Perhaps it is because the physicians try to treat the body as a static thing that they fail to heal the woman; they fail to recognise that the body only lives in transit. It is profoundly locked into temporality, located in a 'space of flows'. It comes to an understanding of itself only in terms of the webs of relation (constantly changing) that are produced and displaced in its being borne by and placing itself within these operations.

The body of Jesus is also situated within various fluid operations. Having no 'place to lay his head', constantly sought after by the multitude and followed after by his disciples, he moves from place to place. Being 'on the way' is a prominent theme in Mark's Gospel.[7] Frequently in the first part of Mark's Gospel Jesus crosses and re-crosses the Sea of Galilee. He is connected to flows of water, bodily fluids like blood and spit (Mark 8.23) and a force, authority or bodily strength (*dunamis*) that passes through him.[8] But he is always in command of these flows and the initiator of operations. That is why this encounter with the woman is so remarkable. For it is the woman's touch that initiates the healing that is discharged through the body of Jesus.[9]

Second, there is a relation between the mobility of these bodies and knowledge. The woman immediately recognises the staunching of the flow of blood, she '*egno en somati*'. And when Jesus is touched in this particular, even intimate way, immediately he *epignous en eauto* – he learns of, recognises an alteration in the currents within which his body is situated. These operations within and between bodies constitute a somatic form of knowing that is not unrelated to physical sensation but the interpretation of which transcends merely registering such sensation. In fact, Mark describes

[7]   See chapter one, pp. 49–52.

[8]   See Ludwig Bieler, *Theios Aner: Das Bild des 'göttlichen Menschen' in Spätantike und Frühchristentum* (Darmstadt: Wissenschaftliche Buchgesellschaft, 1967): 'Was *dunamis* ist, lehrt am besten die Geschichte von der Heilung der Blutflüssigen ... *dunamis* hier die "Kraft" ist' (pp. 80–1). For the relationship between touch, power and the *theios aner* see also K. Kertelge, *Die Wunder Jesu in Markusevangelium: Eine redaktionsgeschichtliche Untersuchung* (Munich: Koesel, 1970), p. 114; and H.-W. Kuhn, *Ältere Sammlungen im Markusevangelium* (Göttingen: Vanderhoeck & Ruprecht, 1971), pp. 192–200.

[9]   A number of commentators have remarked upon how distinctive is this physical touch. We can take Bultmann as illustrative: *The History of the Synoptic Tradition*, tr. John Marsh (Oxford: Blackwell, 1963), p. 214.

two moments in the woman's understanding. For having known in her body what has taken place – '*egno en somati*' – she then grasps what has happened to her – '*eiduia o gegonen aute*'. This second moment is also an embodied knowing, for she is 'trembling with fear'. What takes place in this move from *ginosko* to *oida*? Are they synonyms or is Mark suggesting a move from apprehension to comprehension, a move marked by an outward physical manifestation (trembling) of an inner physical event (the staunching of the flow of blood)? Certainly there is a grammatical move from a past historic to a punctiliar aorist – the second knowing is quite specific and epiphanic – but, either way, this process of knowing and the contents of what is known are both related to the body. For both Jesus and the woman there are significant moments of recognition, there is a knowledge and a knowing that are somatic. Recognition issues from altered states in the flows within which each body is located (and continually being relocated). For the woman this issues in her being able to tell him the whole truth [*pasan ten aletheian*] – where *aletheia* in Mark's Gospel is reserved for the Christ alone.[10]

Third, it is touch that effects these alterations. There is a movement through the senses in this passage. First the woman has heard of Jesus (always in Mark a precondition for believing), then she sees Jesus as one of the crowd, then she touches him. The movement of the senses implicates the woman in an economy of distance – of which more later. It is touch that bridges the different flows within which each body is situated and lives. The bridging disturbs and redistributes the currents. In Mark's Gospel there are 11 references to touch (*apto*) but several scenes in which touch is implied by descriptions of what Jesus does with his hands. In each case bar one there is a cleansing (1.41) or a making whole (3.10; 6.56; 7.33; 8.22). The one exception is 10.13 where Jesus desires that the children are brought to him 'that he should touch them'. Touch initiates transference, involving each in an economy of response that is rooted in the body and calls forth somatic knowledges of recognition. Sometimes, as with the haemorrhaging woman, the recognition is sealed by a naming that indicates a new relation – the woman becomes 'daughter'. Touch gives particular direction to a body continually being situated relationally; it orientates and focuses the various fluid operations. Touch triggers a divine operation, an eschatological operation. It is an operation in which the messianic is performed.[11] The making-whole of the body is a salvific act that translates the recipient into a citizen

---

[10] See Marla J. Selvidge, *Woman, Cult and Miracle Recital*, who also notes that 'blood' is only used in connection with both Jesus and this woman in the Gospel.

[11] For the relationship between Christology and performance see chapter one, pp. 43–9.

of the Kingdom. Proleptically, each one cleansed[12] or made whole receives intimations of their resurrected body. This is significant in a gospel like Mark's where there may be no resurrection scene of the body of Christ. Related to touch is faith, for Jesus redirects each recipient of healing away from the touch to a participation that the touch is an expression of: 'Your faith has cured you.' Faith here is a practice, a form of acting, not a state of mind. For touch enacts trust. To pass over from one's own body to another is an act of entrustment. Entrustment is believing as an action; a believing that the body knows (*ginosko*) and performs before the intellect grasps (*oida*). Faith draws each into the energy flows within which Jesus is situated.[13] Only in Christ in this way can the pronouncement be made of 'Peace', *Shalom*.[14] The levels of entrustment become more pronounced when what is touched is not the garments but the body itself. Consider these two other passages in Mark:

> And they brought to him [Jesus] a man who was deaf, and had an impediment in his speech; and they besought him to lay his hand upon him. And taking him aside from the multitude privately, he put his fingers into his ears, and he spat, and touched his tongue. (7.32–3)

---

[12]   There is a substantial body of literature that treats the uncleanliness issue in this passage. In fact both Tertullian and Chrysostom observed that this woman's condition made her unclean according to the cultic laws laid down in Leviticus 15.25–31. What is not often observed is the enormous importance purity laws give to touch. The Leviticus text explicitly warns against touching anything associated with the woman, for anything touched by her in this condition is rendered unclean. Her touching his garment (Matthew and Luke render this as the hem of his garment and some commentators have made much of the symbolic tassels about the hem of a rabbi's garment) is a sacrilegious act that Jesus turns into a salvific one. The scandal of the touching is another example of the irony and crisis of representation in Mark's Gospel – see the previous chapter. The borders crossed far exceed the permeability of one body by another – as well as the crossing of theological difference (creator–creation) there is also the crossing of sexual difference (man–woman) and cultic difference (clean–unclean).

[13]   Without discussing the economy of the response, Dietrich-Alex Koch remarks on this passage: 'Nicht mehr Jesu automatische wirkende *dunamis*, sondern die *pistis* ist der Grund der Rettung' (*Die Bedeutung der Wundererzählungen für die Christologie des Markusevangeliums*, Berlin: de Gruyter, 1975, p. 137). Power does not operate coercively, it inspires and completes faith, it incorporates. It is in the incorporation that the salvation that Christ brings becomes her salvation (and healing). There has been much discussion among commentators about the role faith plays in this miracle. Kertelge (*Die Wunder Jesu in Markusevangelium*, p. 115), Koch (p. 137) and Nineham (*The Gospel of Mark*, London: A. & C. Black, 1963, p. 158) wish to make faith the dynamic for her healing and suggest Mark does too in order to counter the *theios aner* tradition that emphasised the operation of *dunamis*. But this fails to recognise that the economy of response has two poles – *dunamis* and *pistis*. The woman is healed and knows it *before* Jesus pronounces that it was her faith that made her whole. Jesus only names the practice in which the woman participated such that the *dunamis* was effective.

[14]   Only in Mark's account do we find this confirmation of the woman having come to a new place and well-being.

And they came to Bethsaida. And some people brought to him a blind man, and begged him to touch him. And he took the blind man by the hand, and led him out of the village; and when he had spat upon his eyes, and laid his hands upon him, he asked him, 'Do you see anything?' And he looked up and said, 'I see men; but they look like trees, walking.' Then again he laid his hands again upon his eyes; and he looked intently and was restored, and saw everything clearly. (8.22–5)

There are degrees of intimacy here not found in the passage concerned with the haemorrhaging woman. Flesh makes contact with other flesh, and no doubt this intimacy is possible because the miraculous healing involves two men. Significantly, neither Matthew nor Luke makes any use of these two miracle stories. The personal withdrawal of each man into a secluded space and away from the anonymity of the 'they' who bring these persons to him – 'he took the blind man by the hand' – emphasises that intimacy. Touch is again related to a certain discharge of salvific power. Although in these passages there is no allusion to *dunamis*, the power is materialised instead in terms of a discharge of Jesus's own bodily fluids. But the touch in both accounts is specific. It is directed to the area of the body that is damaged. Jesus reaches into each man's pain, identifies it (and with it). In the first case he actually penetrates the other man's body, crossing into the flesh of the other. The pain is assuaged by the love, care and attention that each is drawn into by that touch. Touch translates the negative into the positive. Touch is a reaching beyond the boundaries of oneself to find a place not yet given, a future not yet received. It is a gesture of overflow.

From the following piece of exegesis we can proceed to develop theologically the three interconnected *topoi* I draw attention to – touch, flows and relation – that will facilitate an understanding of the logic of the incarnation that Christ inaugurates and conducts for the salvation of the world. Touch, flow and relation enable us to develop a Christology in which doctrines of incarnation and atonement become inseparable from doctrines of creation and the Church.

Touch

Let me clarify at the beginning here the mode of touch that I am treating and what I am investigating in this treatment. First: the mode of touch is directly related to the healing of the woman's haemorrhage and any number of uses of touch by Jesus to heal. It is significant in Mark's account of the haemorrhaging woman that two forms of touch are identified, for the woman's touch is distinguished from mere contact. It is the disciples (always in various states of ignorance throughout Mark's Gospel) who draw attention to contact: 'You see the crowd pressing upon you and yet you ask, "Who touched me?"' I am not concerned here with forms of contact – and neither is Mark's Gospel. Aristotle's attention to touch in *De Anima* has been criticised for its 'exclusive concentration on passive rather than active touching'[15] or 'contact sense'. I am far from sure this is a correct evaluation of Aristotle, but it serves to emphasise that the treatment of touch here is exclusively concerned with active touching. In German one can distinguish between two types of body, *Körper*, that is inert, and *Leib*, that is not. *Körper* can refer to the physical bodies of people or animals and can be extended metaphorically to speak of the body of a text (*Textkörper*), for example. *Leib*, on the other hand, bears several interrelated senses. First, it is the precondition for perception. As such it is the German translation of what Merleau-Ponty calls 'body' – that site of crossing between the seeing body and that which is seen, the touching body and that which is touched. Self-reflexivity is the very condition for *Leib*. Second, *Leib* refers on a social level to the complex matrix of relations and circumstances in which individual bodies are implicated. As such, it is only because of this body (as *Leib*) that community becomes possible. The body as *Leib* is political because the body as *Leib* lives (*bios*) whereas the body as *Körper* subsists (*zoe*).[16] Thirdly, *Leib* is, theologically understood, the dwelling-place of the soul.[17]

This examination of touch concerns, then, bodies in the German sense of *Leiber*. Furthermore, it is concerned with the active touching between persons.[18] In the active touching between persons we are examining the intentional structure of touching. 'Intention' here is not simply the conscious motivations for the subject as agent. I use intention in a way developed by Husserl in the fifth of his *Logical Investigations* – the experience of an object of my directed attention (*Gerichtetheit*), an object made meaningful

---

[15] Cynthia Freeland, 'Aristotle on the Sense of Touch' in Martha C. Nussbaum and Amélie Oksenberg Rorty eds., *Essays on Aristotle's De Anima* (Oxford: Clarendon Press, 1992), pp. 227–48, p. 230. See also Jean-Louis Chrétien's excellent examination on Aristotle on touch, 'Body and Touch' in *The Call and the Response*, tr. Anne A. Davenport (New York: Fordham University Press, 2004), pp. 83–131. He agrees that Aristotle is not talking about 'contact' (pp. 116–17), rather 'Touch is the perpetual place of exchange' (p. 117).

[16] For an important discussion of the politics of *bios* and *zoe* and the logic of sovereignty that seeks to produce a biopolitical body, see Giorgio Agamben, *Homo Sacer: Sovereign Power and Bare Life*, tr. Daniel Heller-Roazen (Stanford University Press, 1998).

[17] For an exposition of my view of the soul see essay three.

[18] One could examine intentional touch between persons and animals, for example, though one would have to define how 'intentions' are ascribed to forms of animal behaviour.

for me.[19] These intentions are constitutive of the experience of the perception (apperception) and there is an indeterminacy about them intrinsic to
what is being presented as such. Intentional experiences involve interpretative relations and may become the basis upon which volitional intentions to
act are made by an agent, but are prior to such intentions. Intentional structures, as Husserl wrestled to point out, are complex and multilayered. An
examination of such structures attempts to clarify some of these layers. The
intentional structure of touching cannot simply be examined from the point
of view of the one touching. For it is the nature of this mode of touch (and
Aristotle was certainly aware of this) to affect whatever is touched – as the
example of Jesus's response to the haemorrhaging woman makes plain. As
a swimmer one quickly comes to recognise an accidental 'brush' against
another swimmer and a touch whose intentions are, in some subtle way,
communicated (that is, delivered and received). Those intentions can take
on various communicative shadings – sexual suggestion, aggressive warning,
competitive edge, etc. The context is important: both bodies are exposed,
each to the other. The nakedness renders them both open to the world,
vulnerable to suggestion. What is important for this analysis (and returns us
to the object of this investigation into touch) is how a 'recognition' of the
intentional structure of that touch is produced. What is the operation of
such knowledge, what are its effects, and what are the implications of both
that operation and its effects for a theological anthropology? These are some
of the questions I wish to examine. In the pool much is communicated
between two swimmers about each other, but without words or often distinctive gesturing (for the swimming proceeds through a steady rhythm of
strokes that neither wishes to disrupt). Nevertheless temperament, present
mood, past training, ability, and even levels of intelligence are all communicated through mutual observation (which has always an element of
voyeurism about it). Jean-Louis Chrétien speaks of how 'The flesh listens.
And the fact that it listens is what makes it respond.'[20] The addition of
intentional touch, though, dramatises this communication. It is this drama-
tisation that is being investigated below.

Origen in *Contra Celsum* I.48 writes: 'And they touched the Word by
faith so that an emanation came from him to them which healed them …
[Jesus's] truly divine touch.' He refers to 1 John 1.1 in which the 'Word of
life' is apprehended or 'handled' by three senses: hearing, seeing and touching – handling 'the Word of life'. 1 John continues that there is a bearing

[19] See *Logical Investigations*, vol. 2, tr. J.N. Findlay, second edition (London: Routledge & Kegan
Paul, 1970), pp. 533–659, particularly pp. 552–96.
[20] 'Body and Touch', p. 130.

witness that can take place by describing what the followers of Christ have seen and repeating what they have heard. These acts of representation also disseminate a power that will bring those who picture and hear them into a fellowship, a participation that is ultimately Trinitarian (1 John 1.3). We analysed this *poiesis* and its association with mimesis in the previous essay. But what the witnesses cannot communicate is their touching Christ; for representation distances and renders into a general vocabulary that which was personally experienced. And touch individuates by a bringing into contact and proximity. Touch cannot distance and does not submit to a general vocabulary without ceasing to be what it is. Touch communicates only to the other being touched. It cannot communicate to a third party. A third party may witness touch and draw inferences about it, but s/he has not entered into what was being communicated in the touch. Touch can be described in terms of pleasure, pain, pressure, warmth etc., but that which has been brought into being by the touching cannot be brought into being through the representation of that touch. Touch intimates, it does not speak. Speaking of the child's early tactile experience, the psychologist David Katz uses the term *Eindruck*, an impression, a prehension.[21] The intimacy it creates communicates not a knowledge but a knowingness, an intentionality that expects a response. It brings this knowingness into existence not as creation from nothing but as the realising of the singularity of that which exists. It announces that it is I, in my very corporeal individuality, who is knowing (rather than who knows) you in your very corporeal individuality. As such, this singularising is a bringing forth from an indifference, an indeterminacy, an anonymity. It is not a bringing to identity, for identity is too strong a word for what is only intimated. Rather, it is a bringing into relation because of an intimation of difference. This relational difference is recognised only in a belonging, only in the interchange that in intimating something brings about a transformation in what is perceived and understood in and between the touching and the touched; though the substance of this transformation is only realised in a subsequent reflection.

I would, then, modify what Maurice Merleau-Ponty (for whom also embodied perception is a locus of mystery and enigma) observes about touch and perception when he writes:

> The moment perception comes my body effaces itself before it *and* never does the perception grasp the body in the act of perceiving. If my left hand is touching my right hand, and if I should suddenly wish to apprehend with my right hand the work of my left hand as it touches, this reflection of the body upon itself always miscarries at the last moment: the moment I feel my left

---

[21]   *Der Aufbau der Tastwelt* (Leipzig: Verlag von Johann Ambrosius Barth, 1925), p. 160.

hand with my right hand, I correspondingly cease touching my right hand with my left hand. But this last-minute failure does not drain all truth from that presentiment I had of being able to touch myself touching: my body does not perceive, but it is as if it were built around the perception that dawns through it.[22]

Merleau-Ponty, here as elsewhere in his work, while wishing to move beyond the dualism of mind and body, nevertheless draws a distinction between the body and reflection in which perception is already cognition and prejudgement. This is a model of perception founded upon seeing[23] and I would accept what both Heidegger and Wittgenstein have taught us that we 'see as'. But I suggest that in touch the body does not efface itself. There is an intimation of its very corporeality; as if the body is brought into being by that touch. In fact, in his earlier work *Phenomenology of Perception*, Merleau-Ponty points exactly to that when he writes that in touch, 'I do not only use my fingers and my whole body as a single organ, but also, thanks to this unity of the body, the tactile perceptions gained through an organ are immediately translated into the language of the rest ... Each contact of an object with part of our objective body is, therefore, in reality a contact with the whole of the present or possible phenomenal body.'[24] And so I would correct Merleau-Ponty's later phrase, writing: 'my body *does* perceive and is built around that perception'. The body perceives itself in relation and knows the nature of that relation. If Merleau-Ponty misses that, it may well be because in the left hand touching the right there is no other, both hands are mine. They are 'one sole organ of experience'.[25] There is

---

[22] *The Visible and the Invisible*, ed. Claude Lefort, tr. Alphonso Lingis (Evanston, Ill.: Northwestern University Press, 1968), p. 9.

[23] Chrétien views Merleau-Ponty as making touch fit into his understanding of sight; 'Body and Touch', pp. 100–1.

[24] *Phenomenology of Perception*, tr. Colin Smith (London: Routledge, 1962), p. 369.

[25] Ibid., p. 141. In his late essay 'The Intertwining – The Chiasm' (in *The Visible and the Invisible*), very briefly Merleau-Ponty broaches again the question of 'touching the hand of another' and coins, elliptically, the term 'intercorporeality'. But the model of what he calls 'the circle of the touched and the touching, the touched takes hold of the touching' (p. 141) is founded upon a synergy in which because the organs of my body communicate with each other therefore a transitivity is founded from one body to another (p. 143). In the handshake, then, where each experiences being touched in touching, I 'touch in it the same power to espouse the things that I have touched in my own' (p. 141). In this there is a transcending of difference as each 'address themselves to the body in general and for itself' (p. 143). His account of incorporeal touching is, as he himself claims, curiously locked into the logic of Narcissus. My own account emphasises that touching and being touched by a sentient other goes beyond reflexivity. There is a sense in which Merleau-Ponty's own vocabulary performs a transcendence that he does not investigate beyond an allusive Spinozistic monism; he uses descriptors like 'magical', 'mystery', 'enigma', 'surpassing' and 'miracle'. Even 'vision' in the late essays takes on the gravity of disclosure, revelation and epiphany. He never manages to shake off his Catholic imagination, but he does not reflect upon it either.

what he elsewhere calls the criss-crossing 'of the touching and the tangible',[26] but the touching does not enter a field of intentions and an economy of response, because there is no eros.[27] Consider a different kind of touching of oneself in which there is eros: masturbation. Here the body is effaced and there is no experience of 'touching myself touching', for a distance is opened up by fantasy, erotic scenarios into which the body is inserted; not the physical body but one of the many fantasised bodies we live with. Fantasy consumes the body's perceptions. The body cannot be intimate with itself. Though it can pleasure itself, it cannot singly enjoy the pleasuring of itself without withdrawing from the fantasised scene that supports the pleasuring. The body cannot intimate things to itself.[28] The eros that is conjured in masturbation has first to project and maintain a body image elsewhere. It has to manufacture a distance, an exteriority, for itself such that touching and being touched can take place.

If then the body comes to a sense of itself as different, as singular, as a unity through touch, the economy of that response is governed by desire. Desire issues in a play of nearness and separation, availability and inaccessibility, masking and revealing. If desire can only be desire through an economy of distance, then the economy of response is intertwined with an unfolding of distances, differences, exteriorities that pass in and out of interiorities. This movement in and out, separation and penetration,[29] is not only the heartbeat of the economy of response; it is an exchange, a giving and reception, and a communication. One recalls that the word 'intimate' in its verbal form comes from the Late Latin verb *intimo* – to flow into (Julius Solinus, AD 250), to communicate to the spirit (Tertullian AD 160–240), to put into, but also by AD 400 to narrate, tell, describe, relate. Its adjectival form comes from the earlier Latin *intimus* – innermost or most secret. It is used by Cicero (43 BC) to describe a form of relationship, even a close

---

[26]   Ibid., p. 133.

[27]   Desire arrives late in the economy of perception for Merleau-Ponty. In 'The Interwining', he describes 'the patient and silent labour of desire' (p. 144) that follows touching and is related to articulation. We see this move in much more detail in *Phenomenology of Perception*, where, in the development of his phenomenology of the body, 'The Body in its Sexual Being' (pp. 178–201), he lays the foundation for 'The Body as Expression, and Speech' (pp. 202–32). Although Merleau-Ponty suggests in that volume (p. 178) that an analysis of 'desire or love' will enable us to understand 'the birth of being for us', he views desire as a mode of affectivity, not, as I suggest, the condition for affectivity itself.

[28]   Chrétien concludes: 'Self-touch cannot be the truth of touch'; 'Body and Touch', p. 118.

[29]   Merleau-Ponty observes: 'my own body's "invisibility" can invest the other bodies I see. Hence my body can assume segments derived from the body of another, just as my substance passes into them'; 'Eye and Mind', tr. Carleton Dallery in *The Primacy of Perception* (Evanston, Ill.: Northwestern University Press, 1973), p. 168.

friend. One might also add, a little more felicitously, a relation to *in-timeo*, where *timeo* means to dread, to fear and the prefix *in* negates that experience. I add this last conjectural possibility because intimacy is always ringed with fear, even when it most excludes, and this is part of the way in which desire and distance are interrelated. For intimacy demands the body's openness, its vulnerability. The calibre, or profundity of the giving or reception, depends upon recognising the possibilities of fear, of dread, and negotiating them. The negotiation involves a suffering because I am not the other, and intimacy, while fearing absorption by the other, also suffers the longing for an integration. In Emily Brontë's *Wuthering Heights*, at the climax of an argument between Catherine Earnshaw and Nelly Dean concerning Cathy's obsession with Heathcliff, Cathy shouts out 'I *am* Heathcliff.'[30] But she is not, and that is both her triumph, as a character who epically takes her place at Heathcliff's side, and her tragedy. Intimacy causes a tearing apart, to expose the suffering of longing. Distance, difference are figurations of longing (long-ing) – without them there would be stasis.

Intimacy and distance then require flows, movements, operations and economies. Aquinas provides us with a theological account of this state of things when discussing the divine governance of creation:

> Thus this God does work in every worker, according to these three things. First as an end. For since every operation is for the sake of some good, real or apparent; and nothing is good either really or apparently, except insofar as it participates in a likeness to the Supreme Good, which is God; it follows then that God Himself is the cause of every operation as it ends. Again, it is to be observed that where there are several agents in order, the second always acts in virtue of the first: for the first agent moves the second to act. And thus all agents act in virtue of God Himself: and therefore He is the cause of action in every agent. Thirdly, we must observe that God not only moves things to operate, as it were applying their forms and powers to operation … but He also gives created agents their forms and preserves them in being. Therefore He is the cause of action not only by giving the form which is the principle of action, as the generator is said to be the cause of movement in things heavy and light; but also as preserving the forms and powers of things … And since the form of a thing is within the thing [*est intra rem*], and all the more as it approaches nearer to the First and Universal Cause, and because in all things God Himself is properly the cause of universal being which is innermost of all things [*quod inter omnia est magis intimum rebus*], it follows that in all things God works intimately [*in omnibus intime operatur*].[31]

---

30 *Wuthering Heights* (Harmondsworth: Penguin Books, 1965), p. 122.
31 *Summa Theologiae*, Ia.105.5 responsio.

We will return to this passage. Distance here has only to do with spatiality insofar as spatial images are used to conceive it. But distance cannot be reduced to some mathematical measurement separating two bodies in some pure or idealised space. Bodies can be in close proximity, touching, even interpenetrating, and yet nevertheless distance is experienced. Distance cannot in fact become an identifiable object. Perhaps the closest we get to distance as such is the identification of difference. The distance is intimated to those differences that compose it. This distance is implicated, then, in a common participation, a common recognition of exteriority: I am not the other; the other is not I; the other is not reducible to or measurable by me; and I am not reducible to or measurable by the other. What is intimated in this distance is an excess; the mystery of alterity. Every representation made of this distance must fail if the aim of such representation is to define. For there is no place from which an exhaustive representation is possible, no neutral locus – which again appeals to an ideal, mathematically conceived spatiality. Even the notions of exteriority and interiority lose their meaning, as neither subject has access to this distance outside of partici-pating in it. The memory of that participation may attempt to re-present it – but at best it will be an echo of the experience bouncing back from the walls of a single consciousness. It is not that the distance escapes representation, in fact it demands representation because the distance constitutes a command to communicate. Distance precedes and haunts all communication. But what is intimated in this distance exceeds chains and combinations of signifiers. At best it can imbue signs with a semantic plenitude – like the phrases 'I know you' or 'You know me', spoken by those participating in what Jean-Luc Marion describes as an 'intimate alterity'.[32] These phrases are bridges of suspended steel that open up the distance, sway in the wind and expand and contract with the rise and fall of temperature. The knowledge of distance and its negotiation as it arises in intimacy is a knowledge of difference-in-relation. But, again, this is not a conceptual knowledge, for 'the relation' itself is rendered indefinable in this distance. The relation is always in play, always under construction. Like the distance itself, the relation is never there as an object as such. This is not a conceptual knowing; it is a bodily knowing that is received, given and lived prior to any reflection. The reflection cannot erase the traces of what the body has received, given and lived. In fact, it is these traces that call forth reflection – or rather, meditation, or what the prayerful understand as contemplation.

---

[32]   *L'Idol et la distance* (Paris: Grasset, 1977), p. 199.

We must distinguish here between reflection, as Merleau-Ponty (after Husserl) understands it, and contemplation.[33] For it is in this distinction that the theology of embodiment (and touch as the most fundamental mode of coming to an understanding of being embodied) announces itself most clearly. Following Descartes, to reflect is always to grasp one's own knowing (*cogito ergo sum*), to recognise it as such. Reflection conceptualises and therefore represents certain states and conditions to itself. Its movement is circular in the way phenomenologists since Hegel have recognised the dialectic of In-Itself and For-Itself. To contemplate is to transcend the circularities of reflection; for it is a movement towards the other – a movement that is facilitated, even solicited by that other. It is to be drawn to the other, who is drawn to you. It is a movement without concepts – though images may be used in the first instance (as with an icon). As the goal of reflection is understanding, so the goal of contemplation is a mutual discerning – to know even as I am known. There is not a content to this knowledge. The knowing is a condition of being, a condition in the Johannine texts that is often described as abiding (*meno* – to stay, to stand, but transitively to await, to expect).

Intimacy is mutual abiding, what in John's Gospel is described as the centre of Messianic relationality – I in you and you in me.[34] This relationality participates in and reveals the logic of the incarnation. As the Prologue to the Gospel of St John describes it through a complex combination of prepositions: 'he came into [*eis*] the world. He was in [*en*] the world, and the world came to be [*egeneto*] through him [*di'autou*]' (John 1.9–10). Christ in-dwells that which is already in Christ – the world that was made through him. And so the only-begotten of God begets. The one who, as Origen expounded it,[35] is eternally generated by the uncreated God creates, and then indwells his creation. In this sense we can speak of God's profound touch; the intimacy of his presence as that which touches through maintaining our very existence as an emanation of his own essence. This is at the heart of Aquinas's understanding of divine operations above in which he employs the adjectival form of '*intimo*'. He also explicitly relates the intimacy with the cognates of the verb – to flow into, to communicate to the spirit. In *Summa Contra Gentiles* he observes: 'one finds a diverse manner of

---

[33] We can associate this difference with the difference I allude to in the Introduction (p. 20) concerning the categories 'understanding' and 'discernment'. With discernment and contemplation (rather than understanding and reflection) a religious metaphysics begins to take shape; in this case, a Christian epistemology.

[34] See essay three for a developed exposition of this Johannine theme.

[35] *De Principiis*, I.2.2.

emanation of things [*diversus emanationis modus invenitur in rebus*] and, the higher a nature is, the more intimate to the nature is that which flows from it [*et quanto aliqua natura est altior, tanto id quod ex ea emanat, magis ei est intimum*]'.[36] Gregory of Nyssa in his Eleventh Homily on the *Canticum Canticorum* describes this intimacy as the 'perception of his presence [*aesthesis parousias*]':[37] a perception or feeling (*aesthesis*) in which the remoteness of the uncreated *ousia* of God effects in the soul a profound closeness. If this tension of intense proximity and distance is the very nature of human beings created in the image of God, it issues from the logic of the incarnation. Salvation is to become enfolded within this enfolding logic – to attain the condition of being incarnate as the Word is incarnate, or what Gregory and others termed *theios*. More clearly, human beings have to participate in becoming flesh as he became flesh. Human beings are not truly themselves, are not truly flesh, until they have become flesh as he became flesh. We are, then, seeking a body; through intimacy we seek an intimacy with that source of the 'emanation of things'. It is a body being prepared for us. According to Paul's letter to the Ephesians,[38] it is 'his body, the fullness [*to pleroma*] of him that fills all in all' (Ephesians 1.23).[39] It is a condition of enfleshment that is eschatological – a resurrection body, a new kind of embodiment that in its very singularity indwells or is, to use a term coined by Merleau-Ponty, 'transcorporeal'. Giorgio Agamben describes this condition as being at 'ease': 'The Provencal poets (whose songs first introduce the term into Romance languages in the form of *aizi*, *aizimen*) make ease a *terminus technicus* in their poetics, designating the very place of love. Or better, it designates not so much the place of love, but rather love as the experience of taking-place in a whatever singularity.'[40]

Touch is an orientation towards being incarnate and it finds its true self-understanding in love. Even the touch involved in violence towards, in abuse of, oneself or the other is a call for love, a recognition of its absence. To cut oneself is an attempt to attain some recognition of an embodiment that seems constantly to be under threat of disappearing. It is the mark of the wish to feel again; the recognition of being in a frozen state, without

---

[36] *Summa Contra Gentiles*, IV.11.1.

[37] Werner Jaeger and Hermann Langerbeck eds., *Gregorii Nysseni in Canticum Canticorum* (Leiden: Brill, 1960), p. 324.

[38] I am aware of the arguments among commentators as to whether this letter can in fact be attributed to Paul, but these arguments have no bearing on the Christology announced in this letter.

[39] For a further exposition of the importance of *pleroma* and its association with *kenosis* see chapter nine, pp. 257–61.

[40] *The Coming Community*, tr. Michael Hardt (Minneapolis: University of Minnesota Press, 1993), p. 24.

desire. Touch is always an action, an activity – as distinct from seeing, which is more passive and at my command. As Merleau-Ponty observes: 'In visual experience, which pushes objectification further than does tactile experience, we can, at least at first sight, flatter ourselves that we constitute the world, because it presents us with a spectacle spread out before us at a distance, and gives us the illusion of being immediately present everywhere and being situated nowhere.'[41] Seeing invokes the possibility of pure separation, of exteriority, of rampant individualism, of social atomism, of the society of the spectacle. But touch, adhering as it does 'to the surface of the body',[42] disrupts the 'spectacle' as 'spectacle'. Theologically understood, it disrupts the production of idols – it forestalls reification by the instauration of an economy, a movement, an action. It is at this point that touch is related to flows, for the movement described above as the economy of response (that is inseparable from touching and loving) is a profoundly kenotic movement – the emptying of one towards the other, that is ongoing and endless.

Flows

Two Greek terms are at the theological heart of understanding motion and flows: kenosis and *pleroma*. These terms are also the theological heart for our third *topos*, relation. This is a giving of oneself that can only come from the ongoing and endless reception of the other. This outpouring, both divine and human, is only possible, and for human beings only sustainable, in terms of the infinite plenitude of God's *ousia*. Here lies the basis for a sociality that is the burning vision in all ecclesiological practice. This is very important today, because the unprecedented rise in refugees, exiles, homeless and stateless peoples finds an echo in the growing popularity of ideas like kenosis, emptying, exile and the nomadic among some postmodern philosophers:[43] Michel de Certeau,[44] for example, Mark C. Taylor, [45] Jean-Luc Nancy,[46]

[41] *Phenomenology of Perception*, p. 369.

[42] Ibid.

[43] There is an interesting collection of essays concerning this theme in contemporary continental philosophy: *Letting Go: Rethinking Kenosis*, ed. Onno Zijlstra (Bern: Peter Lang, 2002).

[44] See the later chapters of *The Mystic Fable*, vol. 1: *The Sixteenth and Seventeenth Centuries*, tr. Michael B. Smith (University of Chicago Press, 1992).

[45] See *Altarity* (University of Chicago Press, 1987).

[46] See his notion of the endless diremption of the body: 'Corpus' in *The Birth to Presence*, tr. Claudette Sartiliot (Stanford University Press, 1993), pp. 189–207.

Gianni Vattimo,[47] Emmanuel Lévinas[48] and Jacques Derrida.[49] It is, as we shall see, a kenosis or emptying without telos, an infinite kenosis, a kenosis also that issues from and into absence, not *pleroma*. I will develop what is at stake here with reference to the work of Lévinas.

What characterises philosophy, for Lévinas, is totality: the going out from and the return to the Same in some Hegelian feedback loop. This takes narrative form in in the story of Ulysses 'whose adventure in the world was only a return to his native island'.[50] What his own work defines is the wounding mark or trace of the infinite, the transcendent, an exteriority that forever disrupts this return to the homeland of the Same and therefore totality. This is a thinking orientated towards the wholly other [*autre*], a

> departure with no return, which, however, does not go forth into the void,
> [but] would lose its absolute *orientation* if it sought recompense in the imme-
> diacy of its triumph … As an orientation towards the other … a work is
> possible only in the patience, which, pushed to the limit, means for the agent
> to renounce being the contemporary of its outcome, to act without entering
> the Promised Land.[51]

The orientation towards the other – in which oneself is hostage to the other, totally responsible before this other, accused in the eyes of the other – means for Lévinas that we forever live beyond ourselves. This is the basis for ethics, for him. Not simply an ethics of moral prescriptions, but an ethics commanded by a Good beyond being whose infinity calls all our human productions and fabrications into question. We are summoned to live beyond our home-making, to leave the cities of refuge. This wholly other, in whose wake we follow, is recognised in the face of the stranger, the widow, the orphan; it calls each of us in turn to 'go forth', even if that going forth is not 'into the void'. There is redemption only in this movement out to the other. In a passage entitled '*Pièces d'identité*' Lévinas writes: 'A Jew is accountable and responsible for the whole edifice of creation. Something engages man

[47] See *Beyond Interpretation: The Meaning of Hermeneutics for Philosophy* (Cambridge: Polity Press, 1997) and *Belief*, tr. Luka Disanto and David Webb (Stanford University Press, 1999).

[48] This is a profound and recurrent theme throughout Lévinas's work. It perhaps best finds expression in the section treating 'The Substitution' that began as an essay in 1968 but was incorporated into Lévinas's book *Otherwise than Being or Beyond Essence*, tr. Alphonso Lingis (The Hague: Martinus Nijhoff, 1981).

[49] See in particular 'Sauf le nom' in *On the Name*, tr. John P. Leavey Jr. (Stanford University Press, 1995), pp. 35–85.

[50] 'Meaning and Sense' in *Collected Philosophical Papers*, tr. Alphonso Lingis (The Hague: Martinus Nijhoff, 1987), p. 91.

[51] Ibid., p. 92.

even more than the salvation of his soul. The acts, utterance, thoughts of a Jew have a formidable privilege of destroying or restoring worlds.' '[A]s responsible,' Lévinas writes, 'I am never finished with emptying myself of myself. There is infinite increase in this exhausting of oneself, in which the subject is not simply an awareness of this expenditure, but is its locus and event ... *The glory of a long desire!* The subject as hostage.'[52]

If I am critical of Lévinas, and even more so of other modern philosophers of the kenotic, or endless self-emptying, it is because of the lack of attention they pay to reception. I do not accept that kenosis is the basis of sociality. As the host must receive her guests, the guests must receive the hospitality offered. For Lévinas, this omission is explicable in terms of the attention given to receptivity in Kant and also Husserl's phenomenology; he wishes to examine that which is prior, for him, to receptivity: being obligated or *sub-jectum* to the other. Lévinas is also wishing to describe an economy, a work towards the other, that 'requires the ingratitude of the other'; since gratitude would be the 'return of the movement to its origin'.[53] In other words, in Lévinas's understanding of the economy of the gift there cannot be mutuality or reciprocity. The economy envisaged, and Lévinas is emphatic about this, is 'a one-way movement'. It is not, in my own terms, an economy of response. What this other brings or evokes is desire; 'desire for the other'[54] is key to Lévinas's account of oneself, one's neighbours, God and ethics. The other is recognised in the economy of the desire it evokes. But sociality is not simply desire *for* the other, it is also the other's desire for me. Lévinas conceives that in the unending emptying of oneself, in the way the other empties me, I discover 'ever new resources. I did not know I was so rich'.[55] But from where can these resources spring if the ego is always a hostage, always accused? They can only come from that which is continually being given, such that what I am being emptied of is that which I am being given: the infinite generosity or fullness of God's grace that St Paul conceives in terms of *pleroma*. That sociality, which moves beyond ourselves and into a permanent journeying towards the other, is only possible within an economy of the gift in which I am constituted in the transit of plenitudinous grace. Only then can my desire for the other avoid being endless sacrifice, on the one hand, or a lust that only consuming the other would satisfy. *Pleroma* as infinite, divine generosity makes possible a relationality beyond self-abnegation and beyond appetite. There are alternative economies of the

---

52   Ibid., p. 169.
53   Ibid., p. 92.
54   Ibid., pp. 94, 97.
55   Ibid., p. 94.

gift that do not figure mutuality in terms of a return to the same.[56] This is an economy of the gift that Lévinas inherits from Marcel Mauss, in which giving incurs a debt to be repaid.[57] Giving is fundamentally associated with exchange, so non-reciprocity is needed to forestall a return.[58] But the economy of giving that I am outlining is more akin to the situation between the host and his guests when Abraham welcomes the three strangers into his camp at Mamre (Genesis 18.1–15).[59] Abraham does not give to the strangers because he will get something in return. Though he later receives the promise of Isaac, the service and the welcome he offers are prior to this promise. He receives the strangers as God and in faithfulness to the God who has been with him throughout his journeying. Being faithful is an orientation of being towards God; it determines but is prior to action. Faithfulness is not part of an exchange system. It is excessive to any system since, when nothing appears to be given and one has to live for a future in which others will enter the Promised Land, not you, faithfulness remains.

The giving that operates between oneself, other people (*autrui*) and God as wholly other (*autre*) transcends exchange. Lévinas is right to point out how we do not own ourselves, but I believe his understanding of God as absolutely other is wrong. It is a God who is always absent, whose mark upon creation is only a trace of his passing on ahead; a God who does not return the infinity of one's desire but, in order to remain God and other must be indifferent to our continual attention to his intention in creating us. Now while I hold to the importance of the apophatic tradition in cutting

---

[56]   I am aware here of the extensive debate between Jacques Derrida and Jean-Luc Marion on the gift, John Milbank's rigorous theological analysis of the debate and his own richly suggestive contribution. I have learnt much from engaging with this material, particularly Marion's phenomenological account of donation and reduction in *Reduction and Givenness: Investigations of Husserl, Heidegger, and Phenomenology*, tr. Thomas A. Carlson (Evanston, Ill.: Northwestern University Press, 1998) and *Being Given: Towards a Phenomenology of Givenness*, tr. Jeffery L. Korsky (Stanford University Press, 2002) (both of which are profoundly theologically informed) and Milbank's provocative challenges to it in the name of deeper appreciation of Trinitarian participation.

[57]   Marcel Mauss, *The Gift*, tr. Ian Cunnison (New York: Norton, 1967).

[58]   See Jacques Derrida, *Given Time: I Counterfeit Money*, tr. Peggy Kamuf (University of Chicago Press, 1992).

[59]   'Then the Lord appeared to him [Abraham] by the terebinth trees of Mamre as he was sitting in the tent door in the heat of the day. So he lifted his eyes and looked, and behold, three men were standing by him; and when he saw them, he ran from the tent door to meet them, and bowed himself to the ground, and said, "My Lord, if I have now found favour in your sight, do not pass on by your servant. Please let a little water be brought, and wash your feet, and rest yourselves under the tree. And I will bring a morsel of bread, that you may refresh your hearts. After that you may pass by, inasmuch as you have come to your servant." And they said, "Do as you have said"' (Genesis 18.1–5). One notes how the three strangers constitute for Abraham 'the Lord'. His response is gratitude at being able to serve and the meal he prepares subsequently far exceeds water and 'a morsel of bread'.

through our projections and fetishes of God, nevertheless I would maintain that the infinity of our desire for the other is only possible on the basis of the infinity of the other's desire for me, and that it is only on that basis of participation in that prior divine erotic giving and receiving, that each of us is able to give to each other. Not that this economy of reception between the divine and human is equal, for the God who created and sustains me, and in whose Triune life I live, is both the origin and the end of my desire. But within what John Milbank has rightly termed 'the asymmetrical reciprocity'[60] we are each of us both constituted and all our relationships likewise. Human beings are gifts to each other in an endless economy of God's grace whereby we are given in order to give.

Now why has this investigation into Lévinas's thinking been important? Because this account of the endless journeying into exile, this account of kenosis in which one is always a stranger, is very popular among postmodern philosophers. With de Certeau and with Lévinas it is developed in a theological context such that Lévinas can remark that this 'departure with no return ... however, does not go forth into the void'. It is the theological context alone that saves this journeying from nihilism. Nihilism issuing from an account of being in exile can do nothing for the plight of the refugee. The work of Derrida, Vattimo and Taylor simply announces that we are all dispossessed persons and in a continual state of being dispossessed; we are all nomads. The corollary of that confronts the refugee with the claim: 'You are nothing special. You merely give poignant expression to the condition of being human.' While there is some truth in that, as I have argued above, that is not the whole of the story. As Edward Said has pointed out in his examination of the experience of being the migrant or the refugee, 'To live as if everything around you were temporary and perhaps trivial is to fall prey to petulant cynicism as well as a querulous lovelessness.'[61] That is not a recipe for sociality; only for indifference and accelerated social atomism. Abraham journeys into deeper and deeper exile but always within the context of God's grace and promise towards him. He journeys within the economy of divine giving, of divine loving that is not impassive to Abraham's desire to be faithful. It is this participation that enables him, in exile, to be the host: to welcome the stranger into all the temporary conditions of his own dwelling. Let me put this in another way: Abraham can befriend the strangers because

[60] See John Milbank, 'The Soul of Reciprocity Part One: Reciprocity Refused' in *Modern Theology* 17 (3), July (2001), pp. 335–91 and 'The Soul of Reciprocity Part Two: Reciprocity Granted' in *Modern Theology* 17 (4), October (2001), pp. 485–507.
[61] 'Reflections on Exile' in *Reflections on Exile and Other Literary and Cultural Essays* (London: Granta Books, 2001), p. 183.

he knows that his true dwelling lies in God's love for him, and the strangers can accept and return Abraham's reception for exactly the same reason. The economy of faithful response is excessive to because prior to economies of exchange. In such an economy, to give hospitality also requires us to recognise how we are receiving hospitality: the reception of what is given is also a hosting in oneself of the other. There is no superiority between host and guest. For to host is to allow the guest to be as oneself; and to be a guest is to receive the host as oneself. True justice only operates in obedience to the economy of faithful response that recognises the question in every encounter, 'Who is the stranger?', and realises the answer is: 'Neither of us – while we have each other.' This is the economy of love – that aims always at the perfection and righting of relation. There is no justice, just as there is no beauty, truth or goodness, outside the divine ordering of all relation (or what Pseudo-Dionysius understood as 'hierarchy' and Gregory of Nyssa termed 'order' or *akolouthia*). From the human body in right relation issues the body politic and ecclesial.

We will treat relation itself more fully below. For the moment let us continue this meditation through the association between 'flows' and kenosis (through the metaphorical suggestiveness of the verbs *kenoo* – to empty – and *pleroo* – to fill or make full). This association draws attention to the different forms of flow and flux within Mark's text. For throughout we have been talking about 'operations', 'movements', 'productions' and 'economies'. What is the relationship between the physical issue of blood (which eventually turns into the issue of Christ's own blood, which in terms of the Eucharistic outpouring continues to haemorrhage until his body is complete), the corresponding and countering issue of power and these other dynamisms? Theologically, motion is governed by a teleology – salvation.[62] What is this salvation that physical healing is analogically related to? We can only appreciate the nature of salvation when we understand the origin and end of motion – that is, why there should be a divine creating at all and how that is related to God's own desiring. Motion is ecstatic and ultimately Trinitarian; and the condition for its possibility is distance. We saw above that it is distance that gives intimacy and enables participation. What salvation is then, and what the operations of grace move towards, is an ever-deepening participation in God – the source of life in abundance, resurrection life. Eschatological concepts such as 'peace', 'abiding', 'rest' (as eternal Sabbath) are intimations of the content of this participation, like Agamben's 'ease'. The ecstatic nature of motion requires continual self-abandonment. What Paul

---

[62]   For an excellent genealogy of motion and its relation to the divine, see Simon Oliver, *Philosophy, God and Motion* (London: Routledge, 2005).

calls being a 'living sacrifice' (Rom. 12.1). It stands in contradistinction to what Paul describes as hardening the heart (Rom. 9.18, 11.7, 11.25) – that is, the stasis, the paralysis that issues from self-protection, fear, resentment, anger, narcissism. In fact there is only one motion because there is only one telos – and that motion is, depending upon perspective, kenotic or pleromatic (to coin a word). It is either emptying towards the other or filling with respect to receiving the other. Any notion of participation requires understanding this economy. Not that there is a reciprocity here, finally. For we are given before we learn to give and receive within that ultimate givenness. Divinely understood, there is response not reciprocity proper (though we can use Milbank's felicitous phrase 'asymmetrical reciprocity'). But insofar as God accommodates himself to that which is human, and insofar as we human beings as his creation are 'necessarily ... framed of such a kind as to be adapted to the participation of such good',[63] then it follows that there are both operations of God in the world and discernments of them and a reciprocity of relation among all things mundane (of the created order). In Barth's language, in creation there is both an external and an internal covenant. Christ, as the mediator of God to humankind and humankind to God, makes possible both the asymmetrical and symmetrical reciprocity, for the movements of Christ are both participations in the *perichoresis* that constitutes the impassable triune Godhead and the economic operations of that *perichoresis* with respect to creation itself. Creation in and through the Word is caught up in the flows, emanations and energies that not only keep that creation in existence but also maintain its orders. Gregory of Nyssa, commenting upon a traditional Trinitarian analogy of the relationship of the Father to the Son being like the relationship between mind and word, puts it thus:

> ... the Word of God has been shown not to be this actual utterance of speech, or the possession of some science or art, but to be a power [*dunamis*] essentially and substantially existing, willing all good, and being possessed of strength to execute all its will; and, of a world that is good, this power [*dunamis*] appetitive and creative of good is the cause.[64]

With the word *dunamis* we return to the Gospel passage of the haemorrhaging woman's miraculous healing. Both *kenoo* and *pleroo*, as descriptions of the divine economy and the response it calls forth, are related back to *dunamis*. In the Introduction I commented upon how this word, like *oikonomia* and *energeia*, was central to early Christologies as found in the Apologists. Let me

---

[63] Gregory of Nyssa, 'The Great Catechism' in *Select Writings and Letters of Gregory, Bishop of Nyssa*, p. 478.
[64] Ibid.

take this further in developing a Christology in terms of flow and motion on the basis of the citation from Gregory. As Jean Daniélou points out, following the early Apologists, 'the *dunamis theou* came to be thought of in two successive stages: first, as an impersonal power inherent in the divine nature, and secondly, as the Son of God brought forth specifically for the work of creation'.[65] But this led to varieties of subordinationist thinking. It was Origen who corrected some of the early apologetic (and Gnostic) thinking in which *dunamis* and *energeia* figured by making the generation of the Son from the Father eternal. But, as Michel Barnes has commented, 'where Athanasius and his contemporaries use the doctrine of divine generation to prove that the Father and the Son share the same nature or essence, Gregory uses generation as the basis for distinguishing the Persons [of the Trinity].'[66] Power is the expression of essence or *ousia*. Christ shares in the power of God (as does the Spirit), and it is the unity of the operations of this power that demonstrates the singleness of their nature (*ousia*). We will return to the generation and production of difference in several other essays. For the moment I only wish to pay attention to the way the Godhead is conceived as endlessly appetitive and creative in its operations; and how all these operations are good. Christology has to be conceived in terms of this power and these operations. As such, salvation comes as human beings recognise they exist within this economy of response, this 'eternal power of God which is creative of things that are, the discoverer of things that are not, the sustaining cause of things that are brought into being, the foreseeing cause of things yet to be'.[67] The woman's spring of blood (that has caged her in a concern with herself, with her health, with spending all she has on the care of that self and trying to restore that health) dries up – because she enters into the flows of God's power. Participating now in a new, dynamic economy – living out that appetitive and creative kenosis and *pleroma* – issues in new asymmetrical and symmetrical reciprocities: the relations that constitute the body of Christ. As such, as we saw, some early commentators saw her as a figure of the Church.

---

[65] *A History of Early Christian Doctrine: Volume Two, Gospel Message and Hellenistic Culture*, tr. John Austin Baker (London: Darton, Longman & Todd, 1973), p. 352.

[66] Michel René Barnes, 'Divine Unity and the Divided Self: Gregory of Nyssa's Trinitarian Theology in Its Psychological Context', *Modern Theology* 18 (4), October (2002), pp. 475–96, p. 483. See an earlier article by Barnes for a discussion of the hierarchical process involved in the terms *ousia, dunamis, energeia* and *ergo*, and how Gregory goes against this trend by viewing power as the natural expression of essence – 'The Background and Use of Eunomius' Causal Language' in Michel Barnes and Donald Williams eds., *Arianism after Arius: Essays on the Development of the Fourth Century Trinitarian Conflicts* (Edinburgh: T. & T. Clark, 1993), pp. 217–36. For a much more detailed and fascinating study of *dunamis theou* with particular reference to the theology of Gregory of Nyssa, see Barnes, *The Power of God: Dunamis in Gregory of Nyssa's Trinitarian Theology* (Washington, D.C.: Catholic University of America Press, 2001).

[67] Gregory of Nyssa, 'The Great Catechism', V, p. 478.

Relation

Let us at this point return to the New Testament, and to another account in which touch, flows and relations coincide with Christology. This account is, in some way, the reverse of the scene of the woman with the haemorrhages as it concerns an extravagant outpouring towards Jesus:

> Six days before the Passover, Jesus came to Bethany, where Lazarus was, whom Jesus had raised from the dead. There they made him supper [*deipnon*]: Martha served [*diekonei*], and Lazarus was one of those at table with him. Mary took a pound of costly ointment of pure nard [*pistikes polutimou*] and anointed [*eleipsen*] the feet of Jesus and wiped his feet with her hair; and the house was filled [*eplerothe*] with the fragrance of the ointment. But Judas Iscariot, one of the disciples (he who was to betray [*paradidonai*] him), said, 'Why was this ointment not sold for three hundred denarii and given to the poor?' This he said, not that he cared for the poor but because he was a thief, and as he had the money-box he used to take what was put into it. Jesus said, 'Let her alone, let her keep it for the day of my burial. The poor you always have with you, but you do not always have me.' (John 12.1–8)

We have been concerned with relation throughout the examinations of touch and flows, but from this passage I wish to point to three things pertaining to the Christic operation. The extent to which this Johannine account is related to the accounts in Mark (14.3–9), Matthew (26.6–13), Luke (7.36–50) or some independent source has been fiercely debated by New Testament scholars.[68] I do not intend to enter those debates, which often tend to result in judgements about John's confused blend of traditions. And in moving from the account in Mark's Gospel to John's I have no other purpose than recognising different Christological elements, evident in Mark, pronounced in John.[69] As Rudolf Schnackenburg points out, with John 'the construction and direction of the story ... [has] its clear Christological

---

[68] All commentators enter the debates, cite the various possibilities and come to their conclusions.

[69] Specifically, these concern the paradoxical nature of all relations *en Christo* that participate in the *kenosis/pleroma* economy, as I hope to show. To some extent Mark offers an account that could have achieved most of the same ends insofar as there is a touching, a liturgical pouring out of oil and a relational exchange that is public. This account too then can be viewed as paralleling the account of the haemorrhaging woman. But the woman in Mark anoints Jesus's head, while the anointing is explicitly related to his burial (where he does not receive any anointing). In John, Mary anoints Jesus's feet – it is not an anointing for burial in the same way, since Nicodemus and Joseph of Arimathea anoint Jesus's dead body (John 19.38–40). To my mind, the verbal echoes and explicit mention of location (Bethany) point to John's knowledge of the Markan text. Though some have suggested that the account in Mark is a later addition indebted to John, most see the Markan text as expressing the earliest tradition. My interpretation is foregrounding the Christology here.

tendency'.[70] This account allows me to make a number of points on the economy of relational exchanges; these points draw together the themes of this essay.

First, an economy of love constitutes the relations here (an 'extravagant act of love' – Bultmann[71]). There is a profound return of that which Mary had received. If, with the haemorrhaging woman in Mark's Gospel, *dunamis* flows out from Jesus through touch, here something is bestowed upon Jesus through the pouring of the ointment over his feet. What is bestowed is costly [*polutimou*], much valued, but it is the act itself that bestows most. For it not only anoints Jesus as the Messiah King,[72] and (as the different accounts of the story in the other Gospels express) anoints him proleptically for his burial. There is also here an act of sacrificial worship that confers on Jesus the glory of God. This glorification is important. Throughout the Gospel Jesus glorifies God and God glorifies Jesus. This co-glorification as an economy of response is central to the identification of Jesus as the Christ. Mary's act of glorification, intensified because it takes place in silence and is witnessed in silence, is a participation in the salvific presence (*kabod*) of the divine. Hence the act issues in a perfume that fills the house, akin to the smoke of the glory of God that fills the temple. There is an operation in this economy and a participation in that operation. Throughout the Gospel this divine operation in figured in terms of movements of descent and ascent.[73] Here in Mary's act is a profound obeisance, a descent that imitates and responds to Christ's own kenotic descent. She enacts, at another level, Martha's own serving (*diekonei*). In her descent Christ receives. His passivity is deeply receptive of the acknowledgement of who he truly is. He is lifted up, exalted, by her descent – the pouring of the ointment is a metonymy of

---

[70] *The Gospel According to St John*, vol. 2, trs. Cecily Hastings et al. (London: Burnes & Oates, 1980), p. 371.

[71] *The Gospel of John: A Commentary*, tr. G.R. Beasley-Murray (Oxford: Blackwell, 1971), p. 415.

[72] I am aware some commentators have questioned the kingship theme (championed by C.K. Barrett, *The Gospel According to St John*, 2nd edition (Philadelphia, Penn.: Westminster Press, 1978, p. 409) because, unlike in Mark, it is the feet not the head that are anointed. But this ignores the fact that John (unlike Mark and Matthew) strategically situates this story *before* Jesus's Messianic entrance into Jerusalem and associates it directly with the repeated motif of kingship in John's account of the Passion (John 18.33–40; 19.1–6, 12–16, 19). Some have noted that John's attention to the days on which the supper took place (six before the Passover) may be an allusion to the *Habdalah*, the supper concluding the Jewish Sabbath – a supper which came to be associated with Elijah and the welcoming of the Messiah. See Barrett, p. 411. Furthermore, I argue that the anointing of the feet is an important aspect of the lowliness theme in John's Gospel. Bultmann (*The Gospel of John*, p. 415) and Raymond Brown (*The Gospel According to John*, vol. 1, London: Geoffrey Chapman, 1971, p. 452) both point to the feet having theological significance but fail to elaborate the nature of that significance.

[73] For an excellent theological interpretation and historical account of the exaltation and glorification in John's Gospel see Schnackenburg, pp. 398–410.

the flow of her very self towards him.[74] This letting go occurs in several stages: the anointing of the feet, not the head (that parallels Jesus's own lowliness in the following chapter, where he stoops to wash the feet of the disciples at the Last Supper);[75] the smearing of the feet with the oil; and the letting down of her hair, a thing prostitutes did in the ancient world – as in the Lukan account. This act is, of course, related to the theme of reception and refusal that occurs throughout the Gospel. John insists it is not enough that Christ come to his own; his own must receive him.

But in this reciprocity we must always observe a difference that introduces us to the second observation about the Christic operation. The divine reaches out to the human, first and foremost; the human responds and, cooperating with the divine, glorifies God. The reciprocal relation issues from and is sustained by God. There is a priority here and that means there is a politics. Let me begin to define politics with an observation made by Michel Foucault: 'Power is only a certain type of relation between individuals.'[76] I would wish to take this further and suggest all power concerns relations as such. We will return to the question of reciprocity in a moment, but I suggest every relation (and power can only be powerful with respect to relations) is a power relation insofar as all relation involves the distribution of differences, and some of the differentials (perhaps many) involve inequalities. The inequalities may relate to biology (one having higher energy levels than another), physiology (one being stronger than another), psychology (levels of self-confidence or self-assertiveness), intellectual capacity, economics, class, professional hierarchy, etc. No relation is equal. Reciprocity, then, is either the ideal horizon towards which all relations aspire, or of a different order to personal and social standings; or perhaps both. There are two sets of the politics of relation in this story. There is the politics of what some commentators call the 'family circle' within which this supper takes place. The relations are deliberately politicised. It is uncertain whether Lazarus is both host and guest[77] but Martha's serving and both her and Mary's female presence at such a meal 'is surprising to the Jewish-Christian reader'.[78] But before we jump to the idea of a democratisation we have to recognise social levels of servitude that the Gospel writer disrupts by giving greater

[74]   Brown notes that *myron* came as either a powder or a liquid (p. 448).

[75]   Bultmann notes a rabbinic parallel to this anointing of the feet (*The Gospel of John*, p. 415). The association of this account with the Last Supper is strengthened through the term for the meal (*deipnon*) that is found in John only here, 13.2, 4 and 21.20.

[76]   'Pastoral Power and Political Reason' in Jeremy Carrette ed., *Religion and Culture by Michel Foucault* (Manchester University Press, 1999), p. 134.

[77]   See Brown, p. 448.

[78]   Ernst Haenchen, *John*, vol. 2, tr. Robert W. Funk (Philadelphia, Penn.: Fortress Press, 1984), p. 84.

prominence to the female characters than the male ones (other than Jesus himself). The second set of political relations concerns the emphasising of differentials implicit in various hierarchical structures in the encounter between Mary and Jesus. There is the reclining male and the female at his feet; there is the teacher and the disciple; there is Christ and one of his believers; there is, theologically conceived, God and a human being, the creative Word and the creature. Touch, which here is not a momentary event but a continued action involving anointing and wiping [*exemaxen*],[79] establishes an exchange that does not overthrow the hierarchies; in fact, it confirms them as the order of things – it subtends them. Economies of gift and response constitute a relation in which both figures participate. It is in the participation itself that a reciprocity beneath or beyond personal, social or even theological standings operates. Power is continually displaced because the mutual affirmation that takes place in this event demands a co-dependency. To employ Louis Althusser's term 'interpellation', this event names Jesus as Christ as surely as it names Mary as the lover of Christ, a disciple, a bride, a figure of the Church as the bride. This co-dependency and co-constitution of identity allows for the reversal of roles – which is what occurs in the chapter that follows, when, at the Last Supper, Jesus lays aside his garments and both washes and wipes [*ekmassein*] the feet of the disciples. Touch establishes flows of love concretised in perfumed ointment and water that while affirming difference, are excessive to it.

The radical nature of the relation, the economy of exchange and touch in this passage, are emphasised through a contrasting relation and economy of response introduced with Judas Iscariot. There is a social equality established between him and Jesus, issuing in the way both are able to articulate judgements: Judas's observation that the ointment could have been sold for the poor is countered by Jesus's observation that there will always be poor people. The contrasting judgements about the situation can only be made, for both protagonists, from a position of assumed authority. Judas challenges Jesus and it is in the assumed right to challenge that a social equality is announced. But it is a *primus inter pares* that makes this reciprocity (that democratises Jesus as a man like Judas is a man), and therefore both relation and touch are impossible. Exchange is reduced to a simple material and financial one that is impervious to personal and theological economies of response. Rather than power being displaced it is reified in two antithetical

---

[79] Again some commentators have observed how this account must be a 'confused amalgamation of details' (Brown, p. 452) from the synoptic Gospels because why would someone pour the oil and then wipe it away again. But as my reading emphasises that the pouring and the wiping mirror the washing and the wiping in chapter 13, John is drawing a parallel to make a theological point.

positions. The move from the material specificities of 'this ointment' to the vague abstraction of 'the poor', in Judas's question, is indicative of the disembodiment that accompanies the establishment of political contestation and the hypostasising of democratised differences. This disembodiment is figured in terms of 'theft'. For Judas is a thief on many levels, most profoundly in being unable to return that which most truly belongs to the Christ (in contrast to Mary's sacrificial giving). In the foot-washing of chapter 13 Judas is included in a liturgy of incorporation ('If I wash you not, you have no part with me': John 13.8). Jesus, then, as the Messianic servant, refuses the disembodiment and distance from relation that Judas's refusal to engage installs. But then it is after the foot-washing that Judas 'went out immediately. And it was night' (John 13.30).

These observations on what we might term Christic relations or relations *en Christo* put a different gloss on Paul's statement in the Letter to the Galatians: 'There is neither Jew nor Greek, there is neither slave nor free, there is neither male or female; for you are all one in Christ Jesus' (Gal. 3.28). For that sentiment is read today in terms of a democratising of differences; Christ the leveller of hierarchies, the liberator of the subjugated. And what my reading has sought to point out is how that is not so. The oneness is in Christ and it does not concern the equality of social positions. Jews remain Jews, Greeks Greeks, slaves slaves, freeborn freeborn, males male and females female and all relations between them will reflect levels of social and cultural power, its distribution, its waxing and waning. The Christic operation is not apolitical; it concerns power and its authorisation. The oneness concerns the submission of all social positions (and the politics of identity) to Christ, and the new orders of power (and its polity) that are engendered by this submission. It is an order and a polity that participates in the same oxymoronic condition found in the apophatic observations on knowing by unknowing, grasping by surrendering, fuelling a passion that is apathetic. Here in this economy of descent and ascent, service and kingship, vulnerability and power, framed by a coming crucifixion that is simultaneously a glorification, a giving that is receiving, an intimacy that distances, a kenosis that is plenitude, a laying down that is an exaltation.

The Schizoid Christ

By way of conclusion, let me return to the 'schizophrenisation' that Deleuze and Guattari view as therapeutic.[80] In a chapter, called (after Engels and

---

[80] *Anti-Oedipus*, p. 68.

Freud) 'The Holy Family', they offer a characterisation of one who lives as a schizo:

> These men of desire – do they live yet? – are like Zarathustra. They know incredible sufferings, vertigos, and sicknesses. They have their spectres. They must reinvent each gesture. But such a man produces himself as a free man, irresponsible, solitary, and joyous, finally able to say and do something simple in his own name, without asking permission; a desire lacking nothing, a flux that overcomes barriers and codes, a name that no longer designates any ego whatever. He has simply ceased being afraid of becoming mad. He experiences and lives himself as the sublime sickness that will no longer affect him.[81]

The person is given over to the operations he performs, the desiring he produces and reproduces; as such this one is radically deterritorialised and gives way to the body without organs. What I am suggesting is that Christian theologians might re-think this figure in terms of Jesus as the Christ – viewing Christology as concerned with tracing and understanding the operations of Christ. I make such a proposal on the basis of trying to recover something of the 'otherness' of Christ for contemporary Christology. If Christ reveals to us what it is to be human, we cannot simply project our images of being human onto the figure of Christ. We have then to wrestle with and deconstruct the language and the categories we use to speak about this incarnate one. The early Church Fathers like Tertullian and Athanasius were emphatic that at every moment of his historical existence Jesus Christ did not cease being God.[82] It was by not ceasing to be God that human beings could become deified. The figure of the schizo I take, then, as a figure for the rethinking of what is human – 'do they live yet?' Of course, for Deleuze and Guattari, this experience of schizoid living is the product of capitalism's liberation of the flows of desire. But there is a correlation between the spirit of Christianity and capitalism that Marx, Weber and Benjamin (among others) have noted. Elsewhere I have argued how Marx understood capitalism as fundamentally an idolatrous form of religion – a religion in which the operations of a transcendent God become fetishised in terms of money or gold.[83] But the true schizo living – that Deleuze and Guattari recognise as intrinsic to any social production and reproduction, even in precapitalist times/places,[84] because inseparable from the *socius* as

---

[81]   Ibid., p. 131.
[82]   See Tertullian, *Adversus Marcionem*, ii.27, and Athanasius, *Contra Arianos*, i.42.
[83]   See 'The Commodification of Religion or the Consummation of Capitalism' in Slavoj Žižek and Creston Davis eds., *Political Ontologies* (Durham, N.C.: Duke University Press, forthcoming).
[84]   *Anti-Oedipus*, p. 139.

such – transgresses such fetishism, transgresses all codings of desire. There
might then be theological value in examining further this schizo Christ
who produces, through his unique operations, the deterritorialised Church
– which, if not exactly a body without organs, might, in terms of Paul's first
Letter to the Corinthians (12.12–31), be understood as a body in which the
differences between organs are only epiphenomenal: 'many members, yet
one body'. A schizo Christology, already announcing a theological anthropology, would lead then to a schizo ecclesiology: a true *socius*. But that is
another essay.

Chapter Three

THE BODY OF THE CHURCH AND ITS EROTIC POLITICS

The real presence of diversity in our flesh and blood which are at the same time bread and wine ...[1]

I want to begin with theological accounts of being human that lie at the heart of the Christian tradition and develop their implications both Christologically and ecclesiologically. These accounts can be found in both the Greek and Latin Fathers, in Origen, Gregory of Nyssa, John Damascene and Maximus the Confessor as well as Augustine, Bonaventure, Aquinas and Ignatius of Loyola. They concern a certain confluence between the soul and the body that issues not quite in a doctrine (the accounts are too slim and ambiguous for that) but in what I would term a theological phenomenology of the senses, even a Christian epistemology. Damascene, in his treatise *De Fide Orthodoxa*, puts the matter tersely when he states that sensations of the world, acts of intellection and the stirring of desire all involve 'movements of the soul'.[2] The Greek word is *kinemapsyches* and it is indebted to Aristotle.[3] I want to suggest – contrary to all dualisms of mind and body, *psyche* and *soma* – that it is an investigation into the operations of the soul that will deliver to us a theological materiality. This is not another form of post-Cartesian idealism: the material order is not a construct of mind. For mind,

---

[1] Lines from Czeslaw Milosz's poem, 'Capri', in *Facing the River: New Poems*, translated from the Polish by the author and Robert Hass (Manchester: Carcanet Press, 1995), p. 12.

[2] *De Fide Orthodoxa*, II, 11.22.46, 248 in *Schriften des Johannes von Damaskos*, ed. B. Kotter, vol. 2 (Berlin: Walter de Gruyter, 1973).

[3] Aristotle distinguished between motion, *kinesis*, and actuality or *energeia*. They were not dualistic concepts but constituted two poles of a spectrum. *Energeia* was the perfection or realisation of all that was potential. *Kinesis* was the movement that moved all things towards their formal (in the Aristotelian sense of 'form') completion. The form is the '*logos* of the essence' (*Physics*, II.3.194b27). See L.S.A. Kosman, 'Aristole's Definition of Motion' in *Phronesis*, 14 (1969), pp. 40–62.

as we will see, is only one aspect of being ensouled and being embodied, and the theological materiality of the world is its sheer givenness in wonder. Only having understood this theological materiality – which, at heart, is nothing more or less than incarnationalism – can we appreciate the nature of the Church as the body of Christ and the eros of its political relations.

On the Enmattered Soul

We begin then with the soul, a subject that Aristotle claimed was one of the most difficult to investigate yet one of the most valuable entities to be investigated. Aristotle's own analysis, in *De Anima*, remains important to later Christian conceptions, as Aquinas's large commentary on the text testifies.[4] In fact, the text is being revisited today by a number of contemporary moral and analytical philosophers concerned with overcoming the mind/body dualisms bequeathed by various Cartesians[5] – though wrestled against vigorously, if in the end vainly, by Descartes himself. What Aristotle has to say about the soul is instructive and we shall build upon it.

First of all, while there is no identity there is a profound relationship between the soul and the body such that all 'the affections [*pathe*] of the soul involve the body' (403a16);[6] affections are, in an older translation, 'enmattered'. Even intellection that might be thought to operate independently of the body, does not, because to understand requires imagination and there can be no imagining without the body. As Aquinas concludes: 'Understanding, then, it seems, does not occur where there is no body',[7] though later I wish to reverse the direction of this thinking and suggest all understanding affects the body. Aristotle himself suggests this when he goes on to exemplify

---

[4]   *Commentary on Aristotle's De Anima: St Thomas Aquinas*, trs. Kenelm Foster O.P. and Silvester Humphries O.P. (Notre Dame, Ind.: Dumb Ox Books, 1994). In a somewhat similar manner – though the vocabulary differs from both Aristotle and Aquinas – Maurice Merleau-Ponty has examined the way that 'every thought known to us occurs to a flesh'. See his essay 'The Intertwining – The Chiasm' in *The Visible and the Invisible*, ed. Claude Lefort and tr. Alphonso Lingis (Evanston, Ill.: Northwestern University Press, 1968), p. 146. Other Christian theologians whose reflections upon the soul took the form of commentary upon Aristotle's *De Anima* include Albertus Magnus, Cajetan and Suarez. A number of French phenomenologists, after Merleau-Ponty, have also returned to Aristotle's text – Rémi Brague and Jean-Louis Chrétien among them.
[5]   See Martha C. Nussbaum and Amélie Oksenberg Rorty eds., *Essays on Aristotle's De Anima* (Oxford: Clarendon Press, 1992) and Christopher Shields, 'Some Recent Approaches to Aristotle's *De Anima*' in *Aristotle: De Anima*, tr. D.W. Hamlyn (Oxford University Press, 1993), pp. 257–81.
[6]   I refer throughout to Hamlyn's translation, which has become the standard, scholarly version in English of the Greek text.
[7]   *Commentary*, p. 8.

in a manner that recalls the citation from John Damascene: 'Being angry is a particular movement of the body of such and such a kind' (403a24, see also 408b5). For Aristotle 'the soul, therefore, will be the actuality of the body' (412a16) where actuality is related to potentiality as form to matter. The soul is the body's 'essential whatness'.

Secondly, the soul is the origin of movement: sensation, appetite and thought are each considered movements with respect to the soul (415b8).[8] The body is not, then, self-moving and autonomous. Rather, it participates in motions, engaging in them passively and actively.[9] The soul as the origin of motion is both unmoved and always in motion (408b29). It is 'unmoved' because it is stirred into moving by objects that it recognises as desirable.[10]

Thirdly, the soul is not the mind; cognitive operations take place within, and are governed by, the soul. So that throughout the treatise Aristotle refers to the soul's actuality consisting in its possession of knowledge. It is the 'enmattered' soul that knows; knows in a more profound because more inclusive way than the mind alone knows. The soul's knowledge is also the body's knowledge.

I wish to continue this line of thought because I want to suggest the body is always immersed in what, after Merleau-Ponty, I will call a field of intentions or, otherwise said, a politics that the mind frequently only recognises later, and that this is the fundamental level at which the body operates inter-subjectively. At this level the political engagement is ontological. But we move too quickly. I must first show how the enmattered knowledge of the soul is implicated in this field of intentions. We must define 'knowledge' here because evidently I am not talking about knowledge as a body of facts. In Britain, increasingly, education is being reduced to just this – the impart-ing of information, where information can be quantified as a commodity. That is simply head-knowledge, or what Aristotle will call 'the power to think … [that] alone is capable of existence in isolation from all other psychic powers' (413b24, modified translation). Head-knowledge is know-

---

[8]   Aristotle here is following Plato, who also viewed motion as properly belonging to the soul. See *Phaedrus*, 245c ff. See also *Laws* 897 where Plato recognises motion as not primarily about physical forces (as in Newton), but as emotional and intellectual. It is in and through such motions that there is participation in the Forms, and therefore in the Good as the highest Form.

[9]   My understanding of motion in Plato, Aristotle and Christian theology is indebted to Simon Oliver's immensely interesting study, *Philosophy, God and Motion* (London: Routledge, 2005).

[10]   'The "motion" of the soul is the *energeia* of "seeing" or "understanding" an object as significant so as *then* to initiate *kinesis*,' ibid., p. 47. See also D.J. Furley, 'Self-Movers' in Mary Louise Gill and J.G. Lennox eds., *Self-Motion from Aristotle to Newton* (Princeton University Press, 1994). As Oliver recognises, with Aristotle difference becomes the fulcrum for motion such that all bodies are caught up in matrices of interactive relations. As such, motion is ecstatic (see *Philosophy, God and Motion*, p. 49).

ledge as representation. It is not irrelevant to the condition I am pursuing, but it is not identical with it. The knowledge I am speaking of is more like the knowledge a sports person has with respect to the position of his or her body to a ball, a bat, another competitor. It is frequently said of Tim Henman, Britain's number one tennisplayer, that he is too intelligent and lets his mind rather than his instincts rule his playing. For professional experience has shown that a body that has been highly trained and disciplined in a certain sport knows of itself where it must be in order to win or perform to its very best. The knowledge I am speaking of, then, has much to do with performance, on the one hand, and relation, on the other. Knowledge occurs within a relational process called knowing. It is an active condition. Knowledge here is both an intuiting and a practising, a coming to know and a practical 'knowing how to' that issues from being trained in how to do it. Nobody simply knows how to cook; and to cook so that flavours and textures of foods distinctively offset each other takes practice. Knowledge is inseparable, then, from experience and socialisation; it is always a 'knowing how to'. So I might say I know Arthur Schnitzler wrote a collection of short stories published in 1925 and entitled *Die Frau des Richters*, but what I suggest is happening is that I am actually saying I know how to use the term short story, the numbers composing a date and recognise a name, Arthur Schnitzler, with respect to authoring this work. I know how to employ three forms of speaking in a grammatical unit. I am saying no more than Wittgenstein said here, but unlike Wittgenstein, I want to relate this knowing to the enmattered soul and the politics or field of intentions that are intrinsic to intersubjective living. Knowledge becomes a performance demonstrating that one knows how to. But it is also only relational. That is, *that* performance takes place within the context of other performances and in response to these other performances. Knowing, then, is implicated in economies or movements of response, exchange and declaration. It is continually caught up in communicating and in the communications of others. Even when asleep the ensouled body communicates – by how it lies, turns, moans, snores or is simply still. It communicates with respect to others, in answer to others, as a declaration to others. I am not some monadic centre of my knowing and my knowledge; I am immersed in a transcorporeal exchange of knowledges in which sensing is always simultaneously sensibility. That is what I mean by a field of intentions. I am caught up in an interactive knowing that issues from micro acts of interpretation that concern what the body is in contact with and that become necessary, inevitable, because I am placed within intricate webs of communication. In a final and elliptical essay on the phenomenology of the body, Maurice Merleau-Ponty writes of how 'my own body's "invisibility" can invest the other bodies I see. Hence my body can assume segments derived from the body of another, just as my substance passes into them.'[11] In this transcorporeality the ensouled body is already politicised; for its knowing is politicised — that is, its knowing only issues from that ensouled body being an active participant in a larger social grouping. Its knowing is always political because it is always relational.[12] We could relate the body's knowledge to a gnomic saying by Nietzsche: 'The body is a big reason, a plurality with one sense, a war and a peace, a herd and shepherd. A tool for your body is your small reason, my brother, which you call "spirit", a small tool and toy for your big reason.'[13]

So much, then, for the manner in which the enmattered soul exists politically. But what about eros? How does the appetitive relate to this ontologised, and politicised, epistemology? Let us not speak, as Kant did, of a faculty of desire as if desire was a divisible unit of the soul. The soul is indivisible, as Aristotle demonstrated. On the other hand, in the past I have referred to eros as the animator of intention. On this model, eros would be an animator of movement within the soul, along with thought and sensation. But this now strikes me as a highly mechanistic understanding of desire. It figures desire as a source, a centre from which movement issues. And so we might conceive the soul as constituted by three sources of animation: desire, sensation and thought. This would then lead to three kinds of motion within the soul. But the indivisibility of the soul would suggest this was not the case. It would suggest that desire cannot be divorced from sensation and thought; that desire is actualised only with respect to sensation and thought. Aristotle observes that where there is 'sense-perception, then also [there is] imagination and desire [orexis]. For where there is sense-perception, there is also both pain and pleasure, and where these are, there is of necessity also wanting [epithumia]' (413b16). Orexis is a general. word for longing in which there are three forms of desire: passion (thumia), wishing (boulesis) and wanting (epithumia).[14] Aristotle views only 'wishing' to be associated with the rational part of the soul; passion and wanting are subrational but nevertheless associated with thinking because of the role played by the imagination (433b5). We will develop this line of thinking later. For now what is central is that desire is not a source; it is a condition. If the condition of the soul is both the origin of motion and always in motion, this motion is related to the soul's desiring.

[11] 'Eye and Mind', tr. Carleton Dallery in *The Primacy of Perception*, ed. James M. Eddie (Chicago: Northwestern University Press, 1964), p. 168.

[12] Obviously such relational knowing is also implicated in ethics because of its continual involvement with others.

[13] *Sämtliche Werke, Kritische Studienausgabe*, vol. 4, Giorgio Colli and Mazzino Montinari eds. (Munich: Deutscher Taschenbuch Verlag, 1988), p. 39.

[14] See Hamlyn's translation, p. 92.

What is desired is actuality, the complete realisation of the form of what the body senses. All things move for Aristotle, towards their true *topos* or condition in the world (*Physics* VIII.4). *Kinesis* is then related to desire (III.10.a17–20). Aristotle does not employ the term *eros*[15] (although Plato uses *epithumia* to denote sexual desire), but as the notion of desiring was associated with the Christian command to love from at least the time of Origen,[16] so we find, in Christian theology, much support for the idea of the soul as the seat of transformative and ecstatic love. It is evident in the work of Gregory of Nyssa, Augustine, Pseudo-Dionysius, Bernard of Clairvaux and many of those medieval commentators on *Canticum Canticorum*.[17] The soul is

---

[15]   It is well known that in the *Nicomachean Ethics* Aristotle speaks of friendship or *philia* (Books 8 and 9). He outlines three different *teloi* for philial love – pleasure, usefulness and virtue – which give rise to three modes of behaviour. One might think that these forms of friendship might be connected with the different modes of desiring and *kinesis*: *thumia* and *epithumia* with pleasure (*hedonia*) and usefulness, which are inferior forms of *philia* and the more rational *boulesis* with the virtuous form of *philia*. But, in fact, the main verb throughout for desiring is *boulomai*. Sometimes he uses the middle voice of *ephiemi* or the more acquisitive form of desiring in *orego*, but references to *epithumia* are rare (Book 9.v.3). Earlier he quite explicitly informs us that pleasure (*eudaemonia*) is not itself a motion (1.7). It is an *aspect* of *energeia*, a realisation, an end in itself. Pleasure is not, then, a dynamic aspect of desire – as it is for Plato in the *Symposium*. But Aristotle does not examine this association, and, unlike Plato, he nowhere investigates the difference between *philia* and either *eros* or *agape*. In fact, in Books 8 and 9, although *phileo* is dominant he uses both *agapao* and *erao* as synonyms (8.i.6; 8.iii.1; 9.xii.1), and under *philia* includes *erotikos* and *erastos* (8.iii.5; 8.iv.1; 9.i.2; 9.v.3).

[16]   See Origen's *Commentary on the Song of Songs*, 63–71, for an argument in favour of the use of *eros* by Christian theologians to discuss both God's own loving and the Christian's love of God (made possible on the basis of God as the origin of all possible loving). Origen refuses here to view *eros* as simply an acquisitive and appetitive desire. As in Plato's *Lysis* and *Phaedrus* (though not in the *Symposium*), *eros* is recognised as ecstatic, demanding the forgetting of self and excessive to utilitarian ends. In his own *Commentary on the Songs of Songs*, Gregory of Nyssa goes even further, speaking of *eros* as the intensification or realisation of *agape*: 'The bride is wounded by a spiritual fiery shaft of desire (*eros*). For *agape* which is aroused is called *eros*' (Werner Jaeger and Hermann Langerbeck eds., *Gregorii Nysseni in Canticum Canticorum*, Leiden: Brill, 1960, p. 383). A detailed study of *eros* in the Platonic and the early Christian traditions can be found in J.M. Rist, *Eros and Psyche: Studies in Plato, Plotinus and Origen* (University of Toronto Press, 1964) and Catherine Osbourne, *Eros Unveiled: Plato and the God of Love* (Oxford: Clarendon Press, 1994). Both of these authors are critical of the influential study *Agape and Eros* by Anders Nygren, tr. Philip S. Watson (London: SPCK, 1953). See also James Barr, 'Words for Love in Biblical Greek' in L.D. Hurst and N.T. Wright eds., *The Glory of Christ in the New Testament* (Oxford University Press, 1987), pp. 3–18, for a series of insightful observations on *agape*, *eros* and *philia*. Barr concludes significantly: 'though *eros* is used in disapproved erotic contexts, this in no sense sets it apart from *philia* and *agapesis*, which are typically used also in theologically positive relations' (p. 10).

[17]   For an overall examination of commentaries on the *Canticum Canticorum*, see Denys Turner, *Eros and Allegory: Medieval Exegesis of the Song of Songs* (Kalamazoo, Mich.: Cistercian, 1995). For an excellent reappraisal of 'desire' in Gregory of Nyssa, see Martin Laird, 'Under Solomon's Tutelage: The Education of Desire in *Homilies on the Song of Songs*', in *Modern Theology* 18 (4), October (2002), pp. 507–26. On page 521 he points out how important it is 'to be aware of a certain lack of consistency in Gregory's vocabulary of desire'. For a concise account of 'desire' in Bernard, see Pierre Dumontier, *Saint Bernard et la Bible* (Paris: Desclée de Brouwer, 1953), pp. 39–43.

not the source of desire; to desire is written into the nature of what it is to be ensouled, to participate in the world as one who senses, thinks and creatively responds to what is continually being given. To desire is to be educated, not erased, in Christian praxis; one cannot desire without a body, as one cannot think without a body.[18]

Let me relate this understanding of desire back to my earlier sketch of what it is to know, and suggest the body's knowledge is intimately associated with the movements of desire. It is because of this that I would reject any idea that psychoanalysis murdered the older conception of the soul; psycho-analysis, when it concerns itself with the dream-life and the imaginary as they cooperate with the somatic, offers us tools for what St Paul would call the discernment of the spirits – those movements of affection within the soul. Psychoanalysis becomes a hermeneutical art. But if the body's know-ledge is constituted in and through its negotiations with other bodies *and* is intimately associated with desire, then the economies of response that I out-lined above, those fields of intention, are caught up in complex movements of desiring. Desire then both is politically informed and politically informs. Desire is produced and desire is a work that produces. There is a canny scene in *Star Trek: The Next Generation* where the android Data is captured by the Borg. The queen of the Borg reads a strong determination of Data's desire to experience life as a real (conceived as emotional) human being. She stages this desire for him by electronically mapping onto Data's arm a piece of human skin. The camera closes in for a shot of the taut piece of skin, white (this is Hollywood), pimpled, covered in tiny golden hairs. The queen of the Borg blows softly across these hairs. 'Do you feel that, Data?' she asks, in a voice as warm and deep as seduction itself. 'Was that good for you, Data?' she asks, quickly associating sensation with erotic appetite, her blowing lightly on the hairs of the flesh with having sex. Desire, sensation and thought are inseparably associated here in operations that move across the subjectivies of two bodies. Data's desire to be an affective human is reproduced for him as a desire for sexual satisfaction. This, of course, is another of Hollywood's ideologies. But the point I am wishing to make is only that the body's knowledge is informed by desire while desire is also informed by the way that the body sensuously encounters and negotiates the thoughts and knowledges of other bodies. Desire, that fosters determi-nations for how the body will act, will itself be disciplined by that body's

---

[18] Challenging some earlier readings of the call to *apatheia*, Morwenna Ludlow observes with respect to Gregory of Nyssa that '*Apatheia* is … not the absence of desire but freedom from any *materialistic* impulse or passion'; *Universal Salvation: Eschatology in the Thought of Gregory of Nyssa and Karl Rahner* (Oxford University Press, 2000), p. 58. But the education of materialistic impulses does not deny but intensifies appreciations of embodiment.

engagement in the world. As such, politics is always an impassioned affair; and the movements of desire, sensation and thought within the soul mean the politics of the body's knowledge is continually under revision. Of course this observation would also have come as no surprise to Plato – whose *Republic* is founded upon the city as structured according to the human soul; nor Aristotle, who in *Nicomachean Ethics* conceived politics to be inseparable from *phileo*; nor Perikles, who urged that citizens 'should fall in love with' the city, employing – in his Funeral Oration – the erotic term for lovers, *erastai*;[19] nor Augustine, who represented the city of God as a specific social form organised according to a orientation of desire towards God. A certain analogy governs the relationship between the enfleshed *psyche* and the gathering and negotiation of knowledges in the *polis*. What I am suggesting here is that entwined physical, rational and spiritual growth and nourishment of the 'enmattered soul' is determined by the body's negotiations with other bodies.

On the Eros of the Ecclesial Body

Allow me to step back at this point, because in order to develop this argument in terms of Christology and ecclesiology, I need first to define the formation of a Christian 'enmattered soul', since discipleship implies a formation, a following, a disciplining such that the knowledge attained is a knowledge of Christ. In other words, if the 'enmattered soul' is determined by the body's negotiations with other bodies, then what is distinctive about this determination when those negotiations concern the body of Christ in the threefold sense in which the medievals understood that 'body': as the historical person of Jesus of Nazareth, as the eucharistic elements and as the Church?[20] This is where we must return to those Greek and Latin Fathers who reflected upon the relationship between the physical and the spiritual senses and developed, thereby, a theological phenomenology of embodiment. Let us take a passage from Augustine's *Confessions* as illustrative:

> But what do I love, O God, when I love thee? Not the beauty of a body nor the rhythm of moving time. Nor the splendour of the light, which is so dear

[19] Thucydides, *History of the Peloponnesian War*, tr. Rex Warner (London: Penguin, 1954), p. 149. See also Richard Sennett for an extended analysis of the relationship between the Greek *polis*, desire and nakedness in *Flesh and Stone: The Body and the City in Western Civilization* (New York: Norton Paperback, 1996), pp. 31–67.

[20] See Henri de Lubac, *Corpus Mysticum*: deuxième edition (Paris: Aubier, 1949), particularly 'Le "Corpus triforme" d'Amalaire et ses destinées', pp. 297–342.

to the eyes. Nor the sweet melodies in the world of sounds of all kinds. Nor the fragrance of flowers, balms and spices. Nor manna and not honey; not the bodily members which are so treasured by carnal embrace. None of this do I love when I love my God. And yet I do love a light and a sound and a fragrance and a delicacy and an embrace, when I love my God, who is light and sound and fragrance and delicacy and embrace to my interior man. There my soul receives a radiance that no space can grasp; there something resounds which no time can take away; there something gives a fragrance which no wind can dissipate; there something is savoured which no satiety can make bitter; there something is embraced which can occasion no ennui. This is what I love when I love my God.[21]

Arguments have been conducted about the nature of the relation between physical and spiritual sensing. Balthasar, commenting upon Rahner's account of the five spiritual senses in Origen, denies there is an utter distinction between the body and the soul such that 'both sensibilities [physical and spiritual] are thus, ontically as well as noetically, but different states [*katastaseis*] of the one and only sensibility'.[22] Sin creates a distinction; salvation is a training whereby the physical is transformed into the spiritual. Commenting subsequently upon Rahner's account of the spiritual senses in Bonaventure, Balthasar denies for Bonaventure that there is an ontic and noetic correspondence between the two sensibilities. Spiritual perception is brought about by grace such that 'the "spiritual senses" do not constitute a second higher faculty alongside the corporeal senses [as they do in Origen]'.[23] In effect, Balthasar reverses the judgements of Rahner with respect to the two most important figures in the development of the notion of spiritual sensing. But on the account of the soul that I have outlined above, whether these two Church Fathers have been correctly interpreted or not, the corporeal senses affect movements of the soul; the world is not simply external, it is profoundly internalised. Any operations of grace work with this enmattered and embedded soul. This is how I would interpret the passage from Augustine, for what is evident here is the confluence between body and soul, the external world and interiority, and the two modes of

---

[21] *Confessions*, X.6.

[22] Hans Urs von Balthasar, *Glory of the Lord: A Theological Aesthetics*. Volume I: *Seeing the Form*, tr. Erasmo Leiva-Merikakis (Edinburgh: T. & T. Clark, 1982), p. 369. He is discussing Karl Rahner, 'Le debut d'une doctrine des cinq sens spirituals chez Origene' in *RAM*, 13 (1932), pp. 113–45.

[23] Ibid., p. 372. He is discussing Rahner's second article, 'La doctrine des "sens spirituel" au moyen-age, en particulier chez S. Bonaventure' in *RAM*, 14 (1933), pp. 263–99. For a detailed discussion of the spiritual senses within the Orthodox tradition and theologians between Origen and Bonaventure, see B. Fraigneau-Julien, *Les Sens spirituels et la vision de Dieu selon Symeon le Nouveau Theologien* (Paris: Beauchesne, 1985).

reception – from the world of the senses and from God. The structure of the writing performs a chiasmus rather than a dialectic. In a dialectic one set of statements is confounded by a second. Here one set of negative statements – 'not the' 'nor the', 'none' – passes over into a set of affirmative statements – 'there something is'. From apophasis we move to cataphasis; rather than (as in Pseudo-Dionysius) the opposite. Nor is what the body experiences negated – there is 'beauty' in a body, there is 'splendour' in light, there is 'sweetness' in melody and there is a 'treasure' in carnal embrace. These experiences are themselves good, only they just cannot accurately describe the nature of loving God, who Augustine has learnt over long years to understand is a spiritual not a material being. These experiences of the senses whereby the world is received by the body are translated as the soul receives them from God.

If the body's knowledge is erotic (as in affective), then such knowledge is not only relational, it is tactile. Aristotle observes: 'those living things that have touch also have desire' (414b6). The ensouled flesh comes to an understanding of itself through touch, through contact.[24] Aristotle insists 'with the faculty of touch none of the other senses exists' (414b33) and 'in respect of touch [human beings are] accurate above all others. For this reason [we are] also the most intelligent of animals' (421a16). Aquinas's commentary here is important because of the manner in which the faculties of the senses are often hierarchised.

> Yet it might seem that mental capacity corresponded rather to excellence of sight than of touch, for sight is the more spiritual sense, and reveals better the differences between things.[25] Still, there are two reasons for maintaining that excellence of mind is proportionate to fineness of touch. In the first place touch is the basis of sensitivity as a whole; for obviously the organ of touch pervades the whole body, so that the organ of each of the other senses is also an organ of touch, and the sense of touch by itself constitutes a being as sensitive. Therefore, the finer one's sense of touch, the better, strictly speaking, is one's sensitive nature as a whole, and consequently the higher one's intellectual capacity. For a fine sensitivity is a disposition to a fine intelligence.[26]

---

[24] For a comprehensive survey of touch in Aristotle see Cynthia Freeland, 'Aristotle on the Sense of Touch' in Nussbaum and Rorty eds., *Essays on Aristotle's De Anima*, pp. 227–48.

[25] The priority of 'sight' as the most spiritual sense has a long history in Greek and Christian thought that concerns the nature of light. Sight is related to fire, whereas touch is related to the earth. Light is related to divine illumination and so, for Augustine, it is light that enables the soul to understand at all. It is the key to the intellectual grasp of what is given in the senses. (See *De Genesi ad litteram*, III.5–6.)

[26] *Commentary*, pp. 152–3.

The second reason for the importance of touch is that 'fine touch is an effect of a good bodily constitution or temperament' such that 'those whose touch is delicate are so much the nobler and the more intelligent'.[27] This is a very important comment because it ontologises touch. Touch operates at the juncture between the corporeal and the spiritual. It is more fundamental than sight, which is associated with the epistemological. In fact, we might infer from this that touch is our finest sensibility for apprehending the divine. It is the most immediate of our perceptions since 'touch alone seems to perceive through itself' (435a11). By this I do not imply that God can be directly touched or even directly apprehended. God is not corporeal. I merely suggest the possibility that our profoundest because most immediate understandings of what it is to be incarnate are intuited through touch: where, first, divine spiritual presence (and our participation in it) becomes inseparable from physical existence; and where, second, we are most affected (transformed) by such an intuition. Through touch there is contact, and through contact there is nourishment (or, if the contact is abusive, malnourishment) and nurturing (or violation). Either way, through touch there is movement within the soul such that the whole person is caught up in the circulations of desire – the desire of the other as well as that person's desire for the other.[28] Aquinas calls this 'the mover moved'.[29] The 'intuition' involved is not blind (in the Kantian sense of intuitions without concepts being blind). For since there are forms of desire in both the rational and irrational parts of the soul, according to Aristotle and Aquinas, and 'movement always ... involves imagination and desire' (432b13), then imagination and desire, touch and movement are related. 'Aristotle includes imagination under intellect', Aquinas observes.[30] In fact, intellect and desire are the two forces of movement within the soul and, evidently, not entirely distinguishable because contin-

27 Ibid., p. 153. For the theological importance of touch for Aquinas see John Milbank and Catherine Pickstock, 'Truth and Touch' in *Truth in Aquinas* (London: Routledge, 2001), pp. 60–87; for the theological implications of touch see John Milbank, 'The Soul of Reciprocity Part Two: Reciprocity Granted' in *Modern Theology* 17 (4), October (2001), pp. 485–507. See also Jean-Louis Chrétien, 'Body and Touch', in his *The Call and the Response*, tr. Anne A. Davenport (New York: Fordham University Press, 2004), pp. 83–131.

28 See *De Anima* 433a9–443b21 on the faculty of desire as it relates to motion. Aquinas, in what constitutes a refutation of Lacan (and Žižek), claims: 'It is absurd to say that desire is for the sake of desiring; desire is essentially a tendency to "the other"' (*Commentary*, p. 244).

29 Ibid., pp. 246–7: 'The mover moved is the desire itself; for whatever desires is moved inasmuch as it desires, desire itself being a certain act or movement in the sense that we give the term "movement" when we apply it to activities that are consequent upon actuality (*prout motus est actus perfecti*), such as sensing and understanding.' Later Aquinas outlines how this movement of desire is 'circular'.

30 Ibid.

ually crossed by the operations of the imagination.[31] Contemplation requires images (432a3); so contemplation concerns movement, desire and an intuition that is imagined, imaged. 'The soul never thinks without an image' (431a8); and such thinking is inseparable from being affected physically, even if the intellect can distinguish itself from the flesh (and judge it) (429a29). If such intuition, contemplation, imagination, movement and desire require contact, depend upon touch, then the ensouled flesh is not monadic. It only realises itself in community; in political and erotic communities or *ekklesia*.

I want to suggest that such a construal of the enmattered soul and its desiring can be developed Christologically and ecclesiologically through an examination of the following passage from John's Gospel:

> I am the living bread which comes down from heaven; if anyone eats of this bread he will live for ever; and the bread which I shall give for the life of the world is my flesh [*sarx*]. The Jews then disputed among themselves, saying, 'How can this man give us his flesh to eat [*phagein*]?' So Jesus said to them, 'Truly, truly, I say to you, unless you eat [*phagete*] the flesh of the Son of man and drink his blood, you have no life in you; he who eats [*trogon*] my flesh and drinks my blood has eternal life, and I will raise him up at the last day. For my flesh is food [*brosis*] indeed [*alethes estin*] and my blood is drink indeed [*alethes estin*]. He who eats [*trogon*] of my flesh and drinks of my blood abides [*menei*] in me, and I in him. As the living Father sent me, and I live because [*dia*] of the Father, so he who eats [*trogon*] me will live because [*di'*] of me. This is the bread which came down from heaven, not such as the fathers ate [*ephagon*] and died; he who eats [*trogon*] of this bread will live for ever.' (John 6.51–9)[32]

---

[31]   Aquinas: '[I]ntellect only moves anything by virtue of appetition' (*Commentary*, p. 245); 'the final motive-force derives from the soul itself acting through the appetitve power' (ibid., p. 246).

[32]   This passage is the final section of what has been termed the 'Bread of Heaven' discourses. Commentary on it is manifold. Every aspect of its form, its linguistic structure, its editing has been argued over. That presents difficulties for any theologian wishing to use it – to read it – in a specific way. The literary approach to interpretation that I employ challenges redaction criticism. I am assuming then that this passage is not a later edition (Bultmann, *The Gospel of John: A Commentary*, tr. G.R. Beasley-Murray, Oxford: Blackwell, 1971). I accept P. Borgen's argument for the unity of the discourse (*Bread of Heaven*, Supplements to *Novum Testamentum*, 10, Leiden: Brill, 1965), though not necessarily because of the 'homiletic pattern' he discerns there. A number of scholars have questioned Borgen's suggestions (see Uno Schnelle, *Antidocetic Christology in the Gospel of John*, tr. Linda M. Maloney (Minneapolis, Minn.: Fortress Press, 1992), pp. 196–7 for a summary of these responses). If any redaction has taken place then there is no need to posit Bultmann's ecclesiastic figure. The unity of the chapter is the work of the Evangelist. We are concerned here with another aspect of the miracle of the feeding of the five thousand (6.1–14) and the 'bread of life' discourse (6.35ff), where the strictly Christological presentation develops into that which is inseparable from it: ecclesiological considerations. I accept also what most of the commentators agree upon: that this exposition relates directly to the eucharist and stands in place of an institution narrative at the Last Supper (that John does not provide).

As the disciples are more than aware, 'This is a hard saying; who can listen to it?' But it is significant that they are already employing the word 'listen' in a complex overdetermined manner; a manner more in line with sensations as a movement of the soul. For to listen is not only to understand intellectually; as a mode of being in contact with, a mode of touch, it is to receive, accept, accommodate. The 'saying' here emphatically concerns two things: eating and flesh/blood. What makes this a *hard* saying is the way it evades being read either metaphorically or symbolically. Whether what we have here is the eucharistic language of the Johannine community or an anti-docetic polemic – or both – the sheer physicality of the language is striking. The eucharistic 'body' (*soma*) and 'blood' is now 'flesh' (*sarx*) and 'blood'.[33] Commentators disagree strongly about the impact of this physicality. Bultmann believes the 'suggestion that people are horrified by Jesus's exhortation to anthropophagy ... can hardly be found in the text'.[34] He believes the people are scandalised by the 'absurdity of Jesus's words' given that Jesus is still alive.[35] But Brown points to the later charges of cannibalism brought against Christians and observes 'the Fourth Gospel makes no concession to Jewish sensibilities and insists stubbornly on the reality of the flesh and the blood'.[36] The blood *is* blood, true blood (*to aima ... alethes*);[37] the flesh *is* food, true food (*brosis alethes*). And the consumption moves from a general prescription (*phageo*) to the specific act of chewing or gnawing (*trogo*).[38] *Trogein* is only found here and in 13.18 (another eucharistic allusion); elsewhere in the

---

[33]   I am aware that Bultmann (*Commentary*, p. 235), Brown (*The Gospel According to St John*), p. 285 and Borgen (*Bread of Heaven*, pp. 86–98) all agree the change here reflects a Syrian/Semitic usage, since there is no word in Hebrew or Aramaic for 'body' as we understand the term. There have been suggestions that John's Gospel was translated into Greek from an Aramaic original. Nevertheless all three agree that the physicality of the language is striking.

[34]   Bultmann, *Commentary*, p. 235.

[35]   Ibid., p. 237.

[36]   Brown, *The Gospel According to St John*, p. 292.

[37]   Commentators differ on their interpretations of John's use of *alethes* rather than *alethinos*. The later word has a Platonic resonance – the heavenly reality as distinct from its natural one – whereas the former means much more 'genuine'. Hence Brown views 'Jesus [a]s insisting on the genuine value of his flesh and blood as food and drink' (*The Gospel According to St John*, p. 283). Barrett, *The Gospel According to St John*, seems to see both words as interchangeable and so here it is both genuinely blood and food and also fulfils a heavenly archetype (p. 299).

[38]   Bultmann: 'the offence is heightened in v. 54 by the substitution of the stronger *trogein* for *phagein*. It is a matter of real eating and not simply of some sort of spiritual participation' (p. 236). Brown agrees and see the change as part of John's attempt to 'emphasize the realism' (p. 283). Barrett disagrees with both of them and views the two words as synonyms (see p. 283). For a longer examination of the issue, which still has not convinced all the scholars, see Ceslas Spicq, '*Trogein*. Est-il synonyme de *phagein* et d'*esthien* dans le Nouveau Testament?', *New Testament Studies*, 26 (1979–80), pp. 414–19.

Gospel John uses either *phagein* or *esthien*. If anything is metaphorical or symbolic in this passage it is the bread.[39] As 'living bread' related to God's own self as 'I am [who I am]' it transcends its most common reference in a way that runs contrary to the insistence upon the common reference of 'flesh'. I suggest that it is not so much that cannibalism is suggested here, but something even more unthinkable for the Jew: the flesh and blood of a human sacrifice. Several commentators note the deepening of the scandal when the drinking of blood is referred to – contrary to God's law (Leviticus 3.17 and Deuteronomy 12.23). It is not a lamb, a goat or a bull ritually slaughtered in the Temple precincts, but one made in the image and likeness of God – *ha-adam*, a man. Their response is visceral as they recoil in horror at a theological giving and an exchange beyond anything they could imagine. 'How can this man give us his flesh to eat?' they demand. In fact, after this saying many of his disciples drew back and no longer went about with Jesus (John 6.66).

If we interpret the 'How' of the Jewish question – 'How can this man give us his flesh to eat' – not as a technical question ('in what way') but a hermeneutical question ('in what manner do we understand the offer of his flesh to eat'), we can further appreciate how the materiality of what Jesus is saying offends cultic rationality. What is suggested by this corporeal feeding is not simply absorption, and this is significant. There is an 'abiding' *in* Christ, but there is also an abiding *of* Christ (in the one who eats).[40] This co-abiding is complex and richly suggestive. It is, I suggest, the chiasmic heart of an *ekklesia* performed and constituted through the eucharist. Why chiasmic? Because observe the curious manner of the reciprocal relation. I eat the flesh of Christ. I take his body into my own. Yet in this act I place myself *in* Christ – rather than simply placing Christ within me. I consume but I do not absorb Christ without being absorbed into Christ. Only in this complex co-abiding is there life, nourishment, nurture: because or through or by means of (an instrumental use of *dia*) this feeding there is both participation of human life in God's life and participation of God's life in human life. Something comes into its own in this relationality. Something of what it is to be fully human comes about by an identification with that which is divine; so there is something of what it is to be God that comes about by an

---

[39] Ernst Haenchen, *John*, vol. 1, tr. Robert W. Funk (Philadelphia, Penn.: Fortress Press, 1984): 'The subject of Jesus's discourse is no longer bread but flesh' (p. 294).

[40] Barrett notes 'abiding' (*menein*) is an important word for John. It has Trinitarian reference for it frequently refers to the nature of the relationship between the Father, the Son and the Spirit. The Father abides in the Son (14.10), the Spirit abides with Jesus (1.32), now those who believe abide in Christ.

identification with what is human. Let me develop this further, for it will deeply inform and challenge our understanding of Christ and the Trinitarian God. It would suggest the incarnation is not fully realised by God becoming human (in Jesus of Nazareth). The incarnation is only fully realised by the God-made-man absorbing into himself all human beings, through the offering of his flesh and blood. The incarnation is only fully realised by the participation of God in human life and the participation of human life in God. Käsemann observes: 'Incarnation rather means, as the prologue unmistakeably indicates, the encounter of the Creator with his creation.'[41] Redemption is the fulfilment of the economy of the incarnation, and incorporation into Christ in and through partaking of the eucharist is fundamental to that economy. Two Christological points proceed from this before we start to consider the implications here for ecclesiology. First, Jesus is the Christ only in relation to other human beings; the act of redemption is a relational act; Christology needs to pay more attention not to the identity of the God-man, but to the redemptive operation effected in and through this complex co-abiding. Secondly, though I would insist on a profound difference between the human and the divine, there must exist within the nature and self-understanding of the Trinity, a quality that has affinity with what it is to be human. To create human beings there must abide in God an image and likeness of what it is to be human that Christ incarnates.

Now we can proceed to ecclesiology. A Christology conceived in terms of a redemptive operation emphasises movement. 'I live because [dia] of the Father, so he who eats [trogon] me will live because [di'] of me.' Dia is a word implying the flowing out from a source; transits, movements effected not only within, but also by means of the ensouled body. Let us consider further two characteristics of this spiritual embodiment. Firstly, I embody Christ's body and this body embodies mine. In other words the bodies here are emphatically carnal and carnally relating, but their co-location is unthinkable. We continually return to that chiasmus 'I in you and you in me'. The coming together of the two bodies does not create a third body whose location can be determined. It is exactly the opposite: the coming together of the two bodies effects a reciprocal dislocation of both bodies: I am not in you but you are now in me. There is an 'abiding' (menei) but it takes place in this complex space whose boundaries are folded back upon themselves. One

---

[41] *The Testament of Jesus*, tr. Gerhard Krodel (London: SCM Press, 1968), p. 34. Haenchen, *John*, vol. 1, argues against this view in which Christology becomes inseparable from a developed sacramental theology (pp. 298–300), but evidently my interpretation would develop Käsemann's suggestion.

body relates to the other, but each are relocated with respect to a co-abiding. In this realm, rather than space, the mutual indwelling which characterises what St Paul calls *koinonia* announces the presence of an *ekklesia* always living beyond itself, because always interpenetrated by that which refigures its boundaries. As such, the *ekklesia* is much less the institution and much more the history of a body that continually over-reaches itself, what Nyssa might term the body's *skopos* – a notion that might be rethought in terms of its tradition. It is the history of its co-relation, its indwelling and being indwelt; an erotic history, as I shall outline. In fact, it is the eros that can never fully possess the object of its desire that renders the co-relation dynamic. We saw this above: the circulations of desire in which Christ as other is not consumed but is nevertheless continually in touch and therefore continually causing the movements within the soul. As such the Church has a history, a tradition, a temporality. It is not that location is eclipsed. A location remains, the body or collected bodies of believers, that is/are material and particular. Such bodies constitute and contest social and political meaning, institutional and behavioural norms, with respect to their dwelling in Christ and Christ in them. But the co-abiding is not reducible to the particular and material location or the social and political meanings embedded in them. The *ekklesia* is a location of liminality; a co-relation that lives always on the edge of both itself and what is other. We might see this liminality in action through a peripatetic teacher like St Paul, moving from one ecclesial community to another, from one *koinonia* to another, not simply relating these nodal points but involving them with issues beyond their own frontiers, persuading them to participate in community life in other terrestrial centres. This is the effect, for example, of his plea for money for famine relief. So the Churches of Macedonia are related to Corinth and both to Jerusalem, and greetings are exchanged and hospitality offered.[42]

We can see how, in my first observation, I moved from the relation of the individual believer to Christ to the relation of the individual believer to another believer in and through Christ. This points to my second ecclesial observation. In the complex location of the chiasmus (I in you and you in me), relation itself is changed. The Hegelian and Sartrean relations of towards (or in) oneself and for oneself have no place here. Neither do the relations of subject to object, object to subject. A new relation is born, and through (*dia*) this Christic co-indwelling all relations are transformed with respect to what is other. To borrow from Rowan Williams, the *ekklesia* is

---

[42]   See here Rowan Williams's essay 'Does It Makes Sense to Speak of a Pre-Nicene Orthodoxy?' and the role played in the early Church by the epistolary form in *On Christian Doctrine* (Oxford: Blackwell, 2001), pp. 11–15.

then not 'a "special" system of human relations, but a place where the rationale of all relations is made plain and their deepening and securing made
possible'.[43] I would use the word 'character' rather than rationale. The *ekklesia* is constituted in and through these transformed relations and so renders
carnal the character of relation as such.

The third ecclesial observation follows from this. There is no incorporation here. As I pointed out earlier, I am not absorbed into Christ. I participate. In fact I only have life through this participation, but it remains *my* life. I
do not disappear within this relational exchange. I come most truly to
myself, but not as a monadic nor Cartesian self. Here is an account of human
belonging where the 'I' is continually aware of the other in whom it abides
and who abides in it. This is not the ruptured or the fissured 'I' so beloved of
Emmanuel Lévinas, Paul Ricœur and various neo-Freudians like Julia Kristeva, concerned with the ego in the accusative, oneself as another or the
stranger within. For this other does not violently displace me – rendering me
a hostage and forever accused. My language of dislocation must be understood topographically, not physiologically or psychologically. The language
of this co-abiding is a language of co-existence, mutual indwelling; an
abiding that is profoundly integral to my living at all. Of course what is refigured here in this complex indwelling that extends each body beyond itself,
is the nature of mission and the whole economy of Trinitarian life as both
processio and *missio*. What is also refigured here is the nature of being in exile;
of the Church always in exile, always a disapora, always in some sense not at
home with itself like the migrant who is the 'resident alien'.[44]

Now, how do these observations relate back to desire? First, with respect
to eros: this carnal indwelling and the operations it effects as movements of
the soul *are* intercourse. For this reason *koinonia* understood in terms of participation is frequently conceived in terms of betrothal. In fact, more than
one New Testament scholar has drawn attention to the way St Paul parallels
the cup of blessing of the covenant participation with the wedding contract
(1 Cor. 10.14–22 with 2 Cor. 11.1–2). It is not simply that the only models
we have for conceiving of such a mutuality concern sexual congress, and so
the language of sexual intimacy is employed in an exposition of such texts.
I do not believe for example that the Church Fathers and mystics who use
the language of sexual intercourse to describe their relation to Christ are
using such language metaphorically, as a symbolic resource. To return to

---

[43] 'Incarnation and the Renewal of Community', ibid., p. 226.
[44] There are certain aspects of this relation that might sound Lévinasian; see my essay 'Hospitality
and Justice: A Theological Reflection' (www. katholische-akademie-berlin.de/Veranstaltungen/
2003112729/ward_pdf.pdf) for a more detailed account of why this is not so.

what happens to 'bread' in the passage from John – if anything is symbolic it is the bread not the flesh. In the same way I suggest sexual union becomes a metaphorical act of the relation to Christ. Or rather, the erotic relation to Christ is the completion or perfection of what is most desired in sexual intimacy; sexual intimacy being an intimation of the divine relation that operates between God and human beings. Relation in Christ is 'true relation' in the same way as Christ's body offers 'true food' and 'true blood'. Both the erotic relation and the divine relation are carnal from the human and Christic perspective, for both of them are profoundly related to movements within the enmattered soul; and so both of them are, in their different ways, spiritual. The relation between them is analogical such that this mutual indwelling truly is (*alethes estin*) the erotic relation. And if we return to my second observation about the *ekklesia* embodying the character of all relations, then eros governs the very possibility of true relation.

But eros can also become the basis for a whole set of negative relations – exploitative relations, possessive relations, abusive relations. We return to my earlier account of the enmattered soul where desire and sensation (sensation which for Aristotle finds its organ *par excellence* in touch) are psychosomatic movements and the body is caught up in imaginings, intuitions and therefore knowledges that are inseparable from desire and the politics of relation. Eros renders the boundaries of our bodies porous and malleable. It renders both bodies and souls vulnerable because receptive. With passion there arrives an eros that classically cannot be entirely divorced from suffering and subjection; although this suffering and subjection is not simply passively borne but actively lived (as 'movements of the soul').[45] The suffering is integral to that living on the edge that characterises co-indwelling. The distorted erotic relations return us to those untransfigured relations – those ego-centred relations, those instrumental relations of subject and object, those possessive relations that seek to consume the other. I would argue that each of these distorted erotic relations is an attempt to avoid the suffering that passion demands, that a life centred on touch demands. For touch makes us, in the words of the German Protestant theologian, Friedrich Schleiermacher, 'absolutely dependent'. In terms of both Aristotle and Aquinas, those who avoid the demands of being absolutely dependent that touch fosters, reduce desire to simply the appetite for consumption. And this appetitive desire eclipses rational desire and a longing that relates to both hope and compassion. The true erotic relation, figured on the Christic description I in you and you in me, is not a masochistic relation. The suffering

---

[45]   For a development of this idea see chapter nine, 'Suffering and Incarnation', pp. 248–66.

passion demands is not desired as such. The masochistic relation is love-as-not-having.[46] That, like its counterpart the sadistic relation, is a distorted desire. Our desire, our bodies' knowledge, our relations have to be governed (and transfigured by being governed) by that I in you and you in me chiasmus. But we have no means of characterising and articulating that chiasmus outside of those intersubjective relations I sketched in the first part of my essay: those relations so profoundly caught up in webs of communication that are more primordial than 'the power of thinking' and the circulations of desire. A discernment is necessary; a discernment available only through time and the disciplined practices of piety. It is a discernment that cannot evade or transcend the politics of its own knowledge, the politics of its own hermeneutics, the politics of believing. But this too is living on the edge. In the erotic politics that constitutes the embodied *ekklesia*, a thin line separates truth claim from wish, revelation from projection, the eternity of conviction from the contingency of orgasm. To live in Christ and for Christ to live in us leaves each and all walking on water.

---

[46]   See Hélène Cixous's essay '"The Egg and the Chicken": Love as Not Having' in *Reading with Clarice Lispector*, tr. Verena Andermatt Conley (Hemel Hempstead: Harvester Wheatsheaf, 1990), pp. 98–122.

Part Two

ENGENDERING CHRIST

Chapter Four

REDEMPTION: BETWEEN RECEPTION AND RESPONSE

It is through my body that I understand other people, just as it is through my body that I perceive.[1]

In 1987, Don Cupitt published his book *The Long-Legged Fly*.[2] It was also the year in which Don became my tutor for a paper in the philosophy of religion. *The Long-Legged Fly* was my introduction to Don's theological thinking, and though we would differ on many issues concerning doing theology and possibly philosophy, aspects of that book remain profoundly embedded in my own thought. In particular that book made me realise two important aspects of the doctrine of the incarnation: first, incarnation is radically non-dualistic; secondly, incarnation concerns what Don calls in that book 'The Speaking Body'.[3]

> Through our senses our bodies as it were extend themselves to reach out into the environment. The objects of sense are *felt* as extensions of our bodies, and understood on the analogy of the body to such an extent that every other material object and every other organized system may also be spoken of as a body. The earth is a body, and there are heavenly bodies in the sky ... Like us, society is a body with members, and we also speak of a body of law (*corpus juris*) and of bodies of knowledge.[4]

---

[1] Maurice Merleau-Ponty, *Phenomenology of Perception*, tr. Colin Smith (London: Routledge & Kegan Paul), p. 216.

[2] This essay was written for Don Cupitt's *Festschrift*, *New Directions in Philosophical Theology: Essays in Honour of Don Cupitt*, ed. Gavin Hyman (Aldershot: Ashgate, 2004). In including it in this collection I wanted to retain its origins and testify to my friendship with Don Cupitt despite of and across our differences.

[3] *The Long-Legged Fly* (London: SCM Press, 1987), pp. 91–8.

[4] Ibid., p. 91.

This notion of the body surfaces in my own understanding of 'transcorpo-reality' and the analogical relationship between the physical, social, ecclesial, sacramental and Christic body that governed the thinking in *Cities of God*.[5] In the same way, observations such as 'the body has multiple perceptions and modes of awareness'[6] and 'The body speaks continually, and its forces and feelings are voiced in a manner that makes them cognitions of the world', from the same chapter, find their echoes throughout my current work on a phenomenology of engaging with Christ. So that while Don and I differ theologically there are shared lines of thought fundamental to both of us (and, among others, to Maurice Merleau-Ponty and Gilles Deleuze), and I would like to hope he would approve of any attempt to think through the association between hermeneutics and healing – reception, response and redemption.

★

In literature (particularly in the genres of autobiography, confession, the keeping of diaries and journals, letter-writing and the various forms of *Bildungsroman*), in interpreting the events of a life as a step towards a new integration, a new holism is keenly recognised. By giving structure to a series of occurrences, by choosing these events out of the plethora of all that happens to any one of us rather than those, an interpretation of one's life experience is crafted. Coming to understand is recognised as an important means of resolving questions about an incident or an action in which one has been involved. Writing in this sense, and interpretation is this sense, are therapeutic. Central to Kristeva's understanding of the processes of healing that operate in exchanges between analyst and analysand, her tales of love, is the bringing of what has been abjected and is aphasic into the realm of the symbolic, to negotiate the traumatised and suppressed semiotic drives in and through the symbolic.[7] So in psychoanalysis, as in literature, the association between interpretation and therapy has been recognised, even theorised. In both these examples, the literary and the psychoanalytical, it is to be noted that I am employing a wide construal of 'interpretation' or, rather, I am viewing all acts of coming to an understanding of life, of dreams and drives, as well as more formal acts of reading as interpreting texts. And it is this wider construal that relates hermeneutics to anthropology and various

---

[5]   London: Routledge, 2001.

[6]   *The Long-Legged Fly*, p. 92.

[7]   See *Tales of Love*, tr. Leon S. Roudiez (New York: Columbia University Press, 1987). For a more developed exposition of Kristeva's position see essay seven, '*Allegoria Amoris*'.

phenomenologies (of the social, Hannah Arendt)[8] or the flesh (Michel Henry)[9] – a relationship explored throughout Paul Ricœur's work – that enables me to recover the profound association between interpretation and therapy evident in various exegetical practices found in antiquity and the early Middle Ages. For example, in Plato, there is a disciplining of desire and perception that comes from interpreting the world within the cave according to the light of the sun beyond the cave. This disciplining or, to use the suggestive title of Martha Nussbaum's book,[10] the therapy of desire begins in the training received while in the cave itself – a training in the way things are to be perceived, that is, understood. This wider construal of 'interpretation' enables me to return hermeneutics to a pre-Reformation tradition, relating it to what Michel de Certeau called the practices of everyday life; to examine the relationship between interpretation and formation, and in that way point up what I mean by healing or therapy with respect to a certain teleology of the self. I want to do this not by explicitly examining here the exegetical practices of antiquity and the medieval period – for that will be done in chapter eight, 'Spiritual Exercises' – but by offering a phenomenological account of the economy of response. My account of the way interpretation governs the operation between reception and response will point up how the activity of interpreting is both ethical and therapeutic with respect to the fashioning of the self.

Let me begin by outlining two crucial differences, as I see them, between the post-Reformation tradition of hermeneutics and the economy of response. First, and primarily, I want to develop an account of response that is embodied, and therefore not just historically and culturally determined but both gendered and erotic. Theoretical accounts of interpretation have, under the influence of the architectonics of Kantian reasoning, centred on acts of consciousness, the operations of *Bewusstsein*, the formation of judgements. Consciousness is viewed as transparent and possessing a self-presence that is immediate. This consciousness is reducible to representations, such that the aim of hermeneutics was nothing less than developing a general method of understanding, that is, an account (provided by Kant in his *Critique of Pure Reason*) of the world as constituted by a disembodied but nevertheless unifying transcendental ego. Although Wilhelm Dilthey

---

[8] See *The Human Condition* (University of Chicago Press, 1958).

[9] See *Philosophie et phénoménologie du corps* (Paris: Presses Universitaires de France, 1965) and, more recently, *Incarnation: une philosophie de la chair* (Paris: Seuil, 2000). I discuss Henry's concept of flesh in essay five, 'Divinity and Sexual Difference'.

[10] *The Therapy of Desire: Theory and Practice in Hellenistic Ethics* (Princeton University Press, 1994).

proposed a more sophisticated distinction between acts of explanation and acts of understanding,[11] and although Gadamer took this distinction further by relating understanding to the processes of what he termed effective historical consciousness, both have no account of embodiment, what I want to call the language and knowledge of the body. This is despite the fact that there is a commitment in both thinkers to a *Lebensphilosophie*, an account of *Erlebnis* or lived experience. Gadamer is important for taking hermeneutics beyond the mental acts of individuals and, influenced by Heidegger's accounts of *Dasein*, *Mitandersein*, *Vorgriff* and *Vorhabe*, for recognising interpretation as a social activity – and I will return to this – but the theatre of interpretative action remains consciousness. Put briefly, he is still wrestling with a Cartesian legacy that cannot give an account of the interdependency of the *psyche* and the *soma*. We can see how, with a little help from Stanley Fish, Gadamer's thinking could appreciate interpretative communities;[12] even, with a little help from Michel Foucault, could appreciate both the archaeology and the genealogy of knowledges. But the attention to understanding and what in one essay Gadamer terms 'The Universality of the Hermeneutic Problem' makes all this heady stuff. As Gadamer writes in his Foreword to the second edition of *Truth and Method*, he understands hermeneutics as 'a theory of the real experience that thinking is'.[13] So, if minds are certainly not functioning as brains in vats, they seem unencumbered with legs and arms, breasts or chests either.

Secondly, what an economy of response sets out to demonstrate is that the role of interpretation is not to mediate between the textual and the nontextual, the word and the world, the sign and what it signifies. Somewhat paralleling the Cartesian dualism, post-Reformation hermeneutics drew this distinction between the textual and the non-textual, word and thing, the

---

[11] See 'The Development of Hermeneutics' in *Wilhelm Dilthey: Selected Writings*, tr. and ed. H.P. Rickman (Cambridge University Press, 1976). What is often missed out of the history of hermeneutics is the contribution of phenomenology, particularly Husserl. Husserl's understanding and examination of apperception and intentionality concerned the manner in which objects were taken up into consciousness and made meaningful. Objects never appeared as such, and phenomenology did not treat them as such; objects were already experienced in terms of webs of interpretative relation. Interpretation became a mode of living in and experiencing the world. Nevertheless, it was the unity of consciousness that became the focus for Husserl's hermeneutical epistemology and his investigations into mindedness (*Zumutesein*). In this he was influenced by neo-Kantians like Paul Nathorp.

[12] Stanley Fish, *Is There a Text in This Class? The Authority of Interpretive Communities* (Cambridge, Mass.: Harvard University Press, 1980).

[13] *Truth and Method*, tr. Garret Barden and John Cumming (London: Sheed and Ward, 1975), p. xxiv.

text and either the referent it pointed to or the sense it contained.[14] Representation became both necessary (to present a consciousness of the world) and something to be transcended; it was both tool and impediment. Fundamentally, and philosophically, post-Reformation hermeneutics continued in and developed out of nominalism. The emergence of Reformation literalism (as distinct from the subtle and complex understanding of the *sensus rectus* or the historical sense) is inseparable from the nominalist separation of the word and the world, the sign and its meaning.[15] Post-Reformation hermeneutics had as its task to render an account of how interpretation joined back together again the word and the world. The movement for this joining could, then, only proceed one way – from word to world, sign to meaning. The role of interpretation is then to mediate, to offer a one-way bridge that enables us to grasp that which is immediate and beyond the word, beyond the sign – indeed, beyond interpretation, the end of interpretation: the self-present meaning.[16]

What I wish to outline in this essay is a different approach to hermeneutics that rejects the dualism of *psyche* and *soma*, as it rejects the dualism of sign and the reality that it signifies. I wish to situate the processes of understanding, sign recognition and interpretation in the wider economies of our embodied response to the world. If, following both Heidegger and Wittgenstein, all seeing (and that seeing I suggest embraces touching, smelling, tasting and hearing) is seeing *as*, then we are as sensate creatures continually involved in coming to judgements about our embodied experience in the

---

[14] This is why some of Ricœur's work and Charles Taylor's is so important. In his essay 'The Model of the Text: Meaningful Action Considered as Text' (tr. Kathleen Blamey in Kathleen Blamey and John Thompson eds., *From Text to Action* (Evanston, Ill.: Northwestern University Press, 1991, pp. 144–67), Ricœur pointed out how the interpretation of a text can act as an analogue for the interpretation of social action. This, along with the development by both structuralists and poststructuralists (like Roland Barthes, Claude Lévi-Strauss and Michel de Certeau) of social semiotics, began to break down the barrier between textual interpretation and cultural interpretation more generally. As I noted above, one cannot omit here the importance of phenomenology for both Ricœur and post-war French thinking more generally. Charles Taylor's examination of human beings as interpretative animals again widened the scope of hermeneutics. See his essay 'Self-Interpreting Animals' in *Human Agency and Language: Philosophical Papers: Part I* (Cambridge University Press, 1985), pp. 45–76..

[15] See here my essays, 'To Be a Reader: Bunyan's Struggle with the Language of Scripture' in *Literature and Theology* 4 (1), March (1990), pp. 29–49; and 'Speaking Otherwise: Postmodern Analogy' in Philip Goodchild ed., *Rethinking Philosophy of Religion* (New York: Fordham University Press, 2002), pp. 187–211.

[16] A critique about the possibility of ever being able to arrive at this meaning is at the heart of Derrida's deconstructive analyses of what he terms 'logocentrism'. Nevertheless, he remains caught within nominalism himself; see my 'In the Daylight Forever?: Language and Silence' in Denys Turner and Oliver Davies eds., *Silence and the Word* (Cambridge University Press, 2002).

world and the text; the phenomenological, the social and the corporeal are continually being engaged concurrently – as the quotation from Merleau-Ponty at the head of this essay announces. We never stop interpreting: 'we are condemned to meaning',[17] though 'condemned' is a strong metaphor to employ here, recalling Heidegger's use of 'prison' to describe the language we always indwell. We never get beyond interpretation, we are constantly reading and re-reading – others, ourselves and the furniture around us – but I want to suggest there is a redemption in this. We are continually moving within and handling the operations of reception and response; and in this movement we are both constituted as subjects and coming to a reflexive understanding of who we are. That is something of what it means to be human. What I am wishing to do is give an account of that concurrent engagement. Ultimately, I suggest, this account points to an excess, what Jean-Luc Marion has recently termed *le surcroît*. For him, that is the character of 'saturated phenomena' – playing on the way excess requires us to believe, *croire*, an infinite interpretability that Marion associates with the iconic.[18] My account of the economy of response, therefore, finds its ultimate frame in the theological, in mythologies of the transcendent. The work of Merleau-Ponty, sketching a phenomenology of *le corps propre* in which the body is already a field of intentions such that thinking and knowledge emerge from its immersion in the world; and the last writings of Michel Henry, developing a phenomenology of Merleau-Ponty's self-confessed secularised account of incarnation: both provide resources for presenting an economy of response. Both are aware that such an account must necessarily draw upon and return us to a certain Christian legacy that has refused the dualism of soul and body, mind and world, and, in developing its theologies of incarnation and being human, has sought to think in terms of the ensouled flesh, or the enfleshed soul. I would point to the writings of Gregory of Nyssa, particularly his reflections *In Canticum Canticorum* and Augustine's *De Trinitate*, for example, as textual sites where – though the body is disciplined in and through practices of piety – the *psyche* and the *soma* work one in relation to the other.[19] The soul is formed in and through the body by a participation of both in the economy of grace. In a sense, then, my account of the economy of response is another take on a question that dominated all Augustine's thinking: what is the relationship between the body and the soul? I will suggest towards the end of this essay that the

---

[17] *Phenomenology of Perception*, p. 420.

[18] *De Surcroit: études sur les phénomènes saturés* (Paris: Presses Universitaires de France, 2001).

[19] There has been a notable shift in the recent scholarship on Gregory of Nyssa towards a re-affirmation of embodiment. See Sarah Coakley ed., *Modern Theology* 18 (4), October (2002) for discussions and examples of this shift in critical attention.

kind of therapeutic interpretation that is fashioned by and for and in the self is determined by the nature of the hope towards which understanding aspires. It is exactly at this point that the project of theological hermeneutics announces itself.

But how do we give an account of how we receive, respond and grope towards understanding? There are, it seems to me, three possibilities.

First, I could give an abstract analysis of what is involved in receiving, responding and understanding, treating the moves involved between sensing, interpreting and acting. Charles Taylor has gone some way towards doing this in his fine essay 'Self-Interpreting Animals'.[20] In the development of a philosophical anthropology, Taylor begins by demonstrating how much of our experience involves descriptions that in turn compose judgements about the world.[21] Things have 'import' for us. That is why we register and experience them, and why, in turn, that import tells us something about the kind of people we are.[22] Reasoning is then 'embedded in feeling',[23] and concerns itself with interpretation. Language facility is also then bound up with these feelings and their interpretation. Language is constitutive of our emotional experience and interprets such experience. So, Taylor concludes, 'interpretation plays no secondary, optional role, but is essential to human existence'.[24]

Within the analytical tradition of philosophy Taylor's essay is important for the way it arrives at conclusions paralleling those of the continental tradition with and after Heidegger. It is valuable for the association it makes between two rival schools of modern philosophy. But its problem for answering the question posed here lies with its very abstraction – it does not situate me as a reader, writer and thinker (and, more generally, language-user) with respect to the analysis. My own partial standpoint is erased or forgotten; and so my own acts of interpretation are masked in attempting to articulate the logic of understanding. This approach would remain true to Enlightenment ideologies. It is insufficiently phenomenological.

A second possible approach could then lie with a turn explicitly to the work of phenomenologists. I could begin by detailing the analyses by Merleau-Ponty of the chiasmus or intertwining in which he attempts to explore prereflexive thinking, thinking embedded in an immersion of the perceiving body in the world.[25] I could then take this further by examining

---

[20] See footnote 14.

[21] 'Self-Interpreting Animals', p. 47.

[22] Ibid., p. 58.

[23] Ibid., p. 62.

[24] Ibid., p. 76.

[25] See *The Visible and the Invisible*, ed. Claude Lefort, tr. Alphonse Lingis (Evanston, Ill.: Northwestern University Press, 1968).

both Henry's examination of *la phénoménologie de la chair* and Marion's phenomenological analyses of givenness and saturated phenomena. I could then
point to the silences in their texts – Merleau-Ponty's resistence to treating
excess as supernatural while toying with a certain mystical language, Henry's
appeal to an immediacy and purity of revelation, Marion's abstract formal-
ism (and also appeal to an immediacy and purity of revelation). I must say I
was very tempted to take this approach because it would foreground that my
own reasoning (like anybody else's) works on the basis of reading and rereading. But the problem here is the level of philosophical abstraction that
still remains – I would not to able to demonstrate the embodied nature of
reading and rereading: the operation of desire, for example, in the economy
of response. I would escape what I see as fundamental to the ethics of interpretation – interpretation's fallibility and the finitude it invokes.

So thirdly, I decided the best way to demonstrate the economy of
response is to examine two specific encounters, or rather (since we never
have just encounters as such) two specific readings (and writings) of encounters which I am subsequently rereading, allowing my own 'prejudices' (in
the Gadamerian sense) to structure that rereading. Thus, in this way, I can
open up other ways to interpret these texts and point up the finitude of my
own interpretative reasoning. And since I wish, ultimately, both to con-
tribute to the development of a theological hermeneutics and to be able to
give an account of a specific therapy operative within acts of interpretation, I
have chosen two encounters from the Christian Scriptures.

The first account is Jesus's encounter with Mary in the 'garden':

> Mary stood at the tomb outside, weeping. As she wept, she peered into the
> tomb; and she saw two angels in white sitting there, one at the head, and one
> at the feet, where the body of Jesus had lain. They said to her 'Woman, why
> are you weeping?' She answered, 'They have taken my Lord [*Kurion*] away,
> and I do not know where they have laid him.' With these words she turned
> round [*eis ta opiso*] and saw Jesus standing there, but did not recognise [*edei*]
> him [*Iesous*]. Jesus said to her, 'Woman, why are you weeping? Who is it you
> are looking for?'. Thinking it was the gardener, she said, 'If it is you, Sir
> [*Kurie*], who have removed him, tell me where you have laid him, and I will
> take him away.' Jesus said, 'Mary!' She turned to him and said, 'Rabboni!'
> (which is Hebrew for 'My Master' [*Didaskale*]). Jesus said, 'Touch me no more
> [*Me mou aptou*], for I have not yet ascended to the Father. But go to my broth-
> ers, and tell them that I am ascending to my Father and your Father, my God
> and your God.' Mary of Magdala went to the disciples with the news, 'I have
> seen the Lord! [*Eoraka ton Kurion*]'. (John 20.11–18)

The second passage follows this narrative after a space of five verses:

One of the Twelve, Thomas, that is the 'Twin' [*ho legonomenos Didumos*], was not with the rest when Jesus came. So the disciples told him, 'We have seen the Lord [*Eorakamen ton Kurion*].' He said, 'Unless I see the mark [*tupon*] of the nails on [*en*] his hands, unless I put [*balo*] my finger into the place [*tupon*] where the nails were, and [*balo*] my hand into his side [*pleuran*], I will not believe'. A week [*emeras okto*] later his disciples were again in the room, and Thomas was with them. Although the doors were locked, Jesus came and stood among them, saying, 'Peace be with you!' Then he said to Thomas, 'Reach [*phere*] your finger here: see my hands. Reach [*phere*] your hand here and put [*bale*] it into my side. Be unbelieving [*ginou apistos*] no longer, but believe.' Thomas said, 'My Lord [*Kurios*] and my God!' (John 20.24–8)

In both of these encounters a transaction takes place between self and other that results in a vocalised recognition – 'my master' and 'my Lord'. In both accounts the transaction takes place through emphatic bodily actions and gestures (Mary's turning and embracing; Thomas's reaching beyond the boundaries of his own body to penetrate [*pherao*] and thrust [*balo*] himself into the body of Christ). In both accounts there is an economy of response, a structured dialectic between self and other, in which difference and affinity, distance and proximity is negotiated in a sensuous move from sight to touch.[26]

[26] I am aware there is a tradition of reading these passages such that neither Mary nor Thomas may have actually touched Christ. C.K. Barrett, *The Gospel According to St. John* (2nd edition, Philadelphia, Penn.: Westminster Press, 1978), sums up the difficulty with regards to the phrase '*me mou aptou*' in the account of Mary's encounter: 'The present imperative with *me* in a prohibition signifies the breaking of an action already in progress, or sometimes the attempt to perform an action' (p. 565). To him either reading is valid, though Dodd (*The Interpretation of the Fourth Gospel*, Cambridge University Press, 1955, p. 443), Rudolf Schnackenburg (*The Gospel According to St John*, vol. 2, trs. Cecily Hastings et al., London: Burnes & Oates, 1980, p. 318), and J. H. Bernard (*A Critical and Exegetical Commentary on the Gospel According to St John*, vol. 2, Edinburgh, T. & T. Clark, 1928, p. 408) prefer to view Mary as touching Christ; Bultmann (*The Gospel of John: A Commentary*, tr. G.R. Beasley-Murray, Oxford: Blackwell, 1971, p. 687) inclines to agree. The interpretation I propose would also tend to the first of Barrett's translations, but if it were the other way, then there is a contrast between Mary's desire to touch, as there is an assumption that such touch will be possible once he has ascended (see Barrett and also Loughlin's reading as cited in footnote 30) and Jesus's invitation to Thomas to touch (following his ascension to the Father?). For a discussion of the relationship of resurrection to ascension with respect to this verse see Raymond E. Brown, *The Gospel According to John*, vol. 2 (London: Geoffrey Chapman, 1971), pp. 1011–17. Brown concludes, though, after an exhaustive survey of interpretations, that the verse 'probably implies that she is touching him' (p. 992). 'The resurrection has made possible a new and more intimate spiritual [and carnal – my insertion] union between Jesus and his disciples'; Barrett, p. 566. Barrett raises no question concerning Thomas's touching of Christ, and Bultmann only suggests 'Thomas did not *first* undertake the contact' (p. 694), with the implication that he does so eventually. I should record though that Ernst Haenchen, *John*, vol. 2, tr. Robert W. Funk (Philadelphia, Penn.: Fortress Press, 1984), p. 211 views the abrupt transition from Jesus's offer of his body to Thomas to Thomas's confession of faith as evidence that Thomas 'did not make use of the opportunity he requested to verify the resurrection'. Weighing the evidence presented in the debates, Schnackenburg concludes significantly that contact with Christ 'is not impossible' (p. 332).

In both accounts there is an eroticism, but I will treat that aspect of these texts in the next essay, 'Divinity and Sexual Difference'. For the moment we will focus on the economy of differences and affinities.

The difference and affinity of those involved in the actions are inseparable from speaking, words and the translation of words from one language to another. The knowledge that comes through recognition, through the economy of responding to the other and the other responding in return, is a vocalised knowledge. It takes the form of an exchange. Although, with Thomas, the words are spoken to the disciples directly and, one assumes from the story, overheard in some sense by Jesus who then returns them to Thomas when they meet. The cameos of relations with the Christ are themselves written compositions by 'John' who, throughout his narrative, is conscious of the creative power of language, and thinks powerfully about the nature of signs. He is aware of the theological significance of his own written, semiotic act (John 20.31). The text moves across the Aramaic acknowledged as the language being spoken by the disciples and Jesus, translating those conversations into Greek. It is a text concerned throughout with the act of naming: in the first account there is Jesus as Lord and Master and the response elicited by being called 'Mary'; in the second there is Thomas, called the Twin (*Didymus*), and Jesus is called both Lord and God. Furthermore, the common theme is paralleled in the common structure of these two economies of responding to the resurrected Jesus. On the one hand, there is Mary's inability to recognise who Jesus is; on the other, there is Thomas's inability to accept a man whose radical difference from all other men is manifested in his conquest of death. For each of them a new alienation from someone once familiar is experienced. In both scenarios there is a coming to know through speaking with and understanding the other, through desiring and engaging with the other, through seeing, naming and touching the other. In both accounts a topography of bodies is sketched. Mary stands, stoops to peer, turns, turns again at the mention of her name, moves forward to embrace, moves back from the embrace and withdraws to tell the disciples what she has seen. Jesus stands in the midst, confronting Thomas, then offers his body for examination, Thomas moves forward, extends his finger, stretches out his hand, pushes it into the side of Christ, withdraws. This topography of bodies in both passages focuses on Jesus's body, coming to understand, coming to an identification of who he is through engaging with this body. The knowledge then that issues in identification is both carnal and theological.

Let us follow these economies of response a little further to see how this topography of bodies maps onto a relationality in which difference and affinity, distance and proximity, are understood; let us ask how difference and affinity, distance and proximity are not only established but what they signify about Christian relations. First, we can note the play of absence and presence. When Mary stands at the tomb, Jesus is, in one sense, not there because the tomb (and the positioning of the angels accentuates this) is empty. And yet he is there in Mary herself, contained within her, internalised as Lord and Master (or Teacher). In a revealing passage on the body's knowledge, Merleau-Ponty observes:

> When I imagine Peter absent, I am not aware of contemplating an image of Peter numerically distinct from Peter himself. However far away he is, I visualise him in the world, and my power of imagining is nothing but the persistence of my world around me. To say that I imagine Peter is to say that I bring about the pseudo-presence of Peter by putting into operation the 'Peter-behaviour-pattern' ... Peter in imagination is only one of the modalities of my being in the world.[27]

In the same way Jesus's presence is part of Mary's presence, and it is the physical absence of that presence that remains within her, displacing both a sense of herself and him, and installs her desire. The question the angels ask her elicits a vocalisation of her desire: to have present, even if only as a corpse, the body of Jesus. Jesus himself not only reiterates the angels' question but he elicits a more precise naming of her desire. Like the night watchmen in the *Canticum Canticorum* speaking to the Beloved, he asks 'Whom do you seek?'[28]

Secondly, we can observe the states of knowledge. We begin with incomprehension, because the body is missing while the presence of Jesus in her and to her remains strong. We continue with misrecognition, for she thought it was the gardener. Turning and turning about (where the body imitates a coming to consciousness of what it itself understands),[29] she turns into a hearing of her own name. The calling calls her not only to herself and

---

[27] *Phenomenology of Perception*, p. 210.

[28] See A. Feuillet, 'La recherché du Christ dans la nouvelle alliance d'après la Christophanie de Jo 20, 11–18' in *L'homme devant Dieu* (Paris: Aubier, 1963), I, pp. 93–112, who develops this association and its erotic allusions to the *Canticum Canticorum*.

[29] Most commentators on the Greek in verses 14 and 16 at this point allude to the complex movements involved. To eliminate the vertigo of such turnings, reference is frequently made to a possible Aramaic version of this text (proposed by M. Black in *An Aramaic Approach to the Gospels and Acts*, Oxford: Clarendon Press, 1954) that might read not 'turned' but 'recognised'. The verb has then been mistranslated when the Gospel was put into Greek. The Sinaitic Syriac version of this text would then be the correct one, that replaces 'turned' with 'she recognised him'. What is interesting from my point of view is the relationship between turning and recognition that this textual debate reinforces.

into a new knowledge, but to an identification through his voice of herself with him (in him, if we can understand the name dwelling in his mouth and mind). The absence that previously filled her disappears, and the two bodies come together (again imitating a state of knowledge) as they embrace. The negative command, *Me mou aptou*, installs a distance again, but it is not an absence – although neither is it presence as possession, nor the unity of the identification of herself in him and with him.[30] In a sense, when he speaks her name he speaks her into existence as part of himself; when he explains to her why she should stop touching him he speaks *to* her and so demonstrates they are not one. His speaking *to* her is a communication *with* her, but also a separation *from* her. (Perhaps this is the condition of all theological understanding, that works between a sacramental presence and an inability to grasp fully what faith understands.) Gerard Loughlin has found a most felicitous phrase for this second observation: 'the language of dispossessive affinity'.[31]

Thirdly, we can identify the modes of address as they shift from interrogation to affirmation, to the giving of a command, to the giving of an explanation, to the giving of a commission, to a final acclamation and testimony before witnesses: 'I have seen the Lord.' The topography of bodies maps, then, onto an economy of response that begins with the paralysing contradiction of absence and presence, issuing dramatically into a consummating knowledge which is then followed by a dialectical relation of affinity (or recognition) and difference, knowledge and desire. The economy of response is composed of four complex movements – of bodies, of language, of knowledge and of desire. The movements are not equally distributed between the two figures. The body of Jesus the Christ is more central to the narrative than Mary's body, though it is Mary's body that moves while Jesus's stands still. The language operates upon and within Mary for the most part – she answers or she listens until she makes her statement before the disciples. She does not control the direction of the language. She speaks within a language given to her by invitation (from the angels, from Jesus). The

---

[30] I very much like Gerard Loughlin's 'carnal' and theological reading of this moment in the Gospel: 'Jesus tells Mary not to cling on to him because he has not yet ascended, *as if she might hold him once he has ascended* ... Thus it is that Mary can touch him once he has ascended, once he is with his disciples in their following of him, in their forgiving and feeding of others. It is in their caring for one another, and for others, that they touch the Lord, and he embraces them, holding them in his arms; his touch being their embrace'; *Alien Sex: The Body and Desire in Cinema and Theology* (Oxford: Blackwell, 2004), p. 266. In a footnote Loughlin points to how this theology is in agreement with Gregory of Nyssa's and alludes to Jean-Luc Nancy's book *Noli me tangere: essai sur la levée du corps* (Paris: Bayard Editions, 2003).

[31] Ibid., p. 283.

movement of knowledge is time-bound – *eureka*, I *have* seen. She understands, then, by remembering. Her moment of identification with Jesus is
crossed by an ignorance that he is not yet ascended. She makes no answer to
the account of going to the Father, ascending to God. What is known, then,
is always being crossed by what is unknown. The language says more than is
understood. It operates as an expression of desire as it changes in the moves
from loss and longing, to being united, to being separated and given the task
of going ahead to speak to others. Desire remains because it cannot fully
attain the understanding faith seeks. Desire remains – confused and lacking
an object (fetishising the corpse), finding and uniting with its object, being
displaced on to another object; desire knows difference while knowledge
has identified again what it knows: 'I have seen the Lord.' All the various
aspects of the economy of response are orientated towards a future state.
Mary must go and tell the disciples, Jesus must ascend; the knowledge and
the language are not yet perfect. The body receives and responds (it sees, it
hears, it touches) more than the mind understands, but what the body
knows is not incomprehensible, it merely sketches a knowledge that has yet
to be entered into; and the future is carried on the wings of desire. The very
secret of the structure of time is contained in that moment of embrace and
recognition.

The economy of response in the account of Jesus and Thomas is more
truncated, though also more visceral. The theme of absence and presence
opens this account too, though it is Thomas's absence to begin with, followed by Jesus's absence when Thomas returns to the upper room and the
disciples. There is a different choreography of bodies. But again, Jesus is
present in Thomas, as his pronouncement to the disciples makes evident.
For Thomas rehearses the wounds inflicted on Jesus by the crucifixion. In
fact, he returns us, like the victims of trauma return the trusted enquirer, to
the scene of the crime: the nails hammered into the hands, the lance punc-
turing the side. Jesus's death lives in Thomas; it lives in his memory, his
language and his understanding of who this man is/was. Let us interpret this
generously, as Caravaggio did (see the front cover). This is not atheism, nor
even agnosticism. This is love that cannot come to terms with loss; this is
belief that cannot yet take on the burden of hope. Jesus comes to Thomas as
Thomas imagines him, as Thomas has internalised him. There is no
mention of Jesus's wounds in Mary's encounter, nor in the encounter with
the other disciples that takes place off-stage, so to speak. But something
more is needed than seeing these wounds. These wounds have shaped
within Thomas an understanding of this crucified man; that understanding
must now undergo a transformation. In *Contra Celsum* Origen suggests that
Thomas 'thought that it was possible for the physical eyes to see the body of

the soul in a form in every respect like its former shape'.[32] In other words, he believed in ghosts, and Jesus had to demonstrate to Thomas through being touched – and the Church through him – that he was no disembodied spirit. Jesus invites Thomas to plunge into the very depths of the tortured Messiah that he has internalised. The touch is demanded of Thomas; it was Mary's spontaneous response. Thomas must go where no other man or woman has been allowed to go – into the very flesh of the Christ. He must be brought to a new knowledge and identification through the engagement of bodies. His future in Christ is only possible on the basis of the carnal reception of and response to flesh touching flesh. Touch and identification are, as with the earlier account, inseparable, but a new and more dramatic crossing of bodily boundaries is required. Thomas has to be brought not to announce his desire but to perform it. It is the same desire as Mary's – to be one with Jesus. But in neither case is seeing enough. Mary has to hear first and then embrace. Thomas has to be commanded. Subsequently, he has to submit to that command (which is only voicing what Thomas himself had voiced within himself). Thomas has to be brought to a knowledge; a knowledge Mary seizes in an utter surrender of herself at the call of her name. Caravaggio captures this leading, this manuduction, for it is Christ who guides Thomas's finger into the wound. And the wound is opened by that finger as if lifting the lid of an inner eye, or even parting vaginal lips. Thomas is led to an intimate, carnal and spiritual knowledge; his face is fixed with both a curiosity and an incomprehension. But let us go just a little further – further than Caravaggio's depiction of Thomas, towards Caravaggio's depiction of and response to embodiment itself. For the painting as a whole, Thomas in his context, suggests the touch is commanded, is solicited as an act of love, initiating a process of healing. Is Jesus's pain in being wounded somehow lessened, healed, by that touch of Thomas's? Is that touch akin to those visions of mystics who kiss the wounds of Christ not out of some gruesome masochism, but out of a love that wishes to touch the very place of pain with love, and begin its healing? Thomas's hand remains forever touching the torn flesh of Christ; and when does touch become caress? The composition suggests a healing of relation; a distance remains (registered in the look on Thomas's face of absolute incomprehension), but it is a distance known in proximity.

The four aspects of the economy of response that we have examined are different in this second account: what is being performed by and upon the body; the coming to know [Erkenntnis] and identify; the language which is

---

[32]   Contra Celsum, II.61.

not of interrogation and explication, but of command; and the operation of desire in which the scene is almost freeze-framed as Thomas reaches into the side of Christ. But the telos of the economy is the same – the learning of difference and affinity, distance and proximity through the establishment of a self-transcending relation.

★

So much for the specific analysis. What of the question, then, that gives the *topos* for this essay? Let me draw this conclusion out systematically. First: there are no pure poles of either reception or response. The economy of response is not the same as an economy of reception, but what we treat in presenting an account of the economy of response is the movement 'between' receiving and responding: the body is already a field of intentions. Secondly, when attempting to assess what is involved in the operations of this economy a number of loci become evident: the contingencies of time and the specificities of bodies lived in particular ways (sexed and socialised bodies); the geography of the movements or performances of these bodies; the embodied dialectic between the known and identifiable and the irreducibility of the other's body such that any encounter becomes what I like to call a congress of mysteries; the exchange of signs – gestural and linguistic – that, to employ Kristeva's terminology, conform to a certain symbolic code, but a code never divorced from the motile drives of the semiotic; the operation of a desire that parallels because it is ultimately inseparable from the dialectic of knowledge and mystery, affinity and difference, visible appearance and invisible excess. The operation of desire works with a dialectic of distance and proximity; it is this dialectic, as Gadamer observed, that makes misconstrual, *méconnaissance*, fruitful. In fact, the praxis of interpretation makes nonsense of the Enlightenment distinction between meaning and misunderstanding. As Merleau-Ponty already saw, touch is the very figure of desire's operation; Lévinas would say 'caress'.[33]

My account of economies of response makes interpretation irreducible. Irreducible in two senses. First, that it will never come to an end. Second, that as a practice it is infinitely complex, subtle and only partly conscious of itself – which is why Habermas's understanding of communicative action is too reductive: dialogue between clearly stated and self-reflexive positions is only one aspect of the hermeneutical activity involved in any encounter. I suggest any act of understanding, any act of reading, any act of interpretation

---

[33] For Emmanuel Lévinas on 'caress' see *Totality and Infinity: An Essay on Exteriority*, tr. Alphonso Lingis (Pittsburgh, Penn.: Duquesne Press, 1969), pp. 257–8.

is implicated in these complex embodied operations that constitute the economy of response. But what of the therapy and the formation? How do these relate to this complex and incarnate hermeneutics? Gabriel Marcel, Merleau-Ponty and Henry all see the Christian account of incarnation as paradigmatic of the mystery of human embodiment itself. What is evident from our analyses of Christ's two post-resurrection encounters as represented by the writer of the Gospel of St John, is that there is a specific teleology: Christ himself is the meaning that can never be totally embraced, recognised, known. His is the excessive body, *par excellence*, that organises all the other forms of embodiment. The praxis of interpretation, that proceeds via economies of response, is governed by a Logos that does not give itself as self-presence (and therefore does not fall foul of deconstruction), but gives itself as a sensible transcendence (Luce Irigaray's term),[34] as a saturated phenomenon, as a body whose significance is irreducible, the knowledge of which is precisely that it is irreducible. The praxis of interpretation is involved in the congress of mysteries, having as its goal an understanding that forever eludes its final grasp. It is involved, then, in a search for truth, a struggle to find meaning. Put briefly, interpretation involves a practice of hope. Despair is where interpretation becomes impossible or arbitrary; the place of trauma and aphasia from which emerge Kristeva's tales of love; the frozen wastes of Dante's nether hell. Interpretation is ultimately an eschatological act. It is the teleology of the praxis of interpretation that shapes the lived experience of the one interpreting. It fashions the self while also enabling that self to reflect upon its own condition. It wagers on the operation of a transcendental Good while continually reminding the interpreter of their fallibility and finitude. It is in this sense that hermeneutics is implicated in a science of healing, an economy of redemption, and, I suggest (following an intuition of Schleiermacher here), the moral formation of subjects. On 21 August AD 397, St Augustine preached a sermon in which he raised the question that I believe is at the heart of his work as it is at the heart of this essay. The question is simply: 'What hast thou that thou didst not receive?'[35]

---

[34] This is explored further in the next essay, 'Divinity and Sexual Difference'.
[35] Quoted in Sergei Lancel, *Augustine* (London: SCM Press, 2001), p. 196.

Chapter Five

DIVINITY AND SEXUAL DIFFERENCE

Why is the work of Luce Irigaray potentially a rich resource for rethinking Christology?[1] Fundamentally, because as one of the most profound contemporary feminist philosophers, she recognises the importance for incarnational theology of eros and embodiment. More particularly, living as a woman in the historical context of the European religious tradition and French and Flemish Catholicism, her work – in *An Ethics of Sexual Difference*, *Sexes and Genealogies*, *Marine Lover* and *I Love to You* – has explored something of the relation between divinity and sexual difference.

In Christian theology of the twentieth century Karl Barth and Hans Urs von Balthasar each attempted to situate the creation and vocation of man and woman within their wider systematic concerns.[2] For Barth, sexual difference was a repetition on a horizontal and social level of the vertical covenant between God and human beings. Sexual difference rehearses the

---

[1] This essay first appeared in *Modern Theology* 12 (2), April (1996). Much work has since been done on the writings of Luce Irigaray by feminists concerned with religion. Furthermore, Irigaray herself has written more, some with respect to Christianity. Among the feminist scholars whose work is important for the ways it critiques and develops Irigaray's religious sensibilities I would particularly draw attention to Grace Jantzen's *Becoming Divine* (Manchester University Press, 1998), particularly pp. 88–107; Pamela Sue Anderson, *A Feminist Philosophy of Religion* (Oxford: Blackwell, 1998), particularly pp. 98–118, 234–40; and Morny Joy, Kathleen O'Grady and Judith L. Poxon eds., *Religion in French Feminist Thought: Critical Perspectives* (London: Routledge, 2003), particularly pp. 1–82. When editing this essay for the present collection I decided not to update the Irigaray analysis but instead to focus it more clearly on the question of sexual difference.

[2] For Barth on sexual difference see *Die Kirkliche Dogmatik*, III.1 (Zürich/Zollikon: Evangelischer Verlag, 1953), #41.3; *Church Dogmatics*, III.1, trs. J.W. Edwards et al. (Edinburgh: T. & T. Clark, 1958), #41.3; *Die Kirkliche Dogmatik*, III.2, #45.2 and 3; *Church Dogmatics*, III.2, trs. Harold Knight et al. (Edinburgh: T. & T. Clark, 1960), #45.2 and 3; *Die Kirkliche Dogmatik*, III.4, #54.1; *Church Dogmatics*, III.4, trs. A.T. Mackay et al. (Edinburgh: T. & T. Clark, 1961). For Balthasar on sexual difference see *The Office of St. Peter and the Structure of the Church,* tr. Andrée Emery (San Francisco: Ignatius Press, 1986).

dialectic of the self and the other; the dialectic itself is constitutive of being human. That is, a human being is such only in relation to other human beings. Man and woman together constitute what it is to be human, making marriage fundamental anthropologically as well as theologically.[3] Marriage is the fulfilment of sexual difference; the fulfilment also of a certain *analogia Christi* insofar as it imitates the old covenantal relationship between Yahweh and Israel and the new covenantal relationship between Christ and the Church. In Balthasar, sexual difference is related to the operation of specific offices within the Church – the Marian and the Petrine – which in turn rehearses the difference and hierarchy between Christ and his Church. The male and female perform the twofold character of the Christian life: service and obedience. These are the distinct vocations of men and women, in which women are the answer or response to *Mensch*. Each theologian, as has been remarked by several commentators,[4] struggles with but cannot avoid the hierarchy in which the male has priority. Each theologian also cannot avoid a biological essentialism that structures and determines the difference that is subsequently enquired into theologically. The sexual in sexual difference is fundamentally physiological – it is that which can be read off from bodies, although these bodily signs have first of all to be recognised as significant or determinative in a major way. And, as those historians of medicine and those genealogists of corporeality inform us, we have only been taught to identify and read certain bodily signs as sexually different over the last 150 years or so.[5] Barth and Balthasar's biological essentialism, their beginning with the determining physiological factors of distinct gonads, is itself histor-

[3]   There is an interesting question in Barth's theology of sexual difference concerning 'marriage' as a social, contractual institution and 'marriage' as a covenantal relation. Barth allows for divorce on the grounds that the relation may not have been and was subsequently misunderstood as being covenantal. The 'marriage' seems, then, to be the relation issuing from the consummation of sexual difference; a relation that is ontologically prior to any ceremonial procedure.

[4]   See Tina Beattie, 'One Man and Three Women – Hans, Adrienne, Mary and Luce', *New Blackfriars* 79 (294), February (1998), pp. 95–103; Gerard Loughlin, 'The Erotics of Sex' in John Milbank, Catherine Pickstock and Graham Ward eds., *Radical Orthodoxy* (London: Routledge, 1998), pp. 143–62; Graham Ward, 'Kenosis, Death, Discourse and Resurrection' in L. Gardner, D. Moss and B. Quash eds., *Balthasar at the End of Modernity* (Edinburgh: T. & T. Clark, 1999), pp. 15–68, and *Cities of God* (London: Routledge, 2001), pp. 182–202; David Moss and Lucy Gardner, 'Difference – The Immaculate Concept? The Laws of Sexual Difference in the Theology of Hans Urs von Balthasar', *Modern Theology* 14 (3), July (1998), pp. 377–401, and 'Something Like Time; Something Like the Sexes – An Essay on Reception' in *Balthasar at the End of Modernity*, pp. 69–137; and Rachel Muers, 'A Question of Two Answers: Difference and Determinations in Barth and von Balthasar', *Heythrop Journal* 40 (1999), pp. 265–79.

[5]   There are a large number of books available in the area now, but one of the earliest and most influential was Thomas Lacqueur, *Making Sex: Body and Gender from the Greeks to Freud* (Cambridge, Mass.: Harvard University Press, 1990).

ically and culturally determined. As such their starting point is relative; relative to other future possibilities and other conceptions of the body's determinative signs in the past.

The Divine Subject

Irigaray starts her examination of the relationship between divinity and human sexuality elsewhere, and that is why we will pursue the alternative avenues for thinking incarnation that her work opens up. Religion plays such a central role in her thinking because of its implications for the psycho-sexual development of the subject. As she writes: 'To posit a gender, a God is necessary; *guaranteeing the infinite* ... If women have no God, they are unable either to communicate or to commune with one another ... [A]s long as woman lacks a divine made in her image she cannot establish her subjectivity.'[6] To appreciate her concern with religion and the relationship she draws here between gender, personhood and the divine, two modes of critical enquiry need to be outlined. The first belongs to Louis Althusser and his notions of subjectivity and the ideology of the Subject. The second belongs to the role God-as-Father plays in the morphology of sexuality in Freud.

Althusser expounds his understanding of subjectification in a famous essay entitled 'Ideology and Ideological State Apparatuses'.[7] Here, with explicit reference to Christianity, he describes how the state is able to maintain power over its subjects through a number of 'apparatuses'. These might be repressive (i.e. the judiciary) or creative (i.e. education), but they constitute two economies of production. As Judith Butler succinctly puts it, there is 'a power *exerted on* a subject' and 'a power *assumed by* the subject, an assumption that constitutes the instrument of that subject's becoming'.[8] These apparatuses discipline individuals into viewing and valuing the world and themselves in specific ways; they operate with ideologies. It is at this point, to illustrate such an operation, that Althusser turns to Christianity. In order to create a subject there needs to be a reified Subject, an Absolute Subject who can 'interpellate' the individual. Ideology establishes this normative Subject and, through interpellation, the subject is called to recognise

[6] *Sexes and Genealogies*, tr. Gillian C. Gill (New York: Columbia University Press, 1993), pp. 61–3.
[7] See *Lenin and Philosophy and Other Essays*, tr. Ben Brewster (New York: Monthly Review Press, 1971).
[8] Judith Butler in *The Psychic Life of Power: Theories in Subjection* (Stanford University Press, 1997), p. 11.

himself or herself. As Althusser puts it, 'ideology "acts" or "functions" … by that very precise operation which I have called *interpellation* or hailing, and which can be imagined along the lines of the most common everyday … hailing: "Hey, you there!"' [9] As such, subjects (and their formation) become dependent upon the authoritarian Subject. In terms of Christianity, 'the interpellation of individuals as subjects presupposes the "existence" of a unique and central other Subject, in whose name the religious ideology interpellates individuals as subjects;'[10] they are 'subjected to God, *a subject through the Subject and subjected to the Subject*'.[11] Thus, returning to Irigaray, one can see that without this transcendental Subject (a divine made in her image) female subjects cannot establish their identity.

Central to sexual morphology in Freud are the famous Oedipus and castration complexes, in which the libido of the son for the mother is sublimated, following an identification with his father. Once the son recognises the 'lack' of the penis in his mother/sister, then the father embodies the threat of castration related to the son's incestuous desire for the mother. The castration complex resolves the Oedipal situation because the son now represses his incestuous desire. But the father figure, as third party in the Oedipal triangle, in now cathected into an alter ego – a symbol of omnipotence, threat and ideality. It is in the creation of the father as the other, both beneficent and tyrannical, that the son substantiates his own sexual identity. Following in the footsteps of Feuerbach, Freud understands any human relationship to 'God' as the personification of this infantile condition.[12] Since for Freud libido is masculine, a daughter also comes to her sexual identity and orientation to the father through the Oedipus complex. Her passage through the complex is more difficult. The lack she sees in her mother and herself causes resentment against the deceptions of the phallic mother and thus a re-orientation of desire towards her father. She identifies with her mother as the would-be lover of the father.

In her early work – *Speculum of the Other Woman* and *This Sex Which Is Not One* – Irigaray submits Freud's analysis of the morphology of the feminine to a psychoanalytical reading. She raises the question of a sexual identity built upon 'lack', a male economy and only one libido (the masculine one). Without offering an alternative morphology (because this is impossible, given the relationship between male identification with the father and the

---

[9]   Althusser, *Lenin and Philosolophy*, pp. 174, 176.
[10]   Ibid., p. 178.
[11]   Ibid., p. 179.
[12]   See 'The Future of an Illusion' in *Civilization, Society and Religion*, The Penguin Freud Library volume 12 (London: Penguin Books, 1991), pp. 179–241.

entry into the symbolic order, see below), she poses the question of how a woman can identify herself as such when '[s]ubjectivity [is] denied to the woman'.[13] Hence she arrives at the observation above: '[A]s long as woman lacks a divine made in her image she cannot establish her subjectivity.'

The difference between these two accounts of arriving at a subjectivity – the one by Althusser and the other by Freud – is evident in the language each uses to describe the processes. When discussing the complex (if not downright obscure) economy of the morphology of the female subject, Freud comments (albeit negatively) on work conducted on the chemistry of sexual processes.[14] The libido is not aligned with these possible processes, but the grounds for its entire divorce from them is evidently difficult to maintain. This is because throughout his examination of the Oedipus and castration complexes libido is understood as a biological drive. As such there is always a slippage between the roles of the physiological penis and the psychoanalytic phallus. In Freud, the morphology of the sexed subject, and therefore an account of sexual difference – though never appealed to by either Barth or Balthasar – rehearses the same biological reasoning. Althusser, on the other hand, avoids such naturalism or essentialism by defining the economy in terms of ideologies, apparatuses and internalised symbolic identifications. He emphasises that the identities arrived at are imaginary to the extent that they are constructs of the apparatuses that mask any genuine conditions under which individuals are living.[15]

But Althusser does not deal explicitly with the sexed subject, although one can infer from his position that a new set of questions will emerge with respect to examining sexual difference and the divine. Put in a way that we will return to later, Althusser's thinking would suggest we ask about the production of difference (and, concomitantly, sexual difference) as such. We might list such questions as: How is difference recognised? What facilitates or requires the recognition? What is the effect of the recognition of difference? What is theologically significant about the operations of the recognition of difference?

Irigaray is able to negotiate Freud's sexual morphology with respect to Althusser's analysis of the imaginary function of ideology in constituting subjectivity through her response to the work of Jacques Lacan and the *Ecole*

---

[13] *Speculum of the Other Woman*, tr. Gillian C. Gill (Ithaca, N.Y.: Cornell University Press, 1985), p. 133.

[14] 'Female Sexuality' in *On Sexuality*, The Penguin Freud Library volume 7 (London: Penguin Books, 1991), p. 388.

[15] There is a problem here with a residual naturalism in Althusser that issues from his Marxist understanding of ideology as distortion of the real, but that need not concern us here.

Freudienne de Paris. For Lacan developed Freud's economy of masculine desire in his exposition and examination of what he, following the work of Henri Wallon,[16] described as the mirror stage in the formation of the I. Wallon had already recognised this stage, when the child confronts an image of itself in a mirror, as decisive for the move from the imaginary to the symbolic. As Lacan later saw it, in *Ecrits*, the mirror stage lies at the threshold between nature and culture.[17] In the mirror the child first conceives both separation (a subject outside his or her own, an other) and unity (a whole subject, not fragmented parts of a body). In the imaginary phase, prior to the mirror stage, the child only glimpsed moments of being – it had no unified conception of the experience of itself. At first the mirror image is taken as reality itself, but later the child realises this unified I is not real. The child realises that it is a split subject – both unified and divided. It needs these images, these substituting representations of itself in order to identify itself as a subject at all. This stage, then, in which symbolic substitutions are understood as necessary, prepares the child for entry into the symbolic order, the order of names and languages. For Lacan, this stage begins earlier than the sexual differentiation through the castration complex in the Oedipal scenario. The castration complex completes the entry into the symbolic, for identification with the Father is understood as desiring the Phallus which is the symbol of, the signifier for, gratification. Possessing the Phallus will enable the unification of the split subject; no longer inhabiting a position in-between the imaginary and the symbolic. But the child learns that the Phallus is only a symbolic substitute – the desire for satisfaction, wholeness and gratification will endlessly be deferred. The Phallus of the Father, therefore, acts as a transcendental signifier in the symbolic order. The Name-of-the-Father maintains the separation between the mother and the child, and perpetuates the prolongation of desire. In fact, the axiom of desire is to desire itself. The cultural order, language, mediation and substitution arise in this aporia as the law of the Father is established; a law that can never be transgressed. The child will seek endless substitution, for what gratification there is lies in desiring desire. Otherwise there is only aphasia and stasis. If the child cannot be the Phallus, nor have the Phallus, it will construct its identity in and through the chains of substituting signs which are haunted by the Phallic.

Although Irigaray drew attention to what she termed, punning, the 'hom(m)osexuality' of this Lacanian account of sexual differentiation and

[16] See Elizabeth Rudinesco, *Jacques Lacan & Co.: A History of Psychoanalysis in France 1925–1985*, tr. Jeffery Mehlman (London: Free Association Books, 1990), pp. 142–5.
[17] *Écrits*, tr. Alan Sheridan (London: Tavistock Publications, 1977), p. 7.

the law of the symbolic, emphasising that this makes all culture, forms of mediation and representation a product of the male imaginary,[18] she nevertheless accepted the need for a move from the imaginary to the symbolic. She may suggest that women, like the tain at the back of the mirror, are never visible in themselves; or that it is the mother who stands behind the child as it faces the mirror and therefore supports all male specularisation. She may draw attention to the flatness of the mirror,[19] which would accentuate the women's sexual organs only as a hole; never, therefore, reflecting the woman as a sexed person in her own right, only a subject who lacks what the male possesses. But Irigaray throughout explores the possibility of a female imaginary and a female desire, pushing towards an account of *parler femme*, a 'speaking [as] woman' within a psychoanalytical framework.[20] In an interview in the early 1990s, Irigaray emphasises that 'Women are committed to two gigantic tasks: assuming consciousness of the order of language and of one's tongue as sexualised, and also of creating a new symbolic morphology in which she can say: I, sexual being, woman, assert such and such.[21] Changing both the imaginary and the symbolic order is, for Irigaray, working within Lacanian thinking. The task for women is to re-envisage Lacan's Name-of-the-Father in terms of a Name-of-the-Mother. Hence, when Irigaray calls for a God guaranteeing the infinite in order to 'posit a gender' and enable women 'to communicate or commune with each other', the God who interpellates and constitutes that subject is the deferred other, the psychoanalytical understanding of God. Then the mother as transcendental signifier will govern the morphology of personhood and sexual differentiation, and the entry into the symbolic. Without appreciating the relationship between sexuality, symbolism and the need for an Absolute Subject for the morphology of the sexed subject, the declaration that

---

[18] See 'The Poverty of Psychoanalysis' in *The Irigaray Reader*, ed. Margaret Whitford (Oxford: Blackwell, 1991), pp. 79–104.

[19] *Speculum of the Other Woman*, p. 89.

[20] See my essay 'In the Name of the Father and of the Mother' in *Literature and Theology* 8 (3), September (1994), pp. 311–27. A number of critics have noted the problems for feminist thinking raised by Irigaray's appeals to this framework. For example, to what extent by critiquing Lacan is she reinforcing sexual difference on male terms – women becoming again the silent ones, the ones without a voice? Some feminist critics have commented on the essentialism that still seems to pertain to Irigaray's understanding of male and female because of the psychoanalytic framework. Some feminists like Juliet Mitchell and Jacqueline Rose have fought to show how Lacan is emphasising much more the *symbolic* nature of both maleness and femaleness. For a detailed discussion of Irigaray's movements between the poles of biological essentialism and social constructivism see Tina Chanter, *Ethics of Eros: Irigaray's Rewriting of the Philosophers* (London: Routledge, 1994), chapter one.

[21] See Raoul Mortley, *French Philosophers in Conversation* (London: Routledge, 1991), p. 72.

women need to have a God of their own to speak would be open to being dismissed as counterfactual to the social experience of most women.

All this by way of prolegomenon. For in this essay I do not wish to justify or criticise the legitimacy of Irigaray's claims. Throughout the last twenty years of the twentieth century, among Anglo-American feminists in particular, Irigaray's work has been prosecuted, defended and used to open up investigations into questions of gender. It is the way she opens up new possibilities for understanding Christology and sexual difference that her thinking becomes important for this exploration. Battles over Irigaray's work, as Margaret Whitford has pointed out, can operate a restrictive closure. Now, she suggests, is a time to 'engage with Irigaray and open up the possibility of using her work as a feminist resource'.[22] First, then, I will examine Irigaray's own portrait of Jesus Christ, particularly with reference to her remarks on the feminist theologians Elisabeth Schüssler-Fiorenza and Mary Daly. I will relate this embryonic Christology to what, following the feminist deconstruction of her early work, has become the constructive direction of her project as a whole – the advancement of a sexuate[23] culture. Secondly, I will develop theologically Irigaray's ideas, on Christ, sexual difference and the metaphysics of desire, drawing out their implications for Christology.

Irigaray's Christ

In her long review article of Schüssler-Fiorenza's book *In Memory of Her*, entitled 'Equal to Whom?', Irigaray declares that she began the book with astonishment and joy only to find she was eventually disappointed. Her joy lay in Schüssler-Fiorenza's reconstruction of the women in Jesus's life: 'The way in which they are described in the text bears the hallmarks of Aphroditism.'[24] The text here is the Gospels as Schüssler-Fiorenza read them. By 'Aphroditism' Irigaray refers to a female representation of the divine love

---

[22]   See 'Reading Irigaray in the Nineties' in Carolyn Burke, Naomi Schor and Margaret Whitford eds., *Engaging with Irigaray* (New York: Columbia University Press, 1994), p. 15. Prior to this collection of essays came Margaret Whitford ed., *Luce Irigaray: Philosophy in the Feminine* (London: Routledge, 1991). In the 1980s Irigaray's work was substantially introduced to the Anglo-American public through Toril Moi, *Sexual/Textual Politics: Feminist Literary Theory* (London: Methuen, 1985) and Elizabeth Grosz, *Sexual Subversions: Three French Feminists* (Sydney: Allen and Unwin, 1989).

[23]   The adjective in French is *sexué* or sexed, but it is usually translated 'sexuate'. Similarly Irigaray's *la sexuation* is usually translated 'sexualisation'.

[24]   'Egales à qui?' in *Critique* 480, May (1987), pp. 420–37, p. 424. Translations from this article throughout the essay are my own. An English translation by Robert L. Mazzola is available, 'Equal to Whom?', *Differences* 1 (2) (1989), pp. 59–76.

within whose tradition she believes Christ's female disciples stood. In *Marine Lover* she details the genealogy of the male-god, placing the 'crucified one' in the trajectory of those other representations of male divinity – Dionysos, the god of desire, and Apollo, the god of order and integrated form. Christ is significantly the one who is historically incarnate – *et incarnatus est* is repeated like a refrain through her chapter 'epistle to the last Christians'. Compared with Dionysos and Apollo, he is 'another nature still'[25] – though she does not explore this nature any further. She refers though to a cryptic text in Hölderlin: '"he perfects that which was lacking in others, so that the presence of the Divine Ones might be total".'[26] Jesus Christ's female disciples, then, offer a gendered love that is different from yet complementary to Jesus's own. He is the god of love, and, since love must be incarnated, he has a sexuate body; they incarnate love also, a female love in a genealogy symbolically represented by Aphrodite. Irigaray rejoices, then, that Schüssler-Fiorenza's work opens up a space between Jesus Christ and the Christian Church's appropriation, interpretation and policing of this figure. Following a line of thought in Nietzsche that characterises the Church as a product of *ressentiment* she had written: 'Doesn't Christianity ... [r]emain the prisoner of hate? With its Distance and Difference ... Certainly, Christianity is thus. What about Christ?'[27] Now Schüssler-Fiorenza has helped her towards answering her final question.

Her own portrayal of Christ maintains this space between the Church and its founder. She asks whether we might not interpret the 'Christic symbol as a consecration of love ... as a quest for some incredible nearness in life'. She is struck by his use of touch and how he 'is respectful of bodily space, of sensual space, of openings in the skin'.[28] It is because of this that she asks, rhetorically, 'Was he really untouchable?' This question is part of a larger one: 'What does it really mean that the word was made flesh?'[29] We will return to those questions in a moment. She is also struck by the fact that unlike Dionysos and Apollo, 'this man-god does not exist in a triumphant self-sufficiency'.[30] This man who 'did not wish to enter violently into the body of the other', and who therefore maintains difference, installs it with his presence, is 'herald of an age of love'.[31] She concludes her 'epistle

---

[25] *Marine Lover of Friedrich Nietzsche*, tr. Gillian C. Gill (New York: Columbia University Press, 1991), p. 181.
[26] Ibid., p. 180.
[27] Ibid., p. 183.
[28] Ibid., p. 182.
[29] Ibid., p. 179.
[30] Ibid., p. 182.
[31] Ibid., p. 184.

to the last Christians' with an observation again on the space within which she has reinscribed him:

> But why a god of love, given the effects and the illustrations we know about?
> Unless exclusive love of the Father is only a partial translation of his message
> ... The life of Christ, perhaps, cannot be reduced to the *pathein* of the
> Father's will. It would open the way for the transcendence of the other that
> has always been covered over by the Father–son paradigm ... This reevalua-
> tion is possible only if he goes beyond the Father–son relationship. If he
> announces – beyond Christianity? – that only through difference can the
> incarnation unfold.[32]

It is this idea that incarnate transcendence, the integration of the divine and the corporeal, is only available through the establishment of difference, a sexuate difference, which contrasts Irigaray's approach to Christ with Schüssler-Fiorenza's (and Daly's). For what disappoints her about Schüssler-Fiorenza's account is what she observes as a reduction of the divine (with respect to the women) and a reduction of the human (with respect to Jesus Christ). Schüssler-Fiorenza reduces the divine in women by examining Christ's female disciples simply as a sociological fact which the Church has effaced. She does not read these women theologically, as involved in an economy of responding to the love of Christ with their own love. She does not read their discipleship – I put words into Irigaray's mouth at this point – soteriologically. Irigaray pointedly asks whether Jesus interests himself with women because they were numbered among the poor and oppressed or because they were women. Schüssler-Fiorenza, wishing to develop a femi-nist theology in terms of a more general hermeneutic of liberation, would say the former. But Irigaray believes this is wrong. 'Women, in fact, are not poor people among so many others. Rather, the exploitation of women, as half of humanity, represents human exploitation which makes possible all the other forms. This exploitation is fundamentally cultural and secondarily socio-economic.'[33] The reality of women calls into question the governing male ontology, the hierarchical ontology, which supports such exploitation. And so Irigaray finds Mary Daly's interest in the 'cosmic dimensions of culture' more incisive[34] because it is concerned with the redemption of creation, with divinity materialised. Schüssler-Fiorenza, Irigaray suggests, wishes to divinise Christ but not women. Women therefore have to neuter

---

[32] Ibid., pp. 187–8.

[33] 'Egales à qui?', p. 425.

[34] Ibid., p. 436. Concern for the cosmic dimensions illustrates the way Irigaray's thinking is pro-foundly influenced by her Catholic background, with its notion of the *sacramentum mundi*.

themselves to obtain an 'identification with a masculine gender'.[35] In divin-
ising Jesus Christ she establishes his identity beyond sexuality, thus reducing
his humanity. And so Irigaray asks if Schüssler-Fiorenza sufficiently tackles
the question of incarnation, of sexualised divinity.

To raise and explore the question of sexualised divinity is fundamental to
Irigaray's project. The corollary of this is: 'Christ is not of our sex as he is in
the manner of men … It is impossible to ask that a woman become holy,
absolved of fault, if she does not recognise her mother as potentially holy. A
god-made man or a Father God are not enough to sanctify woman [*le genre
féminin*].'[36] But before we enlist Irigaray in the post-Christian camps of Mary
Daly (or Daphne Hampson) – in which she certainly does not belong – we
need to appreciate her objection to Daly's position. For while she sympa-
thises with the encouragement Daly has given to an *ekklesia* of sisters, Irigaray
questions the value of such a position for religion and women. 'Personally, I
prefer to make every attempt to keep the differences [*la dimension de la
mixité*], because sexual difference seems to me to assure the limits of being
human which allows space for the divine.'[37] Elsewhere, in her essay 'Belief
Itself' and in her chapter 'epistle to the last Christians', Irigaray conceives the
coming of the holy, its incarnation, as only possible in the space between the
wings of the two angels facing each other on either side of the ark of the
covenant. It is important that the wings, arching over to meet each other, do
not touch. Difference is essential: the sexual difference of the couple.

Debates have raged among feminists as to the extent to which Irigaray is
reinscribing a metaphysics of heterosexuality.[38] Evidence for such a metaphysics does seem to become more available in her later work.[39] Some have
seen Irigaray as playing with essentialism as a strategy required at this point
in time for the feminist agenda.[40] I would wish to emphasise a more Lacanian (rather than Freudian) reading. Certainly, I believe such a reading of
her work is more productive for theological thinking and gets us beyond
the theological analyses of sexual difference in Barth and Balthasar. On
this reading, Irigaray juxtaposes to the phallus the two lips of the vagina.
Both the phallus and the two lips are emblematic, not biological. They are
symbolic positions that do not necessarily map onto bodies possessing male

---

[35] Ibid., p. 432.
[36] Ibid., pp. 432–3.
[37] Ibid., p. 435.
[38] See footnote 20.
[39] See in particular *Elemental Passions*, tr. Joanne Collie and Judith Still (London: Athlone Press,
1992); *Je, Tu, Nous: Towards a Culture of Difference*, tr. Alison Martin (London: Routledge, 1993); and
I Love to You: Sketch of a Possible Felicity in History, tr. Alison Martin (London: Routledge, 1996).
[40] See Margaret Whitford in *Engaging Irigaray*, p. 15.

and female genitalia. The proximity of the phallus and the two lips gives rises to the economy of desire, but Irigaray leaves open (certainly in her work in *This Sex Which Is Not One*) whether the sexes involved in the attraction are opposite or the same. In doing this she blurs neat distinctions between sex, gender and sexuality, and raises questions about what it means to be identified as male or female; what it means to *produce* difference.

Where does this situate Christ, then? And where does this leave feminist theology as it wrestles with Christological issues, particularly the issues of incarnation and redemption? Irigaray creates for Christ a space which is quite distinctive; it is a space that opens out suggestively rather than contracts towards some doctrinal prescription. And despite Irigaray's repeated insistence that although Jesus may not have been opposed to women, 'he does not furnish for them specific [*certaines*] representations of themselves, of their genealogy',[41] the space she opens is suggestively inclusive: 'In the body of the Son of Man there appears, in the form of a wound, the place that, in women, is naturally open.'[42] In other words, this 'Son of Man' bears both phallic and two lip markers. No doubt Irigaray is aware of medieval Catholic readings of the wound in the side of Christ as a vagina opening to give birth to the Church, a place where the waters break and the blood flows.[43] On Christ's blessing of the fruits of the earth, wheat and grape, at the Last Supper, Irigaray observes that he is faithful 'to the very old traditions with which he re-establishes, perhaps, a bridge. These traditions are gynocratic and matriarchal. Does he appropriate them to himself or does he make himself the mediator of them?'[44] Irigaray does not answer the question; the question is a methodological ploy to keep the space in which Christ's sexual identity is situated open, to keep possibilities in play. She, like Julian of Norwich on her own meditation upon the wound in the side of Christ,[45]

---

[41] 'Egales à qui?', p. 436.

[42] *Marine Lover*, p. 166.

[43] See the work here of Caroline Walker Bynum: *Jesus as Mother: Studies in the Spirituality of the High Middles Ages* (Berkeley: University of California Press, 1982), pp. 110–69; *Holy Feast and Holy Fast* (Berkeley: University of California Press, 1987), which has a reproduction of Christ as Mother, *The Saviour* by Quirizio da Murano; and *Fragmentation and Redemption* (New York: Zone Books, 1991). Philippa Berry, in her essay 'The Burning Glass: Paradoxes of Feminist Revelation in *Speculum*' (*Engaging Irigaray*, pp. 229–46) draws attention to Irigaray's indebtedness to the mystical writings of the High Middle Ages: Jan van Ruysbroeck, Angela of Foligno, Catherine of Sienna, Teresa of Avila and Marguerite Porete.

[44] 'Egales à qui?', p. 437.

[45] See *Revelation of Divine Love*, ed. Marion Glasscoe (Exeter University Press, 1993), chapters 24–26. Julian of Norwich's tenth revelation of the wound in the side of Christ leads directly to the eleventh revelation concerning his mother, Mary, and the twelfth revelation concerning the Church and its experience of mystical and ineffable love (what Irigaray would term *jouissance*).

moves from the wound to the womb that enfleshed and bore him. 'Mary, the mother of Jesus, represents, perhaps, a figure of Aphrodite.'[46] There is, again, no incarnation of the divine, no operation of the divine, which is simply male-engendered. Difference and the economy of desire that is sexed incarnate the holy. 'It is in this sense that I have suggested that the incarnation of the divine in Jesus Christ is a part of something larger [*est partielle*]', she writes, and adds that this conforms to Christ's own self-presentation in John's Gospel that he needs to depart so the Paraclete may come.

We will return to John's Gospel in a moment, but this is where Irigaray leaves her Christological reflections while recognising that the spiritual understanding of sexual difference 'could be our "salvation" if we thought it through'.[47] Irigaray's work has facilitated that thinking by creating a space for a contemporary redescription of the sacred and the incarnational. Her work has explored, for women, a new transcendentalism (it must therefore have implications for men also). It is a transcendentalism which is opposed to the Gnostic division between the spiritual and the bodily. She explores what she has termed a 'sensible transcendental'.[48] Catholic and Orthodox Christianity has always emphasised its own sacramental and Christological understanding of an embodied divinity, but Irigaray explicitly associates her notion of the 'sensible transcendental' with the difference between sexuate bodies in relation to each other. I have elsewhere pointed to some of the difficulties for theological thinking of Irigaray's concept of transcendence;[49] briefly, it is a question of the relationship between self-transcendence and an encounter with the transcendent God – a question concerning the extent to which this notion is another variation of Spinoza's pantheism. Nevertheless, the divine, operating through an economy of love and desire, is fore-grounded in her work as in Christian theological enquiry, and presents new possibilities for a philosophy of religion (one not founded upon what Genevieve Lloyd has called the 'man of reason').[50]

---

[46] 'Egales à qui?', p. 430.

[47] *An Ethics of Sexual Difference*, tr. Gillian C. Gill and Carolyn Burke (London: Athlone Press, 1993), p. 5.

[48] See *An Ethics of Sexual Difference* where this notion is continually explored in terms of the dynamic relationship between love and the other in dialogue with major philosophical voices of the western tradition.

[49] See footnote 20.

[50] Genevieve Lloyd, *Man of Reason: 'Male' and 'Female' in Western Philosophy* (London: Routledge, 1993). There have been several attempts by feminists to develop such an alternative mode of philosophy of religion. See Grace Jantzen, *Becoming Divine*, and Pamela Sue Anderson, *A Feminist Philosophy of Religion*.

Christology after Irigaray

On the basis of Irigaray's remarks about Christ (and the psychoanalytic and philosophical frameworks within which she develops them) let me, then, begin to think through aspects of Christology. The exploration, it seems to me, must cover three aspects of the person and work of Jesus Christ. Irigaray asks why, when we examine the person of Christ, 'is his sexuate incarnation denied'?[51] So, first, we must begin to open up questions on the sexuality of this Son of God. Secondly, consequently, we need to examine the relation between the divine and human eros. Thirdly, on the basis of these two investigations we need to rethink the doctrines of the Trinity, ecclesiology. For any examination of Christ relates to the nature and operation of the second person of the Trinity; and any examination of the body of Christ relates to the nature and the work of the Church which, following the ascension of the historical body, becomes itself the mystical body. The development, then, of a sexuate Christology, a theology of sexual difference, has wider dogmatic implications.

In the chapter 'The Displaced Body of Jesus Christ', in my *Cities of God*,[52] I treat more extensively both the sexuality of Jesus the Christ and the displacement that occurs in the shift from his historical body to the Church as his ecclesial and sacramental body. In the essay that follows this one I develop some of the cultural and political issues in the construction of the sexuality of Jesus the Christ. So here I wish to focus on the implications of a sexuate Christology for a soteriological economy of response that examines the operation of sexual difference. Similarly, previous essays have explored much more thoroughly the question of the relationship between divine and human eros. So only those aspects of that relationship that bear on a Christocentric account of sexual difference will be examined here – and examined with reference to the two passages from John's Gospel (of Mary's meeting with Jesus at the garden tomb and Thomas's encounter with the risen Christ) at the centre of the Christological investigations of the previous chapter.

(a) The sexuate body of the Son of Man

Can we really speak of incarnation if we castrate the Christ? 'What Christ did not take, he did not redeem', Gregory of Nazianzus (among other early

---

[51] 'Egales à qui?', p. 430.
[52] London: Routledge, 2001, pp. 97–116.

Church Fathers) reminds us.[53] By an evasion of his sexuality are we not already setting our feet, if not on some docetic trajectory, then on a path leading towards Apollonian enhypostasis (the heresy Gregory is countering)? There is a need to explore what it is to be sexuate, a person experiencing all the passions that other human beings have experienced (and yet without sin) – as Hebrews 4.15 puts it – and God. As we have seen, Irigaray does not reduce being sexuate to the categories of physiological sex or gender. Sex is already gendered as gender is already sex. As such, those feminists who opt out of Christianity because of the maleness of its Saviour can be seen as locking themselves into an essentialism her work renders irreducible. Michel Foucault takes this further by pointing out the historical dimensions of the mediation of sex, sexuality and gender.[54] While not then wishing to deny that Jesus has the genitalia of a male, the social construction and representation of his sexual identity (what normally constitutes gender) and the operations of his sexual desire are not so easily determined. We have no access to this Jew from Nazareth outside of discursive accounts of his life and teaching (in the Gospels). We have no way of calculating the extent to which, in the translation from one context (Aramaic-speaking Palestine) to another (the Greek-speaking Jewish-Christian diaspora or Latin-speaking Gentile Rome), his sexuate nature was refigured. The particularity of bodies, including his – their identification, representation and the values assigned to both – is embedded in complex socio-sexual economies or 'force-relations'.[55] What is certain, as Irigaray points out in portraying Christ in terms of both the phallus and the two lips, is that there is no stable atemporal identity available.

In both the Johannine passages we examined in the last essay an erotic economy is evident. The eros is inseparable from the way the author dramatically isolates both figures with respect to the Christ. This is most pronounced in the garden encounter with Mary, since the Thomas pericope has no synoptic tradition behind it, while the visitation to the tomb by women is recorded in all three synoptic Gospels. In Mark three women approach the empty tomb, in Matthew there are two and in Luke the number is uncertain. But in John's account the male company of Peter and

---

[53] *Epistle*, ci: to Cledonius, the priest against Apollinarius.

[54] The attempt to define 'the regime of power–knowledge–pleasure that sustains the discourse on human sexuality,' what he later terms 'bio-history' and examines as technologies of 'bio-power' is the burden of Foucault's *History of Sexuality*. See volume one, *An Introduction*, tr. Robert Hurley (London: Allen Lane, 1979), p. 11.

[55] The term is Foucault's. It is used to describe the multifaceted power mechanisms within which any object is situated and discursively represented. See *History of Sexuality: An Introduction*, pp. 92–102.

John exit stage left and Mary encounters Jesus alone, who enters stage right. The eros of this encounter would be more emphatic if, as has been argued, the resurrected Jesus is naked.[56]

We noted in the last essay how both Mary's and Thomas's encounter with the Christ involves embodiment and (if we take touch as implied in both events) a crossing over from one body to the other. Mary and Jesus embrace in a garden; the pupil–teacher relation is conflated with the relation between a man and a woman that is suggestively mythologised as a return to the Garden of Eden and a reworking of the *Canticum Canticorum*. And stories of Mary's sexual intimacy with Jesus that have issued from readings of this Scriptural text (among others) testify to the awareness of the eroticism – from the Gnostic Gospels to Scorsese's *Last Temptation of Christ*.[57] Thomas touches the raw flesh of Jesus, placing his hand into the very wound that in John is symbolic of the vaginal opening through which the community of Christ's body is born [John 19.34]. The disciples only see, they only behold. A far greater intimacy is granted to Thomas, a more corporeal intimacy than the head of the beloved disciple resting on Jesus's breast [John 13.23]. It is again a suggestively mythologised intimacy – thrusting into the side of the second Adam from which the new Eve issues. Caravaggio captures the eroticism of that action, its carnality, its penetration, in his famous painting of the scene.

In the first passage, to employ an entirely anachronistic word, the eroticism is heterosexual. In the second passage, to employ a similarly anachronistic word, the eroticism is homosexual. In both there is difference, a difference between self and other remaining even in the epiphany of recognition that overcomes, to some extent, that difference. In both accounts what is sex – being male and female, being male and male – is highly ambivalent. It is ambivalent partly because of the suggestive mythologising – Mary as Eve, Jesus as Adam; Jesus as a hermaphrodite and Thomas as opening up the womb of Christ. But then sex is always a mythopoetic affair, riding on fantasy.[58]

The difference, the affinity, the eroticism and the sex of those involved in the actions are inseparable from speaking, words and the translation of words

---

[56] See K. Kästner, 'Noli me tangere', *Biblische Zeitschrift* (1915), pp. 344–53.

[57] For a detailed account of the figure of Mary Magdalene as it developed in the Middle Ages see Katherine Ludwig Jansen, *The Making of the Magdalene: Preaching and Popular Devotion in the Later Middle Ages* (Princeton University Press, 2001). For a survey of the tradition see David Brown, *Discipleship and Imagination: Christian Tradition and Truth* (Cambridge University Press, 2000), pp. 31–61.

[58] See Slavoj Žižek, *Plague of Fantasies* (London: Verso, 1997).

from one language to another. We observed in the last chapter the forms of discursive exchange in both these passages. What is constituted is the economy of these responses is relation; relation called forth by, and subordinated to, the presence of Christ. And the telos of relation is ultimately salvation. We do not see the redemption of either Mary or Thomas – but then what would such a redemption look like? What we see is a healing, like the woman with the haemorrhage is healed and told her faith has saved her.[59] But this telos is inseparable from the learning of difference and affinity, distance and proximity through the establishment of a relation that is erotic beyond being simply sexual.[60]

(b) Divine and human eros

Christological enquiry cannot be divorced from a doctrine of creation. Furthermore, desire is both the creator and the creation of space. Only where there is space, where there is distance, where there is difference, can there be love that desires, that draws, that seeks participation. In one of Balthasar's explorations of pneumatology, he writes: 'The basis of the biblical religion is the *diastasis*, the distance between God and the creature that is the elementary presupposition that makes it possible for man to understand and appreciate the unity that grace brings about.'[61] The doctrine of creation is founded upon a fundamental difference that opens up all possibilities for desire. It is a difference at the heart of any Trinitarian conception of the Godhead; a Trinitarian difference opened up by Christ, the second Person, and interpreted by the Spirit, the third Person. Christ's difference begets the creative circulation of kenotic giving. In the beginning God created by a process of separation. It is the Spirit that brooded over the chaos ready to give birth to form. It is the Spirit that moved upon the seminal waters, separating the genetic blocks of creations. Desire is built then into the substructure of creation; and in that creation is the incarnation of desire and difference within the Trinity itself.

---

[59] See the second essay in this collection, 'The Schizoid Christ'.

[60] See Michel Henry, *Incarnation*, pp. 311–18 for a discussion of the relationship between nihilism and an eroticism that is simply reduced to sexuality. This reduction is found even in Merleau-Ponty, who in his celebrated chapter on sexuality and the body speaks of Eros as Libido.

[61] *Explorations in Theology: Creator Spiritus*, tr. Brian McNeil, CRV (San Francisco: Ignatius Press, 1993), p. 173. See a similar account by Julia Kristeva in *In the Beginning Was Love: Psychoanalysis and Faith*, tr. Arthur Goldhammer (New York: Columbia University Press, 1988): 'In reality, it is the biblical God who inaugurates separation at the beginning of creation. He creates a division which is also the mark of his presence' (p. 31).

It has been argued[62] that certain feminist theologians (Grace Jantzen, Isabel Carter Heywood and Sally McFague are mentioned) have dissolved the particularity of Jesus Christ into the 'Christification of creation'. This is understood to be the attribution 'to world functions' of terms 'which classical theology reserves for Jesus Christ, the Incarnate Word of God'[63] – that is, incarnation, redemption, kenosis, 'begottenness'. The problems of confusing Christ with creation are that Jesus Christ is made an example and there is an exaltation of 'the theologian as the locus for revelation'.[64] But if we are to escape these problems and yet nevertheless affirm the incarnate Word of God in the particularity of Jesus Christ, can we evade examining the operation of desire in him? Since desire is integral to the Trinity, to creation and to being a sexuate creature, can we cordon off discussions of his sexuality?[65]

The same issue can be approached from another angle; and it is this angle that highlights the resources of Irigaray's work for future Christological investigation. This angle is best attained through the question, Where does Christology begin? Where does it take place? I am not asking about the theological discourse and its various points of manifestation over the centuries, but about the place where the divinity of Jesus of Nazareth reveals itself as a meaningful and relevant operation *pro nobis*. It cannot take place solely within himself to himself – for that assumes he lives for himself alone, which is a refusal of difference, a refusal to attend to Irigaray's observation: he 'is respectful of bodily space, of sensual space, of openings in the skin'. This is an observation borne out by the two encounters with Christ we examined in John's Gospel. Revelation of Christ is a revelation of the operation of Christ in opening a relation that recognises difference, and in that recognition there is both redemption and reconciliation. So often modern Christology examines Christ by beginning with his autonomy, by assuming a philosophy of the subject and the cult of the personality that this fostered: Who is this God-man? But this understanding of personhood – 'an inward-

---

[62]   David Scott, 'Creation as Christ: A Problematic Theme in Some Feminist Theology' in Alvin J. Kimel Jr. ed., *Speaking the Christian God* (Grand Rapids, Mich.: William B. Eerdmans, 1992), pp. 237–58.

[63]   Ibid., p. 250.

[64]   Ibid., p. 257.

[65]   See John McIntyre, *The Shape of Christology* (London: SCM, 1966) for a typical line of dogmatic enquiry: 'After redemption, when the image of God is remade in him [Christ] he [generic man] appears to transcend sex ... There is no need to construe [the Creator–creation relation] in sexual marital terms. In fact I doubt such nonsense need detain us' (pp. 110–11). And yet the Christian tradition provides overwhelming evidence of thinking through divinity and sexuality in 'marital terms'.

ness of self-sufficiency, of autonomous powers, of ordering by reason' – is a historical and cultural product.[66] I would suggest that modern Christology has been, for the most part, concerned with the question of who rather than the operations of salvation such that we ask the question who at all. Modern Christology, as such, has been locked into a redefinition of the Chalcedonian formula in terms of the Hegelian Subject as consciousness. This subject was not simply Hegel's. It was, of course, bequeathed to Hegel – by Luther and Melanchthon,[67] by Descartes's *cogito* and Kant's transcendental ego. But Hegel, in the third part of his *Encyclopaedia of the Philosophical Sciences*, described an economic development of the Subject that overcame metaphysical dualism. The stasis of Descartes's *cogito* and Kant's transcendental unity of self-consciousness is now graphed on to a rapacious historical development towards Absolute identity. Metaphysical dualism can only wrestle, Christologically, with old questions that haunted the quarrels with Gnostics, Nestorians and various subordinationists. But personhood, now defined by Hegel in terms of individualised consciousnesses participating within the economy of the Spirit which sublates difference and otherness,[68] offered theologians a model for understanding how the two natures of Chalcedonian Christology were related to 'fully conscious coincidence'.[69] This model and process could articulate a new second Adam Christology: personhood as *homo dialecticus* and Christ as the perfection of humanity who presents an encompassing and unified identity. This is the Christology of Schleiermacher's *Glaubenslehre* (the natural and the supernatural, finite and infinite, in the person and work of Christ as the perfect communication of God-consciousness);[70] the Christology of Barth (as we saw in the Introduction); the Christology of Tillich (Christ as the symbol for the integration of divided and angst-ridden existence with the ground of ultimate reality); the Christology of Rahner (Jesus Christ, the Logos-Person, as the perfection of the relation between transcendentality and historicity); the Christology of Moltmann (Jesus the Son returning an ever-renewing creation to the Father through the Spirit). All these major modern Christologies isolate the figure

---

[66] Charles Taylor, *Sources of the Modern Self: The Making of Modern Identity* (Cambridge University Press, 1989), p. 158.

[67] See B.A. Gerrish, *Continuing the Reformation: Essays on Modern Religious Thought* (University of Chicago Press, 1993), pp. 17–37.

[68] *Lecture on the Philosophy of Religion*, ed. Peter C. Hodson (Berkeley: University of California Press, 1988), p. 469.

[69] The phrase is used to describe Hegel's model by Peter Dews, *Logics of Disintegration: Post-Structuralist Thought and the Claims of Critical Theory* (London: Verso, 1987), p. 31.

[70] See *The Christian Faith*, ed. H.R. MacKintosh and J.S. Stewart (Edinburgh: T. & T. Clark, 1989), pp. 3–31, 374–475.

of Jesus Christ and attempt to find ways of defining this subject as the perfection of subjectivity.

Irigaray is part of that anti-Hegelian trajectory[71] that would include various forms of dialogicalism and negative dialectics. Like Foucault and Kristeva, she wishes to move knowledge from the domain of the rapacious self-affirmation of disembodied consciousness, Hegel's *Geistessubjekt*, and locate it in the space, the interval, the hiatus that Gillian Rose has called the broken middle,[72] the between of the couple. Personhood is not Hegel's *Geistessubjekt*. For Irigaray (and Kristeva would agree with her), personhood is constituted only through participation in an economy of desire for and by the other: an economy of response. It is constituted, and perpetually reconstituted, not in its autonomy but in its difference: a difference that provokes a dynamic form of recognition. For Irigaray it is not that subjectivity is dissolved, but that sexuate subjects are always *sub-jectum*, and as such, are always being called beyond themselves. They live beyond autonomy because of desire of the other (both subjective and objective genitive). They are drawn into and they extend an eros that is both human and divine. The I is always moving in the orbit of the you, creating a space for a 'we' that is neither the dissolution of the I and the you nor a transcendental identity as such, but an opening onto the impossible – the impossibility of that final identification as 'we'. That opening onto impossibility issues from and is maintained by sexual difference. This concept of the ecstatic subject that Irigaray places at the heart of a feminist resistance to *parler homme* demands a new syntax. In some of her essays she struggles to compose such a syntax:

> I carry you with me everywhere. Not like a child, a burden, a weight, however beloved and precious. You are not *in me*. I do not contain you or retain you in my stomach, my arms, my head. Nor in my memory, my mind, my language. You are there, like my skin. With you I am certain of existing beyond all appearances, all disguises, all destinations. I am assured of living

---

71 See Judith Butler's detailed study of the reception of Hegel in France following the lectures of Alexandre Kojève (and the resistances to it), *Subjects of Desire* (New York: Columbia University Press, 1987), particularly section 4.

72 *The Broken Middle: Out of Our Ancient Society* (Oxford: Blackwell, 1992). In an intellectual *tour de force*, Rose defends the thesis that the 'broken middle' is the site of the sacred. Rose, unlike Irigaray, examines the middle in terms of a rereading of Hegel's thought. She ends her book memorably with a move towards negative theology: 'The more the middle is dirempted the more it becomes sacred in ways that configure its further diremption' (p. 307). There are lines of enquiry that open up here between what Rose is suggesting and what I call the economy of distance in the second essay in this collection. See Rowan D. Williams's theological coda to Gillian Rose's work in 'Between Politics and Metaphysics: Reflections in the Wake of Gillian Rose', *Modern Theology* 11 (1), January (1995), pp. 3–22.

because you are duplicating my life ... How can I say it differently? We exist only as two.[73]

If we exist only as two, then Christology must be explored in terms of the interpersonal, the inter-erotic, not the isolated individual, the self-contained one. And so Jesus Christ as God incarnate can of himself only reveal to the extent he is recognised; he can only reconcile and redeem all to the extent he is responded to. Christology begins with the operation of Christ 'between'. We start there because it is only in our relation to him that we can subsequently contemplate all the other questions that Christology calls forth (creation, sin, sanctification, ecclesiology, what it is to be human, etc.). We are attracted to Christ and confronted by him as we draw near in that attraction – like Mary and Thomas. We are caught up in a wonder, a meditation that draws us into the gravitational fields of God's love. To take up a metaphor employed by Kierkegaard, we are caught up in a form of seduction. We desire him; our desire is evoked by his desire for us. Christology begins here in the economy of erotic response. Balthasar often analyses this in terms of the scholastic vocabulary of *processio* and *missio* or vocation (a word that bears comparison with Althusser's 'interpellation'). Personhood is the enactment of one's vocation (or role in the theodrama), but the dynamic for this enactment is the love of God. The work of Christ in Christian salvation is a Trinitarian work, for Christ's *missio* was a expression of his *processio*. Faith, for Balthasar, is 'a movement of love that makes directly towards the person of Jesus, hears his call to follow him and answers'.[74] Like Mary and Thomas, no one stands before Christ as a subject to an object. To use the Pauline phrase, each stands *en Christo* and, as such, reflections upon living *en Christo* (Christology) are ongoing. Christology is rooted in praxis – in liturgy, in prayer, in relation. The nature of Christ is continually being revealed – it is an eternal action that *is* soteriological. The divinity of Jesus of Nazareth is birthed in and by the circulations of attraction, distance and desire, understood as the interplay of divine and human eros. He becomes Christ, that which operates through him is recognised as Christic, in relation to us as he becomes the object of our desire as we are the object of his.

In *An Ethics of Sexual Difference*, Irigaray observes that 'by wishing to give, he or she constitutes the other as receptacle'.[75] The nature of love is not just to give, it is to create a space for reception. It is not simply a pouring out, an

---

[73] 'When Our Lips Speak Together' in *This Sex Which Is Not One*, trs. Catherine Porter and Carolyn Burke (Ithaca, N.Y.: Cornell University Press, 1985), p. 216.

[74] *Explorations in Theology: Creator Spiritus*, pp. 90–1.

[75] *An Ethics of Sexual Difference*, p. 55.

emptying of oneself on behalf of the other, it is the creation, by that kenosis, of a place for the entry of the other, for participation. The kenosis of Christ, his self-abandoning love articulated in Philippians 2.6–11, creates a place within which divinity is made manifest. Jesus of Nazareth is totally enfolded within a Christic operation that reveals itself *in* and *as* that particular one *in relation to* and *in* others: an economy of redemption in an economy of response whereby divine eros transfigures human eros's simple demand for self-satisfaction. It transfigures mutual masturbation into divine intercourse.

Being biologically male, then, does not restrict Jesus's sexuality. Irigaray herself presents us with a description of Jesus Christ in which both his gender and his sexuality seem continually to overflow a particular chromosomal structure. The divine eros is presenced in and through this one man's sexuate spirituality that draws into its orbit both Mary and Thomas. The cross is the final qualification and disruption of Jesus's male biological form. Significantly, the cross, for Irigaray, is a profoundly feminine symbol. For the 'mouth lips and the genital lips do not point in the same direction', she writes. These two 'sets of lips …, moreover, cross over each other like the arms of the cross'.[76] If, in the resurrection, Jesus Christ remains a physical body, it is a wounded body;[77] a body bearing the marks in his flesh of both the male and the female sex – without his being androgynous.

The focus of a Christology and an economy of salvation thought through on the basis of Irigaray's work will not be Jesus Christ, but Jesus-Christ-with-us. Jesus is a historical figure in a Christological and ongoing narrative. His divinity (and ours) is meaningless outside his relation to others and our relations to him: the economy of response. A male figure, then, is not the focus for salvation. There must be installed relation (rather than Hegelian sublation), and that installation requires difference. There can only be salvation with Christ, through Christ, if there is sexual difference.

(c) The Trinity and ecclesiology

Difference, thought theologically, is rooted in the difference of *hypostasis* in the Trinity; the operation of God in the world opens up the recognition

---

76 Ibid., p. 18.

77 The wounded body of Christ, even following the resurrection, can perhaps be understood theologically in terms of a love that cannot operate beyond the violences which are the necessary consequence of the forced relations within which all objects and actions participate. Irigaray's insistence on the primordiality of sexual difference, while still wishing to envisage a utopian marriage, also recognises that the body will always bear its scars. Love can only be operative where there is incompleteness.

of differences-in-relation that is foundational for the sociality of the Church. It is in and through the movement of these relations that salvation announces itself. In thinking this trinodal relation in the wake of Irigaray's work, salvation is not the overcoming of difference, but its celebration. The perichoretic circle of love in and through difference – which is the model for the operation of the Trinitarian *dunamis* in Origen, Gregory of Nyssa and Augustine – offers us a model that has affinities with the spiritual economy of desire as outlined by Irigaray. For love, as the nature of and the creative mechanism for salvation, can only function through the recognition of difference-in-relation. The interdependence of love, faith and hope is manifest in desire that births a faith that cannot but hope. And hope reaches eschatologically towards the perfection of love – the abandonment to difference-in-relation as such.[78] There is no immanent trinity that is not economic – the Godhead holds nothing back in its desire for what it has created. Our experience of salvation in the created order, as Mary and Thomas show us, is always an experience of what Irigaray terms sensible transcendence, a sexuate divinity.

Having examined sexual difference with respect to Christology, at this point we might raise questions Irigaray raises: 'It is true that Christianity tells us that God is three persons, three manifestations, and that the third stage of the manifestation occurs as a wedding between the spirit and the bride. Is this supposed to inaugurate the divine for, in, with women? The female? ... We have no female trinity.'[79] Let us put to one side the suggestions of modalism; the point raised concerns the 'hom(m)osexuality' and the 'hom(m)osociality' of the Christian Trinity. But this is where Irigaray herself needs a better grounding in the tradition and a more self-reflexive understanding of the symbolics of sexuality that she has advocated. As Balthasar writes: 'the only word that can indicate this act whereby the Father is the origin, without having any origin himself, is love'.[80] To return Balthasar's suggestion to Irigaray's questions, love deconstructs the 'hom(m)osexual' representations of the Trinity – for otherness and difference are necessary for the operation of love to proceed. Insofar as female/feminine in Irigaray's thinking moves between the poles of sex and gender and offers a phenomenological description of an alternative understanding of sexuality then alterity is as constitutive of the Trinity as it is of male–female economies of desire. The Trinity requires then a 'female' as well as a 'male' principle.

---

[78] See chapter 3 of my *Cultural Transformation and Religious Practice* (Cambridge University Press, 2004), for an account of transformative practices of hope.

[79] *Sexes and Genealogies*, pp. 62–3.

[80] *Explorations in Theology: Creator Spiritus*, p. 105.

Balthasar writes: 'The masculine and the feminine in the Church are universally feminine under the masculine element of Christ, but Christ's submissiveness in his relationship to the Father through the Holy Spirit is in turn (supra-)feminine.'[81] I can understand Christian feminists wanting no part in an idiom that aligned femininity with submission. Furthermore, if we were to continue and deepen the dialogue between Irigaray's sexuate metaphysics and Balthasar's theology then the logic of Balthasar's vindication of an exclusive male priesthood would have to be examined.[82] But an exploration of the relationship between kenosis, love, difference-in-relation and the Trinity might provide a model for a Trinity and therefore the operations of a God who offered a transcendental horizon for both male and female subjectivity.[83] Submission might then be read, in such an exploration, as expressing the active pursuit of obedience to Christ, of being (in Althusser's language) 'interpellated' by Christ – an 'interpellation' that all Christians must respond to, desirously.

This needs to be examined further, partly by thinking through sexual difference in terms of ecclesiology – the Church constituted and perpetuated through sexual difference as the body of Christ. This would require the articulation of not just an alternative Christological emphasis, but a pneumatological one: an epistemology of embodiment situated within a theology of desire that moves through God and creation while only made possible by the spaces opened up between us. Pneumatology would then articulate what Derrida, describing deconstruction, calls 'a certain aporetic experience of the impossible'.[84] That is, 'the experience of aporia … as endurance or as passion'.[85] Irigaray posits the possibility of 'God subtending the interval, pushing the interval toward and into infinity. The irreducible. Opening up the universe and all beyond it. In this sense, the interval would produce place.'[86] I suggest this is where theological investigation, that takes Irigaray's analysis of sexuate nature seriously, will begin and end.

---

[81]   Ibid., p. 243.

[82]   Daphne Hampson draws critical attention to Balthasar's Vatican-sponsored document, 'The Christian and Chastity', tr. John Riches in *Elucidations* (London: SPCK, 1975), supporting the Vatican's statement on why women cannot be ordained priests, in her *Theology and Feminism* (Oxford: Blackwell, 1990), p. 67.

[83]   I explore this further in chapter seven, pp. 183–218.

[84]   *Aporias*, tr. Thomas Dutoit (Stanford University Press, 1993), p. 15.

[85]   Ibid., p. 19.

[86]   *An Ethics of Sexual Difference*, p. 48.

Divinity and Sexual Difference: Beyond Irigaray

In conclusion, what then do these economies of response with respect to the sexuate body of Jesus, the Christ, enable us to understand about divinity and sexual difference? Let me make three points that, though beginning with Irigaray's thinking, go beyond them.

First, we have observed throughout that the notion of difference parallels that of distance. This is partly because difference is always thought relatively, as distance is. There is no pure difference. Difference *qua* difference is an abstraction no one could recognise. Difference is relative, and distance spatialises that relativity and also suggests the possibility of a temporal dynamic. That is, because distance is relative so also actions with respect to that distance will alter it − reducing or expanding proximity. In the same way, difference now understood not as an abstraction but as an aspect of a temporal situation concerned with the relational spatialising of bodies with respect to each other, admits degrees thereof and modifications to those degrees. To associate difference with distance − that I will go on to suggest is a profoundly theological notion that the early Greek Fathers termed *diastema* − prevents any difference, sexual or otherwise, becoming a stable marker of a living body.

But the question now arises about the adjective 'sexual' with respect to difference. Put plainly, how does difference get sexed? From the analysis above I would suggest (and this is the second point in a developing under-standing of sexual difference) that difference, to the extent that it treats the bodies of other responsive beings, is always erotic and therefore sexually charged to a greater or a lesser degree.[87] This is because it is only constituted in relation, and relations between responsive bodies become increasingly eroticised through proximity. The move from seeing to touching in the encounters from John's Gospel that we examined in this and the last chapter, marks a degree of erotic charge between the bodies as well as a change in what the body knows. The body's knowledge is, I suggest (fol-lowing Merleau-Ponty), profoundly related to desire. Although I would not want to draw a sharp line between the senses of sight and touch − voyeurism

---

[87]   The history of bestiality points to a longstanding awareness of erotic relations between human beings and animals that has, at times, been sexual. Hence I speak about 'responsive beings', but I am also aware others have found erotic relations between human beings and other natural forms, such as trees, water, mountains and landscapes. In the opening sequences of Minghella's adaptation of *The English Patient*, for example, the camera pans erotically over the undulations of the North African desert as if it were the body of a woman. In Nicolas Roeg's film *Walkabout* trees are given a similar erotic charge.

would warn us against doing this – certain forms of seeing can indeed be tactile. There are certain exchanges of glances that can wound or excite, that can caress or puncture the body. A look can make me feel ugly, feel aroused, feel pain. It is somewhere in the engagement between sight and touch that bodies become sexualised, somewhere in the junction between reception and response within the body's own knowing; such that desire for knowing or being with the other is simultaneously attraction to other. Is it in the moment of sexualisation, in the arrival of attraction, that bodies take on a sexual difference? What I am arguing here – and in doing so re-emphasising Irigaray's symbolics of sexuality – is that in the same way as there is no difference as such, then there is no sexual difference as such. Sexual difference is a not a given, a fundament, a starting point. It cannot be read off from a situation, from the bodies of those who encounter each other. Sexual difference is always an 'achievement', in Hegel's understanding of that term – it is produced in and through specific acts of encountering the other. To take this further with respect to Christian theology: there is no theology of sexual difference, then, only the production of sexual difference in a theological relation. The encounter with Christ installs both the difference and its erotic form, its sexuate nature.

Thirdly, the difference that arises from any encounter is sexual regardless of the physiology of the bodies involved. Of course this is not to deny the physiological or the aesthetic (the beauty, which accords with fashion, of this man or this woman). Neither would I want to deny the role having sexual organs plays in the performance of an explicit sexual encounter or the adrenalin rush that comes with stimulation. I have emphasised throughout the exegeses of Mary meeting with Christ at the tomb and Thomas meeting with Christ in the Upper Room an interplay between what the body receives and responds to and what the mind understands.[88] But the bodies themselves, I suggest, become sexualised by the consciousness of being-in-relation – they are not sexualised before it. In other words, there is no pure physiological state. To return to a point I made with respect to the mythologising of relations in Jesus's encounter with Mary in the garden, the erotic experience is already mythopoetic, shot through with images, fantasies and mythemes. Thus when I speak of 'consciousness' here I do not simply refer to a mental state as distinct from a physical state. The work of Irigaray, and this thinking in the wake of that work, rejects the dualism of mind and body, *psyche* and *soma*. Orientating oneself round a city, anticipating other vehicles and pedestrians while driving, reaching for and choosing a shot at tennis in

---

[88] Neither is there any need to label the 'performance of an explicit sexual encounter' the 'consummation' of sex, as if all other forms of erotically relating were inferior to explicit sexual congress.

response to a return, are all examples of the body 'thinking' and consciously moving with respect to other bodies without necessarily reasoning in these situations. The body is taught to 'think' in these ways through habituating practices. One can then 'know' one is in-relation without the physical proximity of the person. And similarly one can know of being-in-relation without necessarily being mentally attentive to the person one is in relation to. Bodies, I suggest, become sexualised through a consciousness of being-in-relation of various kinds, through attentive rationalising and responsive readings of body language. In being sexualised, bodies negotiate both difference and affinity, distance and proximity – they do not just encounter difference/distance. Attraction, key to the dynamic of desire, operates through economies of both difference and affinity, distance and proximity. It then becomes absurd, not just on anachronistic grounds, to label the erotic encounter between Mary Magdalene and Christ heterosexual or the meeting of Thomas and Christ homosexual, because both of these labels treat sexuality as a self-subsisting thing, a property that can be attributable to relations, a predicate of persons that encounter awakens. This is where a difference would open up between my own account of sexual difference and Irigaray's. For Irigaray, like Freud, understands the libido (or desire) as a sub-structure of selfhood. My theological analysis would suggest this is an entirely wrong way of understanding sexuality. The erotic nature of a sexual relation is intrinsic to relating itself. The relation itself, in its constitution, participates in an eros and a pathos pertaining to all relations between responsive bodies. (And I would be at a loss to say at what point an organic body is unresponsive.) Any understanding of sexual difference has to think through what are relation and embodiment as such.

Let me begin with embodiment, and a distinction as important to St Paul who distinguishes body (*soma*) from flesh (*sarx*) as it is, more recently, to Michel Henry who distinguishes flesh (*chair*) from the corporeal (*le corps*).[89] The distinction is this: there is the material order of things and there is what I will term the ethical order of things. A distinction is not a division. I am not suggesting the world of genetic pools and carbon compounds is divorced from the world of values and significances. In fact, what I understand by the theological term 'incarnational' would describe the material order as already inhabiting, because only made possible by, the ethical order of things. But the distinction nevertheless remains a useful strategic tool for disrupting the empirical and positivist assumption that what is real and what is true issue from recognising only what is constituted by the basic elements

---

[89] *Incarnation: Une Philosophie de la chair* (Paris: Seuil, 2000), pp. 7–9.

of carbon and a DNA blueprint. The corporeal (St Paul's *sarx*, Henry's *le corps*) is the material in itself, the pursuit of which for both thinkers is nihilistic and atheistic. The corporeal as such is, on one level, a philosophical abstraction or isolation proceeding from the complex knowledges of the body (St Paul's *soma*, Henry's *le chair*). On another level, the corporeal as such is only possible on the rejection of the theological and ethical orders that give value and significance to the body.

Positivism assumes the opacity of objects; it assumes objects are as they appear. Appearance is the starting place for understanding and thinking about them. Ontology *is* epistemology. It is exactly this assumption that I wish to 'queer' with respect to human bodies and how we reflect theologically upon them. To a certain extent phenomenology has already begun to think this disruption of appearance, by asking not about appearance as such but about the how of an appearance, the intentionality of the gaze. Phenomenology asks a prior question about the object of scientific enquiry. How does it give itself to appear as such? Understanding is not the discovery of what is the state of affairs but an 'achievement' in and through relating to that which gives itself. Phenomenology distinguishes between an object's appearance and its manner of appearing – for Henry there is '*l'apparence*' and there is '*l'apparaître*'.[90] As such, phenomenology does not ask questions about the material composition or contents of the object, it asks about how it gives itself to be understood. The phenomenological investigation, as Heidegger realised, gives way to an ontological enquiry that is distinct while remaining inseparable from that which makes it appearance. The ontological question is then secondary and dependent; the mystery of what gives itself, the mystery that invests what is with its values and significances, the mystery of donation,[91] remains primary.[92]

Now let us take this one step further with respect to embodiment. For what I am suggesting here is that the meaning and significance of bodies are ultimately ungraspable. Their givenness cannot be accounted for – except mythopoetically or theologically – and they cannot account for themselves (as empiricists would like us to believe). If Jesus the Christ can be understood as the second Adam, then incarnation does not just characterise his body but, in some sense, all bodies. This incarnational nature is the mark of

---

[90]   Ibid., pp. 35–6.

[91]   'There is a difference between calling something a gift, and calling it a donation; it can be a gift even before it is given, but it cannot be called in any way a donation unless it has been given.' Augustine, *De Trinitate*, tr. Edmund Hill (New York: New City Press, 1991), Book V.15.

[92]   Lévinas, following Plato – and evidently the Christian tradition has been indebted to Plato – would concur: the ethical (or the Good) is beyond being and prior to the ontological.

the mystery of the body's donation, or what Rowan Williams has called 'the body's grace'.[93] Of course, Christ as the second Adam does not repeat identically the first Adam since Adam was made 'in the image of God'; he was not God. And so when I say all bodies are 'in some sense' incarnational they are not identical repetitions of Christ's body, but nevertheless participate in that incarnation in their own creaturely way. Embodiment therefore is analogically related to incarnation, and it is, as such, that Paul's *soma* can refer both to (a) the historical and physical body each possesses, even Christ and (b) the transhistorical, spiritual body that is Christ's alone but which is made of several members constituting the Church. This rich, analogical understanding of *corpus* is detailed in Henri de Lubac's study of medieval sacramentality, *Corpus Mysticum*.[94] Embodiment maintains its mystery, rendering the particularity of its thereness continually open to a transcorporeal operation.

This transcorporeal operation is not beyond the body or supra-corporeal. The body's transcorporeality is constituted in and through its relations to other bodies. This brings us to the second of the two categories that, from my exegesis, will determine a different, theological account of sexual difference: relation. A body is, if you like, always in transit, always exceeding its significance or transgressing the limits of what appears. The body is constantly in movement and in a movement. It is these complex movements in and upon the body that the economies of response attempt to sketch. Put differently, the body exists fluidly in a number of operations between reception and response, between degrees of desire/repulsion, recognition/misrecognition, and passivity/activity. These operations maintain the body's mystery by causing it always to be in transit. As such a body can only be reduced to a set of identifiable properties of its appearance (such as identifications of sex as 'male' or 'female') by being isolated from these processes and operations; by being atomised. Embodiment maintains its excess, maintains its transcorporeality in and through its congress with the mysteries of other bodies. It is with respect to other bodies that the operations of reception and response, reading and re-reading, acting and withdrawing are not only conducted but also constituted. These operations bring into being systems of dependences and interdependences, which any singular body can always resist but from which no singular body can ever finally extract itself. I suggest it is from within these systems, with respect to these operations, that the sexuality (and therefore sexual differences) of embodiment emerge. The

---

[93] 'The Body's Grace', in Charles Hefling (ed.), *Our Selves and Bodies: Sexuality and the Household of God* (Cambridge, Mass.: Cowley Publications, 1996).

[94] *Corpus Mysticum,:* deuxième edition (Paris: Aubier, 1949).

encounter with Christ, then, that opens up a Christological operation with respect to bodies and relations, will install an eroticism that determines the nature of a manifold difference – a theological difference (Trinitarian), an ontological difference (between the Uncreated and Creation) and a sexual difference (between the symbolics of the phallus and the two lips).

Chapter Six

THE POLITICS OF CHRIST'S CIRCUMCISION (AND THE MYSTERY OF ALL FLESH)

In this essay I wish to raise a question concerning the organisation of an enquiry, any enquiry. My enquiry here is into the body of Jesus Christ. Two different analyses are fundamental not only to the nature and findings of the enquiry, but to the constitution of the enquiry itself. The first set of analyses concerns the why which drives this enquiry; and the second set of analyses concerns the how, the way of proceeding with the enquiry. Although I must distinguish immediately with respect to this second set of analyses between methodological questions (why a certain *type* of or approach to the enquiry is undertaken) and those elements and relations which organise the space of the methodology – perhaps even lend significance to why this methodology is chosen rather than any other. The first set of analyses concerns desire, attraction, and the relation pertaining between the enquirer and the object of the enquiry; the second set of analyses concerns the assumed knowledges governing the enquiry itself.[1] I will treat the first set of analyses cursorily at this point because I wish to return to it more fully having dealt with what is assumed in order for the enquiry to take place at all.

---

[1] As Michel Foucault points out, 'The fundamental codes of a culture – those governing its language, its schemas of perception, its exchanges, its techniques, its values, the hierarchy of its practices – establish for every man, from the very first, the empirical orders with which he will be dealing and within which he will be at home': *The Order of Things: An Archaeology of the Human Sciences* (London: Tavistock Publications, 1970), p. xx. My second set of analyses might be termed an archaeology of the 'fundamental codes of a culture'.

The Enquiry

It should be no surprise to find throughout the tradition of Christian reflection on the body of Christ that sexual language is frequently employed. Therefore it should come as no surprise to find a number of contemporary patristic and medieval scholars from Virginia Burrus, Kate Cooper and Elizabeth Clark to Caroline Walker Bynum, Daniel Boyarin and Mark Jordan drawing attention to this language.[2] The work of queer theorists and the new attention to the different historical and cultural understandings of embodiment have only returned a number of scholars of early Christianity to their treasured texts in an effort to point out that modernity's commitment to the twin-headed heterosexuality and homophobia is a blip in the history of western civilisation. The language of sexuality and queer relations frequently found in accounts of the body of Christ issues from a fundamental erotics driving the enquiry into the body of Christ itself. In the past the enquiry was governed by a calling, a discipleship, a sacrificial obedience, a participation, a desire, an anticipation and relation. The enquiry was conducted within an encompassing affectivity, such that the end of the enquiry (whether it be Tertullian in *De Carno Christi* or Gregory of Nyssa in his commentary on the *Canticum Canticorum*) is identification with the object of the enquiry: to be made one with Christ. Neither the object nor the enquiring subject has a place outside this affective or erotic economy, the economy of response. I enquire into the nature of this body or into those places (the Scriptures, the Church, the Sacraments) where this body may be found, because I am drawn to it – it is the object of a longing to which I abandon myself.

There is introduced with this erotic affectivity a gendering of relations that opens up questions concerning the maleness of Jesus Christ, and the relationship of this maleness to the economy of salvation. The erotic relations transcend the dimorphism of heterosexuality/homosexuality, as they deepen the mystery of sexuality itself. The erotic is excessive to the sexual,[3] bearing as it does upon that *caritas* which is the mode of God's own activity. It is not that our longing to understand Jesus Christ, to embrace and be embraced by that body which is given so completely for us, negates the sexual. The sexual is the very mark of embodiment itself; a mode of relation

---

[2]   See Virginia Burrus, *Begotten Not Made: Conceiving Manhood in Late Antiquity* (Stanford University Press, 2000); Kate Cooper, *The Virgin and the Bride: Idealized Womanhood in Late Antiquity* (Cambridge, Mass.: Harvard University Press, 1998); Elizabeth A. Clark, *Reading and Renunciation: Asceticism and Scripture in Early Christianity* (Princeton University Press, 1999); Caroline Walker Bynum, *Jesus as Mother: Studies in Spirituality in the High Middles Ages* (Berkeley: University of California Press, 1982); Daniel Boyarin, *Carnal Israel: Reading Sex in Talmudic Culture* (Berkeley: University of California Press, 1993); Mark Jordan, *The Invention of Sodom* (University of Chicago Press, 1998).

[3]   See Michel Henry, *Incarnation: Une Philosophie de la chair* (Paris: Seuil, 2000), pp. 311–18.

in which the body experiences itself as such. But desire reorders the sexual as a deeper mystery of embodiment unfolds. Divine embodiment moves us to affirm our own embodiment in a new way – as a temple of the Spirit, to use the Pauline term, as holy, as graced, as transcending our understanding. The gendered relations, as set up by the erotic affectivity within which the enquiry into the body of Jesus Christ takes place, *are* queered. For they render unstable the categories of sexual difference that might attempt to describe those relations or the performance of the enquirer with respect to the gendered body of Jesus Christ. We saw this destabilising of sexual categories when we examined the work of Luce Irigaray in chapter five. It is not that gender disappears. Gender is not transcended. It is, rather, rendered part of a more profound mystery: the mystery of relation itself between God and human beings. Given over sacrificially to God, I am subsequently found in God to be most myself, my sexual, gendered and gendering self. But I have to be taught what it means to be such a self by the Christ who draws me into a kenotic relationship with him. It is then the very maleness of the body of Jesus Christ crucified and resurrected that comes to determine how I understand my own embodiment.

So much then for my first analysis of what pertains to the purpose of the enquiry. Let me turn now to a more detailed analysis of the assumed knowledges which the enquiry demands, having already shown how the affectivity circumscribing the enquiry raises, as it queers, some of the categories involved. While so engaged let me also emphasise that these knowledges may indeed, should indeed, undergo revisions and repudiations as well as affirmations as the enquiry proceeds. Knowledges are never stable. But in order to engage in such enquiry, in order to raise questions such as 'how do we give an account of this body of Jesus Christ?' we have to assume that we have some knowledge of what a body is. We assume we know what being human is and even what being 'God' is, such that this differs from being human. We assume knowledge of what being male is, what it means, how it can be read with respect to Jesus's body – an assumption that further assumes knowledge of what being female is. Several recent socio-historical and anthropological studies have pointed out how each culture figures and understands the body differently.[4] After Foucault, Pierre Manent has called into question our knowledges about being human;[5] and the work of

---

[4]   I cite only two of the most important ones: Thomas Lacquer, *Making Sex: Body and Gender from the Greeks to Freud* (Cambridge, Mass.: Harvard University Press, 1990) and Richard Sennett, *Flesh and Stone: The Body and the City in Western Civilization* (New York: Norton Paperback, 1996).

[5]   For Foucault's reflections of the eighteenth- and nineteenth-century production of 'man', see *The Order of Things*. For Pierre Manent, see *The City of Man*, tr. Marc A. LePain (Princeton University Press, 1998).

apophatic theology has always been to question our assumed knowledges about the divine. Furthermore, how do we read the Jewish maleness of Jesus Christ when we do not have the body itself, only a body of writings? Several sets of cultural assumptions must then inform any investigation into the body of Jesus Christ – even when that investigation is a theological one which roots itself in rehearsing the tradition and creeds (of Nicea or Chalcedon). For example, the nineteenth-century investigations into the historical Jesus, and the type of kenotic Christologies that followed from those investigations, occur at a time of the increasing medicalisation of the body and increasing confidence (following various declarations of rights) about what it is to be human. In this medicalisation, the body is profoundly secularised; in this confidence, to be human is an act of self-assertion, assertion as self-affirmation. In both of these events, the human body becomes a localised site of certain immanent operations. Reduced to what is observable and explicable, the body becomes an organic machine.[6] It takes on a disenchanted opacity; it becomes an identifiable substance, a collection of organs and chemicals. The nineteenth century was also a time when the new muscular masculinities, sketched by the likes of Winckelmann, from Greek statues, were being formed in the German gymnasia and the English public schools.[7] So the theological investigations work with the cultural assumption that bodies and being human are givens, and being manly was to be strong, forthright and self-controlled. These gendered bodies are constituted of brute data that can be empirically registered and positivistically analysed. Gendered human bodies are objects that can be catalogued. So questions of their meaning and the construction of their gender, questions about the cultural specificity of the scientific interpretations of them, are rendered invisible. As such there is little difference between a live and a dead body; and yet what difference there is *is* what being human is all about. The nineteenth-century theologians assumed certain knowledges about Jesus's Jewish embodiment, humanity and sex; on the basis of such assumptions, it followed that his historical existence could be sketched, his biography written, his psychological profile drawn while, throughout, his masculinity rendered invisible questions concerning sexuality and gender.[8]

For several decades the social sciences have been learning how to quarry

---

[6] For the *episteme* of the gaze with respect to the body see Michel Foucault, *Birth of a Clinic: An Archaeology of Medical Perception*, tr. A.M. Sheridan (London: Routledge, 1989).

[7] See George Mosse, *The Image of Man: The Creation of Modern Masculinity* (Oxford University Press, 1996).

[8] For a further example of how socio-cultural conditions mediate our Christologies see Stephen D. Moore, *God's Beauty Parlor and Other Queer Spaces in and around the Bible* (Stanford University Press, 2001), pp. 90–130.

and question their own assumptions and thereby reopen debates once thought to be closed and rethink issues once thought to be settled. Theology too needs to understand how time-conditioned are its language and thought; how what it assumes it knows needs to be critically examined. It needs to understand also the kinds of bodies its own discourse has been implicated in producing. History shows how Christian theology shaped the anorexic body of the Middle Ages and the heterosexual body of the nineteenth century. Christian theology was profoundly involved in biopolitics – it still is. Daniel Boyarin has demonstrated how Jewish theology also played its part in the rise of heterosexuality and the development of Jewish male (and by implication female) bodies.[9] By taking just one of those three assumptions – knowledges of specifically ethnic bodies, being human and sex – for enquiring into the Jewish body of Jesus Christ, we can begin that critical reflection and think through its theological significance. But we can also begin to ask what kind of bodies is theological discourse implicated in producing today.

Philosophically, questions about the meaning, interpretation, presentation and representation of the body do not arise until late developments in phenomenology such as those of Merleau-Ponty. After Merleau-Ponty (and other phenomenologists like Michel Henry[10] and Jean-Louis Chrétien[11]) bodies are not just there. Embodiment can be rethought. The investigations that have been conducted into the body over the last twenty or thirty years in the wake of phenomenological essays such as 'The Intertwining – The Chiasm' have taught us something of the complex politics of bodies.[12] In the work of Foucault and Irigaray – both explicitly indebted to Merleau-Ponty – bodies are no longer simply givens. Nor are they *tabulae rasae* that receive cultural inscriptions. A new perspective arises that emphasises that we have no immediate access to what is most intimate to us.

Let me be clear, at this point: I am not suggesting that contemporary accounts of the body are any more true or more faithful to the truth of embodiment than the accounts emerging from the Renaissance onwards of the body's facticity. Contemporary accounts are figurations and the scientific

---

[9] See *Unheroic Conduct: The Rise of Heterosexuality and the Invention of the Jewish Man* (Berkeley: University of California Press, 1997).

[10] See *Philosophie et phénoménologie du corps* (Paris: Presses Universitaires de France, 1965) and *Phénoménologie materielle* (Paris: Presses Universitaires de France, 1990).

[11] For Jean-Louis Chrétien see *La Voix nue: phénoménologie de la promesse* (Paris: Editions de minuit, 1990); *L'Appel et la réponse* (Paris: Editions de minuit, 1992); *Corps à corps: à l'écoute de l'œuvre d'art* (Paris: Editions de minuit, 1997); and *Entre flèche et cri* (Paris: Obsidiane, 1998).

[12] In *The Visible and the Invisible*, ed. Claude LeFort, tr. Alphonso Lingis (Evanston, Ill.: Northwestern University Press, 1968).

accounts remain significantly institutionalised – by medicine and governments. The point I am making is double-bound: we cannot just assume that we know what a body is; and yet not to assume, not to have any notion of embodiment would stymie any enquiry before it had been undertaken. And so when I came to write my own account of transcorporeality and the body of Christ in the previous essays and chapter of *Cities of God* I was working with narratives of the unbounded body of Irigaray, the imaginary body of Lacan, the performed body of Butler, and was weaving these notions of the body back into older theological accounts of embodiment evident in Tertullian, Augustine and Gregory of Nyssa. Furthermore, I wished to emphasise while composing an argument that it was not an innocent strategy. I was doing no more than offering a Christological interpretation of some continental views of embodiment. Although I related this interpretation directly to the Scriptures, I was not, by doing that, trying to lend my interpretation a divine legitimacy. I was not saying 'this is the nature of Jesus Christ's body and all embodiment' (given that in Christian theology the nature of the world is read in terms of the one through whom and by whom that world was created). I was telling the story of the body of Jesus Christ in another way. Any enquiry into the body of Jesus Christ assumes a knowledge of the nature of embodiment, assumes an account of substance – I was assuming the knowledges of the body that have been fashioned since the phenomenological turn to the body over forty years ago.

This suggests a profound and a productive agnosticism concerning the body itself, to which I will return in the final part of this essay. All we have is a variety of opinions and beliefs that we necessarily assume are true in order to form the basis for the enquiry at all. What we have when we begin the enquiry are culturally mediated models (frequently internalised) that allow us and enable us to make the necessary assumptions. Thus a certain politics is not only evident but inevitable. It is the politics that interests me in this chapter– not the interpretation of the body of Jesus Christ as such. I wish to investigate this politics in what follows to demonstrate (a) how it can be theologically employed and (b) how its employment is part of a larger history of cultural change and transmission – one that demands we ask why are we interested in the body of Jesus Christ today. What does this very enquiry say about where we stand now? Finally I wish also to offer a theological account of both this politics and the history of cultural change and transmission in which it figures. I am aware that this composes a double movement – investigating the cultural politics of the theological representation and then theologically representing the cultural politics itself. I open myself to the criticism of circularity. But I would argue that the criticism of hermeneutic circularity belongs to an ahistorical logic; it is insufficiently materialist. We never step into the same river twice. Similarly we are never in the same position having moved through the reflexive moment. Temporally and contextually we are elsewhere. In confronting the cultural politics within theological reflection and then embracing those politics as something theologically positive, what I am attempting to develop is new methodology for theological enquiry. This methodology would tender a much more public and responsible theology than we are used to.[13] I hope, finally, to spell out more of what I mean by 'public'.

To render my investigation into the politics of the Jewish, male body of Jesus Christ manageable and also specific I will examine the question of circumcision in two representations divided from each other both culturally and historically. I chose circumcision for three pertinent reasons. First, it has always been not only a physiological but a political action, since it marks a boundary of inclusion and exclusion. While the act (the removal of the foreskin from around the penile helmet) has remained the same, the way that act is understood and evaluated shifts continually. The technology for accomplishing the act of circumcision, the context in which it is done and the persons involved in its execution have also changed. Now it is performed, on the whole, in hospitals by the laity, by qualified medical staff. This is mainly because the foreskin is viewed as a potential harbourer of certain infections. The politics implicated in circumcision change with each cultural context. Secondly, circumcision has recently formed a focus of interest in accounts of the Jewish male body by Elliot R. Wolfson[14] and Daniel Boyarin.[15] These accounts detail the theologies of circumcision. They represent the weaving of theological discourse into our present cultural preoccupations with embodiment. Thirdly, circumcision is also viewed in Christian theology as *the* mark of incarnation. That is, the parentage of Jesus of Nazareth may be ambivalent but his circumcision has traditionally been seen as evidence of the humanity of Christ.[16] Circumcision is the first indication of the gendered corporeality of the Christ – for Leo Steinberg this explains the unusual but frequent emphasis in medieval and Renaissance art on Jesus's penis. In my two examples I wish to investigate the different cultural politics in which the circumcision of Jesus is implicated.

[13] This project is developed in more detail in my *Cultural Transformation and Religious Practice* (Cambridge University Press, 2004).
[14] *Circle in the Square: Studies in the Use of Gender in Kabbalistic Mysticism* (New York: SUNY, 1995).
[15] *Carnal Israel*, pp. 197–225.
[16] See Leo Steinberg, *The Sexuality of Christ in Renaissance Art and in Modern Oblivion* (University of Chicago Press, 1996).

Luke's Gospel

My first example is the account of the circumcision itself in Luke's Gospel (2.21), and my first question about this account concerns why it occurs only in Luke's Gospel. What does it signify?[17] Mark's Gospel has no infancy narrative and so the lack of any reference to Jesus's circumcision is readily explicable. John's Gospel contains one reference to circumcision (John 7.22–3), but not an account of Jesus's own.[18] Of course, it could be argued that since there is, at best, only a veiled reference to the birth of Jesus in the prologue to John's Gospel (1.14), as with Mark's Gospel there is no narrative necessity for mentioning the circumcision. Though since scholars often take both Gospels to have been written with the Gentile world in mind, and given the controversies St Paul records in his letters about whether Christians as inheritors of a Jewish messianic tradition should be circumcised or not, it is significant that they are silent on the issue. But of *what* is that silence significant? The question is ultimately unanswerable, but perhaps the very absence of any mention of Jesus's circumcision signals a politics we cannot access now. It is possibly a politics that needs to be taken into account especially when interpreting the silence in Matthew's Gospel.[19] For

---

[17] A number of commentators note the way Jesus being circumcised accords with Jewish cultic observance and how Jesus is therefore seen as fulfilling all that the Torah required. Jack T. Sanders sums up the point they make: 'The infancy narratives … show how totally immersed Christian beginnings were in good Jewish piety'; *Jews in Luke-Acts* (Philadelphia, Penn.: Fortress Press, 1987), p. 161. To go beyond these observations we need to view the incident in the light of the theology of the Gospel and the Acts of the Apostles. But, as we will see, this is highly disputed territory, betraying the politics of interpretation and what Pierre Bourdieu would call the 'habitus' or network of unreflected dispositions that govern any enquiry. For example, Joseph B. Tyson, in his *Luke, Judaism, and the Scholars* (Columbia, S.C.: University of South Carolina Press, 1999), when discussing the major contributions to Lukan scholarship in the twentieth century by Ernst Haenchen (1894–1975) and Hans Conzelmann (1915–89), situates both their approaches in terms of the Jewish question and their association with or disassociation from German National Socialism. Both Haenchen and Conzelmann make much of the anti-Jewish aspects of the Gospel and, particularly, Acts of the Apostles.

[18] John's concern is with the way that in the Jewish law there is a certain overriding or double-play. Commentators (like Barrett, *The Gospel According to St. John*, 2nd edition, Philadelphia, Penn.: Westminster Press, 1978, p. 320) often refer to Mishnah Nedarim 3.11: 'R. Jose says, "Great is circumcision since it overrides the stringent Sabbath".' Nevertheless, in John's Gospel Jesus makes an interesting association between circumcision and being made whole that reinforces certain elements of my argument near the end of this chapter.

[19] The nineteenth-century German exegete, Ferdinand Christian Baur, believed there was a relationship between Matthew's Gospel and the Gospel of Luke as we have it now. In the words of Tyson, Baur believed '[o]riginal Luke was a revision of Matthew that omitted the Jewish-Christian tendencies … A second author, who intended to reconcile the Jewish-Christian and Gentile-Christian wings of the Church, revised original Luke and re-introduced some pro-Jewish sections from Matthew' (*Luke, Judaism and the Scholars*, p. 137). But this is all very speculative.

most New Testament scholars concur that Matthew's Gospel has an implied Jewish-Christian reader. It is also a Gospel with an infancy narrative and a concern to show not only that Jesus is the *fulfilment* of the Jewish law and prophecy, but also that Jesus is the *continuation* of the Jewish tradition. Luke's Gospel and the Acts of the Apostles, on the other hand, have often been viewed as having an implied Graeco-Roman reader, being addressed to Gentile converts who had separated themselves from both the Jews and the Jewish Christians. '[I]n reality, Luke the historian is wrestling, from the first page to the last, with the problem of the *mission to the Gentiles without the law*', writes Haenchen; 'When Christianity comes to be viewed as a religion separate and distinct from Judaism, which is the way Luke viewed it, then someone who tries to be both is, from a dispassionate descriptive point of view, an anomaly, but from a partisan religious viewpoint a hypocritic', writes Jack T. Sanders.[20] Various studies have argued that the Greek of Luke's Gospel is more rhetorically conscious, the vocabulary more sophisticated. So when the circumcision ought to appear in Matthew's Gospel to show that Jesus of Nazareth really did live out the letter of the Jewish law, it does not. It appears in a Gospel seemingly addressed to Gentile outsiders. Why is this? Or more accurately, why might this be?

It is not that answers to this question are impossible to formulate – one only needs to challenge the implied readership and construct another context. In an article published in 1972, Jacob Jervell – in the only study I

---

[20]   Haenchen, *Der Weg Jesu: Eine Erklärung des Markus-Evangeliums und der kanonischen Parallelen*, 2nd edn. (Berlin: de Gruyter, 1968), p. 100; Sanders, *Jews in Luke-Acts*, p. 130. The work of Jacob Jervell contests this perspective. Developing 'God-fearer' into an official term for Gentiles who had attached themselves to Judaism and become proselytes, Jervell claims: 'it is those Jews who are most faithful to the law, the real Jews, the most Jewish Jews, that became believers' (*Luke and the People of God: A New Look at Luke-Acts*, Minneapolis, Minn.: Augsburg Publishing House, 1972, p. 46). By implication, then, the Gospel is addressed to Jewish Christians with a considerable knowledge of Jewish law at a time when they are defining themselves (and the role of Paul's mission) in the context of a growing purely Gentile Church. In fact, the Church for Jervell is the true and restored Israel. It does not matter for this argument which interpretation, or constructed ecclesiastical context, is right. Though it is significant that Conzelmann, in his commentary on Luke, translated by Geoffrey Buswell as *The Theology of St. Luke* (New York: Harper & Brothers, 1960), in supporting the Gentile readership devotes only one paragraph to the infancy narratives in Luke 1 and 2. It is a dismissive paragraph that makes no mention of Jesus's circumcision while recognising that it 'is strange that the characteristic features they [the infancy narratives] contain do not occur again either in the Gospel or in Acts' (p. 172). Each of these commentators is involved in their own cultural negotiations. It does not matter for this argument whether the Gospel speaks to the Gentiles who have left Judaism and Jewish Christianity behind or speaks to an intra-Jewish debate: in either case a readership (and context) have to be constructed – a politics defined – in order for interpretation to proceed. The argument here concerns the politics of the writing and interpretation itself – its inevitability and its irreducibleness, despite the positivistic language of 'in reality', 'Luke the historian', 'the real Jews', and 'the way Luke viewed it'.

am aware of that is explicitly devoted to the circumcision of Jesus in Luke –
makes the verse the crux of his interpretation of Lukan theology.[21] For
Jervell, working in the aftermath of the Jewish Holocaust and busily trying
to revise scholarly attention to Luke's anti-Judaism, this verse becomes the
key to unlocking the conflicting debates about circumcision in the early
Church. In a way that refuses a supersessionist reading of the covenant,
Jervell claims

> Jesus spells salvation for Israel (and salvation also for the Gentiles via Israel).
> Jesus is Israel's Messiah also because he was circumcised. In the view of an
> early Christian or Jewish Christian, an uncircumcised Messiah is a self-
> contradiction. It is only long after Gentile Christians have gained a majority
> in the church and Jewish Christians feel threatened that the time is ripe for
> speaking of Jesus' circumcision.[22]

It is not, then, that an answer to a certain textual problem cannot be found –
in this case, by constructing a different *Sitz im Leben*. What I wish to point
to, though, is how what is missing, present or elaborated in any of the
Gospel accounts of the life of Jesus is governed not simply by a theological
project but also by a cultural politics. If we view every culture as a set of
interrelated symbolic systems, establishing values here, legitimating certain
forms of activity there, denigrating other, opposing values, criminalising
forms of activity inconsistent with the lifestyle being advocated, then with
the overlapping of those symbolic codes certain symbols are given more
priority than others. Certain symbols are key symbols, or foregrounded
symbols, which are used to interpret or order other less valued symbols.[23]
Each person internalises this priority, and its hierarchies, often without
reflection. In this way specific cultural ideologies become normative. Each
person then reproduces, modifies, even possibly critiques such priorities and
hierarchies in the various practices that make up everyday living within any
particular cultural context. I suggest Luke is doing the same with respect to
circumcision; that circumcision becomes not exactly the organising or key
symbol but one that, in the cultural milieu in which Luke's Gospel was
composed (which is wider than any implied readership), took on a certain
weight, a significance that it may or may not have had in the Johannine
community, for example, or the cultural contexts in which both Mark and
Matthew were writing. The circumcision is an important foregrounded

---

[21] 'The Circumcised Messiah', tr. in Jacob Jervell, *The Unknown Paul: Essays in Luke-Acts and Early
Christian History* (Minneapolis, Minn.: Augsburg Publishing House, 1984), pp. 138–45.

[22] Ibid., p. 144.

[23] See *Cities of God*, pp. 21–4.

action for Luke because of its significance to the people he was addressing (whether Gentile-Christian or Jewish-Christian) *and* the wider situation in which he lived (the Graeco-Roman culture). Both these contexts have to be reconstructed in order for any enquiry or argument to proceed; but the proceedings of the enquiry are also governed by a cultural politics of their own – as Jervell's case evidences. What we are concerned with, then, in an examination of the body of Christ is twofold. First, how we gain access to the cultural politics, the movement of social energies which leads Luke to be concerned with the body of Jesus in this way; secondly, the cultural politics that shapes the way we gain such an access.

The circumcision scene itself is given a certain rhetorical prominence. For not only does it parallel and repeat (albeit differently) the circumcision and naming of John the Baptist (Luke 1.59) – where the Baptist foreshadows the perfections of Christ – but it acts as a tiny bridge between two large pericopes, the nativity (Luke 2.1–20; where narrative attention is drawn to the pastoral framing and that which Mary kept pondering in her heart) and the presentation in the Temple (Luke 2.22–40; where Simeon prophesies the piercing of Mary's soul in the context of sacrifice). The circumcision links salvation to naming, weaving a complex relation between Mary's body and Christ's. For the cutting Jesus undergoes Mary herself will undergo when 'a sword will pierce through your soul *also*' (*de*; Luke 2.35). The present event of circumcision dissolves into the future prophecy while it floats upon a past resonant with connotations of shepherd kings and sacrificial lambs. Time is being governed; an explicit sense of providence is performed through certain symmetries: John and Jesus, Mary and Jesus. The brief action takes on a symbolic weight, a diaphanous quality – as if when held up to the sunlight of eternal truth that watermark of what has been and what will come permeates the present significance of the act. The action is weighted with mystery in the process of which the circumcision *has to be* interpreted. We need to understand what occurs to the event itself in its interpretation.

I am unconvinced by those who might suggest this inclusion of the circumcision in Luke's Gospel was an early example of what we have come to term Orientalism:[24] a western European employing western European views of eastern practices in order to add a bit of local colour or novelistic realism. That is not Luke's cultural context. It is the context of nineteenth-century thinkers, narrators and painters such as Holman Hunt. Some have resorted to saying the verse is an interpolation,[25] others to quibbles about

---

[24]   See Edward Said, *Orientalism* (London: Routledge, 1980).

[25]   See H. Sahlin, *Der Messias und das Gottesvolk. Studien zur protolukanischen Theologie* (Uppsala: ASNU 12, 1945), pp. 240ff.

the grammatical structure of the sentence in Greek that focuses on the naming rather than the circumcision of Christ (in fact, the circumcision may have not taken place at all),[26] and still others argue that pre-Gospel material has been incorporated into the narrative, irrespective of the designs of that narrative.[27] Along with several other commentators I would accept that, viewed in the context of the Gospel as a whole, the circumcision forms one of several references by Luke to Jesus's fulfilment of the Jewish law. As Luke writes: 'they [Jesus and his parents] had performed everything according to the law of the Lord' (2.39). As such the event is theologised. Nevertheless, I want to get behind that gesture and think through why it becomes theologised in this way. What I am suggesting is that the circumcision is an event with specific cultural resonance of which we today continue to register the reverberations, but are unsure how to evaluate them.[28] What does it mean to portray the removal of the foreskin from the penis of Jesus the incarnate God? What did it mean for a Gentile-Christian readership or a Jewish-Christian readership, or as a literary offering to a Graeco-Roman audience? As Tyson acutely recognises with respect to Lukan scholarship, 'it may be observed that the perspective of the reader has a great deal to do with the ways in which narratives are perceived, and this perception has a great deal to do with the social setting of the reader'.[29] We know from the Acts of the Apostles[30] (thought by most to have been written by the writer of Luke's Gospel), the Pauline Epistles[31] and Justin's *Dialogue with Trypho* what difficulties circumcision raised in the Gentile world.[32] Furthermore, as Daniel Boyarin argues, 'For the Jews of late Antiquity, I claim, the rite of circumcision became the most contested site ... precisely because of the way that it concentrates in one moment representations of the significance of sexuality,

---

[26]   See the commentaries by G.B. Caird, *The Gospel of St. Luke* (London: Black, 1968), E. Klostermann, *Das Lukasevangelium* (Tübingen: Mohr Paul (Siebeck), 1929) and H. Schürmann *Das Lukasevangelium 1. Teil Kommentar zu Rap. 1, 1–9, 50* (Freiburg: Herder, 1969) on 2.21.

[27]   See R. McL. Wilson, 'Some Recent Studies in the Lukan Infancy Narratives' in *Studia Evangelica* 1, pp. 235–53 and H.H. Oliver, 'The Lukan Birth Stories and the Purpose of Luke-Acts' in *New Testament Studies* 10 (1963–4), pp. 202–26.

[28]   And not only today. The recent puzzlement among exegetes is only mirrored by the difficulties in the textual transmission of this verse, as various Greek sources attest. For the textual variance between these sources, see Jervell, 'The Circumcised Messiah', p. 140.

[29]   Tyson, *Luke, Judaism and the Scholars*, p. 133.

[30]   Acts 7.8; 10.45; 11.2; 15.1, 5; 16.3; 21.21.

[31]   Rom. 2.25; 3.1; 4.10, 12; 15.8; Gal. 2.3; 5.2ff., 11; 6.15; Phil. 3.3; Col. 2.11.

[32]   To appreciate just how high the theological stakes are on this matter, see Trypho's remarks to Justin that not only does Christ's circumcision require all Christians to be circumcised, but that it was this very circumcision and Christ's obedience to the law, rather than the Virgin Birth, that makes him the Messiah at all: *Dialogue with Trypho*, sections 63, 67.

genealogy and ethnic specificity in bodily practice.'[33] So what kind of politics was this account of circumcision implicated in?

The circumcision of Jesus in Luke is associated textually with naming, sacrifice and salvation. These themes were taken up and developed by the early Church Fathers like Ambrose and Augustine in their allegorical readings of the circumcision. As such circumcision was related to three sets of issues. First, it was connected with a set of moral dispositions to be imitated by followers of Christ: kenotic obedience, self-denial, a disciplining of the sensual flesh. Second, it was linked to a set of soteriological criteria and a particular model for the operation of atonement: the bloodletting was a down payment for the redemption to follow, a token of the sacrifice on the cross. Third, it was related to a set of eschatological values: the eighth day on which the liturgy took place was symbolically associated with the final resurrection (the eighth being the day following the last day in the cosmic calendar). From the early sixth century the 1st of January became the Feast of the Circumcision in the Christian Church. It was the great feast (no doubt to replace pagan feasting) between Christmas and Epiphany. And most of the material we have on the theology of the circumcision is found in sermons and homilies preached on this feast day. This allegorising of the surgical event was a continuation of Jewish hermeneutical method. Circumcision was already being employed metaphorically to refer to hearts and ears in the Old Testament; no less a writer than Philo, in his essay *The Migration of Abraham*, proclaimed: 'It is true that receiving the circumcision does indeed portray the excision of pleasure and all the passions, and the putting away of the impious conceit, under which the mind supposed that it was capable of begetting by its own power.'[34]

Now all this is very erudite, but we need to note what occurs in this allegorical move (and, more generally, in the tendering of a 'theological interpretation' to a concrete event). An episode in a narrative is opaque. Its brute factuality interrupts the smooth flow of events such that it draws attention to itself and raises the question about how we are to understand its inclusion. In the face of that opacity we accredit it not just artistic or creative integrity, but, since we are treating a sacred or revelatory text, we accredit it with theological value. That is, we deem its opacity not to be a case of bad writing, or the work of an editor, or aesthetic pragmatism (some local colour to make the account more believable), or the chronicler's addition of another bit of biographical information. We deem the opacity to be theologically significant. However, though we deem it significant, we do not precisely know of *what* it is significant. Hence the critical debates among the exegetes. By wheeling in the allegorical interpretations of the Philos, the Origens and the Gregory the Greats, we are weighing the episode down with symbolic suggestiveness. In other words, we are legitimating its significance by an appeal to the way it encodes transhistorical and eternal verities. To employ good Hellenistic vocabulary, we are translating *historia* into *theoria*. By this move we both transfigure the material – which has been made to render its true form – and displace the act itself. The body begins to disappear so that in the hermeneutical shift towards moral dispositions, soteriology and eschatology, we are no longer talking about the handling and the mutilation of sexual organs. We are treating the preparation of the heart or soul for receiving the divine. We are not talking about the cutting of male flesh, an incision into masculinity itself. In this theologising we both bypass the way circumcision is a bio-political act implicated in issues of gender, genealogy and ethnicity, and we bypass the metaphorics of the theological discourse that has transfigured the event. For concerns with the production of moral dispositions, moral subjects, soteriological models of redemption that revolve around an exchange mechanism between two asymmetrical powers, and eschatological dreams of new forms of embodiment, new liberational *jouissances*, are both freighted with political implications.

I want to suggest that the circumcision of Jesus – the attention to the body of this man – was important for Luke, and not just theologically in terms of Jesus's obedience to and fulfilment of the Torah or the immersion of Christianity in Jewish piety. To speak of the circumcision was making a cultural and political statement. The question is: What kind of statement? I suggest, whatever the implied readership of the text, a statement is being made here about embodiment (as early Christian exegetes understood) and about Jewish masculinity (and by implication femininity). It is a statement not just about religious and ethnic self-identity (as Jervell argues) but about the way certain figurations of the body are invested with cultural status. It says something, then, about the politics of embodiment. For the body, until its medicalisation and dissection in the late Renaissance and early seventeenth century, was not a discrete entity. It was not only malleable, it was mapped onto and composed other bodies larger than itself – social and political bodies.[35] Furthermore, the body established a hierarchical system of values in which the physical was related intimately to the cosmic. The perfection of the physical was an aspiration towards the realisation of political harmony and cosmic beauty. What then does the circumcised body of

---

[35] See Dale Martin, *The Corinthian Body* (New Haven, Conn.: Yale University Press, 1995), pp. 3–103.

the Messiah mean when it is conceived of as figuring the social and political body, or as an analogue of the cosmic or divine body – not simply a physical, ethnic or even spiritual one?

Circumcision in Late Medieval and Renaissance Culture

Let us move now to the second example of the cultural politics of the circumcision of Jesus and its representation/interpretation. This brings us closer to home (historically and geographically) and rescues me from troubled waters of New Testament exegesis and the sharks within those waters ready to take lumps out of unwitting theologians who wander in there untrained, unlettered. The circumcision of Jesus, as already mentioned, has been celebrated by the Church since the sixth century, but it enjoyed a certain cultic fashion in the fourteenth, fifteenth and early sixteenth centuries in particular. Suddenly, additional to the regular sermons still preached all over Christendom at the opening of the year, collections of orations delivered in the Vatican by aspiring theologians like Campano (in his *De circumcisione*), Carvajal (in his *Oratio in die circumcisionis*), Cardulus (in his *Oratio de circumcisione*) and Lollio (in his *Oratio circumcisionis*) were published. A study of them has been made by the historian of rhetoric, John O'Malley.[36] This was a time when Catherine of Sienna claimed a betrothal to Christ that was mystically figured as the wearing of her Lord's foreskin as a ring. Paintings represented this mystical exchange, while several churches claimed to have the prepuce of Christ – most notably St John Lateran. Steinberg has examined how several painters in this period depicted the visitation of the Magi as an inspection of the circumcised genitalia of Jesus. This inspection can be observed, for example, in Botticelli's *Adoration of the Magi* (1470) and in Pieter Bruegel's *Adoration of the Magi* (1564).

Now part of what we are witnessing here is a cultural shift from the medieval period towards a new valorisation of the material, expressed in a new emphasis upon the incarnation. Christ was humanised. No longer portrayed as King and victor, he is shown as the vulnerable human victim. Christ is brother and friend. He was to be lived out in the world, as St Francis preached and practised. Bernardino Carvajal (preaching before Sextus IV) proclaimed: 'By circumcision he showed himself to be truly incarnate in human flesh.'[37] But despite this new turn to embodiment, there

[36] *Praise and Blame in Renaissance Rome: Rhetoric, Doctrine and Reform in the Sacred Orators of the Papal Courts, c. 1450–1521* (Durham, N.C.: Duke University Press, 1979).
[37] Quoted by Steinberg in *The Sexuality of Christ*, p. 63.

was a continuation of the tradition of allegorising the circumcision, emphasising its relation, in the new covenant, to baptism, self-sacrifice and the
glorified resurrected body.

This revaluation of the circumcision was not simply a Christian phenomenon. Elliot Wolfson has demonstrated the way Kabbalists developed what
the Old Testament and Mishnah employed as a trope into the mystical
symbol. In the *Zohar* circumcision is associated with the ability to see the
Shekhinah, the divine presence. The circumcision, as an inscription in the
flesh of the Hebrew letter *yod* (the first letter of the tetragrammaton) 'represents the divine imprint on the body'.[38] The physical opening, therefore, is
the seal that, in its symbolic valence, corresponds to an ontological opening
in God. Furthermore, entering the *Shekhinah* is an erotic experience of penetrating the divine feminine. The Kabbalists, in Wolfson's account, related
the eye and the penis in an expression of how the initiated had the ability to
see mystically and understand. They also related the phallus to the mouth,
'the covenant of the foreskin and the covenant of the tongue'.[39] A secret
wisdom is imparted such that 'the process of circumcision, the removal of
the foreskin and the uncovering of the corona, is a disclosure of the secret. In
the disclosure of the phallus, through the double act of circumcision, the
union of the masculine and feminine aspects of God is assured.'[40]

Yet despite all this cultural attention to circumcision, whenever the naked
member of Jesus is displayed pictorially or in sculpture, it is never a circumcised penis that is revealed. Steinberg lists a number of paintings of the
naked baby Jesus by Cariani, dal Colle, Perugino, Conegliano, Correggio
and others, in all of which Jesus seems to be well over eight days old and yet
never is the penis circumcised. Perhaps more striking are the sculptures by
Michelangelo, especially the Risen Christ and his famous David. These
bodies are not Jewish bodies and neither of them shows a circumcised penis.
Now why, in a culture that found great significance in the circumcision and
the humanity of Christ, is the circumcision itself not physically portrayed,
even when the genitals of Jesus are carefully delineated? Why is circumcision orally and textually proclaimed and physically and visibly masked?
What is organising the denial here, just as, in the account in Luke's Gospel,
what is organising the avowal there?

Again, let me emphasise that it is the politics governing enquiry, not the
interpretation as such, that I wish to focus on here. Politically I am struck by
the rejection of the Jewish body in both the Graeco-Roman period and

[38] *Circle in the Square*, p. 30.
[39] Ibid., p. 42.
[40] Ibid., p. 45.

Renaissance culture. This rejection gave rise in both periods to anti-Semitism and pogroms. Youths being educated in the Hellenistic schools exercised naked, and it is recorded that some Hellenised Jews who attended such schools underwent surgery to replace the foreskin (see 1 Macc. 1.15; Josephus, *Antiquities* 12.241; 1 Cor. 7.18). In the Renaissance period circumcision was mainly associated with Muslims (who were slaves) or with Jews who were associated with the greedy and covetous sides of nascent capitalism. In both cultures the circumcised body is a socially, ecclesially and aesthetically (and therefore also cosmically) inferior body. In both Roman and Renaissance cultures the circumcised body was a mutilated and wounded body, not the kind of body that could function as a microcosm of cosmic and political harmony. Why should the ideal body, that figures the resurrected body of Christ, have its foreskin intact?

The Politics of Embodiment

Let me suggest that we witness Luke's inclusion of an account of the circumcision of Jesus (coy as it is on details) and a spiritual reading of circumcision (rather than its physical inscription) in the fourteenth to sixteenth centuries as political gestures (of different, maybe opposite kinds). They are accounts of the body of Christ that are grounded upon certain cultural assumptions about embodiment. Luke appears to be making a gesture of resistance to a cultural hegemony. The Christology outlined is one in which Christ is a counter-cultural figure, an ally of the poor, the sick, the destitute – all who are socially marginalised. Michelangelo, on the other hand, is inflecting a cultural hegemony in a different manner (after all, the marble bodies of neither David nor the resurrected Christ are Jewish, they are Hellenic). His Christology is one that emphasised Christ as the perfect form of human being. The cultural resources for envisaging such perfection were classical figurations of the young, athletic body. As classical statues were being excavated, rediscovered and collected, so, in what might be termed a historicist move, Michelangelo returns to figurations of the body evident in the time of Jesus himself. In this inflexion the Jewish body is rendered socially, politically, aesthetically and finally theologically invisible. A different cultural politics, a different cultural negotiation, is involved in both accounts of the body of Jesus Christ. Different theological statements emerge in different times, under different circumstances.

The accounts themselves issue from cultural assumptions about the nature, function, even telos of the human body. As I said at the beginning of this essay, these politics of embodiment are inevitable. But let me take this further. If the politics are inevitable how does theology handle the pragmat-ics of its own discourse? To clarify the issue: the recognition of the politics of interpretation must accept that knowledges are local and enquiries into such knowledges are likewise culturally situated. The body of Jesus Christ, for example, will be differently conceived and differently theologised in differ-ent cultures and in different times. How then does Christian theology retain its commitment in faith to the one Logos? It seems to me that two answers are possible, but I can only accept one *for theological reasons*. In the first, theol-ogy accepts a broadly nominalist and later Kantian metaphysics. That is, it accepts that God is totally unknowable, absolutely transcendent, wholly other, and thus all any of us trade in is symbolic exchanges. I would reject that answer for numerous reasons. The most pertinent of these are (a) the nominalist dualism (later the dualism of noumenal and phenomenal) cannot treat embodiment at all. The body in such a metaphysics is at best a machine activated by a mind; (b) the nature of incarnation is such that God does not remain absolutely transcendent, wholly other. The body of Jesus Christ understood theologically is, to use Derrida's term, a 'quasi-transcendental'[41] and, to use Irigaray's term, a 'sensible transcendent'.[42] (c) There is a subtle imperialism at play with the enunciating position of this metaphysics. From whence can the claim be made that God is wholly other and that human beings traffic merely in symbols for a transcendent reality which may or may not correspond with that reality? This first answer to the problem of theol-ogy's production of local knowledges avoids the politics involved in construction, the violence that is ineradicable in rhetoric, by shifting atten-tion to the universal on the other side of the particular.

The second answer, the one I would wish to develop, is to embrace the inevitability of being implicated in a cultural politics; to accept that theo-logical discourses on the body of Jesus Christ, for example, produce local knowledges – they are specific negotiations within specific socio-historical contexts. Both relativism and universalism can be avoided by developing a Christology that takes time and embodiment seriously.

This Christology would emphasise, on the one hand, the continual dis-placement or deterritorialisation of the body of Christ as it is inflected in this place and that, by this Church and that, by this atheist – even – and that. By these means the Christ-effect is disseminated endlessly but not, I would argue, arbitrarily. To return to the analyses of what drives the enquiry into

---

[41] Derrida first uses the term 'quasi-transcendental' in *Glas,* trs. John P. Leavey Jr and Richard Rand (Lincoln: University of Nebraska Press, 1986).

[42] See *An Ethics of Sexual Difference*, trs. Gillian C. Gill and Carolyn Burke (London: Athlone Press, 1993).

the body of Jesus Christ at the beginning of this essay, the dissemination is determined by an erotics, a participation, a relation. The relation holds — focusing all these disseminations back to that which has solicited and produced them: the actual physical body of Jesus Christ. As, in the eucharist, the body is broken and distributed by the Church but also beyond it.

On the other hand, one would also have to emphasise in such a Christology how the body of Jesus Christ, as it operates upon and within and as the social and political body, the ecclesial and sacramental body — in what I have called variously its displacement, expansion, fragmentation and dissemination — participates in the unfolding operation of the Triune God with respect to creation. The politics of interpretation, the endless figurations of the body of Christ are, then, that which constitutes the very participation of the human in the divine, such that in each historical epoch, as in each distinct geographical-cum-ethnic location, something new is expressed, revealed, produced in a divine/human cooperation about the body of Christ. We are called to make meaning in God. That is, Christian theologians have to render visible the operation of the Word, the body of Christ. Nicephorus, the ninth-century apologist for icons, wrote in his *Third Refutation* that following the resurrection Christ's body, although it appears in a most visible and divine form (*theoeidestaton*), remains a body. It does not change itself into the divine essence (*ousia theotetos*).[43] The fact that Christ is no longer known after the flesh (2 Cor. 5.16) does not mean he has abandoned or rejected embodiment. It means he has been released from physical constraints — or physical constraints that have become viewed as such following the mathematical approach to understanding the world.[44] Theological reflection upon that embodiment is itself a participation in that extended embodiment as it moves through time and space and redeems the material. Christian *poiesis* is itself political, for the Logos is not frozen; orthodoxy is not a frozen Logos. The Logos is person and operation. Christology is not a timeless holy grail handed down from fathers to sons in the purity of its form. No doctrine is. A constant shaping takes place in the interstices between human making and *theopoiesis*. What issues from the accumulation (Nyssa might call it *skopos*) of *paradoses* is the profound mystery of embodiment itself; not just the embodiment of Jesus Christ but the ineffable nature of each human person and all forms of embodiment. For the mystery continually exceeds our local constructions of what it presents. What we discern, and the early Church Fathers discerned, about the

---

[43] 3.39. Quoted in Kenneth Parry, *Depicting the Word: Byzantine Iconophile Thought of the Eighth and Ninth Centuries* (Leiden: Brill, 1996), p. 113.
[44] See Michel Foucault, *The Order of Things*, pp. 46–77.

body of Jesus Christ becomes a meditation on the human person created *imago dei* and *as such* being the priest of the created order around them. As priests the human vocation is then to voice the mystery, which becomes a doxology, of materiality itself.

Such a Christology and theological anthropology do not get theologians themselves off the hook for producing racist or sexist bodies of Jesus Christ. The reflexivity involved in embracing the cultural politics implicated in every discursive production requires a moral responsibility (and a humility on the part of the theologian) that is sensitive to how others might receive what has been produced. Some conflict is inevitable, as some violence is inevitable in all rhetorics of persuasion. But in accepting, as Augustine once taught in *De Civitate Dei*, that it is both necessary to make judgements and equally necessary (pending the last and final judgement) to admit ignorance, then all accounts of the body of Jesus Christ remain open for correction, critique and supplementation. None of them is beyond contestation.

To conclude, then, by returning to what I set out at the beginning of this essay. What both Luke's account of Jesus's circumcision and the Renaissance theologies of the circumcision reveal is how theological discourse is part of a much wider cultural politics. Accounts of the body of Jesus Christ draw upon assumptions about both the nature of embodiment and what is valued and/or denigrated with respect to the representation of that embodiment. This involvement in a cultural politics renders theology public in the sense that it cannot ever (logically) simply talk to insiders about the nature of what is believed. It always transcends its implied readership. The language of theology and the categories for its thinking extend its discursive practices far beyond its own sectarian interests. In continually engendering the Christ figure, theological discourse is implicated in the production of bodies, in the bio-politics of such a production. The realisation of this must make theologians responsible to the wider contexts of their productions, more reflexive about the politics and rhetorics of their accounts and claims. Furthermore there are good theological reasons for this reflexivity – to wit, being so implicated is to participate in the unfolding of the Godhead with respect to creation. To accept, reflect upon and work within the cultural politics of any one time and place is an incarnational act itself, a theological materialism in which the body of Christ is constituted. As such, theologians reflecting upon the embodiment of Jesus Christ help to raise the question of the politics of embodiment itself. In doing this those politics become not simply a cultural but a theological issue. There is a politics of faith.

Coda

I realise I leave two significant questions hanging from those raised in the earlier part of this essay. These questions are related: why there has been increasing attention to the nature of Jesus Christ's embodiment since, say, Tom Driver's short but influential article 'Jesus and Sexuality' in 1965;[45] and what kinds of body is Christian theology implicated in producing today. The answers I give are more speculative because the evidence upon which I am relying is more disparate than the rich texts of the ancient or Renaissance pasts. I would suggest the attention to the nature of Jesus Christ's embodiment is part of a wider cultural obsession with the body in affluent locations around the world. This wider obsession that desires to turn the body into the most finely balanced sensorium so that it might experience its own joys and pains to the full is, I suggest, both a response to the fear of the body's disappearance and also a response to the new working conditions created by globalism[46] that demands a machine's optimum efficiency. While the call goes out for new incarnationalisms (from critical theorists like Irigaray, Cixous, Kristeva and Butler), while new health and sports clubs open every week (in the UK), while cooking and the celebrity of chefs are daily taking up more media time, while high street fashions populate the pages of every glossy magazine and film stars parade their designer labels, while films like *Hannibal* are produced reflecting the fears for and fascinations with the consumer body and while the Human Genome Project publishes its regular breakthroughs – the deepening of cyberspace, the multiplication of mobile phones and the endless mobility of peoples make gnostics of us all. Our working is becoming more and more disembodied; and in becoming more disembodied we are each becoming more depoliticised. A profound invisibility is the cost of our society of the spectacle. And the invisibility most affects bodies: the bodies of workers in countries and continents that do not appear on maps of global operations; the bodies of the disenfranchised within our own societies; and our own bodies too. As I said, this is speculative because the evidence is disparate and the examinations of it are being conducted across many different disciplines.

But what kind of bodies is theological discourse – in its very reflections upon, interpretations of, and participations within the body of Christ – producing today? The court is out on this one for the moment. It is the kind of research into contemporary ecclesial studies that needs to be funded. What

---

45 *Union Seminary Quarterly Review*, 20 (March), pp. 235–46.
46 See Colin Crouch, *Post-Democracy* (Cambridge: Polity Press, 2004), pp. 66–7.

seems evident to me is a new malleability, ambiguity, porousness, hybridity and mixing of the organic and the mechanistic. The cyborg and the angels are figures for new bodily perfections, and we theologians are busily inventing queer Christologies that somehow offer Christian models for an incarnationalism or emphasise an embodiment that is culturally more pervasive. Perhaps theology is doing no more than reproducing the bodies that are culturally in fashion. But if so, then theology really has lost its critical way, and needs to return to the wounded and violated body of Christ: the body as always in some sense circumcised and in need of circumcision. What knowledge issues not only from the gendered body and about the gendered body, but from the wounded body about the wounded gendered body? I believe this question to be central for Christian theology today in thinking through the relationship between Christology, ecclesiology and a culture of endless competition whose only value is success. We need to address this question because we can generate such wonderful images of communion, of the eschatological coming together, of paradise regained in the Kingdom of God, of eucharistic communion. Such images can ally themselves with the cult of the perfect body, not the wounded, circumcised, crucified body. Footage of newsreel taken during the siege of the middle school in Beslan, North Ossetia, in September 2004, showed Orthodox priests out in the streets of the town speaking to the crowds of distraught people whose children, friends and partners were tortured, injured, murdered, mutilated, calling them to prayer. The Church is a wounded body for the wounded; a body racked by the burden of a hope borne in a world of violations. Among the saints some have been martyred, and the Lamb on the throne in the Kingdom of God is a lamb that was slain.[47]

---

[47]   See my 'Steiner and Eagleton: The Practice of Hope and the Idea of the Tragic' in *Literature and Theology*, 19 (2) June (2005), pp. 100–11.

Part Three

THE LIVING CHRIST: ECONOMIES OF REDEMPTION

Chapter Seven

ALLEGORIA AMORIS:
A CHRISTIAN ETHICS

Kenosis: Philippians 2.5–11

Much of what follows rests upon an interpretation of seven verses in this Pauline epistle (in the Jewish context of Isaiah's suffering servant). Therefore we begin our exploration of the configurations of the doctrine of kenosis with exegesis. This is not because my exegesis can avoid being any less impartial than anyone else's, but because we need at the outset a detailed map of the kenotic trajectory. In this way we can locate particular emphases placed by theologians on one part of the trajectory and, consequently, critique their blindness to other parts. More importantly, this is not simply an essay in the history of a doctrine from the beginning to the end of modernity. This essay is also an attempt, following Balthasar and developing his insights through the work of Julia Kristeva, to configure a Christocentric doctrine of kenosis which takes Biblical exegesis as its starting point.

According to the *carmen Christi* of Philippians 2.5–11, the *locus classicus* for Christian teaching on kenosis, it is the incarnation, the Word becoming flesh, which allows us to trace an association between kenosis and naming, the event of God's love and the taking of form:

> Have this mind among yourselves, which is yours in Christ Jesus, who, though he was in the form of God, did not count equality with God a thing to be grasped, but emptied himself, taking the form of a servant, being born like other human beings. And being recognised as a man, he humbled himself and became obedient to the point of death, even death on a cross. Therefore God has highly exalted him and graciously bestowed on him the name which is above every name, that at the name of Jesus every knee should bow, in heaven and on earth and under the earth, and every tongue confess that Jesus Christ is Lord, to the glory of God the Father.

In the descent Christ empties himself, makes himself void. The verb *kenoo* is related to the adjective *kenos* meaning 'vain', 'devoid of truth' or 'without a gift'. With the doctrine of kenosis, then, we investigate exactly what it is to be incarnate. Put systematically, Christology grounds a theological anthropology, and a theological account of what we know of God and how we know it. The kenotic myth concerns the nature of theological naming or discourse and the nature of nature itself. As John Macquarrie has observed, the importance of the teaching lies in its insistence upon the material, the historical and the embodied. It offers a 'safeguard against those docetic tendencies which seem to have dogged the classical christology through the centuries'.[1] With this teaching we are concerned with the relationship between the Logos and mediation.

Kenosis is a doctrine of divine representation. But as the account of the act of divine representation it calls into question the nature and status (ontological and epistemological) of human representations before and following the incarnation. Furthermore, if Christology grounds a theological anthropology, the God who becomes form grounds the human capacity to make forms. Being *homo symbolicus* is integral to being made 'in the image of God'. It is therefore significant that the *carmen Christi* of Paul's letter reveals a concern with representations and consciousness, human and divine. 'Be mindful' verse 5 exhorts, and *phroneo* is intellectual understanding and the ability to think. The verse enjoins that we have the same consciousness as Christ. Verses 6 and 7 delineate that consciousness in terms of a certain morphology and a certain action. He existed in the form of God (*en morphe theou*) but in the emptying he became the form of a slave (*morphen doulou*). We will return to these phrases. In this morphology, though he was equal to God he did not reckon (*hegesato*), think or consider that as something to be used for his advantage.[2] In this morphology he took on the likeness (*homoiomati*) of human beings and was found in human form (*schemati*). In verse 7, the 'taking form' and the 'becoming like' are both modalities of the main verb *kenoo*. Christ's kenosis is his incarnation (death and resurrection)[3] – that is the point. It is an operation with respect to the world, it is not con-

---

[1]   John Macquarrie, *Jesus Christ in Modern Thought* (London: SCM, 1990), p. 245.
[2]   See P.T. O'Brien, *The Epistle to the Philippians* (Grand Rapids, Mich.: Eerdmans, 1991), pp. 211–16 on interpretations of this phrase *ouk haragmon hegesato*.
[3]   J. Jeremias, on the basis of a comparison between this action and the pouring out of the Suffering Servant's soul in Isaiah 53, argues that the kenosis is not the incarnation, but only the death. See 'Zu Phil 2, 7 … EAUTON EKENOSEN' in *Novum Testamentum* 6 (1963), pp. 182–8. This would associate him with the culture of necropolis, modernity. Central to my thesis is that an act of incarnation is also an entry into death, but the two moments of this economy are summed up in a third – resurrection, which is an eternal living beyond oneself.

cerned with the abandonment of divine properties. Something about God is revealed in the operation that would otherwise be concealed – his power-lessness in his giving of himself as servant. The effect of kenosis is a renaming of the world, a world embraced by the Word, again. God gives Christ 'the name above all names [*to onoma to uper pan onoma*]'; a name before which all others will bow and each tongue confess (*exomologesetai* – speak out pub-licly) the Lordship of Christ. Again, humiliation or submission (not Christ's this time, but ours) leads directly to acts of representation, to speaking out publicly. The site for the continuation of the renaming of the world in terms of the Word is the Church – its liturgies, its sacraments, its office.

One of the main shifts within the hymn is from the language of form (*morphe* and *schema*) to the act of naming. The act of naming is made to par-ticipate in the form of revelation – for the name revealed, and then confessed, is God's own name, Lord. Furthermore, its concern with repre-sentation and human consciousness is worked out in terms of a poetic performance. The Christian reader learns by reading, as we saw in the first essay and we see again in the next. Reading is part of the theological prac-tice, the theological pedagogy. Since Ernst Lohmeyer's study of the hymn in the 1920s, these lines have been understood to constitute a poetic unit com-posed with ellipsis, 'rhythm, parallelism, and strophic arrangement'.[4] In other words, the hymn re-presents. It is not separated as an act from the action it tells. It is a poetic enactment reflecting upon three enfolded forms of representation – the divine representation of God in Christ, the exem-plary nature and vicarious representation of Christ's self-giving for the Philippians (see 2.1–4), and the act of naming and speaking as a response to the reception of what is given. The hymn is characterised by a self-reflexive meditation upon theological, ethical and linguistic imitation – salvation, the appropriate behaviour of those being saved and language. The kenotic economy turns, then, upon four key words associated with mimesis – *morphe, homoioma, schema* and *onoma*. *Morphe* is an unusual word in the New Testament – it appears only once more in the longer ending of Mark's Gospel (16.12). According to Lightfoot it 'implies not the external accidents but the essential attributes'.[5] Much has been written concerning the dative *en,* and several commentators have stressed its importance for the interpreta-tion of the whole passage.[6] *En morphe theou* – the Godhead as a sphere

---

[4]   O'Brien, *Philippians*, p. 198. Although it still remains contentious how many strophes there are – two (Martin – note 6) or three.

[5]   J.B. Lightfoot, *St. Paul's Epistle to the Philippians* (London: Macmillan, 1894), p. 108.

[6]   R.P. Martin, *Carmen Christi: Philippians 2.5–11 in Recent Interpretation and in the Setting of Early Christian Worship* (Cambridge University Press, 1967), p. 99; O'Brien, *Philippians*, p. 206.

within which Christ dwells – would then be the equivalent of the Johannine 'that glory I had with you before the world began' (17.5). The *en* would then suggest Trinitarian participation by the Son in the Father. Following Lightfoot, a host of more recent scholars have confirmed this reading by pointing out the affinity between *morphe* and *eikon*, where *eikon* suggests not a distinction between form and substance, but a participation of one in the other. Furthermore, *eikon* is associated in both the LXX and elsewhere in the New Testament with the glory of God, his *doxa*.[7] In the kenosis this participation is poured out and Christ clothes himself (*lambano*) in the essential attributes, *morphe*, of slavery. Note the connection here between slavery and glory in the Godhead – both are moments in a Trinitarian procession. As F.F. Bruce put it, challenging nineteenth-century kenotic Christologies which saw in Christ as servant the abandonment of his divine properties in the form of God: 'The implication is not that Christ, by becoming incarnate, exchanged the form of God for the form of a slave, but that he manifested the form of God in the form of a slave.'[8] Bruce pinpoints a certain concealment and therefore agnosticism pertaining to this form which Balthasar's doctrine of analogy develops: 'Christ's *morphe* exists within a tension unique to it which is intelligible only in a Christological sense: it ... presents itself primarily as its opposite and as the uttermost concealment of this divine form.'[9] The Pauline language suggests an antithesis of 'God' and 'slave', but the repetition of *morphe* identifies the two in the way John in his Gospel identifies crucifixion with exaltation.

As this icon of slavery Christ was born in the likeness (*homoiomati*) of humankind. *Homoiomati* is an ambivalent word in the New Testament (and the history of Christological reflection). Battles have been fought over how to translate it. Lightfoot again points the way: 'Thus *homoioma* stands midway between *morphe* and *schema*.'[10] *Schema* denotes the outward appearance, the accidents, in the Aristotelian sense, of human nature. But these appearances are not manifestations of the substance, they are rather signifiers that are distinct from but which detail the signified substance. Human forms, natural forms are neither appearances nor self-defining matter. *Homoioma* operates at the threshold between the essential manifestation of the form,

---

[7]   See Martin, *Carmen Christi*, pp. 99–119 for a detailed discussion of the association. See also 2 Cor. 4.4 and Col. 1.15 for Christ as *eikon tou theou*, developing a second Adam Christology. The association is important for Balthasar's own concept of Christ as the revelation of God's glory.

[8]   'St. Paul in Macedonia. 3. The Philippian Correspondence', in *Bulletin of the John Rylands Library* 63 (1980–1), p. 270.

[9]   *Herrlichkeit* Bd. I (Einsiedeln: Johannes Verlag, 1969), p. 645; *Glory of the Lord: A Theological Aesthetics. I: Seeing the Form*, tr. Erasmo Leiva-Merikakis (Edinburgh: T. & T. Clark, 1982), p. 670.

[10] Lightfoot, *Philippians*, p. 110.

the icon, and the external appearances. The first, *morphe*, is identical with the original, its ontological extension. The second, *schema*, is an image or resemblance, which is emphasised by the comparative *hos* – he was found *hos anthropos*, bearing all the hallmarks of a human being. A note of separation from the essence, the original, is evident. But *homoiomata* can suggest both full identity with and difference from. R.P. Martin, in his extended analysis of the *carmen Christi* in Paul's letter, concludes: 'The sharp alternatives are: its meaning as "identity" or "equivalence" and its meaning as "similarity" or "resemblance".'[11] The dative here, *en homoiomati*, is both a dative of respect ('with respect to being human') and one of participation ('entering into the condition of being human'). 'By *homoioma* ... Paul doubtless wishes to see ... the process whereby the thing itself impresses its form on us on its own initiative [*ein sich-Auspragen der Sache selbst und von ihr selbst her*]' Balthasar remarks, emphasising both similarity and identification.[12]

The move from *morphe*, through *homoioma* to *schemati* expresses a deepening progression towards externality, secondariness and appearance – towards a human externality which manifests the essential nature of being a slave, towards a world in which what appears is not what is. There is a descent from a logic of identity into a world of shifting appearances and, with verse 9, there is a return to the logic of identity when the Father crowns the Son with his name; a name they share, Lord, Yahweh. In this presentation of kenosis, then, an economy of representation is outlined – form, analogy and figuration give way to the stability of denomination and identity, the name above all names. The return to the Father is a return to the 'form of God' from which he descended – the glory of self-identification within Trinitarian difference. This economy of representation is framed within a rhythm of exchange – acts of giving and receiving by both God and Christ. We will return to this later.

There remain, though, two important aporias in this mimetic economy. The first we have drawn attention to – the ambivalent and yet pivotal word *homoioma*, where presence becomes representation for what is absent. For at what point in the word 'likeness' does identity shift towards resemblance? The second aporia also involves an absenting, a cancelling of presence. For the doctrine of kenosis makes inseparable from the incarnation the descent into death. The ultimate descent into non-being and non-identity is part of, though not the end of, the kenotic trajectory. Dispossession lies at the centre of incarnation. This is important for understanding the nature of *homo symbolicus*, the one 'made in the image of' who subsequently makes

---

[11] *Carmen Christi*, p. 200.
[12] *Herrlichkeit* Bd. I , p. 556; *Glory of the Lord*, vol. I, p. 578.

images of or resemblances. It is important because insofar as Christ's humanity is true humanity and true image of God, the kenosis of incarnation
defines the human condition – its physical appearance, its representations of
those appearances – as crucified, as constantly abiding in a state of dispossession and resemblances. We descend, in the hymn, from true presence in God
into the symbolics of being human, into textuality. From textuality we move
out again into the silent margins of death which erases both our humanity
and our representations. Crucifixion presents a moment when the sacramental is eclipsed.

Not that crucifixion, absence and autism is the end of the kenotic story.
There is resurrection, a renaming and a re-empowerment to speak. We pass,
with Christ, through the textuality of the cosmos from one margin of transcendence to another; we move towards and then beyond death. In the
middle, in the textuality of the cosmos, is the incarnation–crucifixion–
resurrection of the form. Of course, the other way of seeing this would be
to say that the textuality of the cosmos is the single aporia transgressed by
the Trinity which frames it. We exist, then, in the aporia created by God in
the initial *diastasis* that opens with creation itself.[13] Only *post-mortem* are we
re-empowered to speak in the name of Christ. Only *post-mortem* is identification possible. As Balthasar writes: 'this inexact [*ungefähre*] word is replaced
by the exact Word [*durch das exakte Wort ersetzt wird*], which is uttered precisely where the word passes over into silence [*ins Todesschweigen*]'.[14] We find
the same sentiment expressed in the Book of Revelation, in the letter to the
angel of the Church at Pergamum: 'To him who conquers ... I will give a
white stone, with a new name written on the stone which no one knows
except him who receives it' (Rev. 2.17). *Post-mortem* one is given the personhood one always knows is possible; *ante-mortem* is a process of becoming
through obedience, humility and descent. *Ante-mortem* is time for realising
our dispossession, our secondariness; realising, what Emmanuel Lévinas
describes as our position as accusative in a transcendental grammar. The dispossession is integral to the fact we are 'in the image of' and image makers.
It is an expression of that initial *diastasis* separating the uncreated creator
from the created creation. The *ante-mortem* realisation of our dependence,
though, and the secondariness of our representations, are lived within the
horizon of *post-mortem* hopes. The economy of our representations and self-
representation is, theologically, inseparable from our eschatological partici-

---

[13] This concept of *diastasis* will become important for our understanding of Balthasar's work.
[14] *Herrlichkeit*, Bd. III.2/2 Teil (Einsiedeln: Johannes Verlag, 1969), p. 76; *Glory of the Lord: A Theological Aesthetics. VII: Theology: The New Covenant* tr. B. McNeil (Edinburgh: T. & T. Clark, 1989),
pp. 84–5.

pation in the Godhead. In the words of Balthasar: 'Only in death, through divine judgement, does a man receive his definitive orientation.'[15]

The final moment of the kenotic economy is, then, the resurrected body of Christ, his Church. Those whose knees shall bow and whose tongues confess that Jesus Christ is Lord. A continuum is established between the named Christ, the true image of God, and those who worship that name through their own acts of naming; being incorporated into that name through their verbalised response to and reception of it. The textuality of the cosmos is woven into the discourse of heaven, the wording of the world is enfolded within the Word of God through this resurrected body of Christ and the Church. The Church's confession and worship of Christ centre on its own act of representation, the eucharist which enacts Christ's kenosis and our kenosis in Christ through the Spirit. Through this representative act the body of Christ is distributed through the body of the Church which is made up of individual bodies located in social and political bodies. The resurrected *corpus Christi* enfolds all other bodies within it, like the Word enfolding all our words. All other bodies become sites of mystery. The Church, in its response of serving the One who became a Servant, receives its identity as the community of the resurrection, a body located within resurrection life which is its truth, its beauty, its goodness. Bodies as such are always transcorporal – being a physical, spiritual, ecclesial, sacramental and verbal body. This transcorporality is the enfleshment of Christ's givenness to the Father. Creation is Christ's eucharistic confession to the Father. It has no independent meaning; there is no *natura pura*. The world is an allegory of love to be interpreted by love.

Kenosis and the End of Modernity

The doctrine of kenosis was not a point of intense theological debate until the seventeenth century, but because here my concern lies with the doctrine at the end of rather than the entry into modernity, we will pick up kenosis as it came to be developed in the nineteenth century by Lutheran theologians. The focus of the doctrine is now upon the religious self-consciousness of Jesus. The contents of Jesus the Christ's consciousness as the focus for understanding the man–God paradox dominate the wave of debate on kenosis; this debate ranges from E. Sartorius's book *Lehre von der heiligen Liebe*, published in 1844, through to W.F. Gess's work *Das Dogma von Christi: Person und Werk* of 1887. The most significant development in this treatment of the

---

[15]   *Mysterium Paschale*, tr. A. Nichols (Edinburgh: T. & T. Clark, 1990), p. 13.

doctrine comes from the contemporary concerns with historicism, biography and *Bildung*. The treatment of kenosis is a theological aspect of the search for the historical Jesus and discussions concerning the evolution of Jesus's Messianic consciousness.

The most systematic and theologically rigorous of these accounts came from Gottfried Thomasius. For Thomasius what Christ 'poured out' were certain properties of his divine nature, two in particular: omnipotence and omniscience. God is treated as absolute subject and the subject is a self with certain dispositions and attributes that are essential to its nature and the way that self will develop. Thomasius does relate kenosis to a Trinitarian operation, for the 'being man becomes a moment of the inner-divine relationship'.[16] But his concept of the Trinity is two subjects (Father and Son) and a relationship (Spirit).[17] He distinguishes between what is an essential attribute and what is a relative attribute in God. The essential attributes are freedom, holiness, absolute truth and absolute love. The relative attributes are omniscience, omnipotence and omnipresence. These God possesses only in relation to the world and it is these that Christ relinquishes.[18] There are obvious theological difficulties with this account, not the least of which is the division in God himself caused by the existence of a world he brought into being. Alois Emmanuel Biedermann's observation is accurate: 'the relative attributes ... [God] can surrender, because the world and thus the relation to it is not necessary to Him'.[19] Biedermann views this as a step on the road to gnosticism.

As far as this essay is concerned, all that needs to be noted is Thomasius's inadequate Trinitarian reading of kenosis, his attention to subject positions with essential and relative attributes and the absence of any necessary connection now between the incarnation and the Passion. Kenosis begins to label a certain diminishment of faculties. Time and creation prevent God from being God. It is human finitude that is uppermost, a human finitude to which his model of Christ draws attention. Death is the release from such finititude. Hence, because of his attention to attributes of Christ as a historical person, the crucifixion is not the final outworking of the incarnation, a movement in God himself, it is merely the cancellation of the human con-

---

[16] *Christi: Person und Werk* (Erlangen, 1853). For a selection from *Christ's Person and Work*, see C. Welch ed. and tr., *God and Incarnation in Mid-century Germany Theology* (New York: Oxford University Press, 1965), pp. 23–101. This quote is from *God and Incarnation*, p. 83.

[17] This is a concept of the Trinity that constitutes one of the backbones of modern theology, particularly Protestant modern theology. There are parallels between this concept and the kinds of Christological thinking I draw attention to in chapter five, 'Divinity and Sexual Difference', pp. 147–8.

[18] *God and Incarnation*, pp. 67–72.

[19] Ibid., p. 303.

sciousness and its limitations. With this attention to the attributes of Christ's person and with the emphasis upon historical contingency in the developing liberal humanist Christologies, the *Myth of God Incarnate* simply awaits its writing. Developments in the doctrine of kenosis will lead to theologies of the death of God, so-called secular theologies.

It was Hegel who first announced this possibility. The tragic fate of the Unhappy Consciousness in which the self aims to be absolute, in which the human absorbs the divine, announces 'the hard saying that "God is dead"'.[20] Hegel prophesies here the atheistic apotheosis of liberal humanism. Prior to Thomasius or even Sartorius, Hegel propounded a view of kenosis in one of the closing sections of *The Phenomenology of Spirit*, 'The Revealed Religion', which was to be highly influential in the development of twentieth-century Christologies. Prior to the mainline nineteenth-century kenoticists, he nevertheless was more radical in suggesting the complete surrender by Christ of all divinity or the complete identification of Christ with all things human.[21] The closing sections of the *Phenomenology of Spirit* are vague, elliptical and suggestive. They are notoriously difficult texts to elucidate. But it is important to understand Hegel's recapitulation of kenosis not only in order to see how modernity's preoccupation with death culminates in the semi-readings of Hegel by death-of-God theologians, but also in order to recognise the parallels between Hegel's thinking and Balthasar's teaching on kenosis.

In *The Phenomenology of Spirit* Hegel employs the word twice in his highly abstract account of Christ's birth, death and resurrection. The abstract nature of the account, while difficult, is methodological – the concern of the dialectical movement of Spirit is always to move beyond its representations of itself. Hegel wishes, then, to concentrate upon what he calls the 'Notion of Spirit' rather than 'picture thinking' – a move similar to Bultmann's project of demythologisation, a move in which (or so it seems) speculative philosophy becomes the hermeneutical key for understanding the revelation of God in the narrative accounts of Jesus Christ. I write 'so it seems' because following the considerable reappraisal of Hegel as a theologian[22] it seems

---

[20] *The Phenomenology of Spirit*, tr. A.V. Miller (Oxford University Press, 1977), p. 455.

[21] 'Hegel ... must be regarded as the primogenitor in modernity of the espousal of a thoroughly radical interpretation of kenosis': Cyril O'Regan, *The Heterodox Hegel* (New York: State University of New York Press, 1994), p. 219. It is significant, though, that Hegel's concept of the Trinity moves closer to an operational one – it is not two persons and a relationship.

[22] See O'Regan and the detailed analysis of the religious context of *The Phenomenology of Spirit* in Laurence Dickey, *Hegel: Religion, Economics, and the Politics of Spirit 1770–1807* (Cambridge University Press, 1988). For theological accounts of Hegel see Albert Chapelle, *Hegel et la religion, t. 1: La problematique; t. 2: La dialectique. Dieu et la Création; t. 3: La dialectique. La Theologie et l'Eglise; Annexes* (Paris: Editions Universitaires, 1963–71); Emilio Brito, *Hegel et la tache actuelle de la christologie*, tr. Th. Dejond S.J. (Paris: Editions Lethielleux, 1979).

that the judgement of Jean Hyppolite – that religion is 'prefigurative representation of philosophical thought'[23] – cannot go unchallenged. The revealed status of the Christian religion for Hegel privileges and universalises its claims to truth. The narrative of Christ can be seen as offering a hermeneutical key for the condition of being human. That is, the Trinitarian account of Christ's kenotic descent and return to the father presents us with an account of selfhood. Rather like Augustine's *De Trinitate*, therefore, it is not the structure of being human which offers us a revelation of the Trinity, but the Trinity which offers us the revelation of the structure of being human. Theology precedes, in this model, and provides the possibility for understanding and the condition for the existence of the philosophical and anthropological.

In developing the Notion of Spirit Hegel draws upon metaphors culled from a Biblical soteriology – Adam's fall, Christ's coming, Christ's return to the Father – and understands the structure of what later was termed *Heilsgeschichte* as the structure of mind itself, our mind and the mind of God. Unlike the Greek religious Spirit which gave rise to an aesthetic representation (in works of art), the Christian man-God was actualised in history. Hegel does not doubt this. In the former religion the absolute self-consciousness of the Spirit is figured forth by the finite Spirit. In the latter the absolute self-consciousness of the Spirit manifests itself. The former represents human knowledge of the divine. The latter is God's presentation of his own self-knowledge. Hence Christianity is a revealed religion and the '*content* of this picture-thinking is absolute thinking'.[24] We can observe here the radical difference between the Lutheran Hegel and Luther's own emphasis upon divine concealment. For Hegel, '[t]his concealment ceases when the absolute Being *qua* Spirit is the object of consciousness'.[25] There are theological, though not philosophical, difficulties here. If all is revealed then there is no transcendence. If there is no transcendence, if all is immanent, then all is indifferent. We will return to this. Death is resurrection for Hegel, but does that mean that there is no distinction? Are we moving towards a form of integration where difference collapses and knowledge is oblivion – a form of death *à la* Spinoza's third degree of knowledge?

Kenosis is used on both occasions in *Phenomenology of Spirit* to express an externalisation of Self that moves consciousness into self-consciousness. This self-consciousness, to become self-consciousness, has to take on form, has to involve itself with representation (*Vorstellung*). It is exactly at this point

---

[23] Jean Hyppolite, *Structure and Genesis of Hegel's Phenomenology of Spirit*, trs. S. Cherwiak and J. Heckman (Evanston, Ill.: Northwestern University Press, 1984), p. 532.

[24] Hegel, *Phenomenology*, p. 479.

[25] Ibid., p. 459.

– the recognition of the centrality of mediation and mimesis – that the focus of Hegel's account of kenosis differs from the Christocentric accounts of the seventeenth- and nineteenth-century Lutherans. This, in turn, is because of the emphatically Trinitarian understanding of both Christ's kenosis and the movement of the Spirit towards the integration of knowing and being in Hegel. Christ is one moment, one figure in a Trinitarian narrative. He alone is not the Saviour, his death is not in some isolated way the summation of our salvation. '[T]hree moments constitute Spirit ...: essence, being-for-self which is the otherness of essence and for which essence is, and being-for-self, or knowledge of itself *in the* "other".'[26] This Hegel relates to a Lutheran emphasis upon the Word. 'It is the word which, when uttered, leaves behind, externalized and emptied, him who uttered it, but which is as immediately heard, and only this hearing of its own self is the existence of the Word.'[27] This pictures a perichoretic Trinity: 'Thus the distinctions made are immediately resolved as soon as they are made, and are made as soon as they are resolved, and what is true and actual is precisely this immanent circular movement.'[28]

We need to elucidate this further in order best to appreciate its implications – for an understanding of both Hegel's theological thinking and the future kenoticists. The main point is that incarnation completes creation.[29] Incarnation reveals the spiritualisation of Nature because it reveals the dynamic whereby the infinite Spirit in its abstraction and alienation enters into living and necessary conversations with the finite Spirit. This raises problems about the freedom of God to create out of nothing that we will examine further in relation to Balthasar's emphasis upon the *diastasis* between Creator and creation. But Hegel's doctrine of kenosis is Trinitarian: the Father abandons in an externalisation of his Spirit his abstract distance, entering into self-consciousness, which, to be self-consciousness must take on concrete representation. The Son, as this concrete representation of the Father, allows himself to be put to death so that the absolute Spirit, which is the continual movement of consciousness to self-consciousness, might be manifest. 'This death is, therefore, its resurrection as Spirit.'[30] This Trinitarian economy parallels creation itself because it was the 'eternal or

---

[26] Ibid., p. 465.

[27] Ibid., p. 465.

[28] Ibid., p. 465.

[29] O'Regan thinks creation and incarnation are given equal weight, that the body of God in creation is identical to the body of God in Christ. I am not sure here.

[30] Hegel, *Phenomenology*, p. 471. Is there too much emphasis upon pneumatology? O'Regan thinks so. But the Spirit only exists on the basis of creation/incarnation. We could say that there is not enough Spirit in Hegel – that the Spirit simply remains as the movement-in-relation operating between the Father and Son; that the Spirit is not a distinct hypostasis. See later in the chapter.

abstract Spirit' becoming 'other' to itself or entering existence, which created the world.[31] Within this world individual selves do not exist as Spirit because they remain bound to the immediacy of the natural. They must become self-conscious, other to themselves, in order to be spiritual. The Fall is therefore inevitable, man 'lost the form of being at one with himself'[32] and began 'this withdrawal into itself or self-centredness'.[33] The withdrawal into oneself is not in itself evil, for Hegel, for in the purity of God's Trinitarian action there is a withdrawal into God's self. But because human self-reflected 'thought stems from immediacy or is *conditioned* thought, it is not pure knowledge'.[34] The move of the finite Spirit is therefore towards the purity of knowledge, *Gewissen* (certainty). The incarnation is a vital stage on this journey because it is with the incarnation that the truth of universal consciousness is revealed, and the certainty is manifest that human beings strive to attain. 'The dead divine Man or the human God is *in himself* the universal self-consciousness.'[35] This is manifest now in the Spirit of the community. An imitation of Christ is necessary and possible. As Jean Hyppolite glosses, 'The movement that took place in Christ must now be executed in the midst of the community and must become its movement instead of being alien to it.'[36] God empties himself out into the human and the human empties itself out into the divine.

'The entire system seems dominated by a meditation on the death *of Christ*.'[37] The secularisation of this subject, subsequently, will only emphasise the death-bound subjectivity we noted earlier. Furthermore, Luther's existential approach to theology is now substantially developed and, along with Schleiermacher's contemporaneous project, the foundations of liberal Protestantism are laid. It is with the apotheosis of such liberalism and the desiring subject, in the death-of-God theologians, that Hegel's concerns with kenosis will be recapitulated.

According to the flight of history as Thomas J.J. Altizer conceives it we are the inhabitants of a profound spiritual darkness which has been enshrouding the world since the death of Christ and is now coming towards its final and apocalyptic conclusion.[38] The Word will have its eschatological

---

[31] Ibid., p. 467.

[32] Ibid., p. 468.

[33] Ibid., p. 468.

[34] Ibid., p. 468.

[35] Ibid., p. 475.

[36] Ibid., p. 567.

[37] Brito, *Hegel*, p. 141.

[38] See his books *History as Apocalypse* (Albany: State University of New York Press, 1985) and *Genesis and Apocalypse* (Albany: State University of New York Press, 1990).

fulfilment. As the history of religions unfolds Christianity is the final one and Christianity can be the final one because the death of God is the centre of that religion. The distinctiveness of Christianity lies in its commitment, through kenosis, to time and creation. The death of God at the crucifixion is emphatically not simply the death of the Son of God, it is deipassionism – a radical working of the doctrine of kenosis. Altizer builds specifically on Hegelian foundations: 'Hegel is the only thinker who made the kenotic movement of the Incarnation the core and foundation of all his thinking.'[39] In Hegel he finds the total eclipse of the transcendent, sovereign and impassive God and the affirmation of the immanence of the world order, a baptised world order. This is the order of what Altizer calls 'total presence'. On the basis of Hegelian kenosis Altizer recommends us, then, to a Christian atheism.

Altizer develops this radical kenosis the furthest, followed by the deconstructive theologians Charles Winquist and Mark C. Taylor.[40] These last two thinkers explicitly relate Altizer's 'theology' with the concerns, and philosophical methods, of post-structural nihilism. How accurate their readings of post-structuralism are is a debate we cannot enter into with this essay. But, for example, in Taylor's work, the eclipse of the transcendent Word is mapped onto a certain reading of Derrida's critique of the relationship between presence and language (logocentrism), Derrida's economy of the endless promotion of differences and deferrals of meaning in language (*différance*) and Derrida's understanding of the continual need of language to supplement itself (dissemination); and so he writes: 'writing is a kenotic process; it empties everything of absolute self-identity and complete self-presence'.[41] In Taylor's work Hegel encounters the linguistic turn. Kenosis is Hegel's immanent process of consciousness becoming conscious of itself and always in the process of surpassing itself reinscribed in terms of textuality. In fact, for Taylor, reality is textuality. But this textuality has none of the allegorical depth and transcendent significance of the Word enfolding all our words – the theme of the kenotic hymn in Philippians. This textuality is all surface, simulacra and façade. As a Christian atheist, Taylor relates this

---

[39] *The Gospel of Christian Atheism* (Philadelphia, Penn.: Westminster Press, 1966), p. 29.

[40] See Charles Winquist's *Epiphanies of Darkness: Deconstruction in Theology* (University of Chicago Press, 1986) and *Desiring Theology* (University of Chicago Press, 1995). For Mark C. Taylor, see *Deconstructing Theology* (New York: Crossroads, 1982) and *Erring: A Postmodern A/theology* (University of Chicago Press, 1984). These theological readings of kenosis are paralleled with several contemporary philosophical ones, as we saw in chapter two, 'The Schizoid Christ', pp. 77–82. Each of them is bound to nihilistic non-foundationalism.

[41] Taylor, *Erring*, p. 118.

dissemination of the presence of the Word to the eucharist as a celebration of dismemberment, dissemination as distribution and crucifixion of the individual self.[42]

Altizer's total presence, like Taylor's linguistic idealism, announces the nihilism of indifference that is the last stage on the road to pure immanence. In Taylor's more performative work we have a vision of the endless, playful erring that fulfils the telos of history as Altizer presents it. Here is total presence – for the writing itself, as it flows along and floats over various ideas and themes, is all there is. The reader constructs and performs and the reading experience of that construction and performance is all the meaning Taylor wishes to promote. Although both atheologians speak of new-found freedoms, particularly freedom from the bondage of a transcendent master God, all value in their worlds is simply local, transient and relative. Liberal humanism – all three thinkers are indebted to the romantic tradition and the theological liberalism of Paul Tillich – has now arrived at the apotheosis of the secular and the superficial. Only the aesthetic, divorced from truth and goodness, remains – Altizer's poetic theology and pastiches of the prophetic, Taylor's commitment to Dionysian wordplay as a form of spiritual exercise.

At the end of modernity, therefore, where does the doctrine of kenosis go? Fundamentally, we have to reappropriate what modernity left behind in its own development and exposition of the teaching. I suggest, with reference to the exegesis of Philippians, that what is absent from modernity's concept of kenosis is the role played by theological discourse as response to a reception of and participation in the divine. For the kenotic economy is redemptive and culminates in a resurrection of the body. In the Pauline narrative, being-unto-death does not expunge the greater movement of being-unto-eternal-life. In refiguring the doctrine of kenosis at the end of modernity Hegel is important here. Hegel drew attention to the importance of representation in the kenotic economy. Furthermore, the reading of Hegel by the death-of-God theologians is a particularly selective one. It is Hegel read through Nietzsche's *amor fati* (a version of the immanence announced in Spinoza's *amor intellectus* – which is also a move towards oblivion) and Zarathustra's pronouncement in the market that God is dead. Hegel rails against those who collapse God into World so that there is too much God – 'God is everything and everything is God' – in the closing pages of his *Encyclopaedia*. He accuses such thinkers of stupidity, falsification,

---

[42] Ibid., pp. 120, 141–2. See the philosophical equivalent to this mode of thinking in Jean-Luc Nancy's essay 'Corpus', in *The Birth to Presence*, tr. Claudette Surtiliot (Stanford University Press, 1993).

and misconception, foreseeing the outcome as 'the secularity of things'.[43] Spinoza's philosophy is listed among such tendencies. Furthermore, Hegel's death of God is not the same as Nietzsche's. Hegel's is more Lutheran and historically concrete – it is the death of the particular incarnation of God in Jesus Christ. Nietzsche's death of God is a metaphor for the end of any transcendent system of values – Goodness, Reality, Truth, Immortality. God for Nietzsche is the figure *par excellence* of what he terms 'metaphysical comfort'.

For Altizer God is a superego, a bigger and more powerful version of ourselves in the sky above – he is overlord. He is, to use the language of Karl Barth (or in a different way entirely, Louis Althusser), Absolute Subject.[44] Hegel's God is much closer to Aristotle's *dunamis* and therefore Aquinas's *actus purus*. Even Feuerbach, as a pupil of Hegel, distinguished between Hegel's God and his own conception of the divine as a human projection.[45] Fundamentally, for Altizer (as for Nietzsche) God is not Trinitarian. It is because of Hegel's insistence upon the Trinitarian distinctions that he is not committed (as Altizer and Nietzsche are) to deipassionism. It is also because of the Trinitarian distinction that the logic of theology for Hegel retains its insistence upon the transcendent (or, at least, self-transcendent)[46] Christ, who existed before all worlds, returning to unity with the Father.[47] In the movement of that giving and return, that mediation of the infinite and the finite, the Spirit is dispensed into the community. There is, then, an immanent *and* an economic Trinity, and so Hegel believes he avoids the atheism of the pantheist as he avoids the docetism of the panlogist. Altizer does not read Hegel in this way. Altizer's reading follows a line of Anglo-American antitheological accounts of Hegel; accounts in which 'Hegel is trimmed and important aspects of his vision shelved, misinterpreted, or explained away'.[48] French and German readings of Hegel tend to have a deeper and more positive evaluation of his theological framework. Nietzsche's much greater presence in the thought of Altizer and the death-of-God theologians is

---

[43]   Hegel, *Philosophy of Mind, Being Part Three of the 'Encyclopaedia of the Philosophical Sciences'*, tr. A. V. Miller (Oxford: Clarendon Press, 1971), pp. 304–5.

[44]   For Barth see the Introduction to this volume. For Althusser see essay five, 'Divinity and Sexual Difference'.

[45]   See Lawrence Dickey, 'Hegel on Religion and Philosophy' in *The Cambridge Companion to Hegel*, ed. Frederick C. Beiser (Cambridge University Press, 1993), pp. 301–47.

[46]   For a discussion of the difference between transcendence and self-transcendence see my 'Sacramentalism or Neopaganism', *Theology* (July 1991), pp. 279–83.

[47]   *Philosophy of Mind*, p. 225. God 'has from all eternity begotten a Son, in whom he, as Spirit, is at home with himself'.

[48]   O'Regan, *The Heterodox Hegel*, p. 86.

evident in talk about being released from bondage to this transcendent God and the new Dionysian life that awaits us all when we move with the flow and pulsations of life. There is an ever greater sense of freedom, these death-of-God theologians argue, as the finite moves towards a greater sense of its particularity and universality. This is a secularised doctrine of atonement and another turn in the Enlightenment dream of human emancipation. But Hegel's concept of necessity means that God has never usurped a position that was not his to begin with. He is as committed to our self-realisation as his own. His freedom and ours are co-implicated. There is a doctrine of participation in the operations of the divine. There is no scope for a release from bondage to the transcendent in Hegel – this is Nietzsche's reading of Hegel's master–slave dialectic in terms of Christian *ressentiment*. In Hegel, we are bound to God as God is to us – necessity led to the incarnation and death of Christ; bound by love. It is this necessary relation, which obviates God's own freedom to chose, and the traditional teaching of creation *ex nihilo*, that will lead Hegel into troubled waters. Primarily, there is the impossibility of grace and the Trinity as an economy of gift. Secondly, there is a compromised transcendence, a univocity in which part and whole, human and divine, share a common ontological foundation. Kenosis operates here – and this is where he differs from Balthasar or, more recently, Jean-Luc Marion[49] – within, not beyond, the philosophical project (metaphysics understood as onto-theology).[50] And with this lies the danger of presenting far too much God, like Spinoza. Hegel is, then, certainly not orthodox, but he is not apostate either. His work stands ambivalently in two historical epochs – the traditional past (late antiquity and medieval) and modernity's present. To refigure kenosis Christologically at the end of modernity we have to develop the Hegel who drew upon the premodern. That will lead us to Balthasar and to poststructural thinkers of kenosis, particularly Julia Kristeva.

---

[49]   Marion develops a *theologia crucis* which rests upon 'une kénose de l'image' which transgresses 'des principes esthétiques' in his book *La Croisée du visible* (Paris: La Différence, 1991). See also Jean-Yves Lacoste's essay 'Jalons pour un traitement kénotique de la question de l'homme' in *Expérience et absolu* (Paris: Presses Universitaires de France, 1994).

[50]   Balthasar wishes to keep metaphysics. In fact, he wants to view the Christian as the guardian of a proper metaphysics of eros, but he distinguishes this metaphysical thinking from the metaphysics which conflates Being with total presence and 'systems of identity': *Herrlichkeit*, Bd. III. Teil 1/2 (Einsiedeln: Johannes Verlag, 1967), p. 978; *Glory of the Lord: A Theological Aesthetics. V: The Realm of Metaphysics in the Modern Age*, tr. O. Davies et al. (Edinburgh: T. & T. Clark, 1991), p. 651.

Balthasar's Kenotic Economy

Kenosis is not simply at the centre of Balthasar's theology. Its economy is both the condition for the possibility of theo-logic itself and its very form (*Gestalt*): 'there is only one way to approach the Trinitarian life in God: on the basis of what is manifest in God's kenosis in the theology of the covenant – and thence in the theology of the Cross – we must feel our way back into the mystery of the absolute'.[51] 'This primal kenosis [*Ur-Kenose*] makes possible all other kenotic movements of God into the world; they are simply its consequences.'[52]

As with the early Fathers he quotes (Cyril, Gregory of Nyssa, Hilary, Chrysostom) kenosis is a Trinitarian event. Laconically, Balthasar writes: 'the Son's *missio* is his *processio* extended [through desire, *verlängert*] in "economic" mode; but whereas in his *processio* he moves towards the Father in receptivity and gratitude, in his *missio* ... he moves away from Him and towards the world'.[53] We can elucidate this account of Trinitarian processions with reference to a prayer Balthasar composed which describes the self-emptying love within the Trinity from which creation and incarnation proceed. 'You, Father, give your entire being as God to the Son; you are Father only inasmuch as you give yourself; you, Son, receive everything from the Father and before Him you want nothing other than one receiving and giving back, the one representing, glorifying the Father in loving obedience; you, Spirit, are the unity of these two mutually meeting, self-givings, their We as a new I that royally, divinely rules them both.'[54] Kenosis, then, is not the act of the Son (as with Luther and the Lutheran kenoticists of the seventeenth and nineteenth centuries). Such a Christology Balthasar would view as Christomonistic. Kenosis is the disposition of love within the Trinitarian community. It is a community constituted by differences that desire the other. For the Father surrenders himself utterly to the Son who is 'the infinitely Other *of the Father*',[55] making all subsequent separation (and suffering) possible. I will develop this notion of suffering in the final essay, 'Suffering and Incarnation'. For the moment what is important in the Son's response to this paternal surrender is an eternal thanksgiving (*eucharistia*)

---

[51] *Theodramatik*, Bd. III (Einsiedeln: Johannes Verlag, 1980), p. 301; *Theo-Drama: Theological Dramatic Theory: IV: The Action*, tr. G. Harrison (San Francisco: Ignatius Press, 1994), p. 324.

[52] *Theodramatik*, Bd. III, p. 308; *Theo-Drama*, vol. IV, p. 331.

[53] Ibid., p. 332/p. 356.

[54] *The Von Balthasar Reader*, pp. 428–9. eds. Medard Kehl and Werner Löser, trs. Robert J. Daly and Fred Lawrence (Edinburgh: T. & T. Clark, 1982).

[55] *Theodramatik*, Bd. III, p. 302; *Theo-Drama*, vol. IV, p. 325.

that enacts, albeit differently, its own surrender. The Spirit maintains and embraces the infinite distance between Father and Son, opening the love that fills that distance to creation. 'Here we see both God's infinite power and powerlessness; he cannot be God in any other way but in this "kenosis" within the Godhead itself'.[56] The 'generation' of the Son makes possible the creation of the world. The circulation of divine desire is the *processio*. Obedience to that desire to abandon oneself is the nature of one's calling or *missio* – for the going out or the *missio* is always the act of love towards the other. Both *processio* and *missio* exemplify kenosis, and this kenosis is the operation that enjoins the immanent Trinity to the incarnation. Thus there arises an analogy of natures between the form of God and the form of a servant. All incarnation is kenotic; all Word becoming flesh, all acts of representation, are kenotic. This will have significant consequences for our understanding of *homo symbolicus*. For the moment it is important to grasp that kenosis always made possible the sacrifice of Jesus Christ on the cross; for Christ was sacrificed before the foundations of the world in his utter givenness to the Father. The cross is not, then, an event that can be isolated and made the fulcrum for all theological understanding. Not only is the event of crucifixion, the death of God, part of a trajectory moving from incarnation to resurrection (and Pentecost). It is the outworking of a soteriological economy inaugurated with creation: 'all the world's darkness is only permitted because of the antecedent *idea*, *offer* and *mission* of the Lamb, which undergird it and make it possible'.[57] Creation is made possible by intra-Trinitarian difference. Creation is completed in the incarnation just as the incarnation is completed in the eucharist. God becomes Form and he, the Son, becomes the transcendental signifier, the name above all names.

For we who are made 'in the image of', kenosis is a mode of living the eternal life of God which sin destroys. Our kenotic action is not identical to Christ's kenotic action with reference to the Father. Ours is a secondary Yes of consent (summed up in Mary's acquiescence to receive God into herself) made possible on the basis of Christ's primary self-offering. We live analogously, and kenosis is both the condition of this living and our understanding of it: this is the mode of all Christian action and ethics. With this notion of difference, of an unassimilable alterity, the teaching of kenosis moves beyond modernity's concern with epistemology (Kant), metaphysics (Hegel) and phenomenological existentialism (Heidegger). Kenosis is the form, character and praxis of a theo–logic that lies outside of, and illuminates, all human logics.

56   Ibid., p. 303/p. 325.
57   Ibid., p. 335/p. 360.

We return to the doctrine of kenosis as it was expounded in premodernity, by the early Church, in the work of Origen, Athanasius and Cyril among the Alexandrians, Gregory of Nyssa among the Cappadocians, and Hilary of Poitiers. Beset as it was by the dangers of subordinationism, modalism and deipassionism, the kenosis of Christ was depicted then in terms of a Trinitarian operation,[58] what Maximus the Confessor called 'an eternal movement of love'.[59] With Palamas a distinction was drawn between God in himself – who was unknowable and inaccessibly concealed in mystery – and those divine energies or operations whereby he is manifested and gives himself to us. Thus Palamas wishes to speak of a 'divine power and energy common to the nature in three'.[60] This force or energy whereby there is communication and the gift of God was understood as the operation of love within the Trinity, the abandoning of one to the other; and salvation issued from a participation within this intra-Trinitarian procession. It is a participation made possible through the incarnation of Christ, the revelation of the true image of God possessed by all. We are redeemed and deified through the economy of love. The distinctive nature of love is to give – a continual act of self-abandonment. It is this abandonment in love which characterises kenosis. To paraphrase Karl Barth's understanding of kenosis, God's freedom to love is a self-giving not a giving up.[61] The doctrine of kenosis outlines, then, the giving of the gift of life – a giving that cannot be given if the giving is not part of an economy that includes reception; an

---

[58] See Origen, *De Princip.*, 1.II.8 and Nestorius, *Liber Heraclides*, 1.I.61.

[59] Quoted by Vladimir Lossky, *Mystical Theology in the Eastern Church* (London: James Clarke, 1957), p. 60. P.T. Forsyth's analysis of kenosis (which he understands as part of a dialectic that embraces the plerosis of self-fulfilment of Christ) draws upon the notion that divine love is the dynamic of action: 'Love alone has any key to those renunciations which do not mean suicide but the finding of the Soul' (p. 320). This analysis, in the first decade of the twentieth century, did not fully articulate a Trinitarian basis for the operation of this love while observing that the kenotic act 'was the most condensed expression of holy love' (p. 316). Nevertheless, Forsyth's main focus remains a psychological account of the reduction in divine qualities – the effects, that is, of Christ's eternal knowledge becoming 'discursive, successive, and progressive' (pp. 310–11), *The Person and Place of Jesus Christ* (London: Independent Press, 1930). For an earlier theological development of the doctrine of kenosis in British theology that also was locked into modernity's metaphysics of selfhood, see Hugh Ross Mackintosh, *The Doctrine of the Person of Jesus Christ* (Edinburgh: T. & T. Clark, 1912). For a very lucid overview of the doctrine of kenosis and its theological importance see Sarah Coakley, 'Kenosis and Subversion: On the Repression of "Vulnerability" in Christian Feminist Writing' in *Swallowing a Fishbone: Feminist Theologians Debate Christianity*, ed. Daphne Hampson (London: SPCK, 1996), pp. 82–111.

[60] Lossky, *Mystical Theology*, p. 70. For an extensive analysis of Palamas's distinctive contribution to Trinitarian thought see Rowan Williams, 'The Philosophical Structures of Palamism', *Eastern Churches Review* 9 (1–2), (1977), pp. 27–44.

[61] *Church Dogmatics*, IV.1, p. 184.

economy of response. It is this giving-in-through-and-beyond-reception that *is* the kenotic economy: grace. It is a pneumatic economy, for the new dimension Christ has opened up the Spirit maintains and presents 'at our disposal as a new, open space'.[62]

This kenotic presentation of the Trinity – *missio* issuing from *processio* – is the basis for Balthasar's theological aesthetics concerned as it is with 'seeing the form': the form of God, the form of revelation, the form of faith and the mediation of those forms. Kenosis is a theological economy of represen-tation – where representation covers both the vicarious representation of Christ dying *pro nobis*[63] and the creative mimesis. Christ the Word descends into all the eloquence, rhetoric, mimesis and endless deferral of meaning in human signs. He is erased by them and through them on Good Friday before sinking down into the silence and the absence of Holy Saturday. But for Balthasar it is in this descent into Hell, 'the dying away into silence … that we have to understand precisely his non-speaking as his final revelation, his utmost word'.[64] Through the cross, judgement falls on all eloquence, rhetoric, mimesis and the endless deferral of meaning in signs. Representa-tion experiences its crisis. And a new word appears, 'his utmost word', on the far side of the death's profound *passio*. Only in and through the cross, the death of God, is there redemption and an ability to 'see the form'.

'Seeing the Form [*Schau der Gestalt*]' is the subtitle to volume one of *The Glory of the Lord*. In that volume Balthasar begins to describe the relationship that exists between *pistis* and *gnosis*, faith and knowledge, in a way that refig-ures Hegel on the basis of his Christological refocusing of *analogia entis*. Faith cannot operate without love (or hope) for Balthasar. Faith, understood as trustful self-abandonment in obedience, is intrinsic to the kenotic economy of desire in the Trinity. He writes: 'the Spirit is not so much a divine object of faith as the divine medium of the gift of faith made to the Father in the Son'.[65] Our faith is the human response to God's faith, a response of obedi-ence which enables our participation in God's triunal and kenotic love.[66]

---

[62]   Balthasar, *Spiritus Creator, Skizzen zur Theologie III* (Einsiedeln: Johannes Verlag, 1967), p. 153; *Explorations in Theology III: Creator Spirit*, tr. B. McNeil (San Francisco: Ignatius Press, 1993), p. 169.

[63]   See Balthasar's essay 'On Vicarious Representation', in *Pneuma und Institution, Skizzen zur The-ologie IV* (Einsiedeln: Johannes Verlag, 1974), p. 401; *Explorations in Theology IV: Spirit and Institution*, tr. B. McNeil (San Francisco: Ignatius Press, 1993), pp. 415–22.

[64]   *Mysterium Paschale*, p. 79.

[65]   *Spiritus Creator, Skizzen zur Theologie III*, p. 107; *Explorations in Theology III*, p. 118.

[66]   See Kristeva's definition of faith in *In the Beginning Was Love: Psychoanalysis and Faith*, tr. Arthur Goldhammer (New York: Columbia University Press, 1988), p. 24: 'faith could be described, perhaps rather simplistically, as what can only be called a primary identification with a loving and protective agency'.

Through and with and in this faith the 'light of grace comes to the aid of natural ability: it strengthens and deepens the power of sight'.[67] We see and know differently because the realm of signs surrounding us is read through the hermeneutic of God's poured-out love: 'a synthesizing power to penetrate phenomena, a power that derives from God and is capable of interpreting phenomena so that they disclose what God wishes to reveal of his own depths in them'.[68] In this epistemology of faith, opinion or view [*Ansicht*] is transformed into true sight [*Sicht*]; the images [*Abbilder*] of the world become true pictures [*Urbilder*] of God. Balthasar's *analogia entis* draws close to Barth's *analogia fidei* at this point. In the Introduction we saw the tensions in Barth's understanding of analogy; Balthasar's construal does not have these tensions because, for him, *analogia fidei* cannot dispense with a relationship between creator and creature; a creator who gives and maintains the existence of creation, who is, in his ontological difference, absolute Being. The transfiguration of images of the world [*Abbilder*] into true pictures of God [*Urbilder*] parallels the transfiguration of the human form of Christ into the glory of God and human *autarkia* into human *theosis*: 'For now the "prototype" [*Urbild*] (the eternal Son, enjoying Sonship with the Father) has indwelt [*eingebildet*] the copy [*Abbild*] and stamped his divine form [*Form*] upon it once and for all.'[69]

This relationship between Christology and mimesis has further corollaries. One can see the form of God not only in the works of human beings – the music of Mozart, the paintings of Christ-clowns by Rouault – but in the style of the lives of those who have given themselves over to imitating him. The life of Elizabeth of Dijon 'became a sacrament'.[70] She fulfilled an office and a charism. The track of her becoming, her vocation, announces a doctrine, a teaching, carved out in, through and upon her body. 'Her mission was to approach, by way of contemplation, the source of all grace, and so to be a conduit of its flow to the Church.'[71] With Theresa of Lisieux 'it is not so much her writings as her life itself which is her doctrine'.[72] '[S]he stands in exactly the same relationship towards her own being as a writer does towards his novel or a sculptor to his statue.'[73] The form again reveals the

---

[67] *Herrlichkeit*, Bd. I, p. 169; *Glory of the Lord: A Theological Aesthetics*, vol. I, p. 175.
[68] *Spiritus Creator, Skizzen zur Theologie III*, p. 38; *Explorations in Theology III*, p. 42.
[69] *Theodramatik*, III, p. 355; *Theo-Drama*, vol. IV, p. 381.
[70] Balthasar, *Elizabeth of Dijon*, tr. A.V. Littledale (London: Harvill Press, 1956), p. 63.
[71] Ibid., p. 53.
[72] Balthasar, *Therese von Lisieux* (Cologne: Jakob Hegner Verlag, 1950), p. 24; *Therese of Lisieux*, tr. Donald Nicholl (London: Sheed & Ward, 1953), p. xxi.
[73] Ibid., p. 47/p. 17.

glory of God for those who can read it. By extension, the style of a theo-logical discourse betrays the extent to which the theologian is obedient to the call upon his life. For the theologian's task is not only to expound the Form of God, it is to be abandoned unto God so that the Form of God may be impressed upon the discourse itself, the doing of theology itself. Kenosis operates here as the condition for the possibility of theological method. The Passion of Christ has therefore effected an ontological shift, but this 'primal form can never be adequately and exhaustively reproduced by any rational construction [*Gebilde*]'.[74]

Without faith as kenotic, self-abandoning love we are simply left in the strident darkness of clashing empty symbols; we are left stranded on Matthew Arnold's 'Dover Beach'. 'In this amorphous condition, sin forms what one can call the second "chaos" (generated by human liberty).'[75] This is the Hell Christ descended into on Holy Saturday and from which the redemption of form and representation will issue on Easter Sunday. Christ descends into the hiatus, the aporia, the margins. It is precisely here that non-speaking becomes 'his final revelation'.[76] Death is the autistic state where meaning dissolves into the seas of the chaotic as Christ descends into the depths of the abyss. But this God who can separate himself from himself, the basis of a Trinitarian distinction between the Father and the Son, brings into this abyss a boundary, a limit. 'God himself has proven to be Almighty who is able to safeguard his identity in nonidentity.'[77] That new and para-doxical 'identity' rises to the world again, and so a new discourse announces itself which is theological: 'In the presence of the hiatus, the "logic" of theology can in no way rest on the (unbroken) continuity of human (and scientific) logic, but only on that theo"logic" established by God himself in the hiatus of the "death of God".'[78] This is the death of the sign – its silenc-ing, its judgement – which only faith in the transcendent meaning of a love which frames the text can read aright. Language too must experience its Passion – that is, the central intuition of the economy of representation, the movement towards naming, which the doctrine of kenosis expresses. In the words of Emmanuel Lévinas, language 'expresses the gratuity of sacrifice'.[79]

---

[74] *Herrlichkeit*, Bd. I, p. 205; *Glory of the Lord: A Theological Aesthetics*, vol. I, p. 212.

[75] *Mysterium Paschale*, p. 173.

[76] Ibid., p. 79.

[77] *Pneuma und Institution, Skizzen zur Theologie IV*, p. 399; *Explorations in Theology IV: Spirit and Institution*, p. 413. This phrase sums up Balthasar's rejection of a Christology locked into the meta-physics of modern selfhood.

[78] *Mysterium Paschale*, p. 79.

[79] *Otherwise than Being or Beyond Essence*, tr. Alphonso Lingis (The Hague: Martinus Nijhoff, 1981), p. 120.

In experiencing its Passion, it experiences its redemption, and this is because the Spirit recapitulates always the entire economy of salvation, expressing 'the pneumatic unity of Cross and Resurrection'.[80] As a further corollary, 'Hell is a *product* of the Redemption'.[81] Passion is understood here as ambivalent – the word ties together the twin themes of love and suffering, crucifixion and exaltation. We must always recall that what is poured out is love, a love that in giving itself suffers, and through that suffering is able to name. What persists when the continuity of human discourse and reasoning comes to its end or reaches its edge, is the economy of love: 'the continuity is the absolute love of God of man, manifesting itself actively on both sides of the hiatus (and so in the hiatus itself), and his triune Love in its own intrinsic reality as the condition of possibility for such a love for man'.[82] Balthasar concludes: 'Everything turns on his inner-Trinitarian Love.'[83]

As we saw in the exegesis of the kenotic hymn in Philippians the linguisticality of God (in Christ) and human beings (in their response to that Word) – indeed the linguisticality of the Church – is prominent. It is precisely with linguisticality, the textuality of living, that post-structural accounts of kenosis have been concerned. It is with reference to these accounts that we can not only develop Balthasar's own position but also locate the theologian with respect to contemporary philosophical, anthropological and psychological concerns. The existential has always played an important part in Balthasar's theological account of what it is to be human, open to the transcendent, creative and artistic. This existentialism may be the liberal weak-point in Balthasar's conservative theology; it is he rather than Karl Rahner who is more indebted to Heidegger. 'A non-existential theology, therefore, remains unworthy of belief because it is not capable of making anything really visible.'[84] Nevertheless, Balthasar's work breathes in a certain rarefied atmosphere, a post-resurrection perspective, as if the work was composed on the frosted heights of Thomas Mann's magic mountain. The social, the political and the physical orders of being proceed somewhere in the plains at the foot of the escarpment. This need not be. Balthasar's own gaze may be fixed on the transcendental categories of the good, the beautiful and the true, but his work endorses no gnosticism and warrants no docetic concentration upon the spiritual. His theology sacralises, through Christ, the historical and

---

[80] *Theodramatik*, III, p. 360; *Theo-Drama*, vol. IV, p. 386.
[81] *Mysterium Paschale*, p. 79.
[82] Ibid.
[83] Ibid., p. 81.
[84] *Herrlichkeit*, Bd. III. I/2 Teil (Einsiedeln: Johannes Verlag, 1967), p. 579; *Glory of the Lord: A Theological Aesthetics. V: The Realm of Metaphysics in the Modern Age*, tr. O. Davies et al. (Edinburgh: T. & T. Clark, 1991), p. 602.

concrete, giving back soul to the historical and concrete. The concrete and historical take on a certain permeability while remaining quite emphatically material, corporeal. As he himself describes it, through Christ mundane reality is delivered from self-glorification[85] – that is, empiricism, naive realism, positivism. In bringing Balthasar's work into an examination of poststructural concerns with textuality, I am, then, simply extending and applying it. That is, I am reading, on the basis of faith, the watermark of God's glory in the experience of being 'made in the image of'. Theology precedes and makes possible an anthropology which emphasises the nature of the symbolic worlds we construct. This is how Augustine comes to relate the Trinity to his concept of personhood, theology to psychology, in *De Trinitate*. We are going to make a similar move, for what is at stake is the ineradicable correlation between what I called in chapter one Christology and mimesis. The notion of *homo symbolicus* (that cannot be separated from a *homo hermeneuticus*), kenosis and an anthropology grounded upon the mission of Christ can be seen more clearly by developing Balthasar's understanding of God's kenotic love through an examination of Kristeva's phenomenology of desire. Most particularly, we need to examine her work on the relationship of love to language, the order of the symbolic to the abject.

Kristeva's Kenotic Economy

We can legitimately develop Balthasar's work through Kristeva's because they share so much. Let me briefly point to four fundamental parallels. First, there is a common appeal to the primacy of love as an anthropological root. Balthasar develops this through his notion of the *imago dei* and divine eros, based upon his work on Gregory of Nyssa. Kristeva develops this from the attention given by psychoanalysis to sexual desire and, more specifically, Freud's discussion of narcissism and the Oedipal triangle. Secondly, for both of them the relationship of mother and child acts as the locus for a metaphysical analysis of living towards transcendence. Balthasar begins his exploration of the wonder of Being and the awareness of our radical contingency with relation to this transcendent horizon. Kristeva explores the nature of the unfathomable and the mystery of identity beginning with the mother–child unity. Thirdly, they share an understanding of selfhood as caught up in and constituted by wider economies of desire than simply the

---

[85]   *Herrlichkeit*, Bd. I, p. 566; *Glory of the Lord: A Theological Aesthetics*, vol. I, p. 589.

intentions of an I, modernity's subject. For Balthasar the significance of human eros (man/woman, mother/child, self/neighbour) is located in the larger economy of divine eros, and so self-autonomy is always fissured: one moves towards a realisation of personhood in following Christ and obeys the call to intra-Trinitanarian participation. Here an *anthropologia crucis* is sketched, which can only enter the condition of an *anthropologia resurrectionis* through entering the divine operation of redemption. Nevertheless the condition of *anthropologia crucis* is the existential condition for the possibility of entering this economy of resurrection life. For Kristeva, the ability to love oneself aright is dependent upon loving others. The ego is not the *ego cogito* of Enlightenment reasoning, but the *ego affectus est* of Bernard of Clairvaux. The self is always in process, always part of an ongoing performance, always being displaced, because it is always only constituted in relation to being affected by that which is other. Finally, Kristeva herself recognises the connections between her own semanalysis — the analysis of the semiotic traces rippling the symbolic surface of a text — of amatory discourse, kenotic abandonment and Christ's Passion. In her short book *In the Beginning Was Love*, she writes:

> Christ's Passion brings into play even more primitive layers of the psyche; it thus reveals a fundamental depression (a narcissistic wound or reversed hatred) that conditions access to human language. The sadness of young children just prior to their acquisition of language has often been observed; this is when they must renounce forever the maternal paradise in which every demand is immediately gratified. The child must abandon its mother and be abandoned by her in order to be accepted by the father and begin talking ... [L]anguage begins in mourning ... The 'scandal of the cross', the *logos tou staurou* or language of the cross ... is embodied, I think not only in the psychic and physical suffering which irrigates our lives ... but even more profoundly in the essential alienation that conditions our access to language, in the mourning that accompanies the dawn of psychic life.

She goes on to conclude in a way that returns us from Lacanian psychology to Balthasar:

> Christ abandoned, Christ in hell, is of course the sign that God shares the condition of the sinner. But He also tells the story of that necessary melancholy beyond which we humans may just possibly discover the other, now in the symbolic interlocutor rather than the nutritive breast.[86]

---

[86] *In the Beginning Was Love: Psychoanalysis and Faith*, tr. Arthur Goldhammer (New York: Columbia University Press, 1988) pp. 40–1.

In what follows the theological implications of this astonishing passage will be drawn out in relation to Balthasar's depiction of Christ's kenotic love and the aphasia of Holy Saturday, and the descent towards the name and beyond the figurative in Paul's letter to the Philippians. For what Kristeva presents us with is an account of the inseparability of a morphology of selfhood from a theory of representation on the basis of kenosis. We recall that there is a concern with the morphology of selfhood in Paul's *carmen Christi* – with the move towards one's true identity *post-mortem*. For Kristeva, our initial entrance and any subsequent entrance into language is an experience of kenosis. But unlike the economies of lack and negation which characterised Hegelian kenosis – and characterise also the psychological economies of Freud and Lacan, founded as they are upon a similar notion of progress through negation and rejection (*Verneinung* and *Verwerfung*), the symbolics of castration – Kristeva's emphasis is upon resurrection. 'I see symbolic castration less as asceticism than as an expansion – through asceticism – toward an endless poiesis ... my own path to vitality.'[87] This growth, this movement beyond the death-drive, comes in and through the advent of language that Kristeva is all too aware parallels the Advent of the Word. This advent of language, and this constitution of personhood, are situated initially within the nexus of relations that comprise the Oedipal triangle and the movement from the imaginary to the symbolic order through the mirror stage.

We have treated Lacan's mirror stage in chapter five, 'Divinity and Sexual Difference'. Developing out of Freud's meditation on primary narcissism, we noted that this stage describes the effects of that scene when the child confronts its image in a mirror. Before this stage, the child occupies an imaginary phase in which it experiences, produces and stores up various images of itself and its body through mobilising any number of identifications it makes of the world around it.[88] This imaginary level, closely associated for Kristeva with the rhythms, pulsations and drives of the psychobiological, provides the foundation for the subject of enunciation, the entry into discourse. For Kristeva this imaginary remains present in discourse itself as the semiotic as distinct from (but not polarised to) the semantic. 'I therefore distinguish between the *semiotic*, which consists of drive-related and affective *meaning* organized according to primary processes whose sensory aspects are

---

[87]   *New Maladies of the Soul*, tr. Ross Gubermann (New York: Columbia University Press, 1995), p. 90. Both Irigaray and Cixous have continued in their own work to stress the difference between feminine economies of desire – emphasising extravagant giving and excess – and masculine economies of desire – characterised by lack and anal retention. For a concise expression of this theme see Cixous's essay '"The Egg and the Chicken": Love Is not Having', *Reading with Clarice Lispector*, tr. Verena Andermatt Conley (Hemel Hempstead: Harvester Wheatsheaf, 1990), pp. 98–122.
[88]   *New Maladies*, pp. 103–4.

often nonverbal (sound and melody, rhythm, color, odors, and so forth), on the one hand, and *linguistic signification* that is manifested in linguistic signs and their logico-syntactic organization, on the other.'[89]

As we noted earlier, with the mirror stage the child enters into the symbolic order. It recognises both its own need for symbols and yet also its own separation from full identity because of the uncrossable bar between the symbolic and the real (Lacan's S/s). It is at this stage that Kristeva places the child's descent into depression. The realisation of separation is a profound realisation of loss – a loss which is continually sublimated by the employment of symbols or language. Semanalysis is, for Kristeva, the inquiry into the relationship between that which is sublimated – which she terms the semiotic – and that which is being symbolised. This fundamental sense of loss, which Kristeva associates with the Passion of Christ and which I am describing as a kenotic economy, Kristeva terms abjection. 'Abjection,' she writes, 'or the journey to the end of the night.'[90]

The economy of abjection outlines the logic of separation that begins earlier and then informs Lacan's mirror stage. *Anthropologia crucis* is a condition established primordially in the individual's life with separation from the body of the mother, the abjection of the mother, and the move towards the law of the Father. For the Father governs the creation of firm identities in the realm of the symbolic. Kristeva views this separation from the body of the mother as a separation from the semiotic *chora*. This has to occur prior to the move through the thetic or image stage and the arrival at the semantic concern with the proper name. Abjection institutes an exclusion which marks a beginning and a boundary. On one level, abjection marks the beginning of the social order by defining that which is forever external, distinct and threatening its domain. On another level, abjection marks the initiation into subjectivity as the I discovers what is not-I, what is other (both the semiotic body of the mother and the imaginary father). On a final level, abjection marks entrance into the symbolic order. It marks out that which we necessarily leave out, that which remains but is silent, in order to construct. In all these cases, abjection both constitutes the possibility for the autonomy of the order – social, subjective, symbolic – while haunting such order by identifying its frailty, its instability, its ephemerality. As such, abjection constitutes what Kristeva calls 'the margin of a floating structure'.[91]

The effect of this separation Kristeva discerns in the melancholia which affects children just prior to entrance into language, prior, that is, to entering

---

[89]   Ibid., p. 104.

[90]   *Powers of Horror*, tr. Leon Roudiez (New York: Columbia University Press, 1988), p. 58.

[91]   Ibid., p. 69.

the realm of the symbolic.[92] The separation institutes primary narcissism and also creates a space. The child as presubject enters an emptiness which will lead to the entry into the symbolic order at the mirror stage. Kristeva locates, in this emptiness and the separation which precedes it, a primary identification with what she terms the 'imaginary father' – that is, the loving Father/husband of the Mother. These are troubled waters in studies of Kristeva, for the 'imaginary', loving Father prepares the subject for desiring the Phallus which provides the dynamic for entry into the symbolic order and the Oedipus complex. For our purposes, this haunting by the 'imaginary' father – whatever the coherence of the idea in Kristeva's work and her dialogue with Freud and Lacan – is another example of how Kristeva's morphology of the self parallels the doctrine of kenosis in the *carmen Christi*. Frequently Kristeva likens the operations of this imaginary father – the entry of the third party that comes from outside, or above, the dyad of mother–child – to the Christian God. The triune economy of love is explicitly compared with Christian *agape*.[93] It is not the maleness as such that the imaginary father figure installs. Another woman might play this loving role in the life of any particular family. This pre-Oedipal father combines both genders. And as Kelly Oliver remarks in her commentary upon Kristeva's work: 'The irrepresentable that makes representation possible is represented ... by the imaginary father ... It is only in the context of "his" love that the symbolic can become meaningful.'[94] Through agapaic love Kristeva weaves this making meaningful of the symbolic into the psychic process of identification, where (in one form of identification) there is a recognition and participation of one subject in another. The eucharist figures large in such discussions. In fact, Kristeva's notion of the meaningful sign, the affected respresentation, the effective symbol, is trans-substantiation. As the eucharist is a participation in eternal life and fosters resurrection, so does involvement with language. The eucharist, as an emblem of the kenotic economy, is always both a giving of life and a sacrifice, a loss, an act of violence.[95]

The melancholy moment before entering language is a moment where the meaning is lost. It is not only in children learning to speak that this occurs, and so Kristeva's work is not limited to the psychology of child development. The loss of meaning, and its consequent relinquishing of

---

[92] It must be admitted here that Kristeva provides us with no clinical evidence to support such a claim.

[93] *New Maladies*, pp. 121–3, 179–80.

[94] *Reading Kristeva: Unravelling the Double-Bind* (Bloomington: Indiana University Press, 1993), pp. 63–4.

[95] *New Maladies*, p. 183.

desire, is found paradigmatically in depressive states of all kinds. It is constantly having to be negotiated as the self-in-process grows in and through its misidentifications with others. It is negotiated in all transference and countertransference (or all economies of response). This loss, this use of symbolic substitutions, and the dialectic of demand and desire in which all representations participate place the self always in process, always searching for a place to belong to, always experiencing a certain dis-possession.

What is important, in terms of Kristeva's semanalysis, is that representation remains infected by that which is abjected.[96] The semiotic drives operate dialectically within and upon the symbolic, so that 'writing causes the subject who ventures into it to confront an archaic authority'.[97] The corollary of this is that the melancholy moment where meaning is lost is rediscovered and performed in every form of mimesis. Some acts of representation appeal to that suppressed melancholy more than others. Hence, when discussing Holbein's *Dead Christ* in *Black Sun*, Kristeva writes: 'very much like personal behaviour, artistic *style* imposes itself as a means of countervailing the loss of other and of meaning'.[98] The death of Christ becomes a portrayal of a paradox – representing the erasure of beauty, transcendence and form; presenting ironically an icon of that which is iconoclastic. The experience of depression, of descent into emptiness, is endemic to the economy of representation as it is also to the self-in-process – both of which are constantly searching for, but can never attain, stable identity. Such stability, the stability of a proper Name not infected by the body of the mother, the semiotic *chora*, remains forever futural and eschatological, while being constitutive of the present as hope and promise. Holbein's presentation of Christ in the tomb, then, leads us 'to the ultimate edge of belief, to the threshold of non-meaning'.[99] Non-meaning causes frigidity and paralysis. According to Irenaeus, throughout this time in the tomb Jesus looked upon chaos.[100]

We saw with Balthasar that 'the death of Jesus, like his incarnation, was a function of his living, eternal love'.[101] Similarly, for Kristeva, the logic of

---

[96] Semanalysis treats three interrelated forms of representation: 'representations of words (close to the linguistic signifier), representations of things (close to the linguistic signified) and representations of affects (labile, psychic traces subject to the primary processes of displacement and condensation)': *In the Beginning*, p. 4.

[97] *Powers of Horror*, p. 75.

[98] *Black Sun*, tr. Leon Roudiez (New York: Columbia University Press, 1989), p. 129.

[99] Ibid., p. 135.

[100] *Ad. Haer.* 4 c 22 n. 1.

[101] *Pneuma und Institution, Skizzen zur Theologie IV*, p. 398; *Explorations in Theology IV: Spirit and Institution*, p. 412.

separation, the necessary recognition of *diastema* (with attending plurality and heterogeneity) – which provides the possibility for the ongoing configuration of self-in-relation-to-others in and through language – are part of a more general economy of love. Loss must lead to a renewal; death to resurrection. The psychologist's work is installed here where the movement breaks down, where the dead body of the mother is buried within and brings death to the soul, silence and autism to the speaking subject. Resurrection comes with becoming reconciled to the loss, the attachment to the mother, and searching for new identifications in and through discourse with the ideal and loving father. This Kristeva depicts in terms of the love of the mother for and by the father. Participation in and desire for complete reconciliation with this love – the economy of response – functions as the utopian horizon that makes psychological healing possible. Without this economy there is only abjection and melancholy; the material world is without meaning, for it cannot signify at all.

This concern to re-establish the primacy of a transcendental love is yet another reason why Christianity haunts her own analyses and why her work can be paralleled with Balthasar's. She asks what psychoanalysis is 'if not an infinite quest for rebirths through the experience of love'.[102] Psychoanalysis never probes the genesis (for we are born into a love always already in operation) but the *dunamis* of love. This is the economy of desire which, for Kristeva, we enter with that primordial separation from the mother. We are born to love because we are born divided. As Kristeva writes, elliptically: 'Love is a death sentence which causes me to be.'[103] The ego issues, then, from a transcendental economy of love and death (as separation) already in operation. Since this issuing is inseparable from entering the symbolic order, it is the economy of love which infects the symbolic order with its desire for identification with the other. All discourse, then, is amatory discourse: 'The speaking subject is a loving subject.'[104] All representation is a kenotic act of love towards the other; all representation involves transference – being caught up in the economy of giving signs. Kristeva, taking up Lacan's structuralist understanding of language, views metaphor as the condensation of this love present in discourse and desire for the other as the operation of displacement or metonymy. '[W]riting serves as a resurrection.'[105] As she herself concludes, in a way which returns us to theology: 'the literary experience stands revealed as an essentially amorous experience, unstabilizing the

---

[102] *Tales of Love*, tr. Leon Roudiez (New York: Columbia University Press, 1987), p. 1.

[103] Ibid., p. 36.

[104] Ibid., p. 170.

[105] *New Maladies*, p. 181.

same through its identification with the other. In this it emulates theology, which, in the same field, has strengthened love into faith.'[106]

These two elements of Kristeva's semanalysis – the relation between abjection, the symbolic and descent into non-meaning (the logic of separation), on the one hand, and the relation between representation and transcendental economy of love (the logic of identification), on the other – not only parallel the doctrine of kenosis in Paul's *carmen Christi* and Balthasar's analysis of Holy Saturday. Kristeva's work, I wish to argue, roots a theological examination of the doctrine in an anthropology that relates the fundamental experience of human existence as one of dispossession (or in Schleiermacher's term, 'absolute dependence') to our nature as the creators of signs and symbols. We are makers of images because we are 'made in the image of'. Of course, while pointing to a triunal economy in Kristeva, a distinction must be made between this and Balthasar's Trinitarian theology. It is a distinction between the way difference is understood and championed in Kristeva's work (as in Lévinas's, Derrida's, Irigaray's and Cixous's) and theological difference. Heidegger's ontological difference is the site for both their meeting and their departure from each other. Theological difference, Trinitarian difference, is other than ontological difference while being the condition for the possibility of ontological difference in Balthasar. But ontological difference characterises the human situation – summed up in Mary's open womb – and one could say it was this difference which post-structuralism teaches us about.

The kenotic economy becomes the very root of sign production and therefore theological discourse. In fact, Kristeva privileges the Bible as a place where this economy is most evident. Of course, it could be argued that what Kristeva presents us with is a demythologised, psychoanalytic reading of the Christian faith. This would identify her work as continuing the project of modernity. And there are emphases in her work that support the view that psychoanalysis 'explains' religious phenomena – codes of practice, liturgies, symbols, narratives – which make up Christianity. There are other, more recent, emphases which recognise parallels between the work of the analyst and the work of the priest (and between the work of the psychoanalytical theorist and the theologian). Karl Jaspers was among the first to suggest that psychoanalysists replace the traditional priest and sacramental confession, but Kristeva does not seem to wish to secularise a religious praxis. As a therapist, she works for the resurrection of the subject, through bringing that subject into a participation, in love, in an economy of response to the Word. She does this by fostering desire and vitality on the far side of

---

[106] *Tales of Love*, p. 279.

depression and descent into a death-like asymbolia. She accepts that theologians have resolved many of the 'maladies of the soul' by 'granting their subjects a single object in which to delight – that is, God (as Saint Augustine said, *res qua fruendum est*)', but recognises that 'If God no longer exists, the unconscious must reassemble the fragments of hysterical heterogeneity and its masks.'[107] Therapy seems to function, then, as establishing subjects within a kenotic economy of love and its representation at a time when theology no longer has cultural dominance and when many can no longer believe in God. A time perhaps when Christian theology has given itself over to secular logics – such as the work of the death-of-God theologians we saw earlier. Therapy helps those who are outside faith, outside communities of those practising faith; those who are left washed up on the beach after the wave of secularism has crashed and ebbed away. Furthermore, Kristeva is aware that psychoanalysis cannot become a metanarrative, a master discourse which can explain away religious discourse which is also founded upon establishing persons in the economy of love. '[P]sychoanalysis ... is an art – I admit, an artifice – that may allow the men and women of our modern, sleek, lofty, costly, and profitable cities to preserve a life for themselves.'[108] Psychoanalysis is an artifice, 'an imaginary discourse that serves as truth',[109] for assisting modernity's ego in its search for a lost soul, for facilitating a transposition from necrophilia to resurrection life. Kristeva's own theory of the dialectical relationship between the semiotic and the symbolic would, in fact, militate against placing psychological discourse above theological discourse; giving symbolic priority to one form of language. To make such a claim 'creates the danger of transforming psychoanalysis not only into an ideology but also into a religion'.[110] Certainly, Kristeva's reflections upon her Catholicism have caused embarrassment among several of her admirers and critics.[111] But if Kristeva is right, then, on the basis of the theological account of kenosis, we can understand each act of signification (speaking or writing) and each act of performing that act (reading, liturgical practice) as a move in love, a kenotic giving towards an ineffable Word, a name above all names, a name which gathers up all our naming and within which we too

---

[107] See 'The Semiotics of Biblical Abomination' in *Powers of Horror*, pp. 90–112, and 'Reading the Bible' in *New Maladies*, pp. 115–26. 'The Bible is a text that thrusts its words into my losses' (*New Maladies*, p. 119). This remarkable essay argues for psychoanalysis as 'post-Catholic' and demonstrates the analyst's continuing dependence upon Biblical rigour, logic and love.

[108] *New Maladies*, p. 76.

[109] Ibid., p. 44.

[110] Ibid., p. 123.

[111] *In the Beginning*, p. xi. Kelly Oliver has spoken of Kristeva's 'nostalgic relation to Christianity' and how her work 'privileges and recreates the Christian imaginary' (*Reading Kristeva*, p. 128).

are named (*en to onomati Jesou*). On the basis of her work we reopen the relation of Christology to mimesis. If she is also right that this descent to the marginalised is a movement towards the recovery of the lost semiotic body of the mother, then Christianity must possibly rethink its doctrine of the Trinity in terms of sexual difference – as we saw in chapter five.

Transcorporality

The Godhead, who makes us in his image, circumscribes all human creativity, human *poiesis*. This creativity receives its transcendental meaning (truth, beauty, goodness) only in its relation to him. We are makers because we are made 'in the image of', and our making (insofar as it configures God's own making) is redemptive. To be redemptive, to participate in the economy of redemption opened and perfected by Christ the form of God's glory, our making cannot be in our name. Our making cannot, like the builders of the Tower of Babel, make a name for ourselves. Our making cannot reify our own autonomy. Such making is only death and idolatry. Our making must be in and through an abandonment to an operation that will instigate the crisis of our representations. Our making has to experience its Passion, its descent into the silent hiatus. 'God "judges" all human thoughts that strive upwards of themselves to attain the utmost, and requires of them something that they can accomplish only in self-denial.'[112] This crisis and Passion is, in fact, the condition of all human making – Derrida's '*Kenosis* of discourse' – but we can only understand this crisis and Passion aright if they are read in terms of a theology of kenosis. The endless differing and deferral of meaning read philosophically will only return us to the tragic vision of Hegel's Unhappy Consciousness.[113] To be redeemed, the chaotic and febrile semiosis has to be bounded by the Trinitarian operation as we saw in chapter one. To this extent, kenosis in Lévinas, Derrida, Irigaray, Cixous and Kristeva requires the theological framework they allude to and employ metaphorically in order for the 'resurrection', the 'eschatology', the 'utopia' of which they speak to be possible. Balthasar's work explicitly announces this – metaphysics is only possible on theological conditions. The trinodal economies found in Kristeva (and Lévinas and Derrida[114]) require a theological reading, require the

---

[112] Balthasar, *Herrlichkeit*, Bd. III. I/2 Teil, p. 13; *Glory of the Lord: A Theological Aesthetics. V: The Realm of Metaphysics in the Modern Age*, pp. 15–16.

[113] I will develop this idea in the final essay, 'Suffering and Incarnation'.

[114] For a discussion of these trinodal economies in Lévinas and Derrida see my *Barth, Derrida and the Language of Theology* (Cambridge University Press, 1995), pp. 164–70, 247–8.

difference they speak of to be a theological difference. Without this reading, post-structural economies of the sign simply point towards the aporia of alterity without end. With this reading, then, all accounts of meaning and sign-giving, accounts of the economy of response, are coherent in terms of the incarnation. The incarnation of the Word reveals the ineradicable theological nature of all our wording. The intratextuality of human existence is grounded in the groundlessness of the divine. As such all discourse is theological discourse. The subject of theology, on the basis of the relationship between kenotic Christology and mimesis, is the economy of the gift, or, more accurately, the economy of giving, receiving and responding. This economy of the gift, which is inseparable from the exchange and economy of the signs, is the very crux of the incarnational problematic, the crux of the question concerning mediation. Read theologically, discourse is always a meditation upon, as it is also an operation within, the divine–human exchange. Derrida has observed that a gift is never pure.[115] There is no pure giving of the gift, its recognition and reception as gift involve it within an exchange and economy. Nevertheless, there is what he calls 'continuity with respect to [the] difference'[116] between giver–gift and receiver.[117]

What is Christian theology about for Balthasar? It is about the play, the irresolvable dialectical play, between presentation and representation, between divine disclosure and reception. It is about the economy of grace; an economy inseparable from our own attempts to grapple with and grasp the meaning of that grace. It is not only a meditation upon grace (then it would place itself above grace); rather, it is also a meditation from grace and within grace. As such, discourse read theologically is a means of grace; of incorporation into that which is given. If Derrida is correct and the gift cannot be given without obligation, then our human condition before the Godhead (as conscious recipients of grace, made conscious, that is, by faith) is one of being under obligation (there are echoes here of Lévinas's exploration of ethics and Derrida's exploration of negotiation as it issues in and through intratextuality[118]) and God's grace cannot operate without prior

---

[115] *Given Time: I Counterfeit Money*, tr. Peggy Kamuf (Chicago: University of Chicago Press, 1992), chapter 2.

[116] Ibid., p. 57.

[117] See Jean-Luc Marion 'In the Name: How to Avoid Speaking of Negative Theology' in J. Caputo and M. Scanlon eds., *God, the Gift, and Postmodernism*, (Bloomington: Indiana University Press, 1999), for a debate between Marion and Derrida on the gift. See also, in the same volume, 'On the Gift', pp. 54–78.

[118] For Lévinas's understanding of the ethic of being under obligation, *Otherwise than Being*, pp. 9–11. For negotiation in Derrida see his essay 'En ce moment même dans cet ouvrage me voici' in *Psyche* (Paris: Galilée, 1987), pp. 159–202.

and eternal covenant. The question then emerges as to who or what maintains the continuity in difference, the *sine qua non* of any exchange, in a
theological investigation of the divine and human kenosis. If the incarnation
provides the primary example, then God becoming form in Christ provides
the ontological possibility for such a continuity. The continuing noetic possibility is the work of the Spirit of Christ through the Church's *eucharistia*.
The Trinity is the condition for a transcorporality that is the hallmark of not
only Jesus Christ's historical existence but also human existence *tout court*.

Kristeva provides Balthasar with an anthropological account of transcorporality; Balthasar provides Kristeva with the Catholic theology that
operates in the silent white margins of her own texts. The human eros is
made part of a wider economy of desire – the desires of other people propelling my desire and the divine eros drawing me out in love, worship and
obedience, pouring me into a Trinitarian kenosis. Kristeva demonstrates
how language is motivated by and abides within desire. Discourse, then, is
always an amatory discourse proceeding through a never-to-be-entangled
interplay of human and divine desire. It is a desire which both affirms and
requires representation and yet denies and puts representation into crisis. Its
enfleshment, its incarnation, is both its sanctioned limitations and its possibility of freedom. To employ one of Kristeva's definitions of psychoanalytic discourse, theology is a 'discourse[s] of love directed to an impossible
other'.[119] It is both a meditation and a mediation; a coming to understanding and a participation; knowledge as love. We gain access to God and God
to us through a transferential discourse. It has been recognised by many
theologians (George Lindbeck and Nicholas Lash most recently) that theology is a second-order reflection and redescription upon the faithful practice
of the Church. Hans Frei sums up this observation: theology 'is an enquiry
into the logic of the Christian community's language – the rules, largely
implicit rather than explicit, that are exhibited in its use of worship and
Christian life, as well as in the confessions of Christian beliefs'.[120] These
rules constitute the cultural linguistics of the Christian religion. What this
essay outlines is an expansion of, by detailing the economy of, that 'logic of
the Christian community's language', placing it within what Balthasar
would call the theo-logic of Trinitarian love. As such, Christian theology is
not secondary but participatory, a sacramental operation. It is a body of
work at play within the language of the Christian community. Our physical
bodies are mediated to us through our relation to other physical bodies and
the mediation of those relationships through the body of the signs. Thus we

---

[119] *In the Beginning*, p. 7.
[120] *Types of Christian Theology* (New Haven, Conn.: Yale University Press, 1992), p. 20.

are mapped onto a social and political body. The meaning of these signs is mediated to us through the body of Christ, eucharistic and ecclesial, so that we are incorporated into that spiritual body. Transcorporality is the hallmark of a theological anthropology.

We noted, when discussing Paul's *carmen Christi*, that we can either view the images, forms and deferrals of meanings, the textuality of this world, as caught between two aporias – incarnation and death – or we can view the textuality of this world as a hiatus within the economy of love within the Trinity. The textuality of this world is a product of the *diastasis* stamped upon the human creativity because we are made 'in the image of'. As the creature is made so the creature makes. Discourse issues from this *diastasis*, this space created by the love that gives and the love that responds; where giving and responding are two sides of the same act of abandonment. The space emerges in our abandonment to another; a womb from which the Word of God and the word of being human both are birthed; a name in which I too am named. Discourse, read theologically, is constitutive of personhood *en to onomati Christo*. Here the *I am* is named; and the *I am* is God in me, and me (I in the accusative) in God. Practising theology, engaging in theological discourse as writer and reader (and any reader re-writes just as any writer reads), becomes an act of faith (and faithfulness). It is an ongoing liturgical act, a sacramental and soteriological process in which knowledge of God is inhabited rather than possessed. Put briefly, what is suggested by transcorporality is that *en Christo* it is by our sign-giving and receiving, by our wording and reading, that we are redeemed. Every particular body participates in the universal form because it participates in the eschatological reordering of creation through Christ. As Christians, then, we are caught up not in a knowledge but a knowing of God, a revelation of God about God, that issues from the movement of his intra-Trinitarian love. Epistemology and ontology as conceived in modernity by Kant and Hegel fall as metaphysical idols before the economy of God's love. We are not brought to know without also being brought to understand that we are known. We do not grasp the truth without being grasped by what is true. Our knowledge of God is, then, both active and passive, a knowing as a being known; a form of incorporation coupled with the realisation we are incorporated. The kenotic economy is the narrative of transcorporality. It narrates a story of coming to know through coming to love – love given, love endured. Creation is an *allegoria amoris* in which we not only participate, we perform.

Chapter Eight

SPIRITUAL EXERCISES: A CHRISTIAN PEDAGOGY

Wim Wenders's film *In weiter Ferne, so nah!* (*Faraway, So Close*), which won the Grand Prix du Jury at Cannes in 1993, opens with a quotation from Matthew's Gospel: 'if your eye is healthy, your whole body will be full of light; but if your eye is unhealthy, your whole body will be full of darkness' (6.22). The film narrates the story of one angel's experience, Cassiel's. So concerned is he with humankind that he asks to become human, and his wish is granted. Separated from his angelic state and angelic company he experiences the nature of being human. He sinks into drink and despair. He prays to his angelic friend Raphaela: 'We humans are confined by what is visible, Raphaela! Only what we can see matters. It is all we believe in. Invisible things don't count. Only the things we touch truly exist for us.' The film offers a beautiful and imaginative critique of materialism along the lines of Walter Benjamin's belief that 'Materiality – but here soulless materiality' is the home of the satanic.[1] Benjamin calls for a reassessment of allegory as a form of cultural critique countering that materiality which is 'emancipation from what is sacred'.[2] Wim Wenders suggests something similar: we have to learn to see things otherwise – we have to remythologise.

The title for this essay bears the traces of its genealogy. With the association of allegory and spiritual reading I am interweaving my text with those medieval forms of interpretation which, drawing upon the exegetical methods of the Alexandrine School, systematised a fourfold reading of Scripture: the historical, the allegorical, the tropological, and the anagogical.[3] The central division was between the literal and the spiritual senses. As Aquinas

---

[1]   *The Origin of German Tragic Drama*, tr. John Osborne (London: New Left Books, 1977), p. 230.
[2]   Ibid.
[3]   The definitive, and exhaustive, study of this tradition belongs to Henri de Lubac. See *Exégèse médiévale, les quatre sens de l'écriture*, IIe partie, livre I (Paris: Aubier-Montaigne, 1961), livre II (Paris: Aubier-Montaigne, 1964).

notes, and here he is only following in the wake of a pronounced tradition, 'Of these four, allegory alone stands for the three spiritual senses.'[4] It is important for what I wish to argue for here – a Christological (and Trinitarian) understanding of materiality or phenomena – that allegory as such was intimately connected in the medieval mind with a doctrine of creation. The second discourse my title is associated with is the set of meditations composed for the training of the Jesuits by their sixteenth-century founder St Ignatius Loyola. These meditations, entitled *The Spiritual Exercises*,[5] employ imagination as a methodical principle. The Scriptures, particularly the Gospels as they relate to the life of Christ, are not simply read: they are internalised as prayer. Reading here is not a process of decipherment and the Biblical text does not stand as an object before a subject. Reading here is a spiritual exercise; it is a form of 'touching, as being touched,' to cite the French philosopher Jean-Luc Nancy.[6] Subject and object both possess permeable membranes, and the reading effects a displacement and a transpositioning (in the full, rich meaning of that word). The third discourse my own text is in dialogue with is the work of the Dutch-American literary critic and theorist, Paul de Man. De Man, in 1979, published an influential volume on the work of Rousseau, Nietzsche, Rilke and Proust entitled *Allegories of Reading*.[7] With the work of Paul de Man we move towards postmodern understandings of *allegoria*: an *allegoria* which returns to a reappraisal of the ancient and medieval practices of allegorical composition and interpretation after the Enlightenment and Romantic denunciation of allegory in favour of the symbolic. What I wish to argue for in this essay is a turn from the stasis of analogy and symbol (important categories for modernity) to the dynamism and semiosis of allegory. But, importantly, the semiosis of allegory is read theologically as concomitant with a doctrine of creation. For outside of such a theological reading semiosis in itself simply announces an aesthetics of nihilism – an announcement encountered many times with poststructural accounts of the free-floating sign. But the move from static atemporal discussions of analogy and symbol to allegory will lend itself to a rather different model for the hermeneutical task, one that is founded upon narrative, representation and participation and one which presents a more dynamic view of the relationship between revelation (the event of Christ), disclosure (a participation in that event), mimesis and knowledge.

---

[4]   *Summa Theologiae*, I.Q.1.10.

[5]   Tr. Thomas Corbishley S.J. (Wheathampstead: Anthony Clarke, 1973).

[6]   *The Birth to Presence*, tr. Brian Holmes et al. (Stanford University Press, 1993), p. 198.

[7]   *Allegories of Reading: Figural Language in Rousseau, Nietzsche, Rilke, and Proust* (New Haven, Conn.: Yale University Press, 1979).

Introducing the Theme

If revelation is understood as the self-giving of God in Christ such that we have knowledge of him, then our truth-claims concerning God must have their origin in an event God himself executes. The structure of revelation is therefore Trinitarian. Though whether the event of Christ is an open one (a present continuous action) or a closed one (a punctiliar aorist action) we leave undecided as yet. If hermeneutics is concerned with interpreting the testimonies to that event – insofar as any experience of God has to be mediated, that is attested to, in some discursive form – then Christian hermeneutics must begin with the Biblical forms of such testimony: i.e. the Gospels.[8] Though whether hermeneutics is integral to that continuing event (a theological hermeneutics) or treats the mediation of that event as its object (a universal hermeneutics), we also leave undecided as yet. The preface to Luke's Gospel expresses the need to build upon the testimonies of those who experienced the events:

> Inasmuch as many have undertaken to compile a narrative [*diegesin*] of the things which have been accomplished [*peplerophoremenon*] among [*en*] us just as they were delivered [*paredosan*] to us by those who from the beginning were eye witnesses [*autoptai*] and ministers [*huperetai genomenoi*] of the Word, it seemed good to me also, having followed [*parekolouthekoti anothen*] all things closely [*akribos*] [for some time past], to write an orderly [*kathexes*] [account] for you, most excellent Theophilus, that you may know [*epignos*] the truth [*asphaleian*] concerning the things of which you have been informed [*katechethes*]. (Luke 1.1–4)

What Luke's preface also proclaims is something of the complex nature of that testimony. The RSV translation portrays Luke's Gospel as a modern form of historiography. It is concerned with the sacrosanct hallmarks of

---

[8] This raises a thorny though pertinent question – the question of the relationship between the Gospels and the Pauline epistles as testimonies to the event of Christ. I am suggesting here, counter to a Protestant emphasis on the priority of Paul, that the Gospel narratives inasmuch as they represent the life and work of Christ, are disclosive. That is, they enable the reader as a practitioner of faith to participate in the ongoing Trinitarian outworking of the incarnation, death and resurrection of Christ. The question as to whether the Pauline epistles (or the Revelation of St John) also facilitate such a participation immediately arises. I would answer no insofar as these deal only indirectly with the event of revelation. They can be disclosive to the reader as a practitioner of faith but the character of that disclosure has to be understood on the basis of the Gospels. In other words, and I am in no doubt that this is controversial, the Gospels have to interpret the rest of the Bible. In the Gospels the canon has a molten core from which it receives the light by which it can be read by faith. For the Gospels present us with he with whom we have to do as creatures – the Christ.

such historiography: empirical evidence gathered from first-hand sources or the archives they left behind them, the correct ordering of this evidence, its careful researching, its verification and its reliability. A positivism remains paramount, and it is the positivism which is to persuade the contemporary reader that these were and are indeed the facts of the case. A certain employment of technical or official terms and a certain appeal to the Hellenistic genre of scientific prefaces appears to be there in the Greek, but not unambiguously. In a recent appraisal of Luke's preface[9] aporias are emphasised: 'the effect of the long words is to obscure the thought Luke is trying to convey. Obscurity is deepened by the amphibolous position of several words.'[10] Others scholars have attested the seemingly pretentious, over-inflated style, the ambiguities of diction and syntax, the allusiveness of meaning and the 'double focus in assessing the significance of Luke's words'.[11] It is easy to pass this off as Luke's white-collar worker Greek education – shorthand for bad writing.[12] But what is evident is that the scientism of modern historiography is not present in the Greek: 'most of the varied approaches to reading Luke-Acts as "history" in the Greco-Roman tradition are based on a misreading of the preface ... Luke promises not independent "investigation" but faithful recording of received tradition (verse 2); he does not challenge his predecessors but ranges his own work alongside theirs.'[13]

Luke emphasises, then, that what is to follow is a narrative within which events will be arranged. The conditions governing the arrangement are not divulged. Representations of time play an important function in Luke, as the dating and paralleling of John's birth and Jesus's indicate, but 'the "order" that he promises is probably no more than the inevitable concomitant of the move from oral storytelling to written narrative'.[14] Even so, this narrative is not composed of just any set of events, they are events which have come to full measure: *plerophoreo* is linked to that favourite Pauline verb *pleroo*, it carries the associations of to fill up, to pervade, to perfect, to consummate. It is the opposite of *kenoo* – to pour out. I will say more about this opposition in chapter nine, 'Suffering and Incarnation', but for the

---

[9]   My discussion of this preface is heavily indebted to the two most thorough analyses of Luke 1.1–4 in English: H.J. Cadbury, in F.J. Foakes-Jackson and K. Lake eds., *The Beginnings of Christianity*, vol. II, (London: Macmillan, 1922), pp. 401–20; Loveday Alexander, *The Preface to Luke's Gospel* (Cambridge University Press, 1993). The interpretation of this passage is solely my responsibility.

[10]   Alexander, *Preface*, pp. 104–5.

[11]   Ibid., p. 123.

[12]   Ibid., pp. 105, 168–86.

[13]   Ibid., pp. 200–2.

[14]   Ibid., p. 202.

moment what is important is that if Luke is the author of Acts then he had close contact with the Pauline community and Paul himself. For Paul, Christ is the fullness of God towards the salvation of the world. These events announce a spiritual, soteriological fruition; they have borne (*phoreo*) or conveyed a fullness within which we have participated (*en hemin*). 'The phraseology of verses 1 and 2 clearly implies two groups of people, those among whom the events were "accomplished" and those to whom the tradition was handed down, and the same pronoun is used of both. There must therefore be a reference to the *corpus christianorum*.'[15] The verb is passive, the community (we) have received these things and been consumed by them. Furthermore, Luke makes plain that as he is communicating these events through his narration to Theophilus, so these events were communicated (orally?) to those like Luke. The verb *paradidomai*, while certainly meaning 'to hand down' (Mark 7.13; Acts 6.14) and suggesting a teaching (and charism?) passed on in a fashion similar to the doctrine of apostolic tradition, also suggests being placed in the hands of a higher power. It is not simply a delivery, but also a delivering up. The verb is used in all four gospels to talk about the handing over of Jesus to the Roman and Jewish authorities. Is there also a hint of betrayal or the recognition of a potential betrayal? That is, as Christ is delivered 'into the hands of sinful men' (Luke 24.7), is not the narration of the events of Christ's life, events which communicate because they disclose a redemptive operation, also being handed on to those who may treat these things disrespectfully? Paul will talk of not discerning the body of Christ and consuming the eucharist unworthily. Is there a betrayal also possible here in hardening one's heart to the power of God as it is disseminated in the telling of these events; a telling by *autoptai* (not eye-witnesses so much as those with first-hand experience of the facts[16]) and ministers of the Word? These witnesses subordinate themselves to the Word – their testimonies are such that the Word speaks through their words; their creation becomes creative. They attest the message Jesus himself proclaimed (the Word is also used to describe Jesus's own message in Luke 8.11–21); they retell a telling. This is discipleship, the following in the wake of and the passing on of that which has been received (and responded to). Luke announces his own participation in this (and therefore the participation of his narrative?) when he uses the verb *parakoloutheo* – 'to follow after,' or 'to follow faithfully'.[17] H.J. Cadbury, back in 1922, suggested translating this (and the following word 'all' (*pasin*)) as 'having participated in

15   Ibid., p. 112.
16   Ibid., pp. 120–3.
17   Ibid., pp. 128–30, for the several interpretations of this word.

[them] all'.[18] Following is a synonym for discipleship, obedience, subordination to the Word (Luke 5.27). There has been some discussion here of whether Luke is falsely claiming that he too is one of the eye-witnesses. Those opposed to this idea wish to translate his use of the verb as 'to investigate'. But there is no need for such contortions. Luke stands in the line of those whose lives have been caught up with the salvific events that are being spoken of and written about. His following is a writing or a rewriting of the original Word, writing of the living out of the faith. This writing as praxis demands for Luke a written account, just as the following of the witnesses demanded an oral account. The event of revelation enjoins a dissemination. Both tellings are related to the advent, the giving of the Word. Both tellings disseminate the salvific fullness of that Word. *Akribos*, then, might also carry the sense of 'diligently' – that is, it might describe a moral and behavioural disposition akin to servant and follower, as well as an evaluation of the precision of the research (or the account, if 'accurately' is a description of the writing).

The emphasis of this whole sentence devolves upon the final *hina* clause and the knowledge that Theophilus will attain through this telling. It is a knowledge distinct from that gained through oral teaching (*katecheo*).[19] There is something certain and established by this knowledge. But what? The events or the account of the events? *Asphaleian* is 'assurance' or 'security' about this truth that is not systematically taught. The assurance here need not concern simply the contents of the account nor the writing of the account as superior to its oral narration.[20] What may be assured is not an intellectual understanding, but a redemptive communication, a disclosure of or participation in the operation of a revelation. There is a knowledge of God, a disclosure, and it pertains to the telling of the story, the narrative, the writing which is also an obedient following after. The telling itself partici-

---

[18]   Cadbury, *The Beginnings of Christianity*, p. 502.

[19]   There is an interesting ambivalence which emerges through this word, which has also been understood as 'report' – evil reports about the Christian sect presented to the Roman official Theophilus. Whether Theophilus had such an official status is doubtful (Alexander, *Preface*, pp. 187–200), but the semantic ambivalence of the word does relate to whether Theophilus is an insider (a Christian) or an outsider (someone to whom a Christian apologetic has to be made). This is not irrelevant to the doubleness of much of this preface. While not employing explicit Christian terms (as if then the narrative was aimed at fostering relations with Hellenistic non-Christians) there are words that do have Christian connotations, as we have seen. It is as if, should Theophilus be a Christian, the Gospel is directed to someone over his shoulder who is not. If Theophilus is not a Christian then this is *apologia*, appealing to Hellenic officialdom by the employment of a neutral, even scientist, rhetoric. Either way, the Gospel has another intention, an allegorical intention.

[20]   Alexander, *Preface*, p. 192.

pates in it and produces a divine pedagogy. The writing itself only has such a power because it participates in the truth it announces. As such, knowledge of God in and through Christ is not a seizing and possessing, but a following in the wake of, an ongoing activity, a lifestyle.

Development of the Theme: Aristotle, *Mimesis* and Knowledge

It is this kind of knowledge, a practical knowledge in the Aristotelian sense of *phronesis* that will direct the thinking of this essay. For Aristotle there is a clear link between knowledge, mimesis and the nature of analogy. This inter-association connects his eudaemonistic ethics to *therapeia*, rhetoric to catharsis, logic to stylistics – as we shall see. And, by extension, this cluster of notions has political consequences. Hence, of tragedy, Aristotle writes that 'by means of language enriched with all kinds of ornament ... it represents men in action ... and through pity and fear it effects relief to these and similar emotions'.[21] If we work backwards from the sequence here announced, knowledge begins with experience, the excitation of the passions common to all, and is expressed through the symbolic form of utterance. In *De Interpretatione*, Aristotle elaborates by emphasising that spoken words are symbols and written words are symbols of those symbols.[22] The exchange value of these symbols is established by convention: their meaning is defined and confirmed within social practices. There is no natural relation between names and things in themselves.

Where a gap opens between our naming and our experience of the world, the communication of meaning is paramount, and therefore Aristotle calls for a style which is proper for the subject-matter to be conveyed. Analogy, a subset of metaphor (being a metaphor of proportion) in *Poetics*, is viewed as the most important kind of figure in Book III of *Rhetoric* because of its facility to communicate a subject vividly and actively: 'expressions represent a thing to an eye when they show it in a state of activity'.[23] The point of communication is impact and event: 'such expressions arrest the hearer's mind, and fix his attention'.[24] So the rhetorician aims at *pathos*, the dialectician aims at *pistis* (conviction), and the syllogist aims at *episteme* (knowledge) and scientific demonstration. In *Poetics*, 'under the head of

[21] *Poetics*, 1449b21–8.
[22] *De Interpretatione*, 16a3–7.
[23] *Rhetoric*, 1411b2.
[24] *De Interpretatione*, 16b19–22.

Thought' Aristotle conceives each of these aims in terms of a specific linguistic effectivity, as 'all the effects to be produced by language'.[25] If 'purity of style consists in calling things by their own proper names'[26] this is not because things have a direct correspondence to their proper names, but a style of communication is advocated which is appropriate to the experience and communication of those things.[27] Mimesis is effective, imitating and conveying an action, to the extent that its metaphors are proportional (analogical). This connection between language, meaning and action can be seen as a development of Aristotle's argument in *De Interpretatione* that independently neither a noun nor a verb has meaning (16a19–27 and 16b6–8, 19–22). Communication arises only in their association as name (*onoma*) and expression (*rhema*); only as such is there *logos* (significant meaning).

There is no absolute distinction that can be made, then, between analogy as a mode of argumentation (what Aristotle terms an *enthymeme*) and analogy as a mode of metaphorical expression. Logic and rhetoric are inseparable from the appropriate style necessary for the communication of meaning; just as a virtuous act is one appropriate to the situation. In fact, 'It is the logician, capable of examining the matter and forms of a syllogism, who will be in the highest degree a master of rhetorical argumentation.' Thus even in speculative philosophy, where the definition of words is essential to clarity of demonstration, concern is expressed for 'those unacquainted with the power of names',[28] 'actual definitions [where] equivocation slips in unnoticed'[29] and the ineradicable use of words whose meanings are neither univocal nor equivocal. These words Boethius called modes of equivocation *a consilio*; more recent scholars have called them *pros hen* equivocals.[30] A metaphoricity remains constitutive of all communication; what is to be discerned is the proportionality in the metaphoric, the appropriateness of the style to the contents of the communication. The distinction between speculative and poetic discourse, for Aristotle, is more a matter of the relationship

---

[25] *Poetics*, 1456a38–b1.

[26] *Rhetoric*, 1407a3.

[27] Sr Miriam Theresa Larkin C.S., *Language in the Philosophy of Aristotle* (The Hague: Mouton, 1971), p. 51. On Aristotle's understanding of language and how it was received and understood by patristic, medieval and Enlightenment exegetes, see Hans Arens, *Aristotle's Theory of Language and its Tradition* (Amsterdam: John Benjamins, 1984).

[28] *Sophistical Refutations* I.165a1–18.

[29] *Topica* I.100b6.

[30] See Larkin, *Language in the Philosophy of Aristotle*, p. 75 and her conclusion: 'Aristotle uses the term "metaphor" in such a way that the term itself is a *pros hen* equivocal', p. 101. See also Ricœur's analysis of paronyms in *The Rule of Metaphor*, tr. Robert Czerny (London: Routledge, 1978), pp. 259–72.

of function to ends, *ergon* to *telos* or, as Wittgenstein might put it, language-games.[31]

The point at issue here is that, for Aristotle, analogy is part of a larger symbolics of action and effective communication. It is both a rhetorical and a logical tool – though as a logical tool it is less effective for strict demonstration of the truth because as an *enthymeme* it lacks or presupposes a fundamental premise. As one scholar puts it: 'an argument from analogy assum[es] the validity of a regular induction and demonstrat[es] a mere probability'.[32] The aim of effective communication is wisdom and the wholeness that acts as the goal in the pursuit of the good. Communication is an ongoing work within the symbolic, a work corresponding to Aristotle's conception of the material world as a world in motion; a work corresponding to Aristotle's *ergon* argument.[33] As Ricœur puts it, 'Wherever something is in a state of becoming, predication is possible: predication is based on physical dissociation introduced by motion.'[34] The question is, in order for us to have true knowledge of our experience of the world, what gives the endlessly conceptual labour a direction and a structure? Or, put in another way, what acts as non-discursive interpretants for this chain of symbolic, arbitrary (in the Saussurean sense) substitutions? There are two answers: a semantic hierarchy (related to the categories and Aristotle's twin concerns for logical coherence and clarity of definition) and a moral teleology. These provide the vertical and horizontal axes that, it is hoped, contain the slipping, the ambiguity, the equivocation of meaning.

We can approach the spinal cord of semantic hierarchy through Aristotle's discussion of paronyms at the beginning of *Categories*. 'When things get their name from something, with a difference of ending, they are called *paronymous*. Thus, for example, the grammarian gets his name from grammar, the brave get theirs from bravery.'[35] There are primary and derivative meanings. If there is to be a distinction drawn between paronymy and analogy then this semantic hierarchy appears to offer it. Paronymy relates a series of different relationships to the same thing. Analogy, it might be said, discovers comparative identities between different things. This distinction maps closely on the medieval distinction between *analogia proportionalis* (where comparative terms share proportionally the same predicate) and *analogia attributionis*

---

[31] For how this concept of *mimesis* relates to appropriate ethical action, *phronesis* and Aristotle's concept of the mean, see Stephen R.L. Clark's chapter 'The Doctrine of the Mean' in his book *Aristotle's Man: Speculations upon Aristotelian Anthropology* (Oxford: Clarendon Press, 1975), pp. 84–97.

[32] Larkin, *Language in the Philosophy of Aristotle*, p. 52.

[33] See Clark, *Aristotle's Man*, pp. 14–27.

[34] *The Rule of Metaphor*, p. 268.

[35] *Categories*, 1a12–15.

(where one term possesses the predicate properly and the other only by extension). But this is not a distinction Aristotle himself drew, and his definition of analogy as proportional metaphor confounds the scholastic distinction.[36]

Most notably for Aristotle 'being' itself is paronymous.

> There are several senses in which a thing may be said to be, as we pointed out previously in our book on the various senses of words; for in one sense it means what a thing is or a 'this', and in another sense it means that a thing is of a certain quality or quantity or has some such predicate asserted of it. While 'being' has all these senses, obviously that which is primary is the 'what', which indicates the substance of a thing.[37]

The burden of *Metaphysics* is the elucidation of the relationship between the many and the primary with respect to the first philosophy, an examination of being *qua* being. For each substance is individual, and Aristotle writes that 'we seem to be seeking another kind of substance, and this is our problem, i.e., to see if there is something which can exist apart by itself and belongs to no sensible thing'.[38] Through the paronymy of 'being' Aristotle attempts to map the semantic hierarchy onto an ontological hierarchy, 'the most unchangeable principles, being and unity',[39] and there is a recognition that if this cannot be done, if this ordering cannot be established, then nothing can be known in anything but a particular and limited way. 'A further difficulty is raised by the fact that all knowledge is of the universal and of the "such", but substance does not belong to the universals, but it is rather a "this" and separable.'[40] The intellectual wrestling is explicit. Aristotle will advert to his difficulties and, while advocating that there 'is a principle in things', admits that 'About such matters there is no proof in the full sense ... For it is not possible to infer this truth itself from a more certain principle.'[41]

Several aporias reveal themselves: the aporia of the individual substance and the universal presents an aporia of the noetic and the ontological. Both these are further related to 'Another aporetic [which] exists between signification (with real reference) and predication (which tends to leave it

---

[36] See G. Patzig's 'Theology and Ontology in Aristotle's *Metaphysics*', in Jonathan Barnes, Malcolm Schofield and Richard Sorabji eds., *Articles on Aristotle*, vol. 3, (London: Duckworth, 1979), pp. 48–9.

[37] *Metaphysics*, 1028a10–15.

[38] Ibid., 1060a10–12.

[39] Ibid., 1060a37–8.

[40] Ibid., 1060b20–2.

[41] Ibid., 1062a2–5.

behind)'[42] – between symbols and the things they symbolise. What does this add up to? One scholar concludes: 'Aristotle's reflections on substances promised that the aporia would be finally resolved, if only language could be made to circumvent its own disutilities.'[43] But language cannot circumvent its own disutilities, it seems, despite Aristotle's constant return to signification and definition (1062a14–16). In fact, aporias are 'impressionistically linked through the facilities of language'.[44] Analogies drawn from colour, letters of the alphabet, ensoulment of the body, medicine and mathematics replace demonstration. We find the same method employed earlier in *Metaphysics* when Aristotle attempts to distinguish between 'actuality' and 'potentiality' only to conclude that 'we must not seek a definition of everything but be content to grasp the analogy'.[45] It now transpires that what began as an examination of the ontological order for the purpose of stabilising the logic of paronymy, suffers inversion. As one scholar notes: 'the logic of paronymy becomes indispensable; it is the clamp that prevents ontology from disintegrating'.[46] And ultimately, this paradox is only resolved in the turn towards God as the principle of that 'which can exist apart and is immoveable',[47] as the primary and prior source of all derivation.

The necessary relation between the noetic and the ontological, the solution to the universal knowability of the individual substance, rests, finally, upon the rhetorical and the theological. But the turn to God only opens the old debate between whether 'first philosophy' is ontology or theology. Because unless it can be demonstrated that ontology is theological for Aristotle – that is, God is the primary substance from which all other substances are derived – then a further aporia opens between being *qua* being and the divine. Earlier in *Metaphysics* (books VII–IX) it is unclear whether God as prime mover is also creator and cause of all that is: 'the connection between theology and ontology was abandoned'.[48] On the other hand, *Metaphysics* XII 6–7 suggests an eternal unchanging substance different from the two natural substances. And the relationship between the two natural substances and the third unchanging one is paronymous. 1072b13–15 famously states: 'On such a principle, then, depend the heavens, and nature.' No doubt the debate on the relation of theology to ontology in Aristotle's thinking, and

---

[42]   Edward Booth, *Aristotelian Aporetic Ontology in Islamic and Christian Thinkers* (Cambridge University Press, 1983), p. 17.

[43]   Ibid., p. 8.

[44]   Ibid., p. 17.

[45]   *Metaphysics*, 1048a36–7.

[46]   Patzig, *Theology and Ontology*, p. 39.

[47]   *Metaphysics*, 1064a29–1064b14.

[48]   Patzig, *Theology and Ontology*, p. 47.

whether this relation changed over the writing of the different section of *Metaphysics*, will continue. Ironically, if Aristotle systematically followed through a hierarchical relationship between primary, secondary (the terms are found in *Categories*, where Aristotle also denies that there are degrees of substance – 3b33f) and even tertiary substances, he would be affirming rather than rejecting the Platonic relationship between Matter and Form. For us the question of resolving the relationship between theology and ontology in Aristotle is significant, but not essential. What is essential is the extent to which substance can be substantial when so much depends upon the distinction between primary, secondary and tertiary, and yet, as Alexander of Aphrodisia (one of Aristotle's first commentators) notes, 'the principles [of substance] are not made known through axioms, as they are not demonstrable'.[49] What remains when logic and the categories fail to produce knowledge (*episteme*)? Only, I suggest, the unstable nature of analogy itself – hovering between being a mode of argumentation that cannot, finally, be given ontological validation (and therefore constitute a form of knowledge as Aristotle understood knowledge) and a mode of rhetoric. Furthermore, analogy is located within a wider symbolics which responds via social consensus, use and convention to the larger temporal movements and *erga* which characterise the physical world as Aristotle conceives it. What remains is allegory.

In the light of this, what, then, is philosophy for Aristotle but a way of living among the names and things which constitute the world, ever evaluating, defining and interpreting them? This is the human *ergon* as a language-animal contextualised by a world governed by a principle of movement,[50] situated within time. This *ergon* marks out the path of purposeful pedagogy. Analogy is part of this wider and ongoing pedagogical scheme in which identities can never be fixed and definitions only approximated. I use the word allegory with relation to this pedagogical path because specifically, as Paul de Man has pointed out, allegory constitutes a rhetoric of temporality. Allegory 'always corresponds to the unveiling of an authentically temporal destiny'.[51] The moral philosopher and classicist Martha Nussbaum points up the ethics of this Aristotelian notion of dialectic as ongoing clarification within a 'therapeutic community', linking it quite specifically to the rela-

---

[49]   Quoted by Booth, *Aristotelian Aporetic Ontology*, p. 28. Abstracts from Alexander of Aphrodisia's *Commentary on Metaphysics* can be found in W.D. Ross, *Aristotelis Fragmenta Selecta* (Oxford University Press, 1955).

[50]   *Metaphysics*, 1075b37.

[51]   *Blindness and Insight: Essays in the Rhetoric of Contemporary Criticism* (London: Methuen, 1983), p. 206.

tionship between rhetoric and emotion. Emphasising that Aristotle's lectures 'do not claim finality'[52] and that emotions have an intimate relation both to belief and judgement,[53] Nussbaum argues that the purpose of rhetoric is to create, take away and modify emotions 'by discourse and argument'.[54] In this way emotions, closely bound to judgement and therefore affected by modifications of judgement, are educated and 'brought into harmony with a correct view of the good human life'.[55] Hence literature has an important part to play in providing examples in the *Nicomachean Ethics*, and Aristotelian mimesis concerns itself with the creation of dramatic unity (of action, time and place) and presenting universals as particulars.[56] Thus the discourse of poets attempts a task Aristotle set himself to accomplish as a philosopher in *Metaphysics* – and possibly Sophocles fulfils the task much better.[57] *Praxis* and *poiesis* draw close to one another. The latter can affect the former and the former is that which is imitated by the latter. They are not the same, but only to the extent that doing-as-becoming and making are distinct activities.[58] They are the same as two dynamic responses to and participations within the cosmic movement. They are both expressions by which the soul may arrive at truth.[59]

By viewing the human being's work as a journey through a conceptual allegory that requires judgement and clarification (providing a role for philosophy as a critical discourse) I am not suggesting the world is appearance. We will leave that to some Platonists. The world is not appearance for Aristotle; the world is substance, we can trust our perceptions of this world and we develop notions of experience from repeated familiar perceptions of the sensuous and emotional. Intellectual activity abstracts from sensation, but the concrete particular which gives rise to sensation remains. The intellectual abstraction aims at grasping the universal in the concrete particular, and

---

[52] *Therapy of Desire: Theory and Practice in Hellenistic Ethics* (Princeton University Press, 1994), p. 76.

[53] Ibid., p. 80. See also Clark on perception, *Aristotle's Man*, pp. 69–83 and the work of the contemporary American neurologist, Antonio Damasio. In several works – including *Descartes' 'Error': Emotion, Reason and the Human Brain* (New York: HarperCollins, 1995) and *Looking for Spinoza: Joy, Sorrow and the Feeling Brain* (New York: Harcourt, 2003) – Damasio demonstrates how profoundly the mind and the body are related.

[54] *Therapy of Desire*, p. 83.

[55] Ibid., p. 96.

[56] *Poetics*, 51a36–51b10.

[57] See Gerald Else, *Plato and Aristotle on Poetry* (Chapel Hill: University of North Carolina Press, 1986), where he argues for the connections between poetic structure and the syllogistic form, pp. 110–12, 128–9.

[58] For a more detailed discussion of the relationship between *praxis* and *poiesis* see my *Cultural Transformation and Religious Practice* (Cambridge University Press, 2004), pp. 6–8, 139–42, 165–8.

[59] *Nicomachean Ethics*, VI.3.

however aporetic Aristotelian ontology and epistemology are at this very point, nevertheless with Aristotle there is an intense concentration upon the embodied. The embodied is transfigured when its universal form is understood. It is taken up into and receives its full significance through the universal. As such, substance always retains a certain permeability. Linguistic symbols are always symbols of this sensible permeability. Furthermore, as symbols they are interpretations of experience, 'symbols of affections'.[60] Wisdom and the pursuit of the good life invoke a process of rational discrimination which structures, clarifies, interprets and evaluates these symbols, these interpretations of this permeable substance. Aristotle listens through the language to what the world announces about its structures, its balances, its movements, and the divinity of its end. Matter finds its fulfilment in receiving form and 'The Ultimate form it "hopes" to receive ... is the divine life of the Prime ... and it is insofar as we too receive that form that we can understand the world.'[61] Both creation and creature have a vocation within the purview of this dynamic.

Development of a Second Theme: Gregory of Nyssa, *Allegoria* and the Spiritual Sense

Having examined the association of mimesis, *praxis* and knowledge, we return to the original focus of this study – the reading of Scripture and the nature of God's revelation attested there. In introducing Gregory of Nyssa's work at this point, the intention is not to establish a comparison and contrast between Aristotle and Gregory. It would be important to do such work – examining the similarities and differences of their thinking on the pursuit of the good life, their anthropologies, ontologies and epistemologies. Others have demonstrated how profoundly Gregory has been influenced by Aristotle and how un-Platonic is the general character of his thought, despite several critiques of Aristotelian *technologia* in *Contra Eunomium*.[62] The intention here is to develop Aristotle's appreciation of the inseparability

---

[60] *De Interpretatione*, 16a3.

[61] Clark, *Aristotle's Man*, p. 67.

[62] See Hans Urs von Balthasar's study of Gregory of Nyssa's work, *Presence and Thought: An Essay on the Religious Philosophy of Gregory of Nyssa*, tr. Mark Sebane (San Francisco: Ignatius Press, 1995) (first published in 1942). Also E. von Ivanka, 'Vom Platonismus zur Theoriemystik. Zur Erkenntnislehre Gregors von Nyssa', *Scholastik* 11 (1936), pp. 163–95. D.L. Balas is right when he states that Gregory's knowledge of philosophy included middle Platonism and early Neoplatonism as well as strong Aristotelian and Stoic elements (*Theologische Realenzyklopädie*, Bd. XIV, Berlin: de Gruyter, 1985, p. 177). The work of Heinrich Dorrie has emphasised the parallels with Plato's work – the *Phaedo* on Gregory's *De Anima* and *Timaeus* on Gregory's exegesis of Genesis. (See here also

of mimesis and *phronesis*, rhetoric and logic, the temporality and movement of matter and the universal speculation of *theoria* in terms of an allegorical reading of the Scriptures. This reading will, in turn, imply and issue from a theology of representation and reading, as we will see. From analysis of the metaphysics, ethics and aesthetics of representation we move to the practice of reading, the inner dynamics of reader–author–text installed by narrative. We will proceed through an examination of that classic spiritual interpretation of the Scriptures found in *The Life of Moses*.[63]

In Book I of that study, Gregory retells the story of Moses as it can be pieced together from the Books of Deuteronomy and Numbers, the Letter to the Hebrews and Jewish Midrashim. The emphasis is upon the historical and the psychological. Where he deviates from the Scriptures he is concerned with painting a certain realism, a concreteness, about this figure and a plausibility about the events within which he participates. Before the smoking Mount Sinai, Moses's 'whole being so trembled with fright that his faintness of soul was not concealed from the Israelites, but he was as terrifed as they were, at what he saw and his body shook violently'.[64] Corporeality may exist without appetitive passion, sustained without food or drink, for forty days and nights while Moses was wrapped in the darkness of God on the summit of Sinai (I.58, 60), but Gregory nevertheless wishes to affirm the historical particularity of this man and his actions. It is only on the basis of such that he can move from the material and mutable to the practical wisdom, the general outline of the perfect life. Like Aristotle, it is the particular that must embody the universal. 'Always remaining the same, [Moses] preserved in the changeableness of nature an unchangeable beauty.'[65]

It is in Book II that 'a more figurative spiritual sense' (literally 'a more tropical theoria')[66] is worked out. The soul is to be trained in an ascent towards divine illumination, just as in Plato's Cave allegory the philosopher

---

Monique Alexandre, '*L'exegèse de Gen. 1, 1–2a dans l'*In Hexaemeron *de Grégoire de Nysse: deux approches du problème de la matière*', who argues that Gregory's concept of matter is thoroughly Aristotelian: *Gregor von Nyssa und die Philosophie*, eds. Heinrich Dorrie, Margarete Altenburger and Uta Schramm, Leiden: Brill, 1976, pp. 159–92.) Nevertheless many other scholars have pointed out Gregory's indebtedness to Aristotelian vocabulary and concepts. From his work Werner Jaeger infers that 'Gregor hat die aristotelische Kategorienlehre offenbar gut studiert': *Gregor von Nyssa's Lehre vom Heiligen Geist* (Leiden: Brill, 1966). Jean Daniélou, examining Gregory's understanding of *theoria* 'comme méthode discursive pour arriver à une connaissance sure' points that that 'c'est à Aristotle que se rattache la méthodologie de Grégoire': *L'Etre et le temps chez Grégoire de Nysse* (Leiden: Brill, 1970), p. 5.

[63]   Throughout this essay I am making reference to the translation by Abraham J. Malherbe and Everett Ferguson (New York: Paulist Press, 1978).

[64]   Ibid., I.43.

[65]   Ibid., I.76.

[66]   Ibid., II.43.

king is to be trained. Once Moses has been illuminated at the burning bush he is to liberate the Hebrews from Egypt in the same way as the philosopher king is to return to the Cave to release the prisoners. The move from bestiality to enlightenment is mapped out metaphorically in terms of transcending the mud, clay and chaff of the sensual in themselves rather than being released from its bondage. This is where Gregory does not follow Plato. In itself this materiality is good. But we must be released from our dependence upon materiality in and for itself: Benjamin's 'soulless materiality'. What affects the transformation is being able to see the invisible as it pertains to the visible creation, to read the Logos in human beings and the wider world. Creation has to be reread, theologically. We need instruction for this, hence the important role of the teacher and the mode of the teaching (of which we will say more later). For the soul is to be trained in its reading of the world, trained in understanding the perceptions and experiences which inscribe themselves upon that soul. The dynamic of this training is two-fold, the soul's desire for God who is 'alone desirable'[67] and the operation of the Spirit in creation. This philosophy of desire is theologically dependent upon the divine Personhood of the Spirit, which Gregory insisted was necessary for a coherent understanding of the Trinity. Through the Spirit the soul is led to a knowledge of that which subtends all other knowledges and understandings of what is, the Logos: 'It seems to me that at the time the great Moses was instructed in the theophany he came to know that none of those things which are apprehended by sense perception and contemplated by the understanding really subsists, but that the transcendent essence and cause of the universe, on which everything depends, alone subsists.'[68] The condition for ontological and noetic possibility is theological. The recognition of this is both given, via revelation, and earned, by the employment of the intellect. We are enslaved to the material and sensual without the exercise of our rationality (II.46) and without our participation in the eschatological economy of the Spirit. The recognition of the universal and immutable in and through the particular and mutable finds expression in terms of the virtuous life; a life now ordered, orientated and interpreted by that which has been revealed.

The narrative of Moses's life becomes, when interpreted allegorically, a model for our imitation; a paradigmatic form is discerned within the material details. The allegorical text, then, parallels (and it is the nature, operation and significance of that parallel which interests us) the historical people, circumstances and events themselves. Just as these details compose a

---

[67]   Ibid., II.25.
[68]   Ibid., II.24.

reality (for Gregory would not have doubted these things occurred as they were transcribed) which is poised between what Aristotle would call matter and form, so too is the text, as it composes the narrated world, poised between *historia* and *theoria*. Both realities – the concrete universal and the narrative – provide spaces for the operation of what David Tracy terms 'the analogical imagination'.[69] Both in the *actual experience* of Moses before the burning bush, for example, and in the *narrated account* of Moses before the burning bush, a space is opened between sign (or what Aristotle would call symbol) and meaning. Within this space lies what Gregory will frequently term 'a hidden doctrine' ready for disclosure by the reader.

Paul de Man, commenting upon the structure of allegory, states that 'the relationship between the sign and meaning is discontinuous, involving an extraneous principle that determines the point and manner at which the relationship is articulated ... [T]he sign points to something that differs from its literal meaning and has for its function the thematization of this difference.'[70] De Man reappraises and understands *allegoria* within a poststructural view of the construction of all worlds of meaning from the free-floating and endless dance of signs. And this is evidently neither Gregory's cultural context nor anything he would understand by an allegorical appreciation of the world. For Gregory what is allegorical primarily is creation; it is a description of the created order as the invisible is apprehended within the visible. His allegorical readings are readings of the world, but they are also readings of Scriptural texts. The Scriptural texts disclose the nature of the world. Creation is represented in these texts in a way that instructs the soul in the things which are hidden. Scripture is a reading of creation. As such, the discontinuities between sign and meaning in allegory, which de Man alerts us to, are not only evident, they are more complex. Because the sign is not simply the literary sign in the Scriptural text, is it also the body out there in the world that points towards other possible disclosures. So, for example, there is no evident connection between a burning bush and the immaculate conception (II.21), the staff of Moses and the incarnation (II.26, 27), Aaron and the angels (II.51). Yet Gregory insists there is a theological, a hidden, connection. Furthermore, each of these signs can change their meaning as the narrative and interpretation unfolds – the burning bush becomes a picture of the incarnation, the rod becomes 'the word of faith'[71] and then the cross, Aaron is a sign of an angel while he stands alongside

---

[69] *The Analogical Imagination: Christian Theology and the Culture of Pluralism* (London: SCM Press, 1981). I would distinguish, though, between my understanding of 'analogy' and Tracy's correlational understanding.

[70] *Blindness and Insight*, p. 209.

[71] *Life of Moses*, II.36.

Moses before the Pharaoh and a sign of a demon when he leads the Israelites in the worship of idols. Gregory emphasises this discontinuity between object and name, sign and meaning, perception and knowledge: 'The whole creature cannot go outside itself by means of a comprehensive knowledge. It always remains in itself. And whatever it perceives, it forms a perception of by itself. It is incapable of seeing a thing outside its own nature, even if it thinks it is glimpsing an object that goes beyond it.'[72] He associates this with his theology of *diastasis* – the separation between God as uncreated and created human beings.

Let me draw out two consequences of this dislocation between sign and meaning, imaged peception and knowledge, and the allegorical procedure which both creates and perpetuates while seeking to resolve this dislocation. First, with reference to Paul de Man's analysis of allegory, it is the 'extraneous principle' imposing itself upon the object perceived (in Moses's case, the burning bush) or the object depicted which disrupts identification. A is no longer A, A is also B (and C and D). It does not just disrupt once, but having disrupted it continually disrupts. As the narrative continues, the reidentifications, A as B, are not standardised. Shoes with reference to Moses before the burning bush are identified as dead, earthy things which have to be stripped away before illumination is possible. 'Sandalled feet cannot ascend.'[73] Shoes with reference to the eating of the passover are identified as forms of necessary protection against the 'thorns of life'. 'Shoes are the self-controlled and austere life.'[74] In this processive reidentification, nakedness also undergoes a semantic shift. What this affects is an inability to grasp any object as a self-subsisting entity, a body to be owned. There is no stability of the identification. All possession and understanding is provisional, for, as Dorrie points out, 'Nun ist der Logos keineswegs das als solches passive Objekt des Forschens und Suchens.'[75] Allegory as such forestalls what otherwise would be idolatry. We are pushed beyond the symbiotic equation of knowledge and perception because what is seen 'kindles the desire for the hidden through what is constantly perceived'.[76] If the play of the invisible within the visible, the incorporeal within the corporeal, is not perceived there is no perception. There is blindness. Such uninformed perception, such grasping of objects and bodies as if they were self-subsistent entities leads to lust, the misdirection of desire. Gregory speaks of 'the very root of evil – namely, the

---

[72] *Contra Eunomium*, 12, II, 1064 BC

[73] *Life of Moses*, II.22.

[74] Ibid., II.107.

[75] *Reallexikon für Antike und Christentum*, Bd. XII (Stuttgart: Anton Hiersemann, 1983), p. 882.

[76] *Life of Moses*, II.231.

desire which arises through sight'.[77] He follows here a line of theological thinking which has consistently offered a critique against what has come to be called, by Jacques Derrida and Luce Irigaray, ocularcentrism – the ideology and pornography of visibility. Seeing belongs to God alone – *theoria* is associated with *theos*.

Secondly, what determines the multiple reidentifications in Gregory of Nyssa's text is three-fold. There is (a) the iteration of the object elsewhere in the Scriptures – for example, the various emplotments of 'serpent' in the books of Genesis and Numbers and the Gospel of John redefine each other. The serpent that tempted Eve (Genesis) is related to the serpent of bronze in Numbers 2.4–9, which Moses set up to save those bitten by poisonous snakes, which is then related to Jesus's words in the Gospel of John (3.14) predicting his own death. The mention of the word invokes a system of correspondences such that 'you of course understand the "cross" when you hear "wood"'.[78] We might term this the Scriptural principle of intratextuality. Augustine in *De Doctrina Christiana* expounds the principle (and its theology): 'the Holy Spirit has magnificently and wholesomely modulated the Holy Scriptures so that the more open places present themselves to hunger and the more obscure places may deter a disdainful attitude. Hardly anything may be found in these obscure passages which is not found plainly said elsewhere.'[79] This principle blurs distinctions between primary text and secondary interpretation and the hierarchy which privileges one text above another. Intratextuality presents a flat field of signs and displays a constant trafficking between one text and another through the processes of allusion, citation, iteration, reinscription and rewriting, examples of all of which Gregory of Nyssa's text provides. Then there is (b) the tradition of the Church Fathers or the rule of faith. For the staff's transformation into a snake as a sign of the incarnation appears in Irenaeus, *Adversus Haereses* 3.28, and it will appear later in Cyril of Alexandria, *Glaphyra in Exodum* 2.299. We can include here Gregory's appeal to Jewish Midrashim and his indebtedness to the allegorical reading of Philo. We might, following the work on reader–response theory by Stanley Fish, term this an appeal to the interpretive community, if Fish's understanding of this operation was not in fact a secularised notion of *ecclesia* and *paradosis*. Such communities stabilise, by authorising, certain meanings; they create certain ideological readings and in shaping these readings they shape, at the same time, the readers.[80] We will

---

[77] Ibid., II.304.

[78] Ibid., II.132.

[79] *De Doctrina Christiana*, II.6.

[80] *Is There a Text in This Class? The Authority of Interpretive Communities* (Cambridge, Mass.: Harvard University Press, 1980), p. 336.

return to the politics of this 'readings shaping readers' and the relationship between the operation of the analogical imagination and ideology later. Gregory also (c) employs theophany itself as determining reidentifications, just as in his telling of Moses's life there are three moments of revelation – the light of the burning bush, the darkness on Mount Sinai and the view of God's back as he passes by. As a theophany this last episode, which is God's response to Moses's desire to see him, is most significant. The first theophany is mediated (through the bush). The second on Mount Sinai is an entry into darkness and incomprehensibility. This third theophany is the only one where Moses 'sees' God, but not face to face. Throughout his work Gregory emphasises that God is 'The-Always-Greater'[81] and the soul will never reach its final perfection.[82] Only a spiritual rewriting of 'God's back' as the traces of God's operations in the world restores the narrative's intention. The revelation, then, turns out to be a figure for God's mediated presence, a representation of a representation. As theophanies the three events do not suggest the immediacy of knowing God. There is always a distance, a *diastasis*, traversed by representation and desire. Moses's final contact with God is his subsumption into heaven 'leaving behind no sign on earth nor any grave as a memorial'.[83] These theophanies, then, are emphatically moments of negative knowledge, knowledge beyond intelligible knowing, knowledge only *that* God is and not *what* God is. Nevertheless, the theophanies are disclosures of ultimate truth, moments of authorisation that hold the whole narrative progress in order. The meaning and unfolding structure of the action (the history) and the contemplation (the spiritual interpretation) circulate about these moments; moments when the narrative is suspended, frozen in light or darkness. This suspension of the narrative is not, though, accompanied by lacunae in the telling, the writing itself. However filled with light or consumed by darkness, however ineffable – Gregory's language still proceeds. Theology, attestation, requires its rhetoric: oxymoron, paradox and analogy take over. The writing is necessary 'to signify our reasoning',[84] to trace the allegorical in both the Scriptural text and Moses's experience. We write as we reason and this is our teaching. The presence of God is staged; his passing is performed.

Where knowledge, perception, representation and true presence coincide is in the Logos. Heinrich Dorrie notes: 'Folgerichtig fordert Gregor, das Bild Christi in der eigenen Seele aufzusuchen und es von aller Verdunklung

---

[81] *In Canticum Canticorum*, 8; I, 941 B.
[82] *Contra Eunomium*, 1, II, 340 D.
[83] *Life of Moses*, I.75.
[84] *De Hominis Opificio*, VIII.2.

und Verunklarung zu reinigen und zu befreien.'[85] '"The senses of the soul" are pleasured by the charm of the apple tree of the Word.'[86] What is finally revealed to Moses, having been led towards it by trumpets that signified preaching and prophecy, 'the Spirit through his instruments',[87] is the Word itself. The Word is a two-fold divine form of writing. First, there is the Logos presented through the representation, the analogy, of the heavenly tabernacle. The divisions within the tabernacles correspond to Christ's human and Christ's resurrected body (II.174). In II.216 the incarnation is pictured as God writing upon human material. Again the presentation is not finally perspicacious, the rhetoric slides – as the narrative and the exegesis follow each other the tabernacle is also the celestial world (II.179), the Church (II.184) and the human body (II.245). Perhaps this semantic slipping is why prayer and praise even in the tabernacle are described as 'a verbal sacrifice'[88] – the meaning of the words is handed over, abandoned, from the moment of their utterance. Words, like the Word, experience a kenosis.[89] Secondly, there are the tablets of stone written by God which are also a picture of the soul. These are first written upon by the hand of God and subsequently rewritten upon by the action of the Word (II.316). At the pinnacle, holding the rest in order, the form to which all aspires is writing itself, divine and human interwoven, one providing the conditions, even necessitating, the other. *Scriptura, écriture.* 'The Holy Spirit is called "finger" in many places in Scripture'; Gregory notes that revelation is written.[90]

Despite the Platonic/Neoplatonic motif of ascent and the disciplining of the senses through eros, there are sufficent parallels here with Aristotle's understanding of the relationship between mimesis, *theoria*, metaphysics and theology. Not least is the concern to affirm the corporeal, not disregard it. The aporetics of ontology and epistemology are also evident in Gregory's allegorical reading of the pursuit of truth and the virtuous life. We will develop this. These aporetics follow, as I said, from the ultimate *diastema* between creator and creation. They lead to a process of coming to know, not a knowledge. They announce a new kind of space for reflection. Allegory –

---

[85] *Reallexikon*, p. 882.

[86] *In Canticum Canticorum*, 4; I, 844 B.

[87] *Life of Moses*, II.159.

[88] Ibid., II.182.

[89] See here II.247, where no fewer than 18 redefinitions are given for 'the opening in the rock' into which Moses retreated when God passed by.

[90] Ibid., II.216. Philo's work also stressed the written form of revelation, unlike Clement of Alexandria who, later, drew attention to the voice as revelatory. See David Dawson, *Allegorical Readers and Cultural Revision in Ancient Alexandria* (Berkeley: University of Califonia Press, 1992), especially pp. 73–126 and 183–234.

by opening the semiotic can of worms, disassociating sign from meaning, installing an ontological and noetic aporia and indeterminacy – both creates this space and seeks to work productively within it, containing the arbitrary. The opening of this new spatiality through allegory is clearly presented in Gregory's interpretation of the ascent of Moses up the mountain and into the darkness of God (II.152–69). For as the narrative proceeds upwards so the allegorical interpretation, which views this ascent as an interiorised event of illumination beyond sense impressions and reasoning, speaks of penetrating depths and elevation of the mind. If allegory always operates beyond real time (see de Man), transposing and disrupting the historical, it is also a strategy for the disruption of geographical space, installing a deliberate obfuscation of spatial dimensions. A sacred space is opened, what Gillian Rose has called the 'broken middle'.[91] This is a space which is constantly transgressing its own dimensions, a space that cannot be located 'here' or 'there' because it is a space that cannot be contained, a space that deconstructs its boundaries. '[I]n speaking of "place" he [Moses] does not limit the place indicated by anything quantitative (for to something unquantitative there is no measure).'[92] This space can neither be limited nor defined. It is a space for dispossession. Read in terms of ecclesiology, this is a liturgical space.[93] Read theologically in terms of contemplation, this is a place for the interpretative play within representation itself. As such, *allegoria* is like the convex mirror at the centre of Jan van Eyck's famous painting of *The Arnolfini Marriage*. It announces a certain reflexivity about representation and interpretation itself; a self-consciousness, within mimesis, of the dialectic between semiosis and interpretation; a self-consciousness about the way representation constructs our worlds, our notions of identity and reality and how that linguistic construction remains continually open to being rewritten, reinterpreted. The allegory, the hidden doctrine, of the created orders themselves and the allegory of the representation of those orders draw attention to the rhetoric of our knowledge of God's world, its metaphoricity. Furthermore, *allegoria* offers a reflection upon reading itself – the reading which always rewrites, performs the textual score in its own key, according it its own rhythm, with its own attention to certain details and blindness to others. It is in this sense that Paul de Man calls allegory 'metafigural'[94] – it is

---

[91] *The Broken Middle: Out of Our Ancient Society* (Oxford: Basil Blackwell, 1992). See especially pp. 277–96.

[92] *Life of Moses*, II.242. See II.243 for a temporality which is eternal: 'how the same thing is both a standing still and a moving', like Aristotle's concept of God.

[93] See Jean-Yves Lacoste, *Expérience et Absolu* (Paris: Presses Universitaires de France, 1994) for an exploration of how personhood experiences a dispossession and kenosis in and through liturgy.

[94] *Allegories of Reading*, p. 275.

both a strategy of reading and writing and a reflection upon the act of representation itself with respect to reading and writing. *Allegoria* provides Hermes with a mirror in which to contemplate his own character as messenger of the gods, diplomat, trickster and thief.

What then of the reader, who is also pupil, the one under instruction, both for Aristotle and for Gregory of Nyssa? Daniélou notes how Gregory's concept of *akolouthia* depends upon Aristotle's.[95] It is important to point out that allegory never speaks in its own name. The principles of intratextuality and interpretative communities, and the advent of the theophanous, are appeals by the exegete to symbolic fields larger than the single reader, other voices that keep a check upon the arbitrary. The self as author is authored and given authorisation from elsewhere. Ethically, in destabilising identity, allegory destabilises selfhood. The 'I' dissolves into the others which speak in, through and for the I. Allegory creates not only reading but readers, it is a form of discursive power like prayer and confession,[96] rhetoric in the service of soul-making. The 'I' is led on a narrative of purification; the reading is a spiritual exercise, for in the reading the 'I' enters this space of dispossession and is continually renamed – as Moses, as an Egyptian, as an Israelite, as a pillar, as a sanctuary light. 'For not everyone is named brother or friend or neighbour in a good sense by Scripture. It is possible to be both brother and foreigner, both friend and enemy ... Scripture ... gives indication of the double meaning of brotherhood, that the same word does not always signify the same thing but may be taken with opposite meanings.'[97] Reading as contemplation is a form of ethical praxis, integral with the pursuit of the virtuous life. The place and identity of the 'I' is ambivalent, it is an ambivalence which results from a disassociation of name and meaning. This engineers a space for the operation of the Spirit and what Balthasar, discussing the work of Gregory, terms a 'knowledge by desire' as distinct from a 'knowledge by image'.[98] Gregory names God as 'You whom my soul loves' and emphasises that in desire alone do we see God, insofar as we can.[99] Not that representation can be transcended, as we have seen, only that representation can be transfigured through and in desire, through and in the Spirit.

[95] *L'Etre et le temps chez Grégoire de Nysse*, pp. 43–5. This word returns us to Robert Scharlemann's term 'acoluthetic reasoning', explored in the first essay, 'Christology and Mimesis'.

[96] See Michel Foucault, *The History of Sexuality*, vol. 1, tr. Robert Hurley (London: Penguin Books, 1981) for a discussion of confession as social engineering (pp. 18–21, 60–1). Also Talal Asad, *The Genealogies of Religion: Discipline and Reasons of Power in Christianity and Islam* (Baltimore, Md.: Johns Hopkins University Press, 1993), pp. 83–167.

[97] *Life of Moses*, II.208, 210.

[98] *Presence and Thought*, p. 133.

[99] See *In Canticum Canticorum*, 8; I, 941 AB and 12; I, 1024 BC.

It is at this point that we can only appreciate Gregory's concern with allegorical reading of creation and text, and the destabilisation of identity, within wider systematic concerns in his theology. Primarily, there is his concern with the Trinity as the community of processive love. This is linked to his desire to establish the deity of the Holy Spirit, who as union of Father and Son is Person, and who, as processing from the Son, also crosses the *diastema* of creator/creation. This leads Gregory to begin his theology from an existential philosophy of desire as we have seen elsewhere in this collection, and a theological understanding of human beings made in the image of God. We are created with passions that we might be drawn to love God.[100] The operation of this desire will move us beyond the inertia and lust of 'soulless materialism' towards deification.

Where narrative, allegory, knowledge and virtue meet is in this theological understanding of personhood. Here what is 'I', what is identified, what is named – 'all names have equally fallen short of accurate description, both those recognized as insignificant as well as those by which some great concept originated in sense impression'[101] – finds its place in 'the power which encompasses the universe, in which lives the fulness of the divinity, the common protector of all' (II.177). There is here a doctrine of participation, but to enter into the possibilities of that participation, to begin to ascend towards the truth and the good life, requires faith and free-choosing. Symbiotic analogies of God and creation are not self-evident. An irreducible opposition between God and human beings prevents such a natural theology. A space remains, a distance, and it is this space which *allegoria* installs and works productively within so that it may be resolved. The presence of God pervades creation, and our knowledge of that presence develops in, through and as the vocation to true personhood, the move towards becoming a person in Christ. All exists within the Word. The Word is unitary. All things find their definition then in and as the Word. Knowledge of God comes through illumination, the employment of one's reason towards that which is invisible and the necessary dispossession this precipitates. Revelation in all its forms is the continual perichoretic receiving and pouring out of love which is the Trinity and within which all things move. As such, divine disclosure *occurs* only in and as time and narrative, *as* history, *as* metonymy or the ongoing chain of signs. Just as salvation is a matter of the body and the soul, so revelation *is* story, our story within God's own story. The metonymic and horizontal axis of movement into the future from out of the past has a vertical, metaphoric or analogical axis, a transcendent reference. Both are

---

[100] Ibid., 4; I, 844 B.
[101] *Life of Moses*, II.176.

required. Analogy cannot present a frozen glimpse of the eternal truth. It is part of a larger and more dynamic symbolics. Knowledge of God can only issue from allegory, an allegory created as the invisible operates through the visible, an allegory created by infinite love: God's love for us and our desire to close the space which separates our signs from their meaning, our desire for the first, last and only Word. Within a doctrine, then, affirming that 'the term "Godhead" is significant of an operation, and not of nature',[102] narrative – the representation of an action – is not simply the vehicle for disclosure (that is, a divine disclosure is contained within it and is extractable by some hermeneutic process), nor the means for disclosure (that is, illumination uses the form of narrative as an instrument for its own purposes). Both these understandings of the relationship of divine communication to narrative are docetic – the body of the text is epiphenomenal. Rather, narrative as the allegorical representation of God and human salvific action in the world *is* disclosive – for the disclosure itself is not an event but an eventing, an always in the process of coming to be. The disclosure is the continuing outwork through the Spirit of God's revelation of Himself in Christ. The operation of the Logos is not yet complete – that is why allegory remains; the work of Christ is unfinished until human beings through an economy of response are deified: 'all will be one body and one spirit'.[103]

Recapitulation

There is not an attempt in this essay to harmonise Aristotle and Gregory of Nyssa. There are links between Aristotelianism and Neoplatonism.[104] Gregory was profoundly influenced by Aristotelian notions of the temporal, the dynamic, the universal and the corporeal. His was a doctrine of embodiment that took seriously the roots of Christian revelation in the historical and the concrete. Christianity needs, then, to read the spiritual, the universal in such a way as not to denigrate or dissolve the historical and concrete. Discovering the eternal and unchanging within the particular and temporal is the axiomatic concern of Christology, incarnation and sacramentalism. Aristotle provides us with a welcome metaphysics of embodiment. The aporetic character of that metaphysics is also significant, for Christianity cannot found a metaphysics on the equation of reason and Being, as

---

[102] 'On "Not Three Gods"' in *Select Writings and Letters of Gregory, Bishop of Nyssa*, trs. William Moore and Henry Wilson (Oxford: Parker and Company, 1893), p. 333.

[103] *In Canticum Canticorum*, 15; I, 1117 A.

[104] See Booth, *Aristotelian Aporetic Ontology*.

Gregory reminds us with his emphases on the *diastema* between the un-created Creator and the orders created out of nothing. Ours has to be a metaphysics of the saints, not the metaphysics of modernity.[105] The incorporeal is always discovered in the corporeal, the invisible within the visible. Furthermore, Aristotle's emphasis upon the dynamism of creation, on time, on becoming, or the teleology of the good life, could all find a place within Christianity's concern with history, the transience of all things, eschatology and redemption. But, more significantly, this essay has been concerned to develop Aristotle's understanding of the relationship between mimesis, metaphysics, ethics and theology (a relationship which hinges on the nature of analogy) through Gregory of Nyssa's theological understanding of allegory as analogical discourse. On the basis of this development several observations can be made about the relationship of narrative both to revelation, in the exclusive sense of God's revelation in Christ, and disclosure, the mediation of that revelation through the Spirit in creation.

What remains and is safeguarded in allegorical reading is textuality itself, writing, the body of the Scriptural text. The letteral (though not the literal, which is already an interpretation), the written, is affirmed in its materiality. The allegorical simply extends the letteral, supplements it in the sense both of adding to it and altering it. It sucks as a child on the textual breast, and as Gregory states: 'the Word ... changes His power in diverse ways to those who eat. He knows not only to be bread but also to become milk and meat and greens and whatever else might be appropriate to and desired by the one who receives him.'[106] As such, interpretation cannot dissolve the letteral into the meaningful. As Augustine exclaims concerning the Scriptures, 'The surface meaning lies open before us and charms beginners. Yet the depth is amazing, my God, the depth is amazing. To concentrate on it is to experience awe.'[107] The reading shapes and reflects the reader Christocentrically, provoking the desire to understand, provoking the supplementation, the further writing. Language and the circulation of immanent and transcendent desires (human and divine eros) – these remain central to appreciating the relation between narrative and revelation, time, becoming and personhood. That is why we need to explore the work of Lacan, Kristeva and Irigaray alongside the theologies of Barth and Balthasar. We get confused by our grammar, taking 'revelation' as a substantive. As such revelation becomes an event of making something known. We ask about the

---

[105] See Balthasar, *The Glory of the Lord*, vol. 5, tr. Oliver Davies et al. (Edinburgh: T. & T. Clark, 1991), pp. 48–140, 'The Metaphysics of the Saints'.

[106] *Life of Moses*, II.140.

[107] *Confessions*, tr. Henry Chadwick (Oxford University Press, 1992), p. 254.

contents of such knowledge. This has led some to view revelation as propositional.[108] Theophanous events do occur in Scripture, Gregory is drawn towards them. But they occur within a temporal movement that is not, in itself, insignificant. The theophanous event is the result of all that has proceeded it and will in itself be partial, for it will be followed by all that comes as a consequence of it. It is an event within an ongoing chain of events. The creature 'never halts at what it has reached, but all that it has acquired becomes by participation a beginning of its ascent to something still greater'.[109] Moses did not stop in his ascent. The theophanies were stages within revelation, not punctiliar moments of perfect realisation (II.227). Disclosure is an action, not an event – the continuing, generative action of revelation in the temporal and material. It is an action we are a part of and therefore even our attempts to extract ourselves from time and space and examine the content of any experience, moments of self-reflection, are part of the revelatory dynamism. The contents are continually contextualised and, as such, the meaning we give to them shifts, changes. If God transcends our ability to know him even in Christ then divine revelation cannot be the communication of knowledge such as we are used to deducing and inferring from our experience. Illumination can only be the communication of the form, the mediation of God. What we see of this form and what we are to understand by it is akin to the division between sign and meaning in language, in mimesis, which allegory draws attention to. Any contents, any understanding of our experience, is provisional and reinscribed elsewhere, rewritten. Gregory writes: 'This truly is the vision of God: never to be satisfied in the desire to see him.'[110] As such what is revealed in revelation is the nakedness of one's continual desire to see, to understand. What is revealed is an eros that transcends us and our grasp of the created order; and only insofar as desire is God himself in his perichoretic triunity is this a disclosure of the form of God. Illumination as the *actio* of revelation continues towards a not-to-be-realised eschatological horizon; it is coextensive with vocation and discipleship. The ethics of such a following – and here again Gregory follows in the footsteps of Aristotle – is the ethics of moderation or the mean (II.288–90).[111] The teleology of all action is, for both philosopher and theologian, conformity to the Good (II.317–18; *Nicomachean Ethics*,

---

[108] Most recently Richard Swinburne, *Revelation: From Metaphor to Analogy* (Oxford: Clarendon Press, 1992).

[109] *Contra Eunomium*, III.6.74.

[110] *Life of Moses*, II.239.

[111] On the theological importance of following in Gregory of Nyssa see II.252 and *In Canticum Canticorum*, 12.

Book X) – though, of course, the nature of the Good is interpreted differently for philosopher and theologian. Mimesis, as Aristotle observed, is both the representation of action and a form of action itself, both a making (*poiesis*) and a doing (*praxis*). The dreams of speculative philosophy for a coherent epistemology are broken. A complete account of the conditions for the possibility of knowledge is aporetic. There is only *phronesis*, practical wisdom, the process of getting to know which is integral to the pursuit of the good life. We who live in the age of the Spirit of Christ, within the redemptive work of the Holy Spirit, must speak of, through and by revealedness. The language we employ, the stories we tell, must be allegorised in order to open up a space between what we think we know and what is true, between what Aristotle would call *deutera ousia*, the socialised concepts which name our impressions of it, and the *prote ousia*, the substance beyond substance which is God. Allegory brings together rhetoric, aporetics, temporality and transcendence. It is a Christocentric pedagogy, a teaching, a spiritual exercise. The reading that surrenders itself, its certainties, its grasp of things, is contemplation, is praying, as St Ignatius and, more recently, Hélène Cixous,[112] understood. The final responsibility belongs both to the reader and the operation of grace that rends the equivalence of perception and understanding – that is what allegory pronounces. Gregory concludes his *Life of Moses* by turning to his reader. '[I]t is time for you, noble friend, to look to that example and, by transferring to your own life what is contemplated through spiritual interpretation of the things spoken literally, to be known by God and to become his friend.'[113]

If we relate this conclusion to the vexed question which often dogs the story–revelation debate – is it just as theologically and spiritually valid to read Proust as to read the Gospel of St John? – I would have to answer in terms very close to Clement of Alexandria (terms evident in Augustine's *Confessions*): 'if Hellenistic philosophy comprehends not the whole extent of the truth, and besides, is destitute of strength to perform the commandments of the Lord, yet it prepares the way for the truly royal teaching, training in some way or other [*hame ge pe*], and moulding the character, fitting him who believes in providence for the reception of the truth'.[114] It follows that it is in our experience of the world (which to be understood as experience must be represented), it is in our wording and our reading, in

---

[112] See *Reading with Clarice Lispector*, tr. Verena Andermatt Conley (Hemel Hempstead: Harvester Wheatsheaf, 1990) and my essay 'Words of Life: Hosting Postmodern Plenitude', *The Way*, 36 (3), July (1996), pp. 225–35.

[113] *Life of Moses*, II.320.

[114] *Stromateis*, 1.16.80.6.

our storytelling, that we are redeemed.[115] The triune God, by his revelation in Christ and through his Spirit, moves within the processes of time and human desire itself. Because we are made *in the image of* then are we destined to be *homo symbolicus*. My argument presupposes that the Godhead is an operation, not an object, not a subject, and, therefore that his revelation of himself in Christ is a continuously unfolding process, within an eschatological horizon. This unfolding process is the *dunamis* of love itself and therefore the content of such revelation is a getting to love, a pedagogy in adoration, a plotting of praise, a liturgy not an intellectual property. As such our creative storytelling takes place within the operation of God's triune loving; we exist in God's endless impartation of himself.

Coda

At the end of Wim Wenders's film, Cassiel, having sacrificed himself for a little girl, returns to the angelic realm. The closing shots follow the main human characters as they sail towards new horizons. Cassiel and Raphaela conclude the film with a voice-over:

> You. You whom we love. You who do not see us. You who do not hear us. You imagine us in the far distance, yet we are so near. We are the messengers who bring closeness to those in the distance. We are not the message, we are the messengers. The message is love. We are nothing. You are everything to us. Let us dwell in your eyes. See your world through us. Recapture through us that loving look once again. Then we'll be close to you and you to Him.

This is the film's final and most poignant statement against 'soulless materialism'. Again it follows, albeit without any reference, Walter Benjamin's recognition that 'allegories fill out and deny the void in which they are represented, just as, ultimately, the intention does not faithfully rest in contemplation of the bodies, but faithlessly leaps forward to the idea of resurrection'.[116]

---

[115] There is a further implication here. The Scripture's close correlation between the Christ-event and representation is going to make Scripture the most redemptive form of *mimesis*. But there are, after all, narratives of evil. On this account of the relationship between story and revelation, the extent to which something is recognised as good or evil will depend upon spiritual discernment or theological perception. That is, whether the divine can be seen within the ordinary, the invisible in the visible. Nothing by necessity is evil either in creation, experience or representation.

[116] *The Origin of German Tragic Drama*, p. 233.

Chapter Nine

SUFFERING AND INCARNATION: A CHRISTIAN POLITICS

The concern of this essay lies with a comparison and, ultimately, a confrontation between two cultures: the secular and the Christian, with respect to the character and economies of pain and pleasure, suffering, sacrifice and ultimate satisfaction. Not that that the relationship between these cultures is simply oppositional or even dialectical. The character of Christianity today cannot be extracted from its wider cultural contexts. Christianity, though rooted in all its various previous forms and traditions, is conceived in the cultural terms available, the cultural terms that maintain its current relevance and render it comprehensible (and believable) in contemporary society. There is, then, no homogeneous Christian culture, as there is no pure form of secular culture. Contemporary western 'secular' culture is effervescent with religious symbolics and the face of religion is being made ever visible in the public sphere.[1] But we can distinguish them as standpoints,[2] as different modes of viewing the world – modes that affect the values held and produced and the actions taken with respect to those values. They are implicated in different cultural politics concerning the institution of the good life. It is as such that we can compare their notions of pain and pleasure, suffering and sacrifice, while recognising that to undertake such a comparision is also to be implicated in *Kulturkritik*. That is, we not only define certain forms of cultural politics, we engage them, critically.

We need to begin with the corporeal since it is the body that registers suffering and it is the theological nature of embodiment itself which is the concern of incarnation. Suffering is a mode of embodied experience: a

---

[1]   See 'Religion as Special Effect' in my *True Religion* (Oxford: Blackwell, 2002), pp. 114–53.
[2]   For an analysis of 'standpoint-projects' see my *Cultural Transformation and Religious Practice*, (Cambridge University Press, 2004), pp. 72–97.

theological account, then, of suffering must concern itself with what it means to be a soul enfleshed. As we saw in chapter two, 'The Schizoid Christ' and chapter three, 'The Body of the Church and its Erotic Politics', touch as the fundamental sense exposes the body to the world. The body is orientated towards what is external to itself, caught up in economies of exchange and response. Jean-Louis Chrétien, after Aristotle, writes: 'The first evidence of soul is the sense of touch.'[3] The character of bodily experience is registered according to a pain–pleasure calculus. Those of us who are academics spend much of our time, I suggest, experiencing the extremes of neither. Because we touch the world continuously, for the most part we are not attuned to our embodied experience and therefore forget our corporeality since it is the tactile, as we saw, that gives to us the recognition of our embodiment. It is only at the extremes that we register the way touch spreads the soul throughout the body.[4] Perhaps most people only take account of their embodied soul when the body demands account to be taken because its experiences register the intensity of suffering or the delights of bliss. '[W]e feel only what exceeds us.'[5] In beginning with the corporeal let me emphasise first what I am and second what I am not doing.

First, I am rejecting any mind–body dualism. There are intellectual pleasures (as Kantian aesthetics and the joy of reading evidence) and there is intellectual pain (as existentialism emphasised and psychiatry treats). To draw upon a distinction St Paul makes, and which we will return to later, perhaps most of us inhabit the body (*soma*) rather than the flesh (*sarx*), or the symbolics of embodiment rather than its sensate materiality. The reason for this lies in the difficulty of registering sensation as such. That difficulty is at least twofold. On the one hand, to experience the body's continuous immersion in the world there has to be a recognition of what is other and external. We cannot feel ourselves as such. We are given to ourselves first, that we then might recognise that it is 'I' who is embodied. We register sensation then only in encounter. On the other hand, the body's sensations experienced in that encounter are registered through cultural prisms and personal expectations. The raw givenness of the body and its experiences are already encoded. Judith Butler neatly sums this up in her book *Bodies that Matter* through a play on the word 'matter' as it refers to both materiality and something of significance. That which is matter already matters, is

---

[3] 'Body and Touch' in *The Call and the Response*, tr. Anne A. Davenport (New York: Fordham University Press, 2004), p. 85.

[4] The metaphor is employed by the eighteenth-century French philosopher Yves Marie de L'Isle André in his treatise on the union of the soul and the body. See 'Body and Touch', p. 97.

[5] Ibid., p. 99.

already caught up in the exchanges of signification.[6] The soul enfleshed (where 'soul' has much wider connotations than just the mind's cognition, as we saw in chapter three, 'The Body of the Church and its Erotic Politics') is the only 'body' we know, and it sublates any mind–body dualism.

Secondly, I am not suggesting that there is a spectrum with pain at one pole and pleasure at another. Since early modernity, the Protestant awareness of the transcendence of the divine beyond human reasoning, accounts of peering into the infinite reaches of the heavens, and aesthetic descriptions of the sublime have each appealed to experiences that are simultaneously both painful and consummately beatific.[7] The mystic's cry of ecstasy,[8] the mathematician's speechless awe at the dark spaces between the stars,[9] the exquisite intellectual confusion as the experience of what is beautiful sheers towards the edge of the *tremendum*[10] – each testifies to experiences that exceed the neat categorisation, the twin-poled spectrum, of pain and pleasure. Though it does seem to me, and we will return to this in the last section of the essay, that to conflate suffering and bliss can also be a sign of decadence announcing a sado-masochistic culture.

Contemporary Pain and Pleasure

For some time now, at least since the 1960s and 1970s (though their roots lie in Hegel's *Phenomenology of Spirit*), intellectual debates concerned with the economies of desire – whether in Deleuze, Lacan, Lyotard, Barthes, Foucault or Žižek – have been oriented around the notion of *jouissance*. Suffering constitutes itself as the lack or absence of *jouissance*. Bliss, as one translation, is the ultimate human goal. With Lacan and Žižek the lack itself is pleasurable. They would argue that what we desire is not the fulfilment of our desire, but the desiring itself, the prolongation of desire. To attain our desire would collapse the distinction between the imaginary and the symbolic. The extended game of hunt the slipper would come to an end. Desire

---

[6]   *Bodies that Matter: On the Discursive Limits of 'Sex'* (London: Routledge, 1993).

[7]   See my essay 'Language and Silence' in Oliver Davis and Denys Turner eds., *Silence and the Word* (Cambridge University Press, 2000), pp. 159–84; John Milbank, 'Sublimity: The Modern Transcendent' in Paul Heelas ed., *Religion, Modernity and Postmodernity* (London: Routledge, 1998), pp. 258–84.

[8]   See Michel de Certeau, *The Mystic Fable*, vol. 1 *The Sixteenth and the Seventeenth Centuries*, tr. Michael B. Smith (University of Chicago Press, 1992).

[9]   See J.V. Field, *The Invention of Infinity: Mathematics and Art in the Renaissance* (Oxford University Press, 1997).

[10]   See Immanuel Kant, *Critique of Judgement*, tr. James Creed Meredith (Oxford: Clarendon Press, 1952).

only operates if there remains an *objet petit a*, a hole, a gap, a void, a loss that can never (and must never) be fully negotiated or filled. As so we fetishise – turn the hole itself into what we desire: 'in fetishism we simply make the cause of desire directly into our object of desire'.[11] But since the hole itself cannot be negotiated, then objects substitute for and veil this ultimate void. Bliss is then endlessly deferred yet remains the telos and organising point for any local and ephemeral construction of the meaning of embodiment. Lacan (and Žižek) develop into a sacrificial logic the system of compensations and substitutions that Freud increasingly recognised as symptomatic of the way the libidinal drive operates alongside the death drive in the economy of desire. Civilisation, for Freud, is founded upon its profound and ineliminable discontent. In this sacrificial logic we are caught up in a denial of what we most want and produce substitutionary forms, objects, laws, empty symbols for that which is unsubstitutional. And so, we deny – sometimes even murder – what we most value, in order to maintain our fantasies about it.[12] There takes place here a renunciation in the form of a negation of negation. It is this sacrificial logic that I wish to examine.

It finds similar forms in other poststructuralist discourses. Derrida's accounts of the economy of the sign, the economy of *différance* and the logic of the supplement, are also a sacrificial economy. In his essay 'How to Avoid Speaking' (*comment ne pas parler*), he coins the word 'denegation' (*dénegation*) or the negation of negation, to describe the effects of *différance* in discourses of negative theology. Writing in the interstices between the story of Abraham and Isaac in the Old Testament and Kierkegaard's reading of the story in *Fear and Trembling*, Derrida emphasises

> The trembling of *Fear and Trembling*, is, or so it seems, the very experience of sacrifice … in the sense that sacrifice supposes the putting to death of the unique in terms of its being unique, irreplaceable, and most precious. It also therefore refers to the impossibility of substitution, the unsubstitutional; and then also to the substitution of an animal for man; and finally, especially this, it refers to what links the sacred to sacrifice and sacrifice to secrecy … Abraham … speaks and doesn't speak. He speaks in order not to say anything about the essential thing he must keep secret. Speaking in order not to say anything is always the best technique for keeping a secret.[13]

[11]   Slavoj Žižek, *The Fragile Absolute – or Why Is the Christian Legacy Worth Fighting For?* (London: Verso, 2000), p. 21.

[12]   See Žižek on the relationship between Clara and Robert Schumann in *Plague of Fantasies* (London: Verso, 1997), pp. 66–7, 192–212.

[13]   *The Gift of Death*, tr. David Wills (University of Chicago Press, 1995), pp. 58–9.

Speaking in order not to say is the work of *différance* such that deconstruction produces a specific kind of syntax: in *The Gift of Death* it is 'religion without religion'; in *The Politics of Friendship* it is 'community without community' and 'friendship without friendship'; elsewhere it is 'justice without justice'. The syntagma of this sacrificial economy, which keeps concealed what it most wishes to say, is 'X without X'.[14] It conceals a continual wounding presented as a perpetual kenosis, the kenosis of discourse.[15] The sign is always involved in a diremption of meaning as it differs and defers in its logic of sacrificial substitution and supplementation. It is this which brings *différance* into a relation with negative theology (a saying which cannot say). The sign yields up its significance in what Derrida terms a *serierasure*. But what governs the yielding is the logocentric promise, the call to come, an eschatology which can never arrive, can never be allowed to arrive. Suffering, sacrifice and satisfaction are intrinsic to the economy of the sign.

> Every time there is '*jouissance*' (but the 'there is' of this event is in itself extremely enigmatic), there is 'deconstruction'. Effective deconstruction. Deconstruction perhaps has the effect, if not the mission, of liberating forbidden *jouissance*. That's what has to be taken on board. It is perhaps this *jouissance* which most irritates the all-out adversaries of 'deconstruction'.[16]

But this is '*jouissance* without *jouissance*', for deconstruction cannot deliver the delay it describes. Thus, a culture is produced which is fundamentally sado-masochistic: it cannot allow itself to enjoy what it most profoundly wants. Derrida composes a scenario:

> What I thus engage in the double constraint of a *double bind* is not only myself, nor my own desire, but the other, the Messiah or the god himself. As if I were calling someone – for example, on the telephone – saying to him or her, in sum: I don't want you to wait for my call and become forever dependent upon it; go out on the town, be free not to answer. And to prove it, the next time I call you, don't answer, or I won't see you again. If you answer my call, it's all over.[17]

Michel de Certeau and Emmanuel Lévinas, in their different models of selfhood with respect to the other, portray the sacrificial logic in terms of an

---

[14] *The Politics of Friendship*, tr. George Collins (London: Verso, 1997), p. 47.
[15] See *On the Name*, tr. Thomas Dutoit (Stanford University Press, 1995), pp. 50–60.
[16] 'An Interview with Jacques Derrida' in Derek Attridge, *Jacques Derrida: Acts of Literature* (London: Routledge, 1992), p. 56.
[17] *The Politics of Friendship*, p. 174.

endless journeying into exile (Certeau)[18] or the position of always being accused by the other (Lévinas).[19] For both, the self can never be at rest. It must always suffer displacement by the other, always undergo a passion. The displacement and suffering is given, in both their accounts, an ethical colouring for it is constituted in and by a Good beyond being (Lévinas) or the utopic horizon of union with the One (Certeau's 'white ecstasy').[20] The suffering is inseparable from accounts of desire, *jouissance* and substitution.[21]

With various modulations each of these discourses operates a sacrificial logic in which love is not-having (Cixous's formulation).[22] The suffering, the sacrifice, the kenosis is both necessary and unavoidable for it is intrinsic to the economy itself. But unlike Hegel's dialectic, the negative moment is not appropriated and welded firmly into both the providential chain of time and the constitution of the subject. The negative moment remains unappropriated, unsublated, impossible to redeem because forever endlessly repeated. Furthermore, because bound to a construal of time as a series of discrete units, each negative moment is utterly singular and utterly arbitrary insofar as the moment is infinitely reiterated to the point that difference between moments becomes a matter of indifference (rendering the utterly singular moment identical and identically repeated). All suffering is both the same and yet singular; renunciation and sacrifice are both universal (in form) and particular. The relation of this operative negativity to the utopic horizon that governs it (*jouissance* in its various guises) is contradictory rather than paradoxical. It governs the suffering as its antithesis, not its telos. An infinite distance, a distance without analogy or participation, is opened constituting the other as absolutely other. In Derrida's words, 'tout autre est tout autre'.[23] As such the dreams of the bliss of union intensify the suffering in the way that Sisyphus is tormented by seeing the goal for which he strives while also knowing it can never be attained. Or, to employ another Greek myth, *jouissance* is the grapes held out to the thirsting Tantalus. And so one

---

[18] See *The Mystic Fable*, pp. 285–93.

[19] See *Autrement qu'être ou au-delà de l'essence* (The Hague: Martinus Nijhoff, 1974), pp. 206–19.

[20] See 'White Ecstasy' tr. Frederick Christian Bauerschmidt and Catriona Hanley in Graham Ward ed., *The Postmodern God* (Oxford: Blackwell, 1998), pp. 155–8.

[21] For this point in Lévinas see *Autrement qu'être*, pp. 116–20, 156–205.

[22] See '"The Egg and the Chicken": Love as Not Having' in *Reading Clarice Lispector*, tr. Verena Andermatt Conley (Hemel Hempstead: Harvester Wheatsheaf, 1990), pp. 98–122. Cixous describes two types of love as not-having – a masculine economy of renunciation and a feminine economy of enjoying that which is always excessive to possession. Lacan himself drew attention to two economies of desire in his later work, notably *Seminar XX: Encore*. See Žižek, *The Fragile Absolute*, pp. 144–8 for an important reading of this shift in Lacan for Christian construals of 'charity'.

[23] *Gift of Death*, pp. 82–115.

is led to ask what the sacrifice achieves in this infinite postponement of pleasure. As an operation, which is no longer governed by a single or a simple agency (for the poststructural subject is profoundly aporetic), it is required by and maintains the possibility of the economy. It is immanent to the economy but unassimilable to it. It resolves nothing with respect to that economy, only fissures it with the aneconomic trauma that allows the economy to proceed. What is produced, and is continually reproduced, then, is the economy itself: the endless production of pseudo-objects. This economy of sacrifice is fundamental to capitalism itself. For it subtends growth, limitless productivity and sustainable development – which is capitalism's profoundly secular fantasy. It repeats, in a socio-psychological, semiotic and ethical key our various monetary projects in which we deny present delights by investing for greater delights in the future (wherein the pleasures we deny ourselves are only utilised by investment banks to further enhance market forces). Sacrifice as enjoying one's own suffering, in this immanent economy of desire, sustains current developments in globalism (and current illusions that such globalism is liberal and democratic).

Christian Pain and Pleasure

What role does suffering play in the economy of Christian redemption? What of its own sacrificial logic? Returning to our opening account of embodiment, the soul and touch, we need to make a distinction between sacrificial suffering (as kenosis and passion), which undoes the economics of sin through a therapy of desire, and the suffering which is a consequence and a perpetuation of sin, which undoes the orders of grace that sustain creation in its being. The body lives beyond itself. In touch it is exposed, naked to the world, its condition is perpetually kenotic and impassioned. This is the body's most fundamental experience of itself as given over to that which is other. This givenness, that comes with recognising that all is gift, each thing is given-over-to, announces a sacrificial logic distinct from a suffering that is the effect of sin (one's own or someone else's). Of course, this distinction is a theological one, maintained by faith and established by eschatological judgement. Living *in medias res*, as Augustine reminds us, 'ignorance is unavoidable – and yet the exigencies of human society make judgement also unavoidable'.[24] Nevertheless, the distinction is important for it marks out a place for suffering as a passion written into creation (the first

---

[24] *De Civitate Dei*, XIX.6.

incarnation of the divine). A cryptic verse from the Book of Revelation announces that Christ was the Lamb 'slain from the foundation of the world' (13.8). Creation, then, issues from a certain kenotic giving, a logic of sacrifice that always made possible the Passion of Jesus Christ on the cross, the slaying of the Lamb. The cross becomes the place where the two forms of suffering – the sacrificial and that which is a consequence of sin – meet. Jesus is both the body at its most exposed and vulnerable, the body that is given on behalf of sinful human beings, and the suffering victim of the disrupted orders of creation brought about by the lust to dominate. The kenotic abandonment assuages and reorientates the powers of disintegration, establishing grace as the principle of nature. But prior to the Fall, to sin, and judgement which installed suffering (and death) as a consequence of disobedience, prior to the judgement on Eve ('I will increase your labour and your groaning' Genesis 3.16) and the judgement on Adam ('You shall gain your food by the sweat of your brow' Genesis 3.19), there was a foundational giving which was extravagant and costly.

We will return to the nature of this primordial suffering later. Evidently it concerns the divine economy with respect both to its internal relations and its creation. For the moment I wish to point out how this logic of sacrifice operates in respect of divine history or *Heilsgeschichte*. For it is that which reveals itself as flesh and history, recorded in the Scriptures, which, for Christians, stakes out the limits and possibilities for theological speculation. And it is in that revelation of God made flesh that the relationship between suffering and incarnation, the mystery of that relationship, can be apprehended.

The suffering that marks the incarnation is figured early in the Gospel narrative of Luke in scenes and tropes of wounding and scarification. John the Baptist's circumcision is reiterated in the circumcision of Christ (1.59 and 2.21); the prophesied rejection of Christ by the world is followed by an oracle to Mary that 'a sword shall pierce your heart also' (2.35). As we observed in a more detailed exegesis of this passage in chapter six, 'The Politics of Christ's Circumcision', circumcision was interpreted by the early Church Fathers as an early blood-letting foreshadowing the sacrifice on the cross. That suffering was also a glorification, for the detail that it took place on the eighth day was traditionally interpreted as a reference to the eschatological day of judgement; the day following the final and consummating Sabbath when the dead rise with new bodies to dwell eternally in the kingdom of light. This paradoxical nature of suffering and glorification is echoed throughout the New Testament. We will meet it in the Pauline Epistles, and in the Gospel of John, where Christ on the cross is portrayed as both the ultimate victim and the exalted ensign for the healing of the nations. In the Book of Revelation the Lamb worshipped and adored, the disseminator of light throughout the Eternal City, remains a Lamb that is slain.

The scenes and tropes of sacrification in those opening chapters of Luke's Gospel focus on other acts of violence with which the incarnation is announced and brought about: the sacrificial offering made by Zechariah the Priest (1.10), the offering of doves or pigeons at the Presentation of Christ (2.24), the terror struck in Zechariah, Mary and the shepherds at the visitation of the angel(s), the striking dumb of Zechariah 'because you have not believed me' (1.20). The suffering of incarnation is registered somatically and psychologically in the flesh of those called to play a part in its human manifestation. The incarnation of Christ intensifies the experience of embodiment through the sufferings it engenders, just as – in an unfolding of the same logic – it is the experience of suffering which most deeply draws the believer to prayer (in the garden of Gethsemane, in the upper room following the death, resurrection and ascension of Christ, in Paul's imprisonment). In suffering the soul is recognised at the surface of the body, the ensoulment of the body is most exposed.[25] With the darkest nights of the soul, in which is evident the inseparability of consciousness, subconsciousness and the sensitivities of the flesh, comes the profoundest awareness of participation in the divine.

There is no deliverance from suffering promised in the New Testament before the Messianic return: 'He will dwell among them and they shall be his people, and God himself will be with them. He will wipe every tear from their eyes; there shall be an end to death, and to mourning and crying and pain; for the old order has passed away' (Revelation 21.3–4). In fact, in his Epistle to the Colossians, Paul cryptically remarks that he rejoices to suffer for the Church at Colossi because 'This is my way of helping to complete, in my poor human flesh, the full tale of Christ's afflictions still to be endured, for the sake of his body which is the church' (1.24). This is a well-wrought translation, but it filters out some of the syntactic and semantic complexity of Paul's Greek. A close, more literal translation would read:

> Now I rejoice in suffering [*en tois pathemasin*] on your behalf and fill up in turn [*antanaplero*] things lacking of the afflictions [*thlipseon*] of Christ in my flesh [*sarxi*] on behalf of his body [*somatos*] which is the Church.

---

[25] This should alert us to other possible readings of Christian asceticism: the putting to death of the fleshly desires in order to focus on the soul's perfection need not entail a body/soul dualism. This would be gnostic. Christian ascetic practices intensify the experience of the body and it is in that intensification that the soul is rendered most visible, is most engaged.

The Greek gives emphasis to three interrelated themes. First, it builds upon and develops spatial and locational figurations that preoccupy Paul through this letter and (possibly) his Letter to the Ephesians. Throughout the letter Paul draws attention to Christ as a cosmic space filled with all the riches and treasures of wisdom and knowledge (2.3), speaking repeatedly of Christians as living *en Christo* or *en auto*, employing a locative use of the dative. All things upon earth and in heaven are reconciled 'in the body of his flesh [*en to somati tes sarxos autou*]' (1.22). Secondly, the Greek emphasises the inter-dependency of bodies and flesh such that there is a series of co-activities between the individual believer and the body of Christ as *both* the Church and the person of Christ. Later in the letter Paul will talk about being co-buried [*suntaphentes*], co-raised [*sunegerthete*], and co-quickened [*sun-ezoopoiesen*] in Christ (2.12–13) such that there is an economy for growth and expansion through 'the operation of him operating in me in power [*ten energeian autou ten energoumenen en emoi en dunamei*]'. The prose borders on poetry, as alliterative and assonantal effects resonate within an iterative litany. Paul's flesh (*sarx*) participates in an unfolding and outworking of Christ's body (*soma*), just as Jesus Christ's own flesh opens up to enfold all things in earth and heaven in one body. Thirdly, the verse picks up a rich and profound play on the verb *pleroo* and the noun *pleroma*. The verb *pleroo* stands as the opposite to the important word for Christ's descent from God in Paul's Letter to the Philippians, *kenoo* – to empty, to pour out.[26] There, as we noted in chapter seven, '*Allegoria Amoris*', Paul exhorts believers to 'Have this mind among yourselves, which is yours in Christ Jesus, who, though he was in the form of God, did not count equality with God a thing to be grasped, but emptied himself, taking the form of a servant, being born like other human beings' (2.5). But with *pleroo* the economics of emptying that governed the incarnation are now reversed. The lack that kenosis brought about is now being satisfied. There is a filling and a fulfilling, not only of Christ but of each believer with respect to Christ. Paul works and prays for the Colossians that 'you may be filled [*plerothete*] with the full knowledge of the will of him in all wisdom and spiritual understanding [*en pase sophia kai sunesei pneumatike*]' (1.9). The *pleroma* is presented as the glory or the wisdom of God filling a space, defining a certain sacred spatiality like the

---

[26] In a highly insightful and technical article on the great kenotic hymn or *carmen Christi* in Paul's letter to the Philippians (2.5–11) by the New Testament scholar C.F.D. Moule, the point is made that 'what is *styled* kenosis is, itself, the height of plerosis: the most divine thing to give rather than to get' ('Further Reflections on Philippians 2: 5–11' in W.W. Groque and R.P. Martin eds., *Apostolic History and the Gospels*, Grand Rapids, Mich.: Eerdmans, 1970, p. 273). I am attempting to develop this insight theologically, while avoiding some of the neater ethical pronouncements 'to give rather than to get' that Moule makes upon its basis.

Shekhinah in the tabernacle in the wilderness. Earlier in the letter Paul writes that in Christ 'all the fullness [*pan to pleroma*]' dwells (1.19). Later in the letter he writes that 'in him dwells all the fullness of the Godhead bodily [*to pleroma tes theotetos somatikos*] and you are in him having been filled [*pepleromenoi*]' (2.9–10). In the verse following 1.24 he presents himself as the minister according to God's economic handling [*oikonomian*] 'to fulfil the word of God [*plerosa ton logon tou theou*]' (1.25) for the Colossians.

Here in 1.24 *antanaplero* is utterly distinctive. Found only at this point in the New Testament, it combines *ana-plero* (to fill up to the brim, to make up, supply, satisfy and fulfil) with the prefix of *anti*. As J.B. Lightfoot pointed out back in 1876, if Paul's meaning was simply to fill up then the prefix is redundant.[27] With the prefix a self-reflexivity is announced. Twice in the verse the word 'on behalf of' [*uper*] is employed: Paul suffers on behalf of the Colossians and on behalf of the body of Christ as the Church. His suffering in the flesh is filling what remains of the afflictions of Christ *as* Christ suffered on behalf of him in his own flesh. Jesus Christ as flesh (*sarx*) is no longer: 'even though we once knew Christ from the human point of view, we know him no longer in that way', Paul tells the Church at Corinth (2 Cor. 5.16). There remains the body of Christ as the Church composed of the flesh (*sarx*) of believers like Paul. Paul's suffering is, then, an extension of and a participation in the suffering of Christ. Now, on one level this is living *imitatio Christi* – the Church suffers persecution as Christ suffered persecution. But, considered in the light of the three emphases we have been outlining – Christ as a cosmic and spiritual space in which the operation of a divine economy of 'filling' engages and makes itself manifest through the embodiment of those believers composing the body of Christ – then we have to ask what the relationship is between suffering and glorification, affliction and fulfilment. For the filling is an activity described in terms of both suffering and full knowledge, wisdom and spiritual understanding. And it is an activity that not only builds up but also defines the operation of the divine with respect to the body of Christ. A suffering inseparable from the incarnation of Christ is experienced in believers as a suffering inseparable from coming to the fullness of the stature of Christ or 'being renewed in the full knowledge according to the image of the creator' (3.10).

Paul's writing is a theological reflection on the economics of divine power with respect to embodiment in Christ. It is a reflection upon divinity as it manifests itself in the concrete historicity of the death, burial and resurrection of Jesus the Christ. It is not speculative in the sense of conceiving

---

[27]   J.B. Lightfoot, *Epistle to the Colossians* (London: Macmillan, 1876), pp. 164–5.

operations in the Godhead on the basis of which earthly events might be explained. Rather, he develops and unfolds the logic of Christ's incarnation and crucifixion, examining the space that has been opened up 'in the body of his flesh through his death' (1.22). This is not, then, an example of *deipassionism* in the sense of God suffering with humankind – the suffering of God described by Moltmann, for example. One recalls how Moltmann reads Elie Wiesel's account of the hanging of a child in the German concentration camp. Wiesel observes how the question of where God is is raised by Jewish onlookers. Moltmann examines this question and Wiesel's own response, in terms of God being in the very suffering of the child.

> To speak here of a God who could not suffer would make God a demon. To speak here of an absolute God would make God an annihilating nothingness. To speak here of an indifferent God would condemn men to indifference … Does the Shekinah, which wanders with Israel through the dust of the streets and hangs on the gallows in Auschwitz, suffer in the God who holds the ends of the earth in his hand? In that case not only would suffering affect God's *pathos* externally, so that it might be said that God himself suffers at the human history of injustice and force, but suffering would be the history in the midst of God himself.[28]

God suffers with us such that the negative moment is taken up into God in the eschatological coming of the kingdom. Moltmann's theology, endorsing a certain interpretation of Hegel's, radicalises God being with us, compromising God's transcendence.

Balthasar's account, of Christ's descent into hell and into solidarity with the most profound alienation from God the father, retains the transcendent and impassable source, opening wide the difference between the Father and the Son, the Trinitarian processions. In the silence of Holy Saturday God is extended to the point where even that which is most remote from the Godhead is incorporated. The depths of abjection are plumbed and God is found there. 'The Redeemer showed himself therefore as the only one who, going beyond the general experience of death, was able to measure the depths of that abyss.'[29] Through Christ's suffering there is redemption, but once redemption has been achieved – the extreme boundaries of hell encompassed – then all is reconciled. 'Hell is the *product* of redemption', Balthasar informs us.[30] Subsequent suffering is not really suffering at all,

---

[28] Jurgen Moltmann, *The Crucified God: The Cross of Christ as the Foundation and Criticism of Christian Theology* (London: SCM, 1974), pp. 273–4.

[29] *Mysterium Paschale*, tr. A. Nichols (Edinburgh: T. & T. Clark, 1990), p. 168.

[30] Ibid., p. 174.

objectively speaking. For the victory has been won in Christ through the events of those three days (Good Friday, Holy Saturday and Easter Sunday): 'Inasmuch as the Son travels across the chaos in virtue of the mission received from the Father, he is, objectively speaking, whilst in the midst of the darkness of what is contrary to God, in "paradise", and the image of triumph may well express this.'[31]

But Paul's account views things differently: subsequent suffering is not epiphenomenal (which Balthasar's account, influenced as it is by Origen's and Athanasius's Christologies, may seem to render it). It participates in a true and ongoing suffering; a true and ongoing passion located in the very Godhead itself. Following this interpretation of Paul we can conclude that there is a suffering that is meaningless because it has no part in redemption. This is a suffering that rejects and fights against redemption. It has no truth, no existence in Augustine's ontology of goodness, because it is privative – it deprives and strips creation of its orders of being, its treasures of wisdom. Suffering that is a consequence and promulgation of sin can find no place in the *pleroma*. And only *pleroma* gives space, provides a dwelling. But there is a suffering that is meaningful because it is a continuation, a fleshing out and a completing of the suffering of Christ.

In several places Gregory of Nyssa will speak of this suffering as the wounding of love (a double genitive). The suffering issues from the experience of the agony of distance that is installed by difference (between the Bride of Christ and the Christ himself) and discerned by love. The agony is the very labouring of love whereby 'the soul grows by its constant participation in that which transcends it'.[32] Nyssa takes up a theological account of circumcision to describe this movement: 'Here, too, man is circumcised, and yet he remains whole and entire and suffers no mutilation in his material nature.'[33] The question raised here, with respect to the sado-masochistic economy of desire informing postmodern secularity, is where does the difference lie, for the internalisation of a pleasurable pain is common to both?[34] For the moment let us allow that question to hang, while I emphasise, again, that only God can discern and distinguish what is true suffering, and therefore what is being outlined here is not a theodicy, nor the grounds for providing theological rationales for human tragedies. Enlightenment

---

[31] Ibid., p. 176.

[32] Nyssa's *Commentary on the Canticle of Canticles* in Herbert Musurillo S.J. ed., *From Glory to Glory: Texts from Gregory of Nyssa's Mystical Writings* (London: John Murray, 1962), p. 190.

[33] Ibid., p. 193.

[34] For a more detailed analysis of this cultural sado-masochism see my 'Theology and Cultural Sadomasochism', *Svensk Teologisk Kvartalskrift*, Årg. 78 (2002), pp. 2–10.

theodicies pre-empt (and therefore in an act of hubris usurp) eschatological judgement. There is a 'filling up' and therefore an end, when 'Christ is all and in all [*panta kai en pasin Christos*]', but that 'filling up' is not yet concluded and we remain caught between contingent knowledges and truth; intuition, ignorance and hope.

If kenosis and completion, emptying and filling, are not two opposite, but two complementary operations of the divine, like breathing out in order to breathe in, then there is no lack, absence or vacuum as such. Both movements are associated with a suffering that simultaneously glorifies. The self-emptying of Christ reaches its nadir in death only to be reversed in a final coronation: 'Therefore God raised him to the heights and bestowed upon him the name above all names, that at the name of Jesus every knee should bow' (Philippians 2.9–10). The 'filling up in turn' [*antanaplero*] also involves 'being empowered [*dunamoumenoi*] according to the might of his glory for all endurance and long-suffering with joy [*eis pasan hupomonen kai makrothumian meta charas*]' (Colossians 1.11). This leads us to the heart of a theological mystery: what it is that constitutes the intradivine passion.[35] That the passion is the basis for the economy of *kenoo* and *plero* and that this economy opens up a space for divine redemptive activity with respect to creation is evident. It is also evident that this passion is grounded in Trinitarian relations. Paul, in his Letter to the Colossians, mainly treats of the relationship between Christ and the Godhead, but the content and dynamic of that relationship he expresses in terms of wisdom, knowledge, glory and *energeia*. There is much debate between and among New Testament scholars and dogmatic theologians over how developed Trinitarian thinking is within the New Testament. Nevertheless it would appear to be true that the passion that is the basis for the economy of *kenoo* and *plero* – with respect to the glorification of all things created – is an intradivine passion that Christians have understood in terms of the differences–in–relation, the differences–in–identity between the Father, the Son and the Holy Spirit.

The suffering comes by, through and with the infinite capacity for self-exposition. It arises from the naked vulnerability of the body to a touch that delivers us the world and the world to us. Taking up the double nature of the genitive in 'the wounding of love', another way of putting this would be to say that the wounding is intrinsic to the operation of love not only between the Bride and the Bridegroom, the Church and Christ, but between the Persons of the Trinity. This is not an account of the self divided from itself – God is one in substance – nor is this an account of the sovereignty of the

---

[35] I employ passion with a lowercase p to distinguish it from the Passion (of Christ on the cross). Evidently I am suggesting the former is the condition for the possibility of the latter.

Father splitting to constitute the Son. The suffering does not issue from any subordination. Father, Son and Spirit are co-constituted; the self-exposition is eternal. But the very equality-in-difference-of-one-substance expresses the creative tensions of loving communion. At the end of his essay on the body and touch, Jean-Louis Chrétien moves from an Aristotelian account of touch and the orientation of the embodied soul to the exterior to show how these affect Aristotelian theology: 'It is through an intelligible grasp of itself as such that the divine mind is actually intelligent.'[36] This is the basis of God as pure, spiritual act. But we have already understood that touch only knows itself as such with respect to there being an external object. Chrétien observes that for Aristotle 'It is through contact with itself as intelligible object, and by allowing itself to be touched, that the divine intellect eternally ignites what comes after it.'[37] Although later he goes on to quote Aquinas, he does not develop the evident Trinitarian implications of this economy of divine contact. The phenomenology of touch opens into a theology of touch in which the Father eternally begets the Son, and through that contact between them the Spirit born of them both endlessly makes known the intelligibility of what they share. For, as John Philiponus's commentary on Aristotle's *De Anima* says: 'Nothing suffers itself [*huph' heautou paskhei*].'[38] The primordial suffering, then, is a passion of utter givenness through the excess of contact within the Godhead itself, which is given expression in the very act of creation so that a certain suffering is endemic to incarnate living, a suffering that always made possible the sacrifice on the cross.

Let us explore this a little further, for we are coming dangerously close to a theological justification for suffering. We need to explore, as Nyssa does, the nature of this suffering as it adheres to the very act of loving and seeks not the possession but the glorification of the other. We need to explore the economy of that loving which incarnates the very logic of sacrifice as the endless giving (which is also a giving-up, a kenosis) and the endless reception (which is also an opening-up towards the other in order to be filled). The suffering and sacrifice which are born of and borne by passion are the very risk and labour of love; a love which is profoundly erotic and, to employ a queer theory term, genderfucking.[39] It is a suffering engendered

---

[36] 'Body and Touch', p. 128. He quotes from *Metaphysics*, 1072B19–21.

[37] Ibid., pp. 128–9.

[38] *In Aristotelis de Anima Libros Commentaria*, 292. Cited in Chrétien, 'Body and Touch', p. 121.

[39] See Stephen Whittle, 'Gender Fucking of Fucking Gender: Current Cultural Contributions to Theories of Gender Blending', pp. 196–214. For a wonderful exposition of queer thinking for Christian theology, see Marcella Althaus-Reid, *The Queer God* (London: Routledge, 2003), particularly 'Queering God in Relationships: Trinitarians and God the Orgy', pp. 46–59.

by and vouchsafing difference; first Trinitarian difference, subsequently ontological difference between the uncreated Godhead and creation, and finally sexual difference as that which pertains most closely to human embodiment. Augustine describes time in creation in spatial terms, as *distentio*, and *distentio* bears the connotations of swelling, of a space that is the product of a wounding: a wounding in and of love. The primordial suffering is the suffering of loving and being loved. Incarnating the divine – which is the nature of all things 'because in him [*oti en auto*] were created all things in the heavens and on the earth, visible and invisible' (Colossians 1.16) – is inseparable, then, from a passion, a suffering whereby we bear fruit, grow (1.6) and glorify even as we are glorified.

The Confrontation

With this in mind let us now return to the point from which we began – the contemporary sacrificial economies of deferred *jouissance* – and engage the cultural politics of these two positions. The profound difference between the Christian economy I have been outlining (and constructing) and post-modern accounts of the negation of negation lies in the perennial suffering and sacrifices of love as not-having (in the contemporary accounts) and the eternal suffering intrinsic to the plenitude of love itself (the Christian account). The agonistic pleasure of enduring the undecideable (Derrida)[40] is akin to being suspended on the brink of orgasm without being allowed the final release of coming. This is the quintessential sado-masochistic ecstasy which, in truth, announces a certain stasis, even paralysis. In contrast, the closing lines of the New Testament resound with the call for Messianic arrival: 'The Spirit and the Bride say, "Come." And let him who hears say, "Come." ... He who testifies to these things says, "Surely I am coming soon." Amen. Come, Lord Jesus' (Rev. 22.17, 20). The Christian always seeks that coming, not to prolong its arrival, but in the belief that proclaiming that coming is itself ushering in its fulfilment.

Žižek, in a remarkable analysis of the Christian economy of charity (which he compares with Lacan's later shift 'from the "masculine" logic of the Law and its constitutive exception towards the "feminine" logic in which there is *no* exception'),[41] writes about its 'subversive core'.[42] In a reading of

---

40 *The Politics of Friendship*, p. 123.
41 *The Fragile Absolute*, p. 116.
42 Ibid., p. 119.

Paul's two letters to the Church at Corinth, he articulates how Christian love 'unplugs itself' from its cultural context, its organic community, and so disturbs the balance of the All, the integration into the One. 'Christianity *is* the miraculous Event that disturbs the balance of the One–All; it *is* the violent intrusion of Difference that precisely *throws the balanced circuit of the universe off the rails.*'[43] Closely reading the famous hymn to *agape* in I Corinthians, chapter 13, Žižek writes:

> the point of the claim that even if I were to possess all knowledge, without love I would be nothing, is not simply that *with* love I am 'something' – in love, *I am also nothing* but, as it were, a Nothing humbly aware of itself, a Nothing paradoxically made rich through the very awareness of its lack. Only a lacking, vulnerable being is capable of love: the ultimate mystery of love is therefore that incompleteness is in a way *higher than completion*. On the one hand, only an imperfect, lacking being loves: we love because we do *not* know all. On the other hand, even if we were to know everything, love would inexplicably still be higher than completed knowledge.[44]

I remain troubled by the language of nothingness and lack, and I am convinced this is a move by Žižek beyond Lacan, but two main points about the Christian economy of desire are sharpened here. First, this passage captures much of what I have been arguing for in terms of the agony of difference constituted by love itself. As such, the Person of the Spirit holds open to creation the love between the Father and the Son, which challenges our understandings of what is intended by words like 'imperfection' and 'incompletion'. Creation too groans in its distinction and its love. As we noted in chapter five, 'Divinity and Sexual Difference', only in the constitution of difference itself can there be *enjoyment* of the other as other – where enjoyment implies active interest, participation without sublation. This is an altogether different account from the sado-masochistic suffering of love as not-having, of enjoying one's own traumatic symptoms. To delight in the suffering of ambivalence that dares not hope for resolution, is to remain within what Žižek calls '*the balanced circuit of the universe*'. For this delight has no future; deferral does not open a future, it only prolongs the present in despair because hope becomes impossible. And what desire desires, in these contemporary accounts of sacrifice and pleasure, is deferral. The logic of sacrifice to appease the terrible ire of whimsical gods is internalised, and appeasement becomes appraisal of endless situational ambivalence and

---

43   Ibid., p. 121. The italics are Žižek's.
44   Ibid., p. 147. The italics are Žižek's.

insecurity.[45] Sacrifice no longer wards off the arbitrary violences of a sadistic deity, but rather finds sado-masochistic pleasure in always only being compromised and ruptured.[46]

Secondly, the Christian account of suffering is not one installed by the suspension of the semantic by the semiotic. Žižek seems to suggest this himself in his analysis of love and knowledge. Not-knowing is not enduring the undecideable. The knowing-in-part reaches beyond itself, so that time, spirit and materiality are all distended. There is a surpassing of what is understood *in* the understanding that is granted.[47] There is here an overcoming of the instrumentality of reason, whereas it is the sheer inability of the reason to be as instrumental as it might wish which creates the lag and deferral that announces *différance*. It is the very construal of reasoning as instrumental that invokes the aporetic, the undecideable.

Of course, with some irony, Foucault laid the blame for sado-masochism (in which he also delighted and deemed creative) at the feet of Christian pastoral practices, technologies of subjectivity honed and devised from Christianity's inception.[48] He was developing here Freud's concept of moral masochism as an unexpungeable and unconscious sense of guilt. But 'genealogy' is a tool of polemic and resistance, not always alert to the subtleties of historical specificity. The Christian economy of suffering and incarnation sketched here is not sado-masochistic for two reasons: First, it does not view difference as rupture and therefore it does not install a (non)foundational violence (the *tout autre*) as the principle for its momentum; a violence which is either projected (sadism) or introjected (masochism). Secondly, the economy of its desire is not locked into love as not-having. Rather, love is continually extended beyond itself and, in and through that extension,

---

[45] Culturally this prepares the ground very well for the politics of fear and terror which are being instituted (and institutionalised) in the West (including Russia too) today. One can take note of the endless suspicion engendered by the Patriot Act in the United States.

[46] Freud recognised the strong association between sadism and masochism. It was the same instinct, the death instinct, operating by either projecting or introjecting violence. Furthermore, in his 1924 essay 'The Economic Problem of Masochism', having distinguished erotogenic, feminine and moral forms of masochism, he pointed to the relationships between masochism and impotence, the masturbatory act of finding sexual satisfaction in oneself and infantile life. *The Complete Works of Sigmund Freud*, vol. XIX, tr. James Strachey (London: Hogarth Press, 1961), pp. 159–70.

[47] That the surpassing of the understanding takes places in what is understood if only partially is fundamental. It is too easy, and my own work has not always avoided this ease, to counter postmodern economies of lack with theological economies of excess. The surpassing of the understanding is not an entry into the mystical sublime, white ecstasy. The surpassing of the understanding is where what is understood by mind and eye intimates a divine depth intuited by what Gregory of Nyssa would call 'the spiritual senses'. See here essay three, 'The Body of the Church and its Erotic Politics'.

[48] *The History of Sexuality: An Introduction*, tr. Robert Hurley (Harmondsworth: Penguin Books, 1981).

receives itself back from the other as a non-identical repetition. Love construed as having or not-having is a commodified product. It is something one possesses or does not possess. It is part of an exchange between object and subject positions. But love in the Christian economy is an action, an economy of response to Christ, not an object. It cannot be lost or found, absent or present. It constitutes the very space within which all operations in heaven and upon earth take place. The positions of persons are both constituted and dissolved. The linearity and syntax of Indo-European languages barely allow access to the mystery of Trinitarian persons and processions: where one ends and another begins. As such, suffering and sacrifice are not distinct moments, *kenoo* is also and simultaneously *plero*. The wounds of love are the openings of grace.

Again, I repeat, this a theological account of suffering and incarnation. There are myriad historical accounts of suffering and numerous philosophical, psychological and sociological analyses. The burden of my argument is that the incarnational view of creation profoundly relates the theological and the historical – bearing both forward (in a hope that, in being ineradicable, is all the more painful to endure) towards an eschatological discernment. But the method of my argument is confrontational, not simply analytical. And the Christian theological nature of that confrontation is important, for, as Žižek himself observes, Christianity has a 'subversive core', a radicality inseparable from its orthodoxy. What the confrontation suggests is that the sado-masochistic economies of desire profoundly at work in contemporary culture are pathological. They are destructive of what is most necessary for our well-being and cosmic flourishing. Surely the economy of incarnate love offers greater resources for social transformation, amelioration. Surely to persist in enjoying the symptoms of a cultural neurosis (which is transcultural insofar as it constitutes the economy of desire operating in global capitalism) is a decadence few can afford at the peril of us all. We need to practise an art of living in the name of a transcendental hope that breaks free of the vicious circularities of the same; to learn about good formations of the soul which produce those places operating a logic that counters the sado-masochistic economy. We need to defend the legacies of those theological traditions that teach us the proper labour of our loving.

INDEX